CFA Institute®
CFA Program

MW01702003

ALTERNATIVE INVESTMENTS

CFA® Program Curriculum
2026 • LEVEL II • VOLUME 8

WILEY

ISBN 978-1-394360-53-6

SKY A90C0444-DCDA-4FB9-BD61-6A20B70785C3_061325

Please visit our website at
www.WileyGlobalFinance.com.

WILEY

CONTENTS

How to Use the CFA Program Curriculum

The CFA® Program exams measure your mastery of the core knowledge, skills, and abilities required to succeed as an investment professional. These core competencies are the basis for the Candidate Body of Knowledge (CBOK™). The CBOK consists of four components:

A broad outline that lists the major CFA Program topic areas (www.cfainstitute.org/programs/cfa/curriculum/cbok/cbok)

Topic area weights that indicate the relative exam weightings of the top-level topic areas (www.cfainstitute.org/en/programs/cfa/curriculum)

Learning outcome statements (LOS) that tell you the specific knowledge, skills, and abilities you should gain from each curriculum topic area. You will find these statements at the start of each learning module and lesson. We encourage you to review the information about the LOS on our website (www.cfainstitute.org/programs/cfa/curriculum/study-sessions), including the descriptions of LOS "command words" on the candidate resources page at www.cfainstitute.org/-/media/documents/support/programs/cfa-and-cipm-los-command-words.ashx.

The CFA Program curriculum that candidates receive access to upon exam registration.

Therefore, the key to your success on the CFA exams is studying and understanding the CBOK. You can learn more about the CBOK on our website: www.cfainstitute.org/programs/cfa/curriculum/cbok.

The curriculum, including the practice questions, is the basis for all exam questions. The curriculum is selected/developed specifically to provide candidates with the knowledge, skills, and abilities reflected in the CBOK.

CFA INSTITUTE LEARNING ECOSYSTEM (LES)

Your exam registration fee includes access to the CFA Institute Learning Ecosystem (LES). This digital learning platform provides access to all the curriculum content and practice questions. The LES is organized as a series of learning modules consisting of short online lessons and associated practice questions. This tool is your source for all study materials, including practice questions and mock exams. The LES is the primary method by which CFA Institute delivers your curriculum experience. Here, you will find additional practice questions to test your knowledge, including some interactive questions.

DESIGNING YOUR PERSONAL STUDY PROGRAM

An orderly, systematic approach to exam preparation is critical. You should dedicate a consistent block of time every week to reading and studying. Review the LOS both before and after you study curriculum content to ensure you can demonstrate the knowledge, skills, and abilities described by the LOS and the assigned learning module. Use the LOS as a self-check to track your progress and highlight areas of weakness for later review.

Successful candidates report an average of more than 300 hours preparing for each exam. Your preparation time will vary based on your prior education and experience, and you will likely spend more time on some topics than on others.

ERRATA

The curriculum development process is rigorous and involves multiple rounds of reviews by content experts. Despite our efforts to produce a curriculum that is free of errors, we must make corrections in some instances. Curriculum errata are periodically updated and posted by exam level and test date on the Curriculum Errata webpage (www.cfainstitute.org/en/programs/submit-errata). If you believe you have found an error in the curriculum, you can submit your concerns through our curriculum errata reporting process found at the bottom of the Curriculum Errata webpage.

OTHER FEEDBACK

Please send any comments or suggestions to info@cfainstitute.org, and we will review your feedback thoughtfully.

Alternative Investments

LEARNING MODULE

1

Introduction to Commodities and Commodity Derivatives

by **David Burkart, CFA, and James Alan Finnegan, CAIA, RMA, CFA.**

David Burkart, CFA, is at Coloma Capital Futures, LLC (USA). James Alan Finnegan, CAIA, RMA, CFA at American Century Investments (USA).

LEARNING OUTCOMES

Mastery	The candidate should be able to:
☐	compare characteristics of commodity sectors
☐	compare the life cycle of commodity sectors from production through trading or consumption
☐	contrast the valuation of commodities with the valuation of equities and bonds
☐	describe types of participants in commodity futures markets
☐	analyze the relationship between spot prices and futures prices in markets in contango and markets in backwardation
☐	compare theories of commodity futures returns
☐	describe, calculate, and interpret the components of total return for a fully collateralized commodity futures contract
☐	contrast roll return in markets in contango and markets in backwardation
☐	describe how commodity swaps are used to obtain or modify exposure to commodities
☐	describe how the construction of commodity indexes affects index returns

INTRODUCTION

1

In the upcoming sections, we present the characteristics and valuation of commodities and commodity derivatives. Given that investment in commodities is conducted primarily through futures markets, the concepts and theories behind commodity futures is a primary focus of the reading. In particular, the relationship between spot and futures prices, as well as the underlying components of futures returns, are key analytical considerations.

What do we mean when we talk about investing in commodities? A basic economic definition is that a commodity is a physical good attributable to a natural resource that is tradable and supplied without substantial differentiation by the general public.

Commodities trade in physical (spot) markets and in futures and forward markets. Spot markets involve the physical transfer of goods between buyers and sellers; prices in these markets reflect current (or very near term) supply and demand conditions. Global commodity futures markets constitute financial exchanges of standardized futures contracts in which a price is established in the market today for the sale of some defined quantity and quality of a commodity at a future date of delivery; completion of the contract may permit cash settlement or require physical delivery.

Commodity futures exchanges allow for risk transfer and provide a valuable price discovery mechanism that reflects the collective views of all market participants with regard to the future supply and demand prospects of a commodity. Given the financial (versus physical) nature of their contract execution, commodity exchanges allow important parties beyond traditional suppliers and buyers—speculators, arbitrageurs, private equity, endowments, and other institutional investors—to participate in these price discovery and risk transfer processes. Standardized contracts and organized exchanges also offer liquidity (i.e., trading volumes) to facilitate closing, reducing, expanding, or opening new hedges or exposures as circumstances change on a daily basis.

Forward markets exist alongside futures markets in certain commodities for use by entities that require customization in contract terms. Forwards are largely outside the scope of this reading and are discussed only briefly. Exposure to commodities is also traded in the swap markets for both speculative and hedging purposes. Investment managers may want to establish swap positions to match certain portfolio needs, whereas producers may want to more precisely adjust their commodity risk (e.g., the origin of their cattle or the chemical specifications of their crude oil).

Commodities offer the potential for diversification benefits in a multi-asset class portfolio because of historically low average return correlation with stocks and bonds. In addition, certain academic studies (e.g., Gorton and Rouwenhorst 2006; Erb and Harvey 2006) demonstrate that some commodities have historically had inflation hedging qualities.

Our coverage of the commodities topic is organized as follows: We provide an overview of physical commodity markets, including the major sectors, their life cycles, and their valuation. We then describe futures market participants, commodity futures pricing, and the analysis of commodity returns, including the concepts of contango and backwardation. The subsequent section reviews the use of swap instruments rather than futures to gain exposure to commodities. We then review the various commodity indexes given their importance as benchmarks for the asset class and investment vehicles. Finally, we conclude with a summary of the major points.

2 COMMODITY SECTORS

☐ compare characteristics of commodity sectors

Commodities are an asset class inherently different from traditional financial assets, such as equities and bonds. These latter assets are securities that are claims on productive capital assets and/or financial assets and thus are expected to generate cash flows for their owners. The intrinsic value of these securities is the present discounted value of their expected future cash flows. Commodities are valued differently. Commodities' value derives from either their use as consumables or as inputs to the production of goods and services. Because a number of commodities need to be processed or have a limited life before spoiling or decaying, an astute analyst will take into account the growth and extraction patterns of the various commodities as well as the logistics associated with transporting these physical goods. Therefore, commodities, while seemingly familiar from everyday life, offer distinct sets of risk exposures for investors.

Fundamental analysis of commodities relies on analyzing supply and demand for each of the products as well as estimating the reaction to the inevitable shocks to their equilibrium or underlying direction. For example, a growing world population demands more crude oil or related products as transportation of goods and people increases. However, technological improvements (e.g., shale drilling or electric vehicles) can disrupt that trend and in the case of armed conflict or adverse weather, for example, may alter it on very short notice! This means that the quantitative analysis of commodities is often imperfect because of high degrees of non-normalcy and shifting correlations. Furthermore, the coefficients to underlying variables are often non-stationary; for example, much corn today is genetically modified to resist heat, rendering drought impact estimates derived from history less predictive. Much of the raw data are held off market by private firms engaged in the commodity industry (such as oil or agricultural companies), which also hinders a purely quantitative approach. Therefore, the framework offered here will be at a high level. We will later provide a breakdown of individual areas for the investor to apply discretionary or quantitative techniques, as circumstances allow. Because the framework can be applied to both supply and demand, we shall set that distinction aside until we focus on individual sectors and commodities. The tools and considerations in fundamental analysis are as follows:

a. Direct announcements: Various government agencies and private companies broadcast production and inventory data that can be used to infer demand, which is often unobservable. Possible public sources include the USDA (US Department of Agriculture), OPEC (Organization of the Petroleum Exporting Countries), the NBS (National Bureau of Statistics of China), and the IEA (International Energy Agency). Setting aside questions of reliability, sometimes estimating current conditions is as straightforward as monitoring official announcements, even with a lag.

b. Component analysis: The more diligent analyst will attempt to break down high-level supply and demand into various components. Applying a stock and flow approach is a logical method. The stock or potential production or demand attempts to set boundaries around what is actually produced or wanted. This can be as general as the amount of arable land in all of Europe or as specific as the current capacity of the Ghawar oil field in Saudi Arabia. The flow considers the utilization of that stock of raw material. Examples include understanding the oil tanker traffic heading to China, estimating the historical yields of US cotton (the amount of fiber per unit of land) in various weather conditions, and estimating the number of piglets per mother hog in Canada.

   These examples lend themselves to historical quantitative or conditional analysis. However, care needs to be taken regarding the qualitative aspects of supply and demand; a new policy such as stricter emissions standards can affect both supply (higher standards often strand lower-quality materials) and demand (not all consumers may be properly equipped to utilize a changing standard). Political unrest may not touch an isolated farm but may disrupt consumption.

c. Timing considerations: Stocks and flows from (b) can be further affected by timing issues—such as seasonality and logistics—and, therefore, price reaction. A shock, by definition, is a sudden timing switch; an earthquake that destroys a pipeline does not affect the stock, but it does halt the flow. A more common consideration is seasonality, such as the growing period for crops and people's demand for winter heat generated from natural gas. This last aspect in particular feeds into the shape of the commodity futures curve, as discussed later.

d. Money flow: Short-term and long-term prices can be affected by sentiment and macro monetary conditions, such as inflation. If investor risk tolerance is particularly high or low, then expecting exaggerated price movements would be rational as fundamental conditions are hyped up or beaten down. Alternatively, capital availability from low interest rates can help trigger the building of new mines and affect future supply. Government subsidies of substitute technologies can limit commodity price appreciation (e.g., available funds for electric cars indirectly affect the price of gasoline).

In summary, although the casual investor can perhaps focus solely on public summary statements, the engaged researcher will apply a framework of examining the stock and flow components and their related timing to better understand and weigh the pressures leading to higher or lower prices.

Commodity Sectors

The world of commodities is relatively broad but can be defined and separated in a reasonable manner. Although there are several ways to segment the asset class by sector, here we use the approach that is the basis for the Bloomberg Commodity Index: energy, grains, industrial (base) metals, livestock, precious metals, and softs (cash crops). This segmentation is more granular than some other indexes but is reasonably consistent with the breakdown in the specialties of most market participants. As noted previously, each sector has a number of individual characteristics that are important in determining the supply and demand for each commodity. A key concept is how easily and cost-effectively the commodity can be produced and stored, as well as such related issues as frequency/timing of consumption, spoilage, insurance, and ease of transportation to consumers. Note that many commodities, such as uranium or water, are traded only in thin, private markets. They are really just individual transactions, as opposed to the markets we are discussing. For the purposes of our coverage, we have to constrain ourselves to primary commodities, recognizing that there are many others that may offer investment opportunities or require hedging. Exhibit 1 reviews each sector and its main characteristics and influences.

Exhibit 1: A Description of Commodity Sectors and Factors

	Energy: Fuel transportation, industrial production, and electrical generation. Primary commodities include crude oil, natural gas, coal, and refined products, such as gasoline and heating oil.	
Primary Influences	Stocks: Discovery and depletion of new fields, economic and political costs/certainty of access to those fields, refinery technology and maintenance, power plant type and construction, economic (GDP) size	Flows: Pipeline and tanker reliability, seasonality (summer/winter), adverse weather (cold, hurricanes), automobile/truck sales, geopolitical instability, environmental requirements, economic (GDP) growth
	Grains: Provide human and animal sustenance but also can be distilled into fuel (e.g., ethanol). Primary commodities include corn, soy, wheat, and rice.	
Primary Influences	Stocks: Arable farmland, storage/port facilities (infrastructure), human and animal population size	Flows: Weather (moisture, temperature), disease, consumer preferences, genetic modification, biofuel substitution, population growth
	Industrial/Base Metals: Materials for durable consumer goods, industry, and construction. Primary commodities include copper, aluminum, nickel, zinc, lead, tin, and iron.	
Primary Influences	Stocks: Mined acreage, smelter capacity, economic (GDP) stage of industrial/consumer development	Flows: Government industrial and environmental policies, economic (GDP) growth, automobile/truck sales, infrastructure investment
	Livestock: Animals raised for human consumption. Primary commodities include hogs, cattle, sheep, and poultry.	
Primary Influences	Stocks: Herd size, processing plant capacity, consumer preferences, feed availability/cost	Flows: Speed of maturation to slaughter weight, economic (GDP) growth/consumer income, disease, adverse weather
	Precious Metals: Certain metals that act as monetary stores of value (as well as industrial uses). Primary commodities include gold, silver, and platinum.	
Primary Influences	Stocks: Mined acreage, smelter capacity, fiat money supply/banking development	Flows: Central bank monetary policy, geopolitics, economic (GDP) growth
	Softs (Cash Crops): Crops sold for income—as opposed to consumed for subsistence—and often originally seen as luxuries. Primary commodities include cotton, cocoa, sugar, and coffee.	
Primary Influences	Stocks: Arable farmland, storage/port facilities (infrastructure), economic (GDP) size	Flows: Weather (moisture, temperature), disease, consumer preferences, biofuel substitution, economic (GDP) growth/consumer income

As noted in this section, each commodity sector is unique in its fundamental drivers but with the overlapping context of economic and monetary data. With this context in mind, we will now examine the life cycle of the sectors from production to consumption—and their interaction—in more detail.

EXAMPLE 1

Commodity Sector Demand

1. Industrial activity *most likely* affects the demand for which of the following commodities?

   A. Copper

   B. Natural gas

   C. Softs (e.g., cotton, coffee, sugar and cocoa)

Solution:

A is correct. Copper is used for construction, infrastructure development, and the manufacture of durable goods, all of which are economically sensitive. B is incorrect because demand for natural gas is driven primarily by weather conditions (heating or cooling) and only secondarily by industrial activity. C is incorrect because demand for softs is driven primarily by global income.

EXAMPLE 2

Commodity Sector Risks

1. Which of the following commodity sectors are *least* affected in the short term by weather-related risks?

   A. Energy

   B. Livestock

   C. Precious metals

Solution:

C is correct. Weather has very little impact on the availability of precious metals given their ease of storage. Inflation expectations, fund flows, and industrial production are more important factors. A is incorrect because energy demand is strongly influenced by weather (e.g., heating demand in the winter or transportation demand in the summer). B is incorrect because the health of livestock is vulnerable to unfavorable weather conditions increasing the risks of death and disease by extreme cold, wet, and heat.

3 LIFE CYCLE OF COMMODITIES

☐ compare the life cycle of commodity sectors from production through trading or consumption

The life cycle of commodities varies considerably depending on the economic, technical, and structural (i.e., industry, value chain) profile of each commodity, as well as the sector. Conceptually, the commodity production life cycle reflects and amplifies the changes in storage, weather, and political/economic events that shift supply and demand. Recall from the earlier discussion that timing/seasonality is, in effect, an overlay on top of the underlying supply/demand factors. A short life cycle allows for relatively rapid adjustment to outside events, whereas a long life cycle generally limits the ability of supply or demand to react to new conditions. These shifts, in turn, feed into the economics for the valuation and shape of the commodity supply and demand curves, plus their respective price elasticities of demand and supply. Understanding the life cycle builds understanding of, and ideally ability to forecast, what drives market actions and commodity returns.

Among the food commodities, agriculture and livestock have well-defined seasons and growth cycles that are specific to geographic regions. For example, by March of each year, corn planting may be finished in the southern United States but not yet started in Canada. Meanwhile, the corn harvest may be underway in Brazil and Argentina given their reverse seasonal cycle in the Southern Hemisphere. Each geographic location also represents local markets that have different domestic and export demand. These differences affect the nature (level and reliability) of demand and the power of buyers to extend or contract the life cycle.

In comparison, commodities in the energy and metals sectors are extracted all year round. Their life cycle changes are generally at the margin of a continuous process, as opposed to being centered at a discrete time or season. But the products from crude oil and metal ore have seasonal demands depending on weather (e.g., gasoline demand in the summer and heating oil demand in the winter) that affect the life cycle and usage of the underlying commodity. And with all the differences between the varieties even within the same sector, the life cycles depicted have to be representative and selective. The life cycles of several key commodity sectors are as follows.

Energy

For an example of the differences within a sector, one need look no further than energy. Natural gas can be consumed almost immediately after extraction from the ground. Crude oil, in contrast, has to be transformed into something else; crude is useless in its innate form. The refined products (e.g., gasoline and heating oil), in turn, have a number of potential processing steps depending on the quality of crude oil input and the relative demand for the various products. The steps for the energy complex can be summarized as shown in Exhibit 2.

Exhibit 2: Steps for the Energy Complex

Step	Title	Description
1.	Extraction	A drilling location is selected after surveys, and the well is dug. Enough underground pressure for the hydrocarbons to come out naturally may exist, or water or other tools may be required to create such pressure. Water is also used for the fracturing process known as "fracking," which breaks up shale formations to allow for oil or gas to be extracted.
2.	Storage	After extraction, crude oil is commercially stored for a few months on average in the United States, Singapore, and northern Europe and is strategically stored by many countries. In addition, oil may temporarily be stored on tanker ships. Natural gas may be delivered directly to the end consumer. Summer-extracted natural gas is often injected into storage for the winter months.
3.	Consumption Stage	Only natural gas is consumed at this stage because it does not need to be refined. Crude oil requires further processing.

Step	Title	Description
4.	Refining	Crude oil is distilled into its component parts via a process called "cracking." Heat is used to successively boil off the components that are, in turn, cooled down and collected (e.g., gasoline, kerosene), until only the remnants (e.g., asphalt) are left.
5.	Consumption Stage	The distilled products are separated and shipped to their various locations—by ship, pipe, train, or truck—for use by the end consumer.

Sources: Based on information from www.eia.gov/energyexplained/index.php?page=oil_refining#tab1, https://en.wikipedia.org/wiki/Petroleum_refining_processes (accessed 23 April 2019), and authors' research.

Refineries are extraordinarily expensive to build—typically costing several billion US dollars—depending on the processes required to purify and distill the oil. Part of the cost depends on the expected specifications of the crude oil input. Generally speaking, a low-grade, high sulfur source would require more investment than one with an assured lighter, "sweeter" source. Pipelines are also very costly: For example, the Keystone XL pipeline expansion between Canada and the United States was originally estimated to cost $5 billion in 2010, but the estimate was doubled to $10 billion in 2014. Even in countries dealing with violent insurrections (e.g., Libya, Iraq, Nigeria), damage to refineries has been generally modest because of their value to all parties. Pipelines, however, are often destroyed or cut off. Although these costs may appear staggering, they actually pale in comparison with the costs (and risks) of oil exploration, especially in deep offshore locations or geographically remote (or geopolitically risky) regions.

The crude oil market has a number of futures contracts and indexes that follow local grades and origins, but the two most commonly traded set of contracts follow the US-based crude oil (West Texas Intermediate, or WTI, crude oil) and the UK-located Brent crude oil from the North Sea. Likewise, there are futures for natural gas, gasoil, gasoline, and heating oil. Each has different delivery locations and standards, but the WTI and Brent contracts represent a high-quality refinery input that exploration and production companies can use as a hedging device.

EXAMPLE 3

Energy Life Cycle

1. Which of the following is a primary difference in the production life cycle between crude oil and natural gas?

   A. Only crude oil needs to be stored.

   B. European companies are the only ones that store crude oil.

   C. Natural gas requires very little additional processing after extraction compared with crude oil.

Solution:

C is correct. Natural gas can be used after it is extracted from the ground upon delivery, but crude oil must first be processed for later use. A is incorrect because both oil and natural gas are stored before usage. B is incorrect because many countries around the world store crude oil, both commercially and strategically.

Industrial/Precious Metals

The life cycle of both precious and industrial metals is probably the most flexible because the ore, as well as the finished products, can be stored for months (if not years) given the relative resistance to spoilage of metals (assuming proper storage). Otherwise, the life cycle parallels the energy one outlined previously, as shown in Exhibit 3.

Exhibit 3: Copper Purification Process

	Step Name	Description
1.	Extracting and Preparing	Ore (raw earth with ~2% metal content) is removed via a mine or open pit. Ore is then ground into powder and concentrated to roughly 25% purity.
2.	Smelting	The purified ore is heated, and more impurities are removed as slag, increasing the metal content to 60%. Further processes increase the concentration to 99.99%.
3.	Storage/Logistics	The purified metal is held typically in a bonded warehouse until it is shipped to an end user.

Sources: Based on information from http://resources.schoolscience.co.uk/CDA/14-16/cumining/copch2pg1.html (accessed 23 April 2019), www.madehow.com/Volume-4/Copper.html (accessed 23 April 2019), and authors' research.

Similar to refining crude oil, creating the economies of scale involved in the smelter and ore processing plants is critical. These are huge facilities for which marginal costs (i.e., the cost to convert the last pound or kilogram of processed ore into a useful metal) decline substantially with both the scale of the facility and its utilization (output as a percentage of capacity). As a result, when supply exceeds demand for a given industrial metal, it is difficult for suppliers to either cut back production or halt it entirely. Overproduction often continues until smaller or financially weaker competitors are forced to shut down. Because demand for industrial metals fluctuates with overall economic growth, as was discussed previously, there are substantial incentives for metals producers to invest in new capacity when their utilization (and profit) is high but huge economic and financial penalties for operating these facilities when demand falls off during an economic downturn. Ironically, given the typical economic cycle and the time lag involved after deciding to expand capacity, new supply often arrives just as demand is declining—which exacerbates pricing and profit declines.

With the lack of annual seasonality in the production of metals and ease of storage without spoilage, much of time variability comes from the demand side of the equation (e.g., construction and economic growth).

EXAMPLE 4

Industrial Metals Life Cycle

1. Because of large economies of scale for processing industrial metals, producers:

   A. immediately shut down new capacity when supply exceeds demand.

   B. have an incentive to maintain maximum operating production levels when demand declines.

   C. find it difficult to cut back production or capacity even when supply exceeds demand or demand slows.

Solution:

C is correct. Given the sizable facilities in which metals are produced and their capital requirements, reducing capacity is difficult when demand slows. A is incorrect because of the time lag involved in responding to reduced demand conditions. B is incorrect because producers would face financial losses if they maintained maximum production levels when there is a decline in demand.

Livestock

Livestock grows year round, but good weather and access to high-quality pasture and feed accelerate weight gain. As a result, there is fluctuation in the availability of animals ready for slaughter. The timing to maturity typically increases with size, with poultry maturing in a matter of weeks, hogs in months, and cattle in a few years. Taking the example of a hog, the life cycle begins with a sow (female hog) giving birth. Normally it takes about six months to raise a piglet to slaughter weight, and during that time it can be fed almost anything to get it up to proper bulk. In mass-scale production, soymeal and cornmeal are the most common foods. In contrast, cattle take longer to raise. For mass-scale breeding, the first one to two years are spent as "feeder cattle," first eating a grass diet in pasture. The next phase covers an additional 6–12 months whereby cattle are in a feed lot being fattened to slaughter weight, generally on a corn-based diet. Note that the various types of feed for these animals are other traded commodities.

The livestock industry in the United States has historically been among the least export-oriented of all the commodities because of the high risk of spoilage once an animal is slaughtered. However, advances in cryogenics (freezing) technologies with regard to chicken, beef, and pork mean that increasingly these products are moving from one part of the world to another in response to differences in production costs and demand. And as emerging and frontier market countries develop middle class consumers capable of purchasing meat protein as a regular part of their diet, there has been increased investment in the livestock and meatpacking industries in such countries as the United States and Brazil. These industries combine low-cost sources of animal feed, large grazing acreage, and strong domestic demand (leading to facilities with substantial economies of scale) as key export points to supply global demand.

Ranchers and slaughterhouses trade hog and cattle futures to hedge against their commitments. Ranchers can hedge both young cattle that are still in pasture (called feeder cattle) and animals being fattened for butchering (called live cattle).

EXAMPLE 5

Livestock Life Cycle

1. The US livestock sector has been among the least export-oriented commodity sectors because of:

   A. low technological innovation in the sector.

   B. high risk of spoilage once animals are slaughtered.

   C. little or no demand for US livestock from outside the United States.

Solution:

B is correct. Livestock incur a high risk of spoilage once they are slaughtered unless the meat is frozen. A is incorrect because advances in cryogenics have improved the ability to export from the United States. C is incorrect because demand for US livestock has expanded internationally, particularly in emerging market countries that are experiencing economic growth.

Grains

Grains in the Northern Hemisphere follow a similar growth cycle, with an analogous but opposite growth cycle in the Southern Hemisphere. Plants mature according to the following steps: (1) planting (placing the seeds in the ground after preparation/ fertilization work); (2) growth (the emerging of the seedling to full height); (3) pod/ ear/head formation (the food grain is created by the plant); and (4) harvest (the collection of the grain by the farmer). The timing in North America is shown in Exhibit 4 to illustrate the time it takes to grow each crop.

Exhibit 4: Timing for Grain Production in North America

	Corn	Soybeans	Wheat*
Planting	April–May	May–June	Sep.–Oct.
Growth	June–Aug.	July–Aug.	Nov.–March
Pod/Ear/Head Formation	Aug.–Sep.	Sep.	April–May
Harvest	Sep.–Nov.	Sep.–Oct.	June–July

* *The hard winter wheat variety, which has a higher protein content, is used here.*
Source: Authors' research.

Because demand for grains is year round, they are regularly stored in silos and warehouses globally. Some countries have a central purchasing bureau, and others depend on local or international trading companies to maintain stockpiles. Poor hygienic standards and logistics can result in a substantial loss of value to grains due to mold or insect/animal infestation. Monitoring the purchasing patterns of these government tenders can assist a research analyst in determining grain demand.

Farmers and consumers can trade futures to hedge their exposure to the crop in question, and the contract delivery months reflect the different times of the growing cycle outlined earlier. Ranchers also can use grain futures to hedge against the cost of feeding an animal.

Softs

Coffee, cocoa, cotton, and sugar are very different soft commodities in this sector, so we will focus on one that is grown and enjoyed broadly—coffee. Coffee is harvested somewhere all year round in the various countries that circle the Equator. After the coffee cherries are picked (still often by hand, to ensure that only ripe ones are taken), the husk and fruit are removed and the remaining bean dried. More than half of coffee uses the dry method in which the harvested cherries are laid out in the sun for two to three weeks. The wet method uses fresh water to soak the cherries, the soft pulp is removed, the bean is fermented for 12–48 hours, and then the bean is dried. The "green" beans are then hulled, sorted, and bagged for their final markets. With most of the consumption in faraway foreign markets, ships are commonly used to transport the beans to their buyer, which may store them in a bonded warehouse. The local buyer roasts the beans and ships them to the retail location (e.g., coffee house or supermarket) for purchase or brewing.

Coffee comes in two main varieties, robusta and arabica, although there are many others. Generally speaking, robusta beans are lower quality with less flavor than the arabica. There are two futures contracts associated with coffee: The robusta variety is traded in London, and the arabica variety is traded in New York. Note that the contracts are for the unroasted or "green" beans. The physical delivery aspect of these contracts allows for sellers to deliver the beans to an authorized bonded warehouse as fulfillment of the contract at expiration. Therefore, farmers and distributors can sell futures contracts to hedge the sales price of production, and coffee roasters can buy futures contracts to hedge coffee bean purchase costs; contract maturities can be selected by each to match their product delivery schedules.

4 VALUATION OF COMMODITIES

☐ contrast the valuation of commodities with the valuation of equities and bonds

The valuation of commodities compared with that of equities and bonds can be summarized by the fact that stocks and bonds represent financial assets and are claims on the economic output of a business, a government, or an individual. Commodities, however, are almost always physical assets. We say "almost always" because some newer classes of commodities, such as electricity or weather, are not physical assets in the sense that you can touch or store them.

Commodities are typically tangible items with an intrinsic (but variable) economic value (e.g., a nugget of gold, a pile of coal, a bushel of corn). They do not generate future cash flows beyond what can be realized through their purchase and sale. In addition, the standard financial instruments that are based on commodities are not financial assets (like a stock or bond) but are derivative contracts with finite lifetimes, such as futures contracts. As with other types of derivatives, commodity derivative contracts can and do have value, but they are contingent on some other factors, such as the price of the underlying commodity. Hence, the valuation of commodities is based not on the estimation of future profitability and cash flows but on a discounted forecast of future possible prices based on such factors as the supply and demand of the physical item or the expected volatility of future prices. On the one hand, this forecast may be quite formal and elaborately estimated by a producer or consumer. One can imagine the detailed inputs available to an oil company based on the labor and capital expenses needed to extract oil, refine it, and transport it to final sale as gasoline in your automobile. On the other hand, this forecast may be instinctively made by a floor trader with little fundamental analysis but instead with professional judgment based on years of experience and perhaps some technical analysis.

As opposed to a stock or bond that receives periodic income, owning a commodity incurs transportation and storage costs. These ongoing expenditures affect the shape of the forward price curve of the commodity derivative contracts with different expiration dates. If storage and transportation costs are substantial, the prices for a commodity futures contract will likely be incrementally higher as one looks farther into the future. However, sometimes the current demand for the commodity can move the spot price higher than the futures price. The spot price reflects the fact that, instead of going long a futures contract, one could buy the commodity today and store it until a future date for use. The expenditure would be the outlay/investment at today's spot price for the commodity along with (or net of) the future costs one would incur to store and hold it. This time element of commodity storage and supply and demand can generate "roll return" and affect investment returns. These and other factors figure into the assessment of futures pricing, which we will cover later.

Some commodity contracts require actual delivery of the physical commodity at the end of the contract versus settlement in a cash payment (based on the difference between the contract futures price and the spot price prevailing at the time of contract expiration). The force of arbitrage—which reflects the law of one price—may not be entirely enforced by arbitrageurs because some participants do not have the ability to make or take delivery of the physical commodity. In these situations, the relationships that link spot and futures prices are not an equality but are a range that only indicates the limit or boundary of value differences that can occur.

There is an important additional consideration concerning the link between spot and futures prices in commodities. Some of the largest users of commodity futures are businesses seeking to hedge price risk when that price is a critical source of either revenue or cost in their business operations. For example, the airline industry is very dependent on the cost of jet fuel for operating planes. The highly competitive nature of the industry results in tremendous price pressure on airfares, with a need for airlines to fill each flight with as many passengers as possible. The futures and swap markets for jet fuel allow airlines to lower the risk of higher fuel costs by hedging the price of future fuel purchases (particularly against surprise shocks in oil prices).

In addition, the price discovery process of the commodity futures markets provides airlines with insights about future fuel prices that help determine what prices to offer their customers for future flights while still making a profit. In fact, airline ticket sales are—in effect—selling a contract at a price set today for future delivery of a service—namely, a plane flight. In this case, the airlines will typically hedge their price risk and uncertainty about future fuel costs by purchasing ("going long") energy futures contracts.

EXAMPLE 6

Commodities versus Stocks and Bonds

1. In contrast to financial assets, such as stocks and bonds:

   A. commodities are always physical goods.

   B. commodities generate periodic cash flows.

   C. commodity investment is primarily via derivatives.

Solution:

C is correct. The most common way to invest in commodities is via derivatives. A is incorrect because although most commodities are physical goods, certain newer classes, such as electricity or weather, are not tangible. B is incorrect because commodities may incur, rather than generate, periodic cash flow through transportation and storage costs (when the commodities are physically owned).

EXAMPLE 7

Spot Commodity Valuation

1. What is a key distinction between the valuation of commodities compared with the valuation of stocks and bonds?
   - **A.** Valuation of commodities cannot be conducted using technical analysis.
   - **B.** Valuation of commodities focuses on supply and demand, whereas valuation of stocks and bonds focuses on discounted cash flows.
   - **C.** Valuation of stocks and bonds focuses on future supply and demand, whereas commodity valuation focuses on future profit margins and cash flow.

Solution:

B is correct. The valuation of commodities is based on a forecast of future prices based on supply and demand factors, as well as expected price volatility. In contrast, the valuation of stocks and bonds is based on estimating future profitability and/or cash flow. A is incorrect because technical analysis is sometimes applied to valuing commodities. C is incorrect for the reasons stated for choice B.

5 COMMODITIES FUTURES MARKETS: PARTICIPANTS

☐ describe types of participants in commodity futures markets

Public commodity markets are structured as futures markets—that is, as a central exchange where participants trade standardized contracts to make and take delivery at a specified place at a specified future time. As mentioned, futures contracts are derivatives because the value of the contract is derived from another asset. Both futures and forward contracts are binding agreements that establish a price today for delivery of a commodity in the future (or settlement of the contract in cash at expiration). As mentioned at the beginning of the reading, the focus of this reading is on futures, with forwards discussed only briefly.

Futures Market Participants

The key differences between futures and forward contracts is that futures contracts are standardized agreements traded on public exchanges, such as the Chicago Mercantile Exchange (CME), Intercontinental Exchange (ICE), and the Shanghai Futures Exchange (SHFE), and gains/losses are marked to market every day. Standardization allows a participant to enter into a contract without ever knowing who the counterparty is. In addition, the exchange oversees trading and margin requirements and provides some degree of self-imposed regulatory oversight. In contrast, forward contracts are commonly bilateral agreements between a known party that wants to go long and one that wants to go short. Because of their bilateral nature, forwards are considered to be OTC (over the counter) contracts with less regulatory oversight and much more customization to the specific needs of the hedging (or speculating) party. Often, the counterparty for a forward contract is a financial institution that is providing liquidity or customization in exchange for a fee. Although futures markets require that daily cash movements in the futures price be paid from the losing positions to the winning positions, forward contracts are usually only settled upon expiration or with some custom frequency dictated by the contract.

Early commodity exchanges operated as forward markets, but too often participants would go bankrupt when unrealized losses became realized at the end of the contract. The futures process was introduced to minimize this risk, with the exchange acting as payment guarantor. The first modern organized futures exchange was the Dojima Rice Exchange in Osaka, Japan, which was founded in 1710, although futures contracts were traded in England during the 16th century. The structure of futures markets is important to understand as a way of understanding the goals and roles of the various participants. When we consider any commodity, for every producer of that commodity there is a consumer. Thus, for participants who are long the physical commodity and want to sell it, there are also participants who are short the physical commodity and want to buy it. Therefore, for fairness between the two sets of participants, longs and shorts need to operate on an equal basis. As a coincident observation, the commodity markets are net zero in terms of aggregate futures positions (futures contract longs equal futures contract shorts). In contrast, in markets for stocks and bonds, there is a net long position because the issued stocks' and bonds' market values are equal to the net aggregate positions at the end of each day. Shorting an equity is constrained by the short seller's need to locate shares to short, the requirement to reimburse dividends on borrowed shares, and requirements to post and pay interest on margin that generally exceeds the margin required for long equity positions (as in the United States under Regulation T). In contrast, shorting commodity futures is much simpler, with short investors selling to long investors directly, and thus short investors post the same margin required of long investors.

There are a number of participants in commodity futures markets. First are *hedgers*, who trade in the markets to hedge their exposures related to the commodity. The second are long-term and short-term *traders* and *investors* (including index investors), who speculate on market direction or volatility and provide liquidity and price discovery for the markets in exchange for the expectation of making a profit. Third are the *exchanges* (or clearing houses), which set trading rules and provide the infrastructure of transmitting prices and payments. Fourth are *analysts*, who use the exchange information for non-trading purposes, such as evaluating commodity businesses, creating products that are based on commodity futures (e.g., exchange-traded funds, swaps, and notes), and making public policy decisions. Analysts also include brokers and other financial intermediaries who participate in the markets but do not take a position. Finally, *regulators* of both the exchange and traders exist to monitor and police the markets, investigate malfeasance, and provide a venue for complaints.

Commodity Hedgers

Hedgers tend to be knowledgeable market participants: One would expect that a company that drills for oil knows something about the supply and demand for oil and related forms of energy (at least in the long run). However, hedgers may not be accurate predictors of the future supply and demand for their product. Consider a baker who buys wheat for future delivery and benefits from a surprise drought (has locked in a low price in a supply-constrained market). However, the baker is hurt if the weather is beneficial (has effectively overpaid during a bumper crop). Given that a hedger can make delivery (if short the futures contract) or take delivery (if long the futures contract), he or she is generally motivated by risk mitigation with regard to cash flow, so the risk is more of an opportunity cost than an actual one.

It is important to keep in mind that hedging and speculating are not synonymous with being (respectively) long or short. As Exhibit 5 illustrates with some examples, both long and short positions can be associated with either hedging or speculating.

Exhibit 5: Examples of Hedging and Speculating Positions

	Long Position	Short Position
Hedging	Food manufacturer seeking to hedge the price of corn needed for snack chips	Gold mining company seeking to hedge the future price of gold against potential declines
Speculating	Integrated oil company seeking to capitalize on its knowledge of physical oil markets by making bets on future price movements	Commodity trading adviser (CTA) seeking to earn a profit for clients via a macro-commodity investment fund

Note also that hedgers tend to speculate based on their perceived unique insight into market conditions and determine the amount of hedging that is appropriate. From a regulatory standpoint in the United States, the difficulty in clearly distinguishing between hedging and speculating, therefore, has resulted in the separation of commodity producers and consumers from other trading participants regardless of whether commercial participants are actually speculating.

Commodity Traders and Investors

The commodity trading community, like other groups of traders, consists of three primary types: (1) informed investors, (2) liquidity providers, and (3) arbitrageurs. Informed investors largely represent the aforementioned hedgers and speculators, including index and institutional investors. With regard to the hedger, as mentioned previously, a company that drills for oil clearly is familiar with the supply and demand for oil and related forms of energy (at least in the long run). But hedgers may not be accurate predictors of the *future* supply and demand for their product.

Speculators, who believe that they have an information advantage, seek to outperform the hedger by buying or selling futures contracts in conjunction with—or opposite from—the hedger. This trading may be on a micro-second time scale or a multi-month perspective. For example, if a speculator has a superior weather prediction process, he or she has an information advantage and will trade accordingly. Alternatively, a speculator may be willing to act as a liquidity provider, knowing that producers and consumers may not be in the market at the same time. By buying when the producer wants to sell and selling when the consumer is ready to buy, speculators may be able to make a profit. In this sense, speculators are willing to step in, under the right pricing circumstances, to provide insurance to hedgers in return for an expected (albeit not guaranteed) profit.

Finally, arbitrageurs who have the ability to inventory physical commodities can attempt to capitalize on mispricing between the commodity (along with related storage and financing cost) and the futures price. They may own the storage facilities (bonded warehouses, grain silos, feedlots) and work to manage that inventory in conjunction with the futures prices to attempt to make arbitrage-style profits.

Commodity Exchanges

Commodity futures markets are found throughout the world. The CME and ICE are the primary US markets, having consolidated the bulk of the various specialist exchanges. Elsewhere in the Americas, the primary commodity exchange is in Brazil, where B3 trades softs, grains, and livestock. In Europe, the London Metal Exchange (owned by

Hong Kong Exchanges and Clearing Limited (HKEX) is the main industrial metals location globally. Energy and shipping are also traded out of London. In Asia, major commodity exchanges include China's Dalian Commodity Exchange and Shanghai Futures Exchange and Japan's Tokyo Commodity Exchange, among others. Finally, Indonesia (palm oil), Singapore (rubber), and Australia (energy, grains, wool) have supplementary commodity futures markets. Given that people all over the world need food, energy, and materials, exchanges have formed globally to meet those needs.

Commodity Market Analysts

Non-market participants use the exchange information to perform research and conduct policy as well as to facilitate market participation. Their activities affect market behavior, albeit in an indirect manner. Research may be commercially based. For example, a manufacturer may want to project and forecast the energy cost of a new process or product as part of an academic study comparing one market structure with another. Commodity prices are a key component in understanding sources of inflation and are used in other indexes that indicate quality of life for consumers and households. Governments that control natural resource extraction (e.g., nationalized oil companies) or tax commodity extraction by private entities are also interested in understanding futures markets to promote or discourage investment and/or raise revenue.

Commodity Regulators

Finally, various regulatory bodies monitor the global commodity markets. In the United States, commodity and futures regulation falls under the Commodity Futures Trading Commission (CFTC), which is a regulatory body separate from the better-known Securities and Exchange Commission. The CFTC delegates much of the direct monitoring to the National Futures Association (NFA)—a self-regulatory body—whose members are the authorized direct participants in the markets with customer responsibilities (e.g., clearing firms, brokers, advisers).

Outside the United States, most other countries have a unified regulatory structure. For example, the China Securities Regulatory Commission regulates both futures and securities (i.e., stocks and bonds). In Europe, most legislation in the area of financial services is initiated at the European Union (EU) level primarily through the European Securities and Markets Authority (ESMA). The Markets in Financial Instruments Directive (MiFID, and subsequently MiFID II), which first came into force in 2007, was a key element of EU financial market integration that focused largely on deregulation (MiFID II took effect in January 2018). Since 2009, existing legislative instruments, particularly for commodity derivative markets, have been revised and new regulations have been introduced with the aim to strengthen oversight and regulation, and they are subject to G–20 commitments. Harmonizing these different regulatory bodies is the International Organization of Securities Commissions (IOSCO), which is the international association of the world's securities and futures markets.

In all regions, the interests of the financial sector strongly influence debates and legislation on financial market regulation, including that of commodities.

EXAMPLE 8

Commodity Market Participants

1. Commodity traders that often provide insurance to hedgers are *best* described as:

   A. arbitrageurs.

B. liquidity providers.

C. informed investors.

Solution:

B is correct. Liquidity providers often play the role of providing an insurance service to hedgers who need to unload and transfer price risk by entering into futures contracts. A is incorrect because arbitrageurs typically seek to capitalize and profit on mispricing due to a lack of information in the marketplace. C is incorrect because informed investors predominantly keep commodity futures markets efficient by capitalizing on mispricing attributable to a lack of information in the marketplace.

6 COMMODITY SPOT AND FUTURES PRICING

☐ analyze the relationship between spot prices and futures prices in markets in contango and markets in backwardation

Commodity prices are typically represented by (1) spot prices in the physical markets and (2) futures prices for later delivery. The **spot price** is simply the current price to deliver a physical commodity to a specific location or purchase it and transport it away from a designated location. Examples of a spot price may be the price quoted at a grain silo, a natural gas pipeline, an oil storage tank, or a sugar refinery.

A **futures price** is a price agreed on to deliver or receive a defined quantity (and often quality) of a commodity at a future date. Although a producer and a consumer can enter into a bilateral contract to exchange a commodity for money in the future, there are (conveniently) many standardized contracts that trade on exchanges for buyers and sellers to use. Recall that a bilateral agreement is a forward contract, compared with a futures contract that is standardized and trades on a futures exchange. One benefit of futures markets is that information regarding contracts (number, price, etc.) is publicly available. In this way, the price discovery process that brings buyers and sellers into agreement is shared broadly and efficiently (in real time) with a global marketplace among the aforementioned market participants. The longest-maturity futures contract outstanding can have maturity extending from about a year (e.g., livestock) to several years (e.g., crude oil).

The difference between spot and futures prices is generally called the **basis**. Depending on the specified commodity and its current circumstances (e.g., supply and demand outlook), the spot price may be higher or lower than the futures price. When the spot price exceeds the futures price, the situation is called **backwardation**, and the opposite case is called **contango**. The origin of the word "contango" is a bit murky, but one theory is that it came from the word "continuation" used in the context of the London Stock Exchange in the mid-1800s. During this period, contango was a fee paid by the buyer to the seller to defer settlement of a trade (hence the near-term price would be less expensive than the longer-term price). The term "backwardation" describes the same arrangement if it were "backward," or reversed (i.e., payment to defer settlement was made by the seller to the buyer).

Backwardation and contango are also used to describe the relationship between two futures contracts of the same commodity. When the near-term (i.e., closer to expiration) futures contract price is higher than the longer-term futures contract price, the futures market for the commodity is in backwardation. In contrast, when the near-term futures contract price is lower than the longer-term futures contract price, the futures market for the commodity is in contango. The price difference (whether in backwardation or contango) is called the calendar spread. Generally speaking and assuming stable spot prices, the producer is willing to take a price in the future that is lower than the current spot price because it provides a level of certainty for the producer's business. The seller of that insurance on the other side of the trade profits because the lower futures price converges to the higher spot price over time. This relationship occurs when future commodity prices are expected to be higher because of a variety of reasons related to economic growth, weather, geopolitical risks, supply disruptions, and so on. As a long owner of a futures contract in contango, value will erode over time as the contract pricing moves closer to the spot price, assuming all else is unchanged. This relationship can be very costly for long holders of contracts if they roll futures positions over time. Although backwardation is "normal" for some contracts, there are other commodities that often trade in contango.

Exhibit 6 is a stylized representation of backwardation in West Texas Intermediate crude oil on CME Group's New York Mercantile Exchange (NYMEX).

Exhibit 6: Backwardation

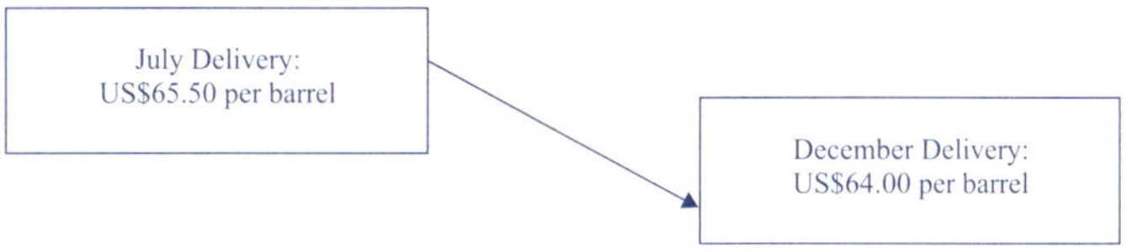

For contracts in a single (common) commodity, such as lean hogs or crude oil, the price differences may be traded as a spread rather than individually.

Exhibit 7 is a stylized representation of contango in lean hogs on the CME.

Exhibit 7: Contango

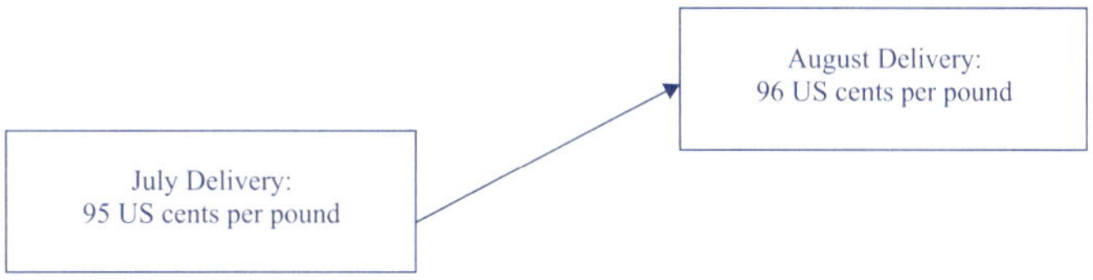

From these examples, the lean hogs July–August calendar spread is −1.0 cent per pound (95 − 96) and the crude oil July–December calendar spread is $1.50 per barrel (65.50 − 64.00).

A positive calendar spread is associated with futures markets that are in backwardation, whereas a negative calendar spread in commodities is associated with futures markets that are in contango. These calendar spreads are traded with their own bid–ask prices, trading range, and order book, similar to the single-month (i.e., nearest to expiration) futures contracts. Note that from this one trade, two contracts (one for each side, or "leg", of the spread) appear on an exchange's trading account and use their respective closing prices to determine profit or loss. Therefore, in the end, all trades and positions are valued at the close-of-day prices.

Commodity futures are settled by either cash or physical delivery. Cash-settled contracts, such as feeder cattle traded on the CME, have no value after the maturity date. Cash settlement is an important innovation in the evolution and development of commodity futures markets. To a certain extent, cash settlement enabled more involvement of two key participants in today's futures markets: speculators and arbitrageurs. It also introduced an entirely new way that hedgers (long or short) could participate in the market to transfer the future price risk of having to sell or buy a commodity without the complications associated with requiring physical delivery. Physical-settled commodity futures contracts require that the title of the actual commodity be transferred by the seller of the futures contract to the buyer at a particular place, on or by a particular date, and of a particular quality specification. For example, under a futures contract with West Texas Intermediate crude oil as the underlying physical commodity, crude oil meeting minimum specifications must be delivered to a particular set of tanks at Cushing, Oklahoma, in the United States. Meanwhile, a similar futures contract with Brent crude oil as the underlying physical commodity has delivery points in the North Sea off the coast of the United Kingdom and Norway. Supply and demand differences at these two faraway geographic locations can cause price divergences despite otherwise similar specifications.

Physical delivery also ensures a convergence of the futures and spot markets, which may not necessarily occur in a cash-settled market. Note that this statement does not imply market manipulation in cash-settled markets, because trading costs or other factors may limit complete convergence. The emergence of central exchanges for trading commodity futures facilitated this convergence with standardized contracts. In addition, these exchanges provided centrally established, publicly available pricing, which quickly replaced private pricing that was dependent on both contract terms and the location where transactions occurred.

Physical delivery can become complicated by such factors as quality or variety differences in the commodity. For example, robusta coffee (traded in the United Kingdom) cannot be delivered for arabica coffee (traded in the United States) because it is a different variety of coffee with a different venue for delivery. Likewise, raw (or unprocessed) sugar that is traded in the United States cannot be delivered for white processed sugar that is traded in the United Kingdom. Futures markets can address some of these peculiarities involving quality or differences in supply. When physical delivery is required, some futures contracts require a premium or discount associated with specifications. For example, arabica coffee prices are automatically adjusted based on the country of origin and the location of the warehouse where delivery is made.

In summary, spot prices are highly localized and associated with physical delivery, limiting the degree to which interested participants can seek to hedge or speculate on their future direction. In contrast, futures prices can be global (and if not, at least regional or national) in scope. They also are standardized for trading on exchanges to promote liquidity; act as a reference price point for customized (i.e., forward) contracts; and generate widely available, minimally biased data for market participants and governments to judge supply and demand and to make planning decisions.

In this manner, futures can be used to allocate risk and generate returns for market participants. On the surface, futures trading may seem muddled and chaotic on a micro level but serves as an overall social benefit by sending signals to producers and consumers for hedging and inventory-sizing purposes and to governments for the potential impact of policy decisions.

EXAMPLE 9

Spot and Futures Pricing (1)

1. The current price of the futures contract nearest to expiration for West Texas Intermediate (WTI) crude oil is \$65.00 per barrel, whereas the six-month futures contract for WTI is priced at \$60.75 per barrel. Based on this information:

   A. the futures market for WTI crude oil is currently in a state of contango.

   B. the futures market for WTI crude oil is currently in a state of backwardation.

   C. the shipping and delivery cost of WTI crude oil for a futures contract expiring in six months with physical delivery to Cushing, Texas, is \$4.25 per barrel.

Solution:

B is correct. Commodity futures markets are in a state of backwardation when the spot price is greater than the price of near-term (i.e., nearest to expiration) futures contracts, and correspondingly, the price of near-term futures contracts is greater than longer-term contracts. A is incorrect because the market would be in contango only if the deferred futures price exceeded that of the nearby futures price. C is incorrect because the shipping and delivery costs associated with physical delivery of a commodity are only one component in determining a commodity futures contract price. Geopolitical, seasonal, and other factors also influence the difference in delivery months.

EXAMPLE 10

Spot and Futures Pricing (2)

1. An important distinction between spot and futures prices for commodities is that:

   A. spot prices are universal across regions, but futures prices vary by location.

   B. futures prices do not reflect differences in quality or composition for a commodity.

   C. spot prices vary across region based on quality/composition and local supply and demand factors.

Solution:

C is correct. Spot prices of commodities vary across regions, reflecting logistical constraints and supply and demand imbalances that hinder the movement of materials. A is incorrect because spot prices tend to vary by region while futures are purposely standardized to facilitate trading. B is incorrect because while futures contracts are based on standardized specifications, composition and quality can be assigned premiums or discounts for delivery.

EXAMPLE 11

Spot and Futures Pricing (3)

1. An arbitrageur has two active positions in the commodity futures markets—one for lean hogs and the other for natural gas. The calendar spread on the lean hogs contract is quoted at –50 cents per pound, and the calendar spread on the natural gas contract is +$1.10 per million BTU (British thermal units). Based on this information, we can say that:

   A. only the spreads of these commodities, and not the individual prices, can be traded in commodity markets.

   B. the lean hogs futures market is in a state of backwardation and the natural gas futures market is in a state of contango.

   C. the lean hogs futures market is in a state of contango and the natural gas futures market is in a state of backwardation.

Solution:

C is correct. The spread is the difference between the current spot price for a commodity and the futures contract price. Because futures markets in a state of contango will have futures prices that exceed the spot price, the spread for these markets is negative. Conversely, in a state of backwardation, the spread is positive. A is incorrect because either the individual contract prices or the combined spreads can be traded. B is incorrect because, as mentioned earlier, the negative sign of the spread of lean hogs futures indicates a state of contango, whereas the positive sign of the spread of natural gas futures indicates a state of backwardation.

EXAMPLE 12

Spot and Futures Pricing (4)

1. A futures price curve for commodities in backwardation:

   A. always remains in backwardation in the long term.

   B. can fluctuate between contango and backwardation in the long term.

   C. reflects structural long-term industry factors, as opposed to dynamic market supply and demand pressures.

Solution:

B is correct. During periods of market stress or fundamental structural change in market conditions, some commodity futures price curves can rapidly shift from contango to backwardation or vice versa. A is incorrect because futures price curves can vacillate between contango and backwardation. C is incorrect because the shape of a commodity futures price curve reflects both long-term industry factors as well as market expectations of future supply and demand of the underlying commodity(ies).

THEORIES OF FUTURES RETURNS

7

☐ compare theories of commodity futures returns

Commodity futures markets have a reputation for volatility, but similar to other asset classes, there are theoretical bases for their long-run behavior. The original purpose of futures markets is for producers and consumers to hedge physical raw materials. In this section, we will discuss the underpinning theories of commodity futures returns, deconstruct the components of futures returns (i.e., at an index level), and close with thoughts on term structure (i.e., contango versus backwardation and implications of rolling futures contracts).

Theories of Futures Returns

Several theories have been proposed to explain the shape of the futures price curve, which has a dramatic impact on commodity futures returns. This reading covers three of the most important theories: (1) insurance theory, (2) hedging pressure hypothesis, and (3) theory of storage.

Insurance Theory

Keynes (1930), the noted economist and market speculator, proposed one of the earliest known theories on the shape of a commodity futures price curve. Also known as his theory of "normal backwardation," Keynes, in his 1930 tome *A Treatise on Money*, proposed that producers use commodity futures markets for insurance by locking in prices and thus make their revenues more predictable. A commodity producer is long the physical good and thus would be motivated to sell the commodity for future delivery to hedge its sales price. Imagine a farmer who thinks that next year she will grow a certain amount of soybeans on her land. She can sell a portion of her crop today that will be harvested months later to lock in those prices. She can then spend money on fertilizer and seed with more confidence about her budget. She may not be locking in a profit, but she would better understand her financial condition. Keynes's theory assumes that the futures curve is in backwardation "normally" because our farmer would persistently sell forward, pushing down prices in the future. Alternatively, this theory posits that the futures price has to be lower than the current spot price as a form of payment or remuneration to the speculator who takes on the price risk and provides price insurance to the commodity seller. The concept of normal backwardation is illustrated in Exhibit 8, using cotton prices pre- and post-harvest.

Exhibit 8: Normal Backwardation

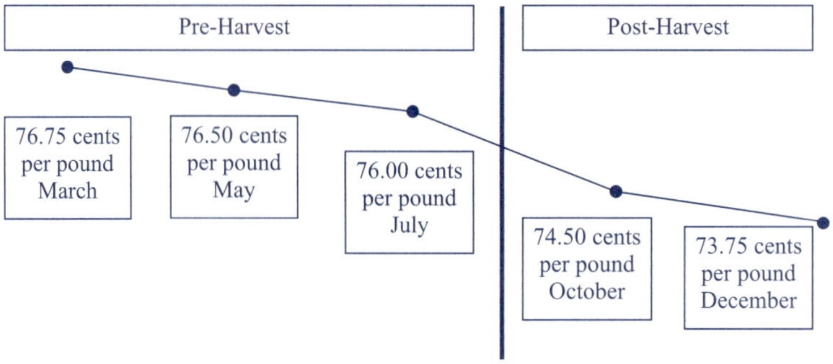

In terms of returns, if the front price is stable (in our example, 76.75 cents), then an investor can buy a further-dated contract (e.g., October) at 74.50 cents and wait for that contract to become the current contract. As the month of October approaches (and assuming no change in front prices), the October contract will reach 76.75 cents at maturity, and the speculator will make a profit of 2.25 cents per pound (note that a contract is 50,000 pounds, so that is a total profit of $1,125 per contract). Even if the contract does not fully converge, this theory holds that there should be positive excess returns (sometimes referred to as the risk premium) via this process to induce buying. As noted earlier, this process acts as a type of insurance for the farmer as well as a return for the investor providing such insurance.

Looking at the evidence, however, markets failed to match Keynes's hypothesis. Kolb (1992) looked at 29 futures contracts and concluded (with some humor) that "normal backwardation is not normal." That is, the presence of backwardation does not necessarily generate positive returns in a statistically significant fashion for the investor (or that contango leads to negative returns, for that matter). This result confirmed other studies, including one by Fama and French (1987). Therefore, a more sophisticated view developed to explain futures markets in contango (i.e., when the shape of the futures price curve is upward sloping with more distant contract dates), recognizing that certain commodity futures markets often show persistently higher prices in the future as opposed to the backwardation outlined by Keynes. This view is called the hedging pressure hypothesis.

Hedging Pressure Hypothesis

This perspective stemmed from multiple works, most notably outlined by De Roon, Nijman, and Veld (2000), who drew from Cootner (1960). Their research analyzed 20 futures markets from 1986 to 1994 and concluded that hedging pressure plays an important role in explaining futures returns. Hedging pressure occurs when both producers and consumers seek to protect themselves from commodity market price volatility by entering into price hedges to stabilize their projected profits and cash flow. Producers of commodities will tend or want to sell commodities forward and thus sell commodity futures. On the other side, consumers of commodities want to lock in prices of their commodity purchases and buy commodity futures. This theory applies to the aforementioned farmer selling a portion of next year's crop today. It can also apply to a central bank that wants to buy gold during each of the next 12 months as part of its monetary operations or a refinery that may want to lock in the price of its oil purchases and, conversely, the prices of its gasoline and heating oil production.

If the two forces of producers and consumers both seeking price protection are equal in weight, then one can envision a flat commodity curve, such as Exhibit 9 illustrates. In this idealized situation, the natural needs for price insurance by commodity buyers and sellers offset each other. There is no discount on the commodity futures price required to induce speculators to accept the commodity price risk because the hedging needs of both the buyer and seller complement and offset each other.

Exhibit 9: Balanced Hedging between Producers and Consumers

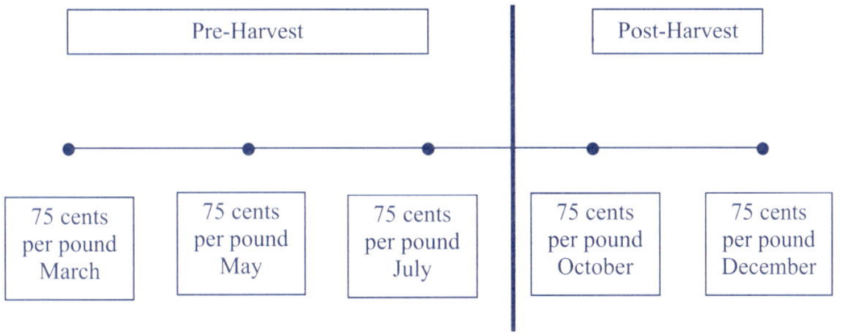

To use a different example, consider the problem of snowfall in the New England region of the United States. On one hand, small municipalities in Vermont, New Hampshire, or Maine may experience high levels of annual snowfall that are a risk to their snow removal budgets. On the other hand, ski resorts in New England have an opposite risk challenge: Low snowfall creates skiing revenue shortfalls (or adds to costs because of the need for man-made snow), whereas high snowfall winters are a potential bonanza for both higher revenue and lower operating costs. This situation is another example of when the hedging needs of two parties can offset each other and create a mutually beneficial outcome.

If commodity producers as a group are more interested in selling forward (seeking price insurance) than commodity consumers (as per the concept of normal backwardation), then the relative imbalance in demand for price protection will lead to the need for speculators to complete the market. But speculators will only do so when futures prices trade at a sufficient discount to compensate for the price risk they will take on. In this case, the shape and structure of the futures price curve can be illustrated as backwardation, as shown in Exhibit 10, which is consistent with Keynes's insurance theory.

Exhibit 10: Commodity Producers Exceed Consumers (Backwardation)

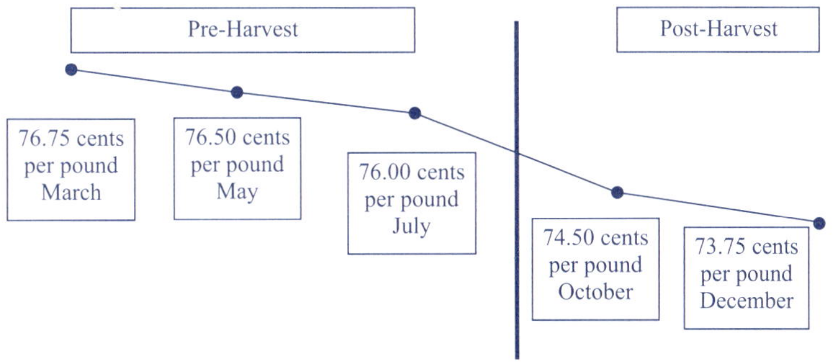

Finally, if the buyers of soybeans (as a group) are especially worried about the availability of the crop in the next harvest but producers of soybeans are less concerned about crop prices, there would be an imbalance in the demand for price insurance away from producers and toward buyers. This situation would lead to a futures price curve that represents a market in contango, as illustrated in Exhibit 11. In this case, the additional demand for price insurance among buyers (versus sellers) of the commodity will lead them to bid up the futures price to induce speculators to take on this price uncertainty risk.

Exhibit 11: Commodity Consumers Exceed Producers (Contango)

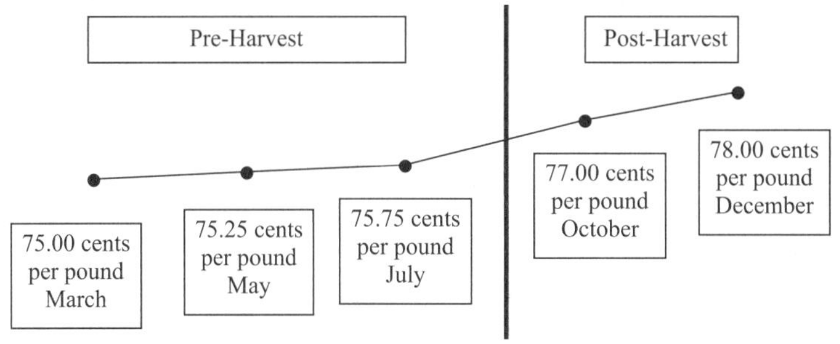

Although this theory is more robust than the Keynes's insurance theory, it is still incomplete. One issue is that producers generally have greater exposure to commodity price risk than consumers do (Hicks 1939). There are companies (as well as countries) that are almost entirely dependent on commodity production and thus are very concentrated in one sector, such as energy (e.g., British Petroleum, ExxonMobil), grains (e.g., Cargill, Louis Dreyfus), and metals (e.g., BHP Billiton, Vale, Rio Tinto, Shenhua).

Commodity consumers, in contrast, are very diffuse and often have other priorities (i.e., few if any individual people hedge their meat consumption or gasoline spending). Companies that purchase and use commodities in their products have a mixed record of price hedging, depending on the importance of the commodities in their cost structure. Clothing companies (e.g., Gap) generally do not hedge cotton because the spending is only a few percentage points of their expense base. Marketing and store experience (seen in rent, occupancy, and depreciation expenses) are much more important. But fast food companies hedge a wide variety of commodity inputs (e.g., livestock, grains, energy) because of the high degree of competition for prepared food at a low price point (e.g., McDonald's, Burger King, Wendy's).

In addition, both producers and consumers speculate on commodity prices, whether it is intended or unintended. Corporate treasury departments that serve as profit centers may adjust their hedges based on their views of the commodity markets. Their primary function may be to hedge, but a profit incentive can lead them to speculate. Individual farmers may not be overly aware of the commodity markets and thus have an inconsistent hedging approach. Trading companies actively trade the futures and physical markets in energy, metals, and grains. The very nature of trading companies is to know what is happening at all times along the value chain of any commodity market and profit from that informational advantage while bringing together buyers and sellers. In their case, profit maximization does not come from the production of commodities but trading around that production. In all of these examples, attempts to hedge may result instead in unintended speculative positions in which a company is not transferring price risk away but instead taking on more risk. The collapse in 1993 of Metallgesellschaft AG, one of Germany's largest industrial conglomerates at the time, from a poorly constructed gasoline, fuel oil, and heating oil hedge is a defining example of flawed commercial hedging.

In summary, despite its intuitive logic, applying the hedging pressure hypothesis remains a challenge because measuring the asymmetry in hedging pressure between buyers and sellers of a commodity is very difficult.

Theory of Storage

This theory, originally postulated by Kaldor (1939), focuses on how the level of commodity inventories helps shape commodity futures price curves. The key issue this theory attempts to address is whether supply or demand of the commodity dominates in terms of its price economics. Recall that commodities are physical assets, not virtual assets like stocks and bonds. Physical assets have to be stored, and storage incurs costs (rent, insurance, inspections, spoilage, etc.). Therefore, a commodity that is regularly stored should have a higher price in the future (contango) to account for those storage costs. In other words, supply dominates demand. In contrast, a commodity that is consumed along a value chain that allows for just-in-time delivery and use (i.e., minimal inventories and storage) can avoid these costs. In this situation, demand dominates supply and current prices are higher than futures prices (i.e., backwardation).

In theoretical terms, available inventory generates a benefit called a convenience yield. Having a physical supply of the commodity available is convenient for consumers of the commodity (e.g., individuals, bread companies, meat processors, refiners) because it acts as a buffer to a potential supply disruption that could otherwise force a shutdown of their operations. Because this type of risk/concern is inversely related to the inventory size and the general availability of the commodity (and confidence in its continued availability), the convenience yield is low when stock is abundant. However, the yield rises as inventories diminish and concerns regarding future availability of the commodity increase.

As a result, the theory of storage states that futures prices can be written this way:

Futures price

= Spot price of the physical commodity + Direct storage costs (such as rent and insurance) − Convenience yield.

This equation indicates that price returns and the shape of the curve can move in conjunction with the changes in the available inventory as well as actual and expected supply and demand. For example, when civil war broke out in Libya in 2011, the production of that country's high-quality crude oil was placed in jeopardy, constricting supply. In reaction, the spot price for high-quality crude oil increased. At the same time, the convenience yield increased in the futures contracts closer to expiration because there was a scramble to tap into alternative oil supplies for European refiners. The high quality of Libyan crude oil also restricted which substitute crude oil supplies could be used to replace production from the blocked oil fields and how soon these replacements could be available. The real-world constraints and complications imposed by geography and the logistics of the oil industry resulted in a multi-month delay for replacement supplies. As a result, in the further-out (i.e., longer time to expiration) futures contracts, the reaction was muted as traders assumed that such replacement supplies would be available. Thus the convenience yield remained lower in the deferred months. For this and other reasons, crude oil was pressured to trade in backwardation during 2011.

Unfortunately, while all these theories are reasonable and attractive, they have components that are unobservable or highly volatile and, therefore, not reliably calculable. Commodity producers and consumers regard storage costs as proprietary information. Events (weather, war, technology) can radically adjust convenience yield in a short time with unknown magnitude. Corn suitable for feed may not be suitable for human consumption, so defining inventories is tricky. In the end, we have frameworks and theories, but they are not easily applied and require judgment and analysis by a trader or a valuation system.

EXAMPLE 13

Theories of Commodity Futures Returns (1)

1. Which of the following *best* describes the insurance theory of futures returns?

   A. Speculators will not provide insurance unless the futures price exceeds the spot price.

   B. Producers of a commodity will accept a lower future price (versus the spot price) in exchange for the certainty of locking in that price.

   C. Commodity futures markets result in a state of contango because of speculators insisting on a risk premium in exchange for accepting price risk.

Solution:

B is correct. Under the insurance theory of futures returns, Keynes stated that producers of a commodity would prefer to accept a discount on the potential future spot price in return for the certainty of knowing the future selling price in advance. A is incorrect because the futures price must be below the spot price (normal backwardation) under the insurance theory of futures returns. C is incorrect because the insurance theory of futures returns implies markets are in backwardation, not contango.

EXAMPLE 14

Theories of Commodity Futures Returns (2)

1. Under the hedging pressure hypothesis, when hedging activity of commodity futures buyers exceeds that of commodity futures sellers, that futures market is *most likely*:

   A. flat.

   B. in contango.

   C. in backwardation.

Solution:

B is correct. Under the hedging pressure hypothesis, a market in contango typically results when excess demand for price insurance among commodity futures buyers drives up the futures price to induce speculators to take on price uncertainty risk. A is incorrect because a flat market would likely exist if futures demand activity largely equaled that of supply. C is incorrect because under this scenario, the futures market would be in contango, not backwardation.

EXAMPLE 15

Theories of Commodity Futures Returns (3)

1. Under the theory of storage, the convenience yield is:

   A. not affected by the supply of a commodity.

   B. typically low when the supply of a commodity is scarce.

   C. typically high when the supply of a commodity is scarce.

Solution:

C is correct. Under the theory of storage, the convenience yield of a commodity increases as supply (inventories) diminish and concerns about the future availability increase. A is incorrect because supply levels have a discernible effect on the convenience yield, as mentioned. B is incorrect because the convenience yield would likely be high, as opposed to low, when supply is limited.

EXAMPLE 16

Theories of Commodity Futures Returns (4)

1. Which of the following represents the formula for a futures price according to the theory of storage?

   A. Futures price = Spot price of the physical commodity + Direct storage costs − Convenience yield.

   B. Futures price = Spot price of the physical commodity + Direct storage costs + Convenience yield.

   C. Futures price = Spot price of the physical commodity − Direct storage costs + Convenience yield.

Solution:

A is correct. According to the theory of storage, the futures price reflects the current spot price as well as costs incurred in actually holding the commodity until its delivery. Such costs include direct storage, such as inventory and insurance costs. Finally, because there is a convenience yield (or benefit) to owning a commodity as a form of insurance against potential supply disruptions, this term is subtracted from the current price of the commodity.

COMPONENTS OF FUTURES RETURNS

8

- ☐ describe, calculate, and interpret the components of total return for a fully collateralized commodity futures contract
- ☐ contrast roll return in markets in contango and markets in backwardation

The total return on a commodity investment in futures is different from a total return on the physical assets. So, why do investors tend to use futures to gain their exposure to commodities? Building on the previous section, one can see that physical commodities need to be stored, fed, or perhaps treated against spoilage. Each commodity can be very different in its maintenance requirements; sustaining a hog in Mexico would be very different from storing crude oil in Nigeria.

The total return on commodity futures is traditionally broken into three components:

- the price return (or spot yield),
- the roll return (or roll yield), and
- the collateral return (or collateral yield).

The price return is the change in commodity futures prices, generally the front month contract. Note that this change is different from the change in the price of the physical commodity because lack of standardization of the physical markets makes that a difficult task. Calculating the price return is straightforward, as shown in the following equation:

Price return = (Current price − Previous price)/Previous price.

In addition, as investors move from futures contract to futures contract, they must "roll" that exposure by selling the current contract as it approaches expiration and buying the next contract (assuming a long position). Depending on the shape of the futures curve, there is likely a difference between the two prices. Thus, a portfolio may require buying more far contracts than the near contracts being sold. Investors can observe this scenario if backwardation is driving the shape of the commodity futures price curve.

Example (stylized): Assume an investor has £110 of exposure in wheat futures and the near contract is worth £10 of exposure (so, the investor has £110 exposure divided by £10 per contract, or 11 contracts), but the far (i.e., longer expiration date) contract is worth only £9 of exposure. Therefore, for the investor to roll forward his contracts and maintain a constant level of exposure, he needs to roll the 11 contracts forward and also buy an additional 1 contract to keep the post-roll exposure close to the pre-roll exposure (£110 exposure divided by £9 per contract equals 12.2, or 12 contracts rounded).

In the opposite case, if the futures price curve shape is being driven by contango—with a higher futures price in the far contract—this scenario will require the purchase of fewer commodity contracts than in the near position.

Example: Assume an investor has £108 of exposure in regular unleaded gasoline (or petrol) futures and the near contract is worth £9 of exposure (so, the investor has £108 exposure divided by £9 per contract, or 12 contracts), but the far contract is worth £10 of exposure. Therefore, for the investor to roll forward her contracts and maintain a constant level of exposure, she needs to roll only 11 contracts and sell the extra 1 near contract to keep the post-roll exposure close to the pre-roll exposure (£108 exposure divided by £10 per contract equals 10.8, or 11 contracts rounded).

Note that this roll return is not a return in the sense that it can be independently captured; investors cannot construct a portfolio consisting of only roll returns. Instead, **roll return** is an accounting calculation used to replicate a portion of the total return for a fully collateralized (i.e., with no leverage) commodity index. As defined, the roll return is effectively the accounting difference (in percentage terms) between the near-term commodity futures contract price and the farther-term commodity futures contract price (note that roll return is sometimes defined in monetary terms rather than as a percentage):

Roll return

= [(Near-term futures contract closing price − Farther-term futures contract closing price)/Near-term futures contract closing price] × Percentage of the position in the futures contract being rolled.

As an example, consider the roll from the March contract to the April contract for WTI crude oil on 7 February 2019 using the S&P GSCI methodology, which rolls its positions over a five-day period (so 1/5 = 20% per day):

March contract closing price: $52.64/barrel

April contract closing price: $53.00/barrel

($52.64 − $53.00)/$52.64 = −0.68% gross roll return × 20% rollover portion

= −0.13% net roll return (note the negative return in contango).

Note that different indexes use different periods and/or weights in their "rolling methodology." In Section 5, we will further discuss the rolling methodology of various indexes.

In his book *Expected Returns*, Ilmanen (2011) made the argument (challenged by others) that roll return is approximately equal to a risk premium. This concept relates back to Keynes and his theory of "normal backwardation." Keynes proposed that speculators take the other side of the transaction from commodity producers—who sell forward to lock in their cash flows—in an attempt to earn an excess return as compensation for providing price insurance to producers. Ilmanen attempted to demonstrate that positive long-run average returns are associated with positive roll return (i.e., in commodities for which futures prices are in backwardation) and negative long-run average returns are associated with negative roll return. However, because 40% of the commodities examined by Ilmanen (p. 255) had negative roll returns but positive total returns, one cannot directly conclude that backwardation earns a positive total return.

The **collateral return** is the yield (e.g., interest rate) for the bonds or cash used to maintain the investor's futures position(s). The minimum amount of funds is called the initial margin. If an investor has less cash than required by the exchange to maintain the position, the broker who acts as custodian will require more funds (a margin call) or close the position (buying to cover a short position or selling to eliminate a long position). Collateral thus acts as insurance for the exchange that the investor can pay for losses.

For return calculations on indexed investments, the amount of cash would be considered equal to the notional value of the futures. This approach means no leverage. For expected returns, commonly, investors should use a risk-free government bond that most closely matches the term projected. Most commodity indexes use short-term US Treasury bills, but if one is forecasting 10-year returns, then for collateral return purposes, a 10-year constant maturity government bond would have a more appropriate term.

Although indexes will be discussed more fully later in the reading, to illustrate the commodity return elements just discussed, one can use an index—in this case, the aforementioned S&P GSCI, which has one of the longest backtested and live history of the investable commodity indexes. Exhibit 12 shows the disaggregation of its return components.

Exhibit 12: Average Annual Return Components of the S&P GSCI, January 1970–March 2019

S&P GSCI Return	Total Return	Spot Return	Roll Return[1]	Collateral Return[1]
Return[2]	6.8%	3.0%	–1.3%	5.0%
Risk[3]	19.8%	19.8%	4.2%	1.1%
Correlation[4]		0.97	–0.11	–0.14

[1] *Roll return is defined as the excess return on the S&P GSCI minus the spot of the S&P GSCI. Collateral return is defined as the total return on the S&P GSCI minus the excess return of the S&P GSCI. The excess return measures the returns accrued from investing in uncollateralized nearby commodity futures.*
[2] *Monthly returns are used.*
[3] *Risk is defined as annualized standard deviation.*
[4] *Correlation with the S&P GSCI Total Return.*
Source: Author's research based on data from S&P Dow Jones Indices.

As can be seen in the table, over the past 40+ years, the S&P GSCI generated 6.8% in geometrically compounded annualized returns, with about three-quarters derived from interest rates (collateral return). The commodity price spot return component of the index (which has varied over time) contributed to approximately 45% of the total return (3.0% out of 6.8%), whereas the roll return subtracted from the overall return by –1.3% (or 130 bps) on an annualized basis. Investors can see the effect of commodities on inflation via the price return.

The volatility and correlations of the components of index returns are driven by the changes in the spot price return (effectively the same annualized standard deviation of 19.8% as the S&P GSCI with a 97% correlation). The roll return and collateral return do not drive, in general, the monthly returns historically. This link between commodity futures prices and commodity total return indexes helps to define commodities as a separate and investable asset class.

In summary, the total return on a fully collateralized commodity futures contract can be described as the spot price return plus the roll return plus collateral return (risk-free rate return). With an index, a return from rebalancing the index's component weights—a **rebalance return**—would also be added. Using historical data (at the risk of it becoming outdated over time), one can demonstratively use the total return deconstruction to analyze commodities.

EXAMPLE 17

Total Returns for Futures Contracts (1)

1. A commodity futures market with pricing in backwardation will exhibit which of the following characteristics?

   A. The roll return is usually negative.

   B. Rolling an expiring futures contract forward will require buying more contracts in order to maintain the same dollar position in the futures markets.

   C. Rolling an expiring futures contract forward will require buying fewer contracts in order to maintain the same dollar position in the futures markets.

Solution:

B is correct. Commodity futures markets in backwardation exhibit price curves in which longer-dated futures prices are priced lower than near-dated contracts and the nearest-dated contract is priced lower than the current spot price. With a lower futures price on the futures curve, rolling contracts forward in backwardation would require purchasing more contracts to maintain the same dollar position. A is incorrect because the roll return is usually positive, not negative, in markets in backwardation. C is incorrect because an investor would need to purchase more, not fewer, contracts in markets in backwardation to maintain his or her total dollar position.

EXAMPLE 18

Total Returns for Futures Contracts (2)

1. An investor has realized a 5% price return on a commodity futures contract position and a 2.5% roll return after all her contracts were rolled forward. She had held this position for one year with collateral equal to 100% of the position at a risk-free rate of 2% per year. Her total return on this position (annualized excluding leverage) was:

   A. 5.5%.

   B. 7.3%.

   C. 9.5%.

Solution:

C is correct. Total return on a commodity futures position is expressed as

Total return = Price return + Roll return + Collateral return.

In this case, she held the contracts for one year, so the price return of 5% is an annualized figure. In addition, the roll return is also an annual 2.5%. Her collateral return equals 2% per year × 100% initial collateral investment = 2%.
So, her total return (annualized) is

Total return = 5% + 2.5% + 2% = 9.5%.

EXAMPLE 19

Total Returns for Futures Contracts (3)

1. An investor has a $10,000 position in long futures contracts (for a hypothetical commodity) that he wants to roll forward. The current contracts, which are close to expiration, are valued at $4.00 per contract, whereas the longer-term contract he wants to roll into is valued at $2.50 per contract. What are the transactions—in terms of buying and selling new contracts—he needs to execute in order to maintain his current exposure?

   A. Close out (sell) 2,500 near-term contracts and initiate (buy) 4,000 of the longer-term contracts.

B. Close out (buy) 2,500 near-term contracts and initiate (sell) 4,000 of the longer-term contracts.

C. Let the 2,500 near-term contracts expire and use any proceeds to purchase an additional 2,500 of the longer-term contracts.

Solution:

A is correct. To roll over the same level of total exposure ($10,000), he will need to do the following:

Sell

$10,000/$4.00 per contract = 2,500 existing contracts.

And replace this position by purchasing

$10,000/$2.50 per contract = 4,000 existing contracts.

9 CONTANGO, BACKWARDATION, AND THE ROLL RETURN

☐ contrast roll return in markets in contango and markets in backwardation

To reiterate, contango and backwardation—and the resulting roll return—fundamentally reflect underlying supply and demand expectations and are accounting mechanisms for the commodity term structure. We can gain a sense of these patterns by again examining the history of an index. Recall that from January 1970 to March 2019, the historical roll return of the S&P GSCI subtracted 1.3% from the average annual total return, with a standard deviation of 4.7%. That historical roll return varied over this time period, as depicted in Exhibit 13.

Exhibit 13: Historical One-Year S&P GSCI Price and Roll Return (Monthly Returns, January 1970–December 2019)

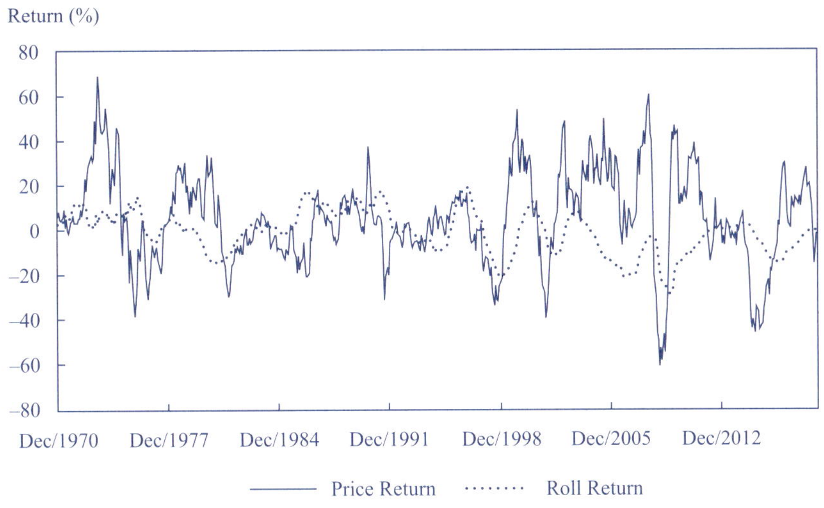

Note: The roll return is rolling monthly.

As the graph shows, periods of either backwardation or contango do not persist indefinitely. A simple review of the Exhibit 13 history demonstrates as much. Furthermore, with a correlation of 3%, roll return is not very indicative of price return, also contrary to popular belief. Positive price returns are associated with negative roll returns as well as positive roll returns. In some cases, certain sectors are indeed associated with contango, as can be seen in Exhibit 14.

Exhibit 14: Average Annual Sector Roll Return and Standard Deviation[a]

	S&P GSCI Total	Energy	Industrial Metals	Agriculture	Livestock	Precious Metals	Softs
Mean roll return (annual)[b]	–1.3%	–1.5%	–1.3%	–4.5%	–1.1%	–5.1%	–5.5%
Standard deviation of the mean (annual)[b]	0.4%	0.8%	0.5%	0.4%	0.5%	0.2%	0.6%
Maximum roll return (annual)[b]	18.9%	31.5%	45.9%	29.2%	35.5%	–0.4%	25.6%
Minimum roll return (annual)[b]	–29.6%	–39.5%	–16.6%	–18.6%	–31.2%	–15.4%	–24.9%

[a] *The periods covered vary by sector:*

- S&P GSCI total: December 1969–March 2019
- Energy: December 1982–March 2019
- Industrial metals: December 1976–March 2019
- Agriculture: December 1969–March 2019
- Livestock: December 1969–March 2019
- Precious metals: December 1972–March 2019

- Softs: December 1994–March 2019

[b] *Calculated using rolling 12-month periods of monthly data.*
Sources: Based on data from Bloomberg and Coloma Capital Futures.

Exhibit 14 highlights a few important factors. First, industrial metals, agriculture, livestock, precious metals, and softs have statistically strong negative mean roll returns. Only energy has a statistical possibility of a positive mean roll return, but that opportunity has diminished after 2010. Note from our comparison of the commodity sectors that industrial metals, agriculture, livestock, precious metals, and softs are stored for extended periods in warehouses, silos, and feedlots. In fact, precious metals historically have had negative roll returns because of gold's perpetual storage as an alternative currency. Historically, energy is consumed on a real-time basis apart from various strategic reserves, with the minimal storage buffer thus creating a lower or negative convenience yield. However, since 2010, the emergence of shale oil production in the United States has increased oil's convenience yield to the point that historical scarcity risk is much lower than before. Also, oil supply risk has shifted to China during this period as that country took over the United States' position as the lead oil importer. Finally, OPEC (with the inclusion of Russia and a few other non-OPEC members) regained some pricing power as the cartel achieved some success with supply restriction. Bringing it all together, one can conclude that indexes and long-only strategies that overweight agriculture, livestock, precious metals, and softs should expect to see negative roll returns (or roll yields). Energy commodities (apart from natural gas) have an opportunity for positive roll return, assuming producers successfully withhold supply from the market.

In conclusion, roll return can have an important impact on any single period return but overall has been relatively modest compared with price return. Furthermore, roll return is very sector dependent, which leads to a conclusion that sector diversification or concentration will have a profound impact on an investor's overall roll return based on a diversified portfolio of commodity futures.

EXAMPLE 20

Roll Return

1. When measuring its contribution to the total return of a commodity futures position, the roll return:

   A. typically has a significant contribution to total return over both single and multiple periods.

   B. typically can have an important contribution to total return in any single period but is relatively modest over multiple periods.

   C. is always close to zero.

Solution:

B is correct. Historically, the roll return has been relatively modest compared with price return but can be meaningful in any single period. A is incorrect because the roll return is typically modest over shorter periods of time, as noted earlier. C is incorrect because futures contracts generate positive or negative roll returns, depending on the commodity and prevailing market conditions.

COMMODITY SWAPS

10

☐ describe how commodity swaps are used to obtain or modify exposure to commodities

Instead of futures, some investors can gain market exposure to or hedge risk of commodities via swaps. A **commodity swap** is a legal contract involving the exchange of payments over multiple dates as determined by specified reference prices or indexes relating to commodities. In the world of commodities, a series of futures contracts often forms the basis of the reference prices. For example, an independent oil refiner may want to hedge its oil purchases over an extended period. The refiner may not want to manage a large number of futures contracts but maintain flexibility with regard to its oil supply source. By entering into a swap contract—particularly one that is cash settled instead of physically settled—the refiner can be protected from a price spike and yet maintain flexibility of delivery.

Based on this example, one can see why commercial participants use swaps: The instrument provides both risk management and risk transfer while eliminating the need to set up and manage multiple futures contracts. Swaps also provide a degree of customization not possible with standardized futures contracts. The refiner in the example may negotiate a swap for a specific quality of crude oil (e.g., Heavy Louisiana Sweet instead of West Texas Intermediate, or WTI) as its reference price or a blend of crudes that shifts throughout the year depending on the season. Customization through the use of a swap may also have value by changing the quantity of crude oil hedged over time, such as lowering the exposure during the planned shutdown and maintenance periods at the refinery.

On the other side of the transaction from the refiner (or other hedging or speculating entity) would be a swap dealer, typically a financial intermediary, such as a bank or trading company. The dealer, in turn, may hedge its price risk exposure assumed in the swap through the futures market or, alternatively, negotiate its own swap with another party or arrange an oil purchase contract with a crude oil producer. The dealer may also choose to keep the price risk exposure, seeking to profit from its market information. A diagram demonstrating this swap transaction is shown in Exhibit 15.

Exhibit 15: Swap Market Participant Structure

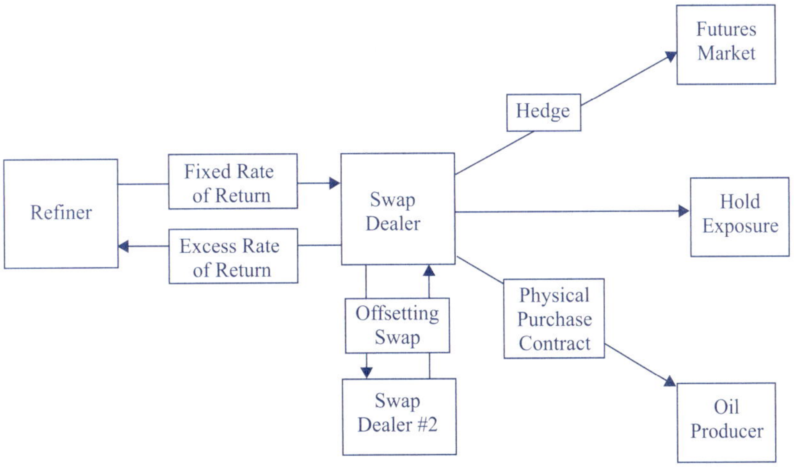

To further understand the diagram in Exhibit 15, assume we had the following scenario:

1. An oil refiner goes long a swap at the end of December that pays the amount exceeding $70 per barrel every month-end through September.
2. The oil refiner would pay a swap counterparty a premium (in this example, $25) for this privilege because it is effectively long a series of call options.

The flow of funds in the swap transaction would be as shown in Exhibit 16.

Exhibit 16: Flow of Funds for Swap Transaction Example

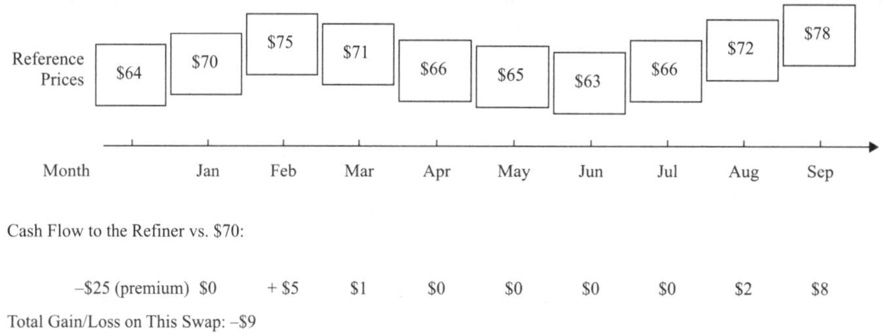

Total gain/loss on this swap to the refiner is –$9 (found by summing the cash flows and ignoring present value calculations or other considerations).

Although this example of a swap lost money and effectively increased the refiner's cost of a barrel of oil by $1 for this time period (given that the net loss on the swap was $9 over nine months), the swap protected the company against the risk of a cash squeeze during those months when an oil price spike could have impaired the liquidity of the company. The swap also defined the cost up front, giving a measure of cash flow predictability. Note that accounting standards and practices for swaps may also have an impact on the attractiveness of swaps. Given that oil prices are subject to many events beyond a company's control, a company looking to protect itself from financing risk may find that a swap can be a valuable tool.

There are many types of swaps available in the marketplace because they are not standardized, exchange-traded contracts like futures. The previous example of the refiner is an example of an "excess return swap." In an excess return swap, the payments to either party are driven primarily by the changes in price of each of the futures contracts that make up the index. The net change in the prices of the underlying futures contracts is defined as the "excess" return, and the excess return is multiplied by the contract's notional amount to determine the payments between buyer and seller.

Total Return Swap

Another common swap in commodities is a "total return swap." In a total return swap, the change in the level of the index will be equal to the returns generated by the change in price of each of the futures contracts that make up the index plus a return based on interest earned on any cash collateral posted on the purchase of the futures contracts that make up the index. If the level of the index increases, the swap buyer receives payment net of the fee paid to the seller; if the level of the index decreases between two valuation dates, the swap seller receives payment (plus the fee charged to the buyer). This type of swap is generally used by large institutional investors (e.g., pension plans) as opposed to commodity producers or buyers. With a total return swap, the investor seeks exposure to commodity returns, often because of the low return correlation of commodities with other asset classes (e.g., stocks or bonds) or as a reflection of the view that commodities provide a valuable inflation hedge for asset/liability matching (ALM). Therefore, such investors would engage in a total return swap that provides them with long exposure to the future returns from a commodity index that is used as the reference price. Again, accounting treatment with respect to futures often drives these decisions.

As an example of a total return swap, assume an investor who manages a defined benefit retirement plan desires commodity exposure for the reasons noted earlier. Given the size of the portfolio manager's plan assets (assume £2 billion), the manager is seeking approximately 5% exposure of plan assets to commodities. More specifically, the manager has decided that this £100 million exposure (5% of £2 billion) should be to the (hypothetical) China Futures Commodity Index (CFCI) and should remain for five years. Based on this decision, the manager issues a request for proposals (RFP) and, after evaluating the various bidders, contracts with a Swiss bank for a total return swap that will provide the desired exposure.

If on the first day of the swap agreement the CFCI increased by 1%, then the swap dealer would owe the manager £1 million (£100 million × 1%). If on the second day the CFCI declined by 5%, then the manager would owe £5 million to the dealer. Commonly, the dealer will hedge its short index exposure with futures or the physical commodity investments. Because the manager would be seeking the risk–return exposure offered by commodities, the manager would not generally hedge its exposure.

Basis Swap

Another common commodity swap is a basis swap, in which periodic payments are exchanged based on the values of two related commodity reference prices that are not perfectly correlated. These swaps are often used to adjust for the difference (called the basis) between a highly liquid futures contract in a commodity and an illiquid but related material. For example, a swap may pay the difference between the average daily prices of Brent crude oil (very liquid) and heavy crude oil available for delivery in the Gulf of Mexico (less liquid). This can be a very valuable arrangement for, in this example, refineries on the US Gulf Coast that have heavily invested in processing cheaper heavy crudes that come from such countries as Mexico or Venezuela. Because prices of these crudes do not always move in tandem with more common crudes, such as Brent, they derive a price basis between the two. It should be noted that "basis" has other meanings as well, depending on the commodity in question. For example, in grains, the basis may refer to the difference between the soybean contract and physical soybeans available for delivery at the Mississippi River.

Variance Swaps and Volatility Swaps

Two final types of relatively common commodity swaps are variance swaps and volatility swaps. Variance swaps of commodities are similar in concept to variance swaps of equities in that there is a variance buyer and a variance seller. Two parties agree to periodically exchange payments based on the proportional difference between an observed/actual variance in the price levels of a commodity (over consecutive time periods), and some fixed amount of variance established at the outset of the contract. If this difference is positive, the variance swap buyer receives a payment; if it is negative, the variance swap seller receives payment. Often the variance differences (observed versus fixed) are capped to limit upside and losses.

Volatility commodity swaps are very similar to variance swaps, with the exception that the direction and amount of payments are determined relative to the observed versus expected volatility for a reference price commodity. In this arrangement, the two sides are not speculating on the level or direction of prices but instead on how volatile prices will be versus expectations. A volatility seller will profit if realized volatility is lower than expectations, whereas the counterparty volatility buyer anticipates higher than expected volatility.

EXAMPLE 21

Commodity Swaps (1)

1. A portfolio manager enters into a $100 million (notional) total return commodity swap to obtain a long position in commodity exposure. The position is reset monthly against a broad-based commodity index. At the end of the first month, the index is up 3%, and at the end of the second month, the index declines 2%. What are two payments that would occur between the portfolio manager and the swap dealer on the other side of the swap transaction?

   A. No payments are exchanged because a net cash flow only occurs when the swap agreement expires.

   B. $3 million would be paid by the swap dealer to the portfolio manager (after Month 1), and $2 million would be paid by the portfolio manager to the swap dealer (after Month 2).

   C. $3 million would be paid by the portfolio manager to the swap dealer (after Month 1), and $2 million would be paid by the swap dealer to the portfolio manager (after Month 2).

Solution:

B is correct. Because the portfolio manager has a long position in the total return commodity swap, he or she will receive payments when the commodity index rises and make payments when the commodity index declines. The payment calculations after the first two months are as follows:

Month 1: $\$100 \text{ million} \times 3\% = \$3 \text{ million}$.

Month 2: $\$100 \text{ million} \times -2\% = -\$2 \text{ million}$.

A is incorrect because swap payments are made periodically (in this case monthly) and not withheld to the end of the contract. C is incorrect because the payments would be in the opposite direction for each month.

EXAMPLE 22

Commodity Swaps (2)

1. In a commodity volatility swap, the direction and amount of payments are determined relative to the observed versus reference:

   A. direction in the price of a commodity.

   B. variance for the price of a commodity.

   C. volatility for the price of a commodity.

Solution:

C is correct. In a commodity volatility swap, the two sides of the transaction are speculating on expected volatility. A volatility seller will profit if realized volatility is lower than expectations, whereas the volatility buyer benefits from higher than expected volatility. A is incorrect because a volatility swap is based on price volatility, not direction. B is incorrect because a volatility swap is based on price volatility as opposed to price variance (price volatility squared).

COMMODITY INDEXES 11

☐ describe how the construction of commodity indexes affects index returns

As in other parts of the investment universe, indexes have been created to portray the aggregate movement of commodity prices, investment vehicles, and investing approaches. In fact, one could say that an asset class does not exist without the presence of at least one representative index.

Commodity indexes play three primary roles in commodity sector investments. First, an index can be used as a benchmark to evaluate broader moves in commodity pricing. Second, as a broad indicator, an index can be used for macroeconomic or forecasting purposes by examining statistically significant relationships between movements in the commodity index and other macroeconomic variables. Finally, an index can act as the basis for an investment vehicle or contract providing the information needed to record, monitor, and evaluate price changes that affect contract value.

Although there are a number of commodity indexes, the following are used most frequently for the purposes just mentioned: (1) the S&P GSCI; (2) the Bloomberg Commodity Index (BCOM), formerly known as the Dow Jones–UBS Commodity Index (DJ–UBS); (3) the Deutsche Bank Liquid Commodity Index (DBLCI); (4) the Thomson Reuters/CoreCommodity CRB Index (TR/CC CRB); and (5) the Rogers International Commodities Index (RICI). The following are key characteristics that differentiate each of these indexes:

- The *breadth* of coverage (number of commodities and sectors) included in each index, noting that some commodities have multiple reference contracts (e.g., for crude oil, the common contracts are for West Texas Intermediate in the United States and Brent crude for Europe).
- The relative *weightings* assigned to each component/commodity and the related methodology for how these weights are determined.
- The *rolling methodology* for determining how those contracts that are about to expire are rolled over into future months. This decision has a direct impact on the roll return (or yield) of the overall commodity. Recall that roll return is one of the three key components of overall commodity returns.
- The methodology and frequency for *rebalancing* the weights of the individual commodities, sectors, and contracts in the index to maintain the relative weightings assigned to each investment. As with stocks and bonds within a portfolio, the opportunity to earn positive rebalance returns for commodities depends on the correlation of the underlying components of the index and the propensity of underperforming components to revert back to the

mean. For example, a drought may cause cotton prices to increase, but a strong crop the following year will cause prices to collapse. A rebalance sale of the overvalued cotton exposure into an undervalued exposure should "lock in" some of that gain. The rebalance return will likely vary depending on the methodology used by the index.

- The *governance* of indexes is important because it is the process by which all the aforementioned rules are implemented. For example, some indexes are rules-based, whereas others are selection-based. The rules-based indexes follow a quantitative methodology, whereas selection-based indexes are more qualitative in that an index committee picks the commodities. Also, governance oversees the independence of index providers so that, according to best practices of the Index Industry Association, the asset price should be independent from the index provider, which, in turn, should be independent from the product provider (e.g., the exchange-traded fund or swap provider).

For the index to be a viable and useful construct, it should be investable; that is, investors or their agents should be able to replicate the methodology outlined to translate the index concept into a representation of the asset class. For this reason, index providers and investors must be mindful of the venues (physical or electronic) for trading each commodity index, the liquidity and turnover of contracts based on each commodity index, and the term structure of each index (i.e., how far into the future the index extends and which months it covers). The weighting method for components in an index is key to diversification and—combined with rebalancing frequency—influences the opportunity to earn positive rebalance returns.

An index that requires investments in exchanges all over the world is more difficult and expensive for an investor to replicate. An emphasis on illiquid contracts has a negative impact on transaction costs. Contracts without a full yield curve may be a challenge to analyze and trade. In other words, seemingly small execution concerns are magnified when constructing a benchmark that represents an entire asset class, such as commodities. And indexes that choose (perhaps inadvertently) contracts that more commonly trade in backwardation may appear to improve forward-looking performance (because this generates a positive roll return), whereas those that more commonly trade in contango may hurt performance. Exhibit 17 summarizes the various elements of the main indexes discussed.

Exhibit 17: Overview of Major Commodity Indexes

	Index				
Element	S&P GSCI	BCOM	DBLCI	TR/CC CRB	RICI
Adoption date	1991	1998	2003	2005 (current version)	1998
Number of commodities	24	23	14	19	38
Weighting method	Production weighted	Production and liquidity weighted	Fixed weight	Fixed weight	Fixed weight
Rolling methodology	Nearby most liquid contract, monthly	Front month to next or second month	Optimized on roll return	Front month to next month	Front month to next month

	Index				
Rebalancing frequency	Annually	Annually	Annually	Monthly	Monthly
Individual investor funds available?	Yes	Yes	Yes	Yes in some jurisdictions as well as an exchange-traded fund on a related index	Yes

Note: Information is as of 30 April 2019.
Sources: Information from respective sponsor websites, Bloomberg, and authors' research.

Exhibit 17 helps distinguish the key characteristics that differentiate these five commercially important commodity indexes. In terms of coverage (the number of commodities and sectors included in the index), all five of these indexes have broad sector coverage, including energy, grains, livestock, precious metals, industrial metals, and softs. The only exception is the DBLCI, which does not have any livestock exposure. At the other extreme, the RICI includes relatively exotic (and thus illiquid) commodities, such as lumber, oats, and rubber. As a further example of its unique nature, the RICI once included adzuki beans (the red beans found in many Asian cuisines) and palm oil.

S&P GSCI

The S&P GSCI is the second oldest of the selected commodity indexes. The index is based on 24 commodities and applies liquidity screens to include only those contracts with an established minimum level of trading volume and available historical pricing. It uses a world production value-weighting scheme that gives the largest weight to the most valuable commodity on the basis of physical trade value. It should be no surprise that crude oil has the highest single weight and energy has the highest sector weight (historically as high as 80%) in this index. This approach is most similar to a market-capitalization weighted index of nearly all major bond and stock market indexes. Like some market-capitalization indexes (particularly in emerging or frontier markets), the resulting weights of the S&P GSCI can be highly concentrated. The rolling methodology focuses on owning the front (i.e., near-term) contracts to address the highest liquidity and where supply and demand shocks are most likely to have an impact.

Bloomberg Commodity Index

The BCOM (formerly the DJ–UBS) is based on 23 commodities. It includes liquidity as both a weighting factor and a screening factor, although the index is selection-based, meaning a committee uses judgment to pick the included commodities. The rules of index construction also place caps on the size of the sectors (33% maximum) and floors on individual commodities (2% minimum). These differences mean that very different index composition and weights can occur. For example, the energy sector currently dominates the S&P GSCI (as high as 80% weight), whereas the BCOM's exposure is much lower (approximately 30%). However, exposure to natural gas as a single component of energy is higher in the BCOM (approximately 9%) than in the S&P GSCI (approximately 3%). Given that natural gas had an annualized roll cost of about 19% (often the highest roll cost of all the commodities), the higher weighting of natural gas in the BCOM implies that the index has to find other sources of return (e.g., price return and rebalance return) to overcome the drag that natural gas inventory storage creates through negative roll return. The rolling methodology focuses on owning the front (i.e., near-term) contracts.

Deutsche Bank Liquid Commodity Index

The DBLCI uses a fixed-weighting scheme to allocate exposure. The most notable/unique feature of this index is its rolling methodology. Instead of focusing on near-term contracts, it is optimized based on the time value of maximized backwardation/minimized contango for the contracts that fall within the next 12 calendar months. As an example, a June 2014 copper futures contract may be at 1% backwardation versus a May 2014 copper contract. But if the July 2014 copper contract is at a 3% backwardation (1.5% per month, or 3% divided by two months) versus the 1% backwardation per month on the June 2014 contract, then the DBLCI will roll to the July 2014 contract in preference to the June 2014 contract. Therefore, one could argue the DBLCI takes an active decision with regard to roll return positioning as compared with the other indexes.

Thomson Reuters/CoreCommodity CRB Index

The TR/CC CRB consists of 19 commodities and is a continuation of the first investable commodity index published by the Commodities Research Bureau in 1978 (although an earlier iteration started in 1957). It uses a fixed-weighting scheme to allocate exposure. An index management committee decides the weights based on a number of factors, including diversification, sector representation, liquidity, and economic importance. It also clusters the fixed weights into a number of tiers. As a result, constituents are moved from tier to tier. The rolling methodology focuses on owning the front (i.e., near-term) contracts that mechanically focus on the front month or second front month and do not require a particular calculation.

Rogers International Commodity Index

The RICI uses a fixed-weighting scheme to allocate exposure among 38 different commodities and was designed by investor Jim Rogers in the late 1990s. An index management committee decides the weights based on a number of factors, including diversification, sector representation, liquidity, and economic importance. Like the TR/CC CRB Index, it also clusters the fixed weights into a number of tiers. As a result, constituents are moved from tier to tier as they gain or lose relative importance as seen by the committee. Energy is the largest weight but is still a highly diversified basket. Some energy constituents are denominated in non-US dollar terms—such as rubber (traded in Japan in Japanese yen) and cocoa (traded in London in British pounds)—which potentially adds a foreign exchange exposure element to the index returns.

Rebalancing Frequency

Rebalancing frequency plays a role in index returns, especially for those indexes that rebalance more frequently, such as the TR/CC CRB and RICI. Theoretically, from portfolio management theory, rebalancing is more important if a market is frequently mean reverting because there are more peaks to sell and valleys to buy. However, frequent rebalancing can lead to underperformance in a trending market because the outperforming assets are sold but continue up in price, whereas the underperforming assets are purchased but still drift lower.

The relative performance of the monthly rebalanced indexes (TR/CC CRB and RICI) versus the annual rebalance of the other indexes will depend on the length of time of price trends: More frequent mean reversions should favor the former two indexes, but a longer-term trend will more likely favor the annually rebalancing indexes. If an index uses a floating weighting scheme, such as production value (fully or partially), then the higher (lower) futures prices usually coincide with higher (lower) physical prices. Therefore, with this kind of approach, the magnitude of rebalancing weights is generally lower than for a fixed-weight scheme because the post-rebalance weights will generally drift in line with the current portfolio weights. As a result, the S&P GSCI and BCOM indexes typically have lower rebalancing costs and—in a trending market—have an opportunity to outperform their fixed-weight index counterparts, particularly those that have a relatively frequent rebalance period.

Commodity Index Summary

There is no dominant index based on a particular methodology. Relative performance will occur based on the circumstances of the markets and the time period examined. Evaluating which index is superior for a *long-term* investment generates modest if any value. Per the authors' research, these indexes all have been highly correlated (well above 70%) with each other and have had low (roughly 0%) correlations with traditional asset classes (e.g., US large-cap stocks, US bonds, international stocks). As with equities, for which there are many different index providers, commodity indexes act in parallel even when their returns (and Sharpe ratios) frequently differ dramatically over time.

EXAMPLE 23

Commodity Indexes (1)

1. All else being equal, compared with an equally weighted commodity index, a production value-weighted index (such as the S&P GSCI) will be:

   A. less sensitive to energy sector returns.

   B. more sensitive to energy sector returns.

   C. equally sensitive to energy sector returns.

Solution:

B is correct. The energy sector will make up a sizable portion of a production value-weighted index and thus will be a meaningful driver of returns for such an index. A is incorrect because a production value-weighted index will be more, not less, sensitive to the energy sector. C is incorrect because a production value-weighted index will be more, not equally, sensitive to the energy sector.

EXAMPLE 24

Commodity Indexes (2)

1. Which of the following statements is *not* correct regarding commodity futures indexes?

   A. Commodity sectors in backwardation typically improve index returns.

   B. An index that invests in several futures exchanges provides a high degree of diversification.

   C. Total returns of the major commodity indexes have low correlation with traditional asset classes, such as equities and bonds.

Solution:

B is correct. Commodity futures exchanges throughout the world are highly correlated and thus provide little diversification benefits. A is incorrect because markets in backwardation typically have positive roll yields and thus will likely improve index returns (although the price return may still not be positive and thus the total return may still be negative). C is incorrect because commodity index returns do indeed have historically low correlation with equities and bonds.

SUMMARY

- Commodities are a diverse asset class comprising various sectors: energy, grains, industrial (base) metals, livestock, precious metals, and softs (cash crops). Each of these sectors has a number of characteristics that are important in determining the supply and demand for each commodity, including ease of storage, geopolitics, and weather.
- Fundamental analysis of commodities relies on analyzing supply and demand for each of the products as well as estimating the reaction to the inevitable shocks to their equilibrium or underlying direction.
- The life cycle of commodities varies considerably depending on the economic, technical, and structural (i.e., industry, value chain) profile of each commodity as well as the sector. A short life cycle allows for relatively rapid adjustment to outside events, whereas a long life cycle generally limits the ability of the market to react.
- The valuation of commodities relative to that of equities and bonds can be summarized by noting that equities and bonds represent financial assets whereas commodities are physical assets. The valuation of commodities is not based on the estimation of future profitability and cash flows but rather on a discounted forecast of future possible prices based on such factors as the supply and demand of the physical item.
- The commodity trading environment is similar to other asset classes, with three types of trading participants: (1) informed investors/hedgers, (2) speculators, and (3) arbitrageurs.
- Commodities have two general pricing forms: spot prices in the physical markets and futures prices for later delivery. The spot price is the current price to deliver or purchase a physical commodity at a specific location. A futures price is an exchange-based price agreed on to deliver or receive a defined quantity and often quality of a commodity at a future date.
- The difference between spot and futures prices is generally called the basis. When the spot price is higher than the futures price, it is called backwardation, and when it is lower, it is called contango. Backwardation and contango are also used to describe the relationship between two futures contracts of the same commodity.
- Commodity contracts can be settled by either cash or physical delivery.
- There are three primary theories of futures returns.

  - In insurance theory, commodity producers who are long the physical good are motived to sell the commodity for future delivery to hedge their production price risk exposure.
  - The hedging pressure hypothesis describes when producers along with consumers seek to protect themselves from commodity market price volatility by entering into price hedges to stabilize their projected profits and cash flow.
  - The theory of storage focuses on supply and demand dynamics of commodity inventories, including the concept of "convenience yield."
- The total return of a fully collateralized commodity futures contract can be quantified as the spot price return plus the roll return plus the collateral return (risk-free rate return).
- The roll return is effectively the weighted accounting difference (in percentage terms) between the near-term commodity futures contract price and the farther-term commodity futures contract price.
- A commodity swap is a legal contract between two parties calling for the exchange of payments over multiple dates as determined by several reference prices or indexes.
- The most relevant commodity swaps include excess return swaps, total return swaps, basis swaps, and variance/volatility swaps.
- The five primary commodity indexes based on assets are (1) the S&P GSCI; (2) the Bloomberg Commodity Index, formerly the Dow Jones–UBS Commodity Index; (3) the Deutsche Bank Liquid Commodity Index; (4) the Thomson Reuters/CoreCommodity CRB Index; and (5) the Rogers International Commodities Index.
- The key differentiating characteristics of commodity indexes are

  - the breadth and selection methodology of coverage (number of commodities and sectors) included in each index, noting that some commodities have multiple reference contracts,
  - the relative weightings assigned to each component/commodity and the related methodology for how these weights are determined,
  - the methodology and frequency for rolling the individual futures contracts,
  - the methodology and frequency for rebalancing the weights of the individual commodities and sectors, and
  - the governance that determines which commodities are selected.

PRACTICE PROBLEMS

The following information relates to questions 1-8

Raffi Musicale is the portfolio manager for a defined benefit pension plan. He meets with Jenny Brown, market strategist with Menlo Bank, to discuss possible investment opportunities. The investment committee for the pension plan has recently approved expanding the plan's permitted asset mix to include alternative asset classes.

Brown proposes the Apex Commodity Fund (Apex Fund) offered by Menlo Bank as a potentially suitable investment for the pension plan. The Apex Fund attempts to produce trading profits by capitalizing on the mispricing between the spot and futures prices of commodities. The fund has access to storage facilities, allowing it to take delivery of commodities when necessary. The Apex Fund's current asset allocation is presented in Exhibit 1.

Exhibit 1: Apex Fund's Asset Allocation

Commodity Sector	Allocation (%)
Energy	31.9
Livestock	12.6
Softs	21.7
Precious metals	33.8

Brown explains that the Apex Fund has had historically low correlations with stocks and bonds, resulting in diversification benefits. Musicale asks Brown, "Can you identify a factor that affects the valuation of financial assets like stocks and bonds but does not affect the valuation of commodities?"

Brown shares selected futures contract data for three markets in which the Apex Fund invests. The futures data are presented in Exhibit 2.

Exhibit 2: Selected Commodity Futures Data*

Month	Gold Price	Coffee Price	Gasoline Price
July	1,301.2	0.9600	2.2701
September	1,301.2	0.9795	2.2076
December	1,301.2	1.0055	2.0307

* *Gold:* US$/troy ounce; coffee: US$/pound; gasoline: US$/gallon.

Menlo Bank recently released a report on the coffee market. Brown shares the key conclusion from the report with Musicale: "The coffee market had a global harvest that was greater than expected. Despite the large harvest, coffee futures trading activity is balanced between producers and consumers. This balanced condition is not expected to change over the next year."

Brown shows Musicale the total return of a recent trade executed by the Apex Fund. Brown explains that the Apex Fund took a fully collateralized long futures position in nearby soybean futures contracts at the quoted futures price of 865.0 (US cents/bushel). Three months later, the entire futures position was rolled when the near-term futures price was 877.0 and the farther-term futures price was 883.0. During the three-month period between the time that the initial long position was taken and the rolling of the contract, the collateral earned an annualized rate of 0.60%.

Brown tells Musicale that the pension fund could alternatively gain long exposure to commodities using the swap market. Brown and Musicale analyze the performance of a long position in an S&P GSCI total return swap having monthly resets and a notional amount of $25 million. Selected data on the S&P GSCI are presented inExhibit 3.

Exhibit 3: Selected S&P GSCI Data

Reference Date	Index Level
April (swap initiation)	2,542.35
May	2,582.23
June	2,525.21

1. The Apex Fund is *most likely* to be characterized as:
   - **A.** a hedger.
   - **B.** a speculator.
   - **C.** an arbitrageur.

2. Which factor would *most likely* affect the supply or demand of all four sectors of the Apex Fund?
   - **A.** Weather
   - **B.** Spoilage
   - **C.** Government actions

3. The *most appropriate* response to Musicale's question regarding the valuation factor is:
   - **A.** storage costs.
   - **B.** transportation costs.
   - **C.** expected future cash flows.

4. Which futures market in Exhibit 2 is in backwardation?
   - **A.** Gold
   - **B.** Coffee
   - **C.** Gasoline

5. Based on the key conclusion from the Menlo Bank coffee market report, the

shape of the coffee futures curve in Exhibit 2 is *most consistent* with the:

A. insurance theory.

B. theory of storage.

C. hedging pressure hypothesis.

6. Based on Exhibit 2, which commodity's roll returns will *most likely* be positive?

A. Gold

B. Coffee

C. Gasoline

7. The Apex Fund's three-month total return on the soybean futures trade is *closest* to:

A. 0.85%.

B. 1.30%.

C. 2.22%.

8. Based on Exhibit 3, on the June settlement date, the party that is long the S&P GSCI total return swap will:

A. owe a payment of $552,042.23.

B. receive a payment of $1,502,621.33.

C. receive a payment of $1,971,173.60.

The following information relates to questions 9-15

Mary McNeil is the corporate treasurer at Farmhouse, which owns and operates several farms and ethanol production plants in the United States. McNeil's primary responsibility is risk management. Katrina Falk, a recently hired junior analyst at Farmhouse, works for McNeil in managing the risk of the firm's commodity price exposures. Farmhouse's risk management policy requires the use of futures to protect revenue from price volatility, regardless of forecasts of future prices, and prohibits risk managers from taking speculative positions.

McNeil meets with Falk to discuss recent developments in two of Farmhouse's commodity markets, grains and livestock. McNeil asks Falk about key characteristics of the two markets that affect revenues and costs. Falk tells McNeil the following:

Statement 1	The life cycle for livestock depends on the product and varies widely by product.
Statement 2	Grains have uniform, well-defined seasons and growth cycles specific to geographic regions.

A material portion of Farmhouse's revenue comes from livestock exports, and a major input cost is the cost of grains imported from outside the United States. Falk and McNeil next discuss three conclusions that Falk reached in an analysis of the grains and livestock markets:

Conclusion 1 Assuming demand for grains remains constant, extreme heat in the regions from which we import our grains will result in a benefit to us in the form of lower grain prices.

Conclusion 2 New tariffs on cattle introduced in our primary export markets will likely result in higher prices for our livestock products in our local market.

Conclusion 3 Major improvements in freezing technology allowing for longer storage will let us better manage the volatility in the prices of our livestock products.

McNeil asks Falk to gather spot and futures price data on live cattle, wheat, and soybeans, which are presented in Exhibit 1. Additionally, she observes that (1) the convenience yield of soybeans exceeds the costs of its direct storage and (2) commodity producers as a group are less interested in hedging in the forward market than commodity consumers are.

Exhibit 1: Selected Commodity Price Data*

Market	Live Cattle Price	Wheat Price	Soybeans Price
Spot	109	407	846
Futures	108	407	850

* *Live cattle:* US cents per pound; wheat and soybeans: US cents per bushel.

A key input cost for Farmhouse in producing ethanol is natural gas. McNeil uses positions in natural gas (NG) futures contracts to manage the risk of natural gas price volatility. Three months ago, she entered into a long position in natural gas futures at a futures price of $2.93 per million British thermal units (MMBtu). The current price of the same contract is $2.99. Exhibit 2 presents additional data about the three-month futures position.

Exhibit 2: Selected Information—Natural Gas Futures Three-Month Position*

			Prices	
Commodity	Total Current $ Exposure	Position	Near-Term Futures (Current Price)	Farther-Term Futures
Natural Gas (NG)	5,860,000	Long	2.99	3.03

* *NG:* $ per MMBtu; 1 contract = 10,000 MMBtu.

The futures position is fully collateralized earning a 3% rate. McNeil decides to roll forward her current exposure in the natural gas position.

Each month, McNeil reports the performance of the energy futures positions, including details on price returns, roll returns, and collateral returns, to the firm's executive committee. A new committee member is concerned about the negative roll returns on some of the positions. In a memo to McNeil, the committee member asks her to explain why she is not avoiding positions with negative roll returns.

9. With respect to its risk management policy, Farmhouse can be *best* described as:

   A. a trader.

   B. a hedger.

   C. an arbitrageur.

10. Which of Falk's statements regarding the characteristics of the grains and livestock markets is correct?

    A. Only Statement 1

    B. Only Statement 2

    C. Both Statement 1 and Statement 2

11. Which of Falk's conclusions regarding commodity markets is correct?

    A. Conclusion 1

    B. Conclusion 2

    C. Conclusion 3

12. Which commodity market in Exhibit 1 is currently in a state of contango?

    A. Wheat

    B. Soybeans

    C. Live cattle

13. Based on Exhibit 1 and McNeil's two observations, the futures price of soybeans is *most* consistent with the:

    A. insurance theory.

    B. theory of storage.

    C. hedging pressure hypothesis.

14. Based on Exhibit 2, the total return from the long position in natural gas futures is *closest* to:

    A. 1.46%.

    B. 3.71%.

    C. 4.14%.

15. The *most appropriate* response to the new committee member's question is that:

    A. roll returns are negatively correlated with price returns.

    B. such roll returns are the result of futures markets in backwardation.

C. such positions may outperform other positions that have positive roll returns.

The following information relates to questions 16-22

Jamal Nabli is a portfolio manager at NextWave Commodities (NWC), a commodity-based hedge fund located in the United States. NWC's strategy uses a fixed-weighting scheme to allocate exposure among 12 commodities, and it is benchmarked against the Thomson Reuters/CoreCommodity CRB Index (TR/CC CRB). Nabli manages the energy and livestock sectors with the help of Sota Yamata, a junior analyst.

Nabli and Yamata meet to discuss a variety of factors that affect commodity values in the two sectors they manage. Yamata tells Nabli the following:

Statement 1 Storage costs are negatively related to futures prices.

Statement 2 In contrast to stocks and bonds, most commodity investments are made by using derivatives.

Statement 3 Commodities generate future cash flows beyond what can be realized through their purchase and sale.

Nabli and Yamata then discuss potential new investments in the energy sector. They review Brent crude oil futures data, which are presented in Exhibit 1.

Exhibit 1: Selected Data on Brent Crude Oil Futures

Spot Price	Near-Term Futures Price	Longer-Term Futures Price
77.56	73.64	73.59

Yamata presents his research related to the energy sector, which has the following conclusions:

- Consumers have been more concerned about prices than producers have.
- Energy is consumed on a real-time basis and requires minimal storage.

After concluding the discussion of the energy sector, Nabli reviews the performance of NWC's long position in lean hog futures contracts. Nabli notes that the portfolio earned a −12% price return on the lean hog futures position last year and a −24% roll return after the contracts were rolled forward. The position was held with collateral equal to 100% of the position at a risk-free rate of 1.2% per year.

Yamata asks Nabli to clarify how the state of the futures market affects roll returns. Nabli responds as follows:

Statement 4 Roll returns are generally negative when a futures market is in contango.

Statement 5 Roll returns are generally positive when a futures market is in backwardation.

As part of their expansion into new markets, NWC is considering changing its benchmark index. Nabli investigates two indexes as a possible replacement. These indexes both use similar weighting and rebalancing schemes. Index A includes contracts of commodities typically in contango, whereas Index B includes contracts of commodities typically in backwardation. Nabli asks Yamata how the two indexes perform relative to each other in a market that is trending upward.

Because of a substantial decline in drilling activity in the North Sea, Nabli believes the price of Brent crude oil will increase more than that of heavy crude oil. The actual price volatility of Brent crude oil has been lower than its expected volatility, and Nabli expects this trend to continue. Nabli also expects the level of the ICE Brent Index to increase from its current level. Nabli and Yamata discuss how to use swaps to take advantage of Nabli's expectations. The possible positions are (1) a basis swap long on Brent crude oil and short on heavy crude oil, (2) a long volatility swap on Brent crude oil, and (3) a short position in an excess return swap that is based on a fixed level (i.e., the current level) of the ICE Brent Index.

16. Which of Nabli's statements regarding the valuation and storage of commodities is correct?

   A. Statement 1

   B. Statement 2

   C. Statement 3

17. Based on Exhibit 1, Yamata should conclude that the:

   A. calendar spread for Brent crude oil is $3.97.

   B. Brent crude oil futures market is in backwardation.

   C. basis for the near-term Brent crude oil futures contract is $0.05 per barrel.

18. Based on Exhibit 1 and Yamata's research on the energy sector, the shape of the futures price curve for Brent crude oil is most consistent with the:

   A. insurance theory.

   B. theory of storage.

   C. hedging pressure hypothesis.

19. The total return (annualized excluding leverage) on the lean hog futures contract is:

   A. −37.2%.

   B. −36.0%.

   C. −34.8%.

20. Which of Nabli's statements about roll returns is correct?

   A. Only Statement 4

   B. Only Statement 5

   C. Both Statement 4 and Statement 5

21. The *best* response to Nabli's question about the relative performance of the two

indexes is that Index B is *most likely* to exhibit returns that are:

A. lower than those of Index A.

B. the same as those of Index A.

C. higher than those of index A.

22. Given Nabli's expectations for crude oil, the *most appropriate* swap position is the:

A. basis swap.

B. volatility swap.

C. excess return swap.

SOLUTIONS

1. C is correct. Commodity arbitrage involves an ability to inventory physical commodities and the attempt to capitalize on mispricing between the commodity (along with related storage and financing costs) and the futures price. The Apex Fund has access to storage facilities and uses these facilities in the attempt to capitalize on mispricing opportunities.

2. C is correct. Government actions can affect the supply or demand of all four sectors of the Apex Fund. With respect to energy, environmental mandates imposed by governments have tightened pollution standards, which have led to increasing processing costs that negatively affect demand. The supply of livestock, such as hogs and cattle, is affected by government-permitted use of drugs and growth hormones. Softs, or cash crops, can be affected by government actions, such as the attempt to maintain strategic stockpiles to control domestic prices. The level of demand and relative value of a precious metal, such as gold, is directly linked to government actions associated with managing to inflation targets.

3. C is correct. Expected future cash flows affect the valuation of financial assets, such as stocks and bonds, but do not affect the valuation of commodities. Financial assets (stocks and bonds) are valued based on expected future cash flows. In contrast, the valuation of a commodity is based on a discounted forecast of a future commodity price, which incorporates storage and transportation costs.

4. C is correct. When the near-term (i.e., closer to expiration) futures contract price is higher than the longer-term futures contract price, the futures market for the commodity is in backwardation. Because gasoline is the only one of the three futures markets in Exhibit 2 in which the near-term futures contract price ($2.2701) is higher than the longer-term contract price ($2.0307), the gasoline futures market is the only one in backwardation.

5. B is correct. The theory of storage focuses on the level of commodity inventories and the state of supply and demand. A commodity that is regularly stored should have a higher price in the future (contango) to account for those storage costs. Because coffee is a commodity that requires storage, its higher future price is consistent with the theory of storage.

6. C is correct. Roll returns are generally positive (negative) when the futures market is in backwardation (contango) and zero when the futures market is flat. Because the gasoline market is in backwardation, its roll returns will most likely be positive.

7. A is correct. The total return on the trade represents the sum of three components: price return, roll return, and collateral return.

   Price return = (Current price − Previous price)/Previous price = (877.0 − 865.0)/865.0

   = 1.387%.

   Roll return

   = [(Near-term futures contract closing price − Farther-term futures contract closing price)/Near-term futures contract closing price] × Percentage of the position in the futures contract being rolled.

   Because the entire position is being rolled, the percentage of the position in the futures contract being rolled is equal to 100%. So:

Roll return = [(877.0 − 883.0)/877.0] × 100% = −0.684%.

Collateral return = [3 months/12 months] × 0.60% = 0.15%.

Total return = 1.387% − 0.684% + 0.15% = 0.853%.

8. A is correct. The total return swap involves a monthly cash settlement (reset) based on the performance of the underlying reference asset (S&P GSCI) given a notional amount of $25 million. If the level of the index increases between the two valuation dates (in this case, May and June), the long position (the swap buyer) receives payment. If the level of the index decreases between the two valuation dates, the swap seller receives payment.

   The return on the reference index for the month of June is [(2,525.21 – 2,582.23)/2,582.23], which is equivalent to –2.2082%. Therefore, the swap buyer (long position) must pay the swap seller a cash settlement for the month of June. The June payment calculation is equal to $25,000,000 × –2.2082%, or –$552,042.23.

9. B is correct. Hedgers trade in the futures markets to hedge their exposures related to the commodity, as stated in Farmhouse's risk management policy.

10. C is correct. The life cycle of livestock does vary widely by product. Grains have uniform, well-defined seasons and growth cycles specific to geographic regions. Therefore, both statements are correct.

11. C is correct. Commodity prices are affected by supply and demand, and improvements in freezing technology can improve the firm's ability to store its products for longer periods and manage the volatility of supply and demand. For example, during times of excess supply, a livestock producer, such as Farmhouse, can freeze its products and offer them during better market supply conditions.

12. B is correct. The futures market for soybeans is in a state of contango because the spot price is lower than the futures price.

13. C is correct. In Exhibit 1, the spot price of soybeans is less than the futures price. This observation can be explained only by the hedging pressure hypothesis. According to this hypothesis, hedging pressure occurs when both producers and consumers seek to protect themselves from commodity market price volatility by entering into price hedges to stabilize their projected profits and cash flows. If consumers are more interested in hedging than producers are, the futures price will exceed the spot price.

    In contrast, the insurance theory predicts that the futures price has to be lower than the current spot price as a form of payment or remuneration to the speculator who takes on the price risk and provides price insurance to the commodity seller. Similarly, the theory of storage also predicts that when a commodity's convenience yield is greater than its direct storage costs, the futures price will be lower than the spot price.

14. A is correct. The total return for a fully collateralized position is the sum of the price return, the roll return, and the collateral return:

    Price return = (Current price − Previous price)/Previous price

    = (2.99 − 2.93)/2.93

    = 2.05%.

    Roll return

= (Near-term futures closing price − Farther-term futures closing price)/Near-term futures closing price × Percentage of position in futures contract being rolled

= [(2.99 − 3.03)/2.99] × 100%

= −1.34%.

Collateral return = Annual rate × Period length as a fraction of the year

= 3% × 0.25

= 0.75%.

Therefore, the total return for three months = 2.05% – 1.34% + 0.75% = 1.46%.

15. C is correct. Investment positions are evaluated on the basis of total return, and the roll return is part of the total return. Even though negative roll return negatively affects the total return, this effect could be more than offset by positive price and collateral returns. Therefore, it is possible that positions with negative roll returns outperform positions with positive roll returns, depending on the price and collateral returns.

16. B is correct. The most common way to invest in commodities is via derivatives, and commodities do not generate future cash flows beyond what can be realized through their purchase and sale. Also, storage costs are positively related to futures prices. Physical assets have to be stored, and storage incurs costs (rent, insurance, spoilage, etc.). Therefore, a commodity that is regularly stored should have a higher price in the future to account for those storage costs.

17. B is correct. The Brent crude oil futures market is in a state of backwardation. Commodity futures markets are in a state of backwardation when the spot price is greater than the price of near-term (i.e., nearest-to-expiration) futures contracts and, correspondingly, the price of near-term futures contracts is greater than that of longer-term contracts. The calendar spread is the difference between the near-term futures contract price and the longer-term futures contract price, which is $73.64 – $73.59 = $0.05. The basis for the near-term Brent crude oil futures contract is the difference between the spot price and the near-term futures price: $77.56 – $73.64 = $3.92.

18. B is correct. The Brent crude oil futures market is in a state of backwardation: The spot price is greater than the price of near-term (i.e., nearest-to-expiration) futures contracts. Commodities (in this case, Brent crude oil) are physical assets, not virtual assets, such as stocks and bonds. Physical assets have to be stored, and storage incurs costs (rent, insurance, inspections, spoilage, etc.). According to the theory of storage, a commodity that is consumed along a value chain that allows for just-in-time delivery and use (i.e., minimal inventories and storage) can avoid these costs. Yamata's research concluded that energy is consumed on a real-time basis and requires minimal storage. In this situation, demand dominates supply, and current prices are higher than futures prices (state of backwardation).

19. C is correct. The contract was held for one year, so the price return of −12% is an annualized figure. Additionally, the −24% roll return is also annualized. Nabli's collateral return equals 1.2% per year × 100% initial collateral investment = 1.2%. Therefore, the total return (annualized) is calculated as follows:

Total return = Price return + Roll return + Collateral return.

Total return = −12% + (−24%) + 1.2% = −34.8%.

20. C is correct. Roll returns are generally negative (positive) when the futures market is in contango (backwardation) and zero when the futures market is flat.

21. C is correct. Index B is likely to have higher performance than Index A in a market that is trending upward. Indexes that (perhaps inadvertently) contain contracts that more commonly trade in backwardation may improve forward-looking performance because this generates a positive roll return. Similarly, indexes that contain contracts that more commonly trade in contango may hurt performance for the same reason (i.e., negative roll return).

22. A is correct. Nabli expects the price of Brent crude oil to increase more than that of heavy crude oil, and Nabli can take advantage of this prediction by entering into a basis swap that is long Brent crude oil and short heavy crude oil. Nabli should take a short (not long) position in a volatility swap to take advantage of his prediction that Brent crude oil's price volatility will be lower than its expected volatility. Nabli should take a long (not short) position in an excess return swap to take advantage of his expectation that the level of the ICE Brent Index will increase faster than leading oil benchmarks.

LEARNING MODULE

2

Overview of Types of Real Estate Investment

LEARNING OUTCOMES

Mastery	The candidate should be able to:
☐	compare important real estate investment features for valuation purposes
☐	explain economic value drivers of real estate investments and their role in a portfolio
☐	discuss the distinctive investment characteristics of commercial property types
☐	explain the due diligence process and valuation approaches for real estate investments
☐	discuss real estate investment indexes, including their construction and potential biases

INTRODUCTION

1

Developed land, including commercial, industrial, and residential real estate, derives its value from existing and expected future economic uses. In contrast to owner-occupied properties, financial investors in this asset class typically seek income from commercial and residential users and potential capital appreciation from a future sale as part of a well-diversified portfolio.

Building on the foundation developed earlier in the curriculum, which introduced the unique attributes of real estate as well as its investment characteristics, we now turn our attention to the key features of real estate relevant to valuation, economic drivers affecting property cash flows and prices, and the unique information challenges investors face when assessing and valuing real estate versus other investments. The valuation process for real estate properties using a discounted cash flow, income, or sales comparison approach is broadly similar to that for public or private companies once these important differences are taken into consideration.

This learning module focuses primarily on investments based on commercial or residential real estate properties that are relatively well developed, are stable, and produce reliable periodic income. Portfolios of investments involving these underlying properties are widely available to investors via equity instruments, such as real estate investment trusts (REITs) and real estate operating companies (REOCs); fixed-income securities, such as mortgage-backed or covered bonds; and index-based products.

LEARNING MODULE OVERVIEW

- Actual and potential economic use of residential or commercial real estate is the primary driver of expected value, with net operating income (NOI) as a common return metric for income-producing property.
- Core real estate investments are classified as equity in firms engaged in operating, developing, or servicing real estate investments or real estate investment trusts (REITs), which directly own and operate properties, and are classified as debt if holding mortgage-backed securities or covered bonds.
- Economic value drivers for real estate include GDP, job, and wage growth; credit conditions contributing to the real estate cycle; and local economic factors.
- Real estate investment features such as levels of current income and expected capital appreciation, inflation hedging properties, diversification, and tax benefits affect the role of real estate in an investment portfolio.
- Commercial real estate investments, such as residential and non-residential properties, face both cyclical and structural factors that impact their economic use, cash flow, and relative risk and return.
- Real estate investments require detailed due diligence with respect to local market conditions, legal and financial aspects, and the physical condition of the property itself.
- Once unique characteristics of real estate are considered, valuation methods resemble those for other financial assets; they include the income, cost, and sales comparison approaches.
- Indexes tracking real estate market risk and return allow for relative performance evaluation, investment, and manager benchmarking, as well as index-based investments. The use of appraisal-based rather than actual sales prices in real estate index construction may introduce biases and may also decrease reported real estate return correlation with other asset classes.

2 REAL ESTATE INVESTMENT FEATURES

☐ compare important real estate investment features for valuation purposes

General Characteristics

Earlier learning modules addressed the unique characteristics of real estate investments, which involve heterogeneous building and property assets in fragmented local markets that are bought and sold infrequently with high transaction costs. Real estate investment characteristics range from relatively stable, income-producing properties, referred to as **core real estate**, to more speculative **opportunistic real estate** investments, typically funded on a private basis, as shown in Exhibit 1.

Exhibit 1: Real Estate Investment Characteristics

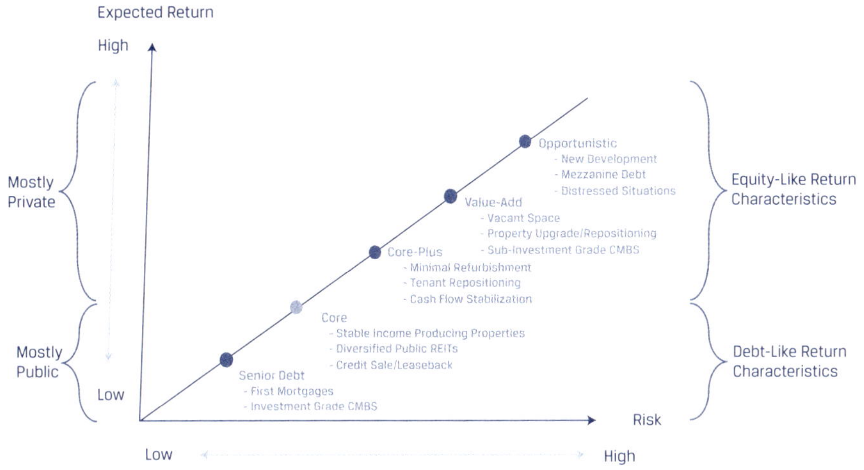

New property developments and those that require substantial improvement associated with opportunistic real estate tend to give such investments more equity-like characteristics, while income-producing real estate assets associated with core investments are more bond-like in nature.

Key characteristics that affect the tradability and rates of return on all real estate investments include a property's current and potential economic uses, expected net cash flows, and capital structure. In this learning module, we focus on developed land, including commercial, industrial, and residential buildings, as opposed to undeveloped land, whose value is most often derived from the timber growth cycle or agriculture.

Economic use of property for residential or commercial purposes is the primary driver of expected income and property price appreciation for real estate investors. Unique features used to evaluate an individual property include its location, size, age, and features and amenities available to users. The price and availability of comparable properties in the same area and the economic environment faced by existing and potential users are important factors affecting property returns. For example, household formation and employment, income, and wealth, as well as the cost and availability of owner-occupied alternatives to rental units, are important drivers of residential real estate. Households also play a critical role in commercial real estate demand in such areas as hospitality and self-storage. Corporate real estate use varies widely, including office space in city centers used by service-based industries, such as financial institutions and health care, to retail shopping centers or industrial or warehouse facilities used in the production and distribution of finished goods.

As in the case of general business conditions, industry-specific dynamics and technological, environmental, and social change are important determinants of pricing and demand, as in the following example.

COMMERCIAL REAL ESTATE TRENDS IN THE WAKE OF COVID-19

The economic lockdowns in many countries due to the COVID-19 pandemic had both immediate and more permanent effects on commercial real estate markets. For example, the shift to fully remote work for many companies during the pandemic led to a sharp drop in office leases, while delays in returning to work combined with more flexible work arrangements had a more permanent effect on office space demand. According to the global commercial real estate service firm Jones Lang LaSalle, global office leasing volume fell from a pre-pandemic high of over 11 million m^2 per quarter to just 5 million m^2 in the second quarter of 2020 and remained well below pre-pandemic levels through 2022.

Online shopping expanded while retail outlets suffered under lockdowns, driving an estimated increase in e-commerce as a percentage of total global retail sales from 15% in 2019 to a record 21% in 2021. As web-based sales remained strong following reopening and companies sought to regionalize supply chains following border closings and lockdowns elsewhere, rents in the logistics and warehouse space rose at double to triple the pace on an annual basis compared to their pre-pandemic growth rates.

Income-producing real estate has cash flow properties similar to most public and private companies but also a number of significant differences. Net cash flows are made up of periodic fixed gross rent or lease cash flows for a given contractual period from one or more tenants plus other income less the fixed and variable costs associated with operating the property. In contrast to measures used in public and private company analysis, such as EBITDA and free cash flow to the firm (FCFF), **net operating income** (NOI) is a commonly used measure of income-producing property returns prior to the inclusion of financing costs or income taxes used in the valuation process. NOI is calculated as shown in Equation 1:

$$\text{NOI} = \text{Effective gross income} - \text{Operating expenses} - \text{Property maintenance allowance.} \quad (1)$$

Periodic real estate cash inflows in the form of lease or rental payments are usually fixed for a period under a contract between a property owner or manager (known as the **lessor**) and a tenant or property user (also referred to as the **lessee**). Owners typically assess a prospective tenant's creditworthiness to gauge their ability to meet future payments from business or personal income and to limit credit risk associated with the lease contract. Contract renewals allow owners to renegotiate rates in response to inflation or rising costs, changes in demand, competition, or market conditions, as well as property upgrades. In some cases, owners may lower rent as an incentive for tenants to accept longer lease terms, while in others, periodic rent increases may be included in contracts to reflect rising costs. Lease terms and conditions vary among property types, as we will show later in the learning module.

Property revenue combines **gross rent**, or the average lease or rental price realized per square foot multiplied by the total rentable space, and other sources of revenue less any deductions for vacancies or concessions to arrive at a property's **effective gross income**. Vacancy rates (or the unoccupied percentage of total rentable space) are of key importance in projecting cash flow along with market rents. Large, multi-tenant residential and commercial properties are rarely fully leased because tenants move and properties are rehabilitated.

Operating expenses include fixed costs such as taxes, insurance, service, and repairs, and variable costs that vary with occupancy levels, such as utilities. These costs may be borne by the owner or partially or fully passed on to tenants based on lease agreement terms.

Property owners must separately allow for expenses to maintain a property's current level of income generation. This **property maintenance allowance** varies among both jurisdictions and types of property. For example, such an allowance is common in European and North American markets but less so in other markets, such as Japan. It may include improvements made to accommodate certain tenants for retail or other commercial uses. Also, while it includes capital expenditures necessary to maintain a property's current economic use, it does not include those capital expenditures that significantly upgrade or change a property's economic use.

As is true of public or private companies, analysts must use judgment to determine the regular and ongoing nature of expenses versus extraordinary items in assessing NOI. Operating expenses and a property's maintenance allowance are subtracted from revenue to solve for this measure, as shown in the following example.

EXAMPLE 1

Wallonia Transit Warehouse Facility

Wallonia Transit is a single-tenant warehouse facility in southern Belgium with 10,000 square meters of rentable space. The facility is fully rented under a five-year lease at an annual rate of EUR52.50 per square meter, and the tenant must cover property taxes and insurance costs. In addition, the lease specifies that the lessor may recover operating expenses of EUR10.25 per square meter per year for property servicing and repairs. Estimated operating expenses and property maintenance expenditures for the year are as follows:

Line Item	Cost (EUR)
Servicing and repairs	120,750
Property tax	12,500
Insurance	40,000
Property maintenance allowance	100,000

1. Solve for Wallonia Transit's NOI, and create a pro forma income statement.

Solution:

Solve for effective gross income (or revenue) by first calculating gross rent:

Gross rent = Base rent (EUR/m^2) × Rentable area.

EUR525,000 = EUR52.50/m^2 × 10,000 square meters.

Combine gross rent with additional sources of revenue and pass-through property tax and insurance costs from the tenant as follows:

Operating expense recovery = Recovery (EUR/m^2) × Rentable area.

EUR102,500 = EUR10.25/m^2 × 10,000 square meters.

Effective gross income = EUR680,000

= EUR525,000 + EUR102,500 + EUR12,500 + EUR 40,000.

Next, solve for operating expenses:

Operating expenses = Service and repairs + Property tax + Insurance

= EUR173,250 (= EUR120,750 + EUR12,500 + EUR40,000).

Recall from Equation 1 that net operating income is calculated as follows:

NOI = Effective gross income – Operating expenses – Property maintenance allowance.

Solve for NOI:

NOI = EUR406,750 = EUR680,000 – EUR173,250 – EUR100,000.

2. Wallonia incurs servicing and repair costs that are 20% above the original estimate. Describe and calculate the effect on Wallonia's NOI.

The pro forma income statement for Wallonia is as follows:

Wallonia Transit Cash Flow	**EUR**
Revenue	
Gross Rent	525,500
Operating Expense Recovery	102,500
Pass-Through Costs	
Property Taxes	12,500
Insurance	40,000
Effective Gross Income	680,000
Less: Operating Expenses	
Services and Repair	(120,750)
Property Taxes	(12,500)
Insurance	(40,000)
Total Operating Expenses	(173,250)
Property Maintenance Allowance	(100,000)
Net Operating Income (NOI)	406,750

Solution:

Wallonia's service and repair costs have risen to EUR144,900 (= EUR120,750 × 1.20), an increase of EUR24,150. Since Wallonia's operating expense recovery for service and repairs is capped at EUR102,500, this increase will reduce Wallonia's NOI by EUR24,150, to EUR382,600.

In addition to profitability for income-producing properties (as shown in the previous example), investors use leverage and coverage measures to assess the creditworthiness of fixed-income investments in real estate.

The capital structure of income-producing real estate investments usually involves a high degree of leverage. Buyers and owners of real estate are often readily able to obtain long-term secured debt funding given the broad ability to use the underlying property as collateral for debt financing and the relatively long useful life of most properties. Mortgage lenders retain a first lien and security interest in collateral, granting them the right to take possession of property for resale upon a borrower default to recover principal and interest.

Recall from earlier lessons that a property purchase typically involves a cash down payment that represents the investor's initial equity position plus a mortgage loan. A primary measure of leverage involves the ratio of mortgage principal outstanding to the property's current value, known as the **loan-to-value ratio** (LTV).

$$\text{LTV} = \frac{\text{Mortgage debt outstanding}}{\text{Current property value}}. \quad (2)$$

While lenders often seek to impose a maximum LTV on borrowers when a loan is extended, LTVs fluctuate as property values change and loan principal is amortized. A lower LTV corresponds to a higher equity position for the borrower.

As in the case of debt coverage ratios among corporate borrowers, the capacity of a property owner to meet debt payments from cash flows is an important consideration. Fixed-income lessons earlier in the curriculum identified the **debt service coverage ratio** (DSC) as a key indicator of credit performance in commercial real estate lending, defined as follows:

$$\text{DSC} = \frac{\text{Net operating income}}{\text{Debt service}}. \quad (3)$$

Debt investors commonly incorporate LTV and DSC measures into loan covenants to protect their interests. The following example demonstrates the relationship between leverage, coverage, and profitability based on the earlier Wallonia Transit example.

EXAMPLE 2

Wallonia Transit Leverage and Coverage

Recall that Wallonia Transit is a warehouse with NOI of EUR406,750 in the current year. Wallonia's owner purchased the facility for EUR3,750,000 at the beginning of the year with a EUR3,000,000 20-year fully amortizing mortgage loan at a 4% annual rate with equal payments at the end of each year.

Martine DuBois is a financial analyst evaluating a commercial real estate debt portfolio that includes Wallonia Transit. She calculates that Wallonia's annual mortgage payment is EUR220,745, which for the first year includes EUR120,000 (= EUR3,000,000 × 4%) in interest.

1. Calculate the LTV for the Wallonia Transit loan at the end of the first year assuming the property value remains constant.

Solution:

Using Equation 2, we can solve for the LTV by dividing the mortgage loan outstanding by the current property value:

$$\text{LTV} = \frac{\text{Mortgage debt outstanding}}{\text{Current property value}}.$$

Mortgage debt outstanding is equal to the original EUR3,000,000 principal reduced by the first year's amortization, or the difference between the annual debt installment of EUR220,745 and interest of EUR120,000:

EUR2,899,255 = EUR3,000,000 – (EUR220,745 – EUR120,000).

Divide the result by the property price of EUR3,750,000 to solve for the LTV:

$$\text{LTV} = 0.773 = \frac{\text{EUR}2,899,255}{\text{EUR}3,750,000}.$$

2. Following a review of recent real estate sales for similar warehouse properties, DuBois concludes that the Wallonia facility appreciated 10% in value. Describe how the LTV will change and calculate the new value.

Solution:

An increase in estimated property value with no change to debt will cause the LTV to fall, indicating a decline in leverage and an increase in owner's equity. In this case, the property value is estimated to have risen to EUR4,125,000 [= EUR3,750,000 × (1 + 0.1)] and the LTV declines to 0.703:

$$\text{LTV} = 0.703 = \frac{\text{EUR2,899,255}}{\text{EUR4,125,000}}.$$

3. Calculate Wallonia's debt service coverage ratio in the first year.

Solution:

Solve for DSC using Equation 3, where debt service equals the annual installment payment, including both interest and principal:

$$\text{DSC} = \frac{\text{Net operating income}}{\text{Debt service}}.$$

$$\text{DSC} = 1.84 = \frac{\text{EUR406,750}}{\text{EUR220,745}}.$$

4. Recall from above a scenario under which Wallonia incurred service and repair costs 20% above original estimates, resulting in a revised NOI of EUR382,600. Calculate and interpret the revised DSC.

Solution:

A decrease in NOI to EUR382,600 reduces the numerator of the DSC calculation and results in a decline in the debt service coverage ratio to 1.73:

$$\text{DSC} = 1.73 = \frac{\text{EUR382,600}}{\text{EUR220,745}}.$$

Higher operating costs reduce a real estate borrower's ability to cover debt service payments from net operating income.

Real estate equity investors may measure returns on a levered basis before or after income tax. For example, investors often consider the first-year return on equity on an income-producing property with debt financing as the **equity dividend rate**, calculated as follows:

$$\text{Equity dividend rate} = \frac{\text{Pre} - \text{tax cash flow}}{\text{Property purchase price} - \text{Mortgage loan}}, \quad (4)$$

where pre-tax cash flow is defined as

$$\text{Pre-tax cash flow} = \text{Net operating income} - \text{Debt service}. \quad (5)$$

Note that in addition to omitting tax effects, this rate of return is solely a cash-based income measure ignoring potential capital gains or losses from a sale.

EXAMPLE 3

Wallonia Transit Equity Dividend Rate

Recall that Wallonia Transit is a warehouse with NOI of EUR406,750 in the first year. Wallonia's owner purchased the facility for EUR3,750,000 using a EUR3,000,000 20-year fully amortizing mortgage loan with an annual mortgage payment of EUR220,745.

1. Calculate the equity dividend rate for Wallonia based on initial equity.

Solution:

Solve for the equity dividend rate using Equation 4 and Equation 5. First, we calculate pre-tax cash flow to derive the numerator of Equation 4:

Pre-tax cash flow = EUR186,005 = EUR406,750 − EUR220,745.

Next, we solve for the denominator by reducing the EUR3,750,000 by the mortgage loan of EUR3,000,000 to get initial equity of EUR750,000. Using Equation 4,

$$\text{Equity dividend rate} = 24.8\% = \frac{\text{EUR186,005}}{\text{EUR750,000}}.$$

2. Calculate the revised equity dividend rate if Wallonia incurs 20% higher service and repair costs and NOI falls to EUR382,600.

Solution:

A 20% rise in operating expenses lowers NOI and pre-tax cash flow:

Pre-tax cash flow = EUR161,855 = EUR382,600 − EUR220,745.

Since the denominator remains unchanged, the equity dividend rate falls:

$$\text{Equity dividend rate} = 21.6\% = \frac{\text{EUR161,855}}{\text{EUR750,000}}.$$

After-tax return measures consider the tax impact of interest and depreciation on cash flows in a similar way to return on equity (ROE) in the case of public and private company valuation.

Given the finite life of most commercial and residential buildings, real estate assets are depreciated over their estimated useful life as in the case for a company's fixed assets, with an important difference. Real estate depreciation occurs on a property's **depreciable base**, which typically includes its construction or original acquisition cost plus any improvements. Allowable depreciation periods vary by jurisdiction and property type but exclude the cost of land, which is assumed to have an infinite life.

Assuming no property purchases or sales, after-tax cash flow is calculated as follows:

$$\text{After-tax cash flow} = \text{Pre-tax cash flow} - \text{Taxes}, \quad (6)$$

where given a tax rate of t,

$$\text{Taxes} = t \times (\text{NOI} - \text{Interest expense} - \text{Depreciation expense}). \quad (7)$$

Taxable income is equal to the term in parentheses in Equation 7. We return to the Wallonia example to compare pre- and after-tax returns.

EXAMPLE 4

Wallonia Transit After-Tax Return

Recall that Wallonia Transit has NOI of EUR406,750 in the first year. Wallonia's owner purchased the facility for EUR3,750,000 with a 20-year EUR3,000,000 fully amortizing loan with an annual installment of EUR220,745, which includes EUR120,000 in interest during the first year. Assume the facility has a 30-year useful life and the estimated cost of the land is EUR750,000. Wallonia's tax rate is 25%.

1. Determine Wallonia's annual depreciation expense.

Solution:

Wallonia's depreciable base equals the original facility purchase price (EUR3,750,000) less the EUR750,000 cost of land, or EUR3,000,000. Straight line depreciation for 30 years allows for a EUR100,000 (= EUR3,000,000/30) depreciation allocation per year.

2. Calculate Wallonia's after-tax cash flow.

Solution:

Solve for after-tax cash flow by first calculating Wallonia's taxes and substituting into Equation 6. Given that Wallonia has NOI of EUR406,750, first-year interest of EUR120,000, EUR100,000 in depreciation allowance from the solution to Question 1, a 25% tax rate, we can solve for taxes using Equation 7, as follows:

$$\text{Taxes} = t \times (\text{NOI} - \text{Interest expense} - \text{Depreciation expense})$$

$$= \text{EUR}46{,}688 = 0.25 \times (\text{EUR}406{,}750 - \text{EUR}120{,}000 - \text{EUR}100{,}000).$$

Recall that pre-tax cash flow equals EUR186,005, or NOI of EUR406,750 minus debt service of EUR220,745. Using Equation 6,

$$\text{After-tax cash flow} = \text{Pre-tax cash flow} - \text{Taxes},$$

$$\text{EUR}139{,}317 = \text{EUR}186{,}005 - \text{EUR}46{,}688.$$

Analysts and investors often focus on pre-tax real estate returns since many real estate investments involve income pass-through features that are taxed at an investor's individual tax rate.

Classifications

The distinct features of real estate require a different approach to investment classification than that introduced earlier in the curriculum for corporate issuers. Recall that firms are grouped based on their principal business activity using commercial classification systems, relative sensitivity to the business cycle, and statistical similarities such as size or financial measures determined to be relevant for performance.

Commercial classification systems such as MSCI's Global Industry Classification Standard (GICS) define the real estate industry as either firms engaged in operating, developing, or servicing real estate investments or entities known as **real estate investment trusts** (REITs), which directly own and operate properties and distribute dividends to shareholders.

Exhibit 2: GICS Real Estate Industry Classification

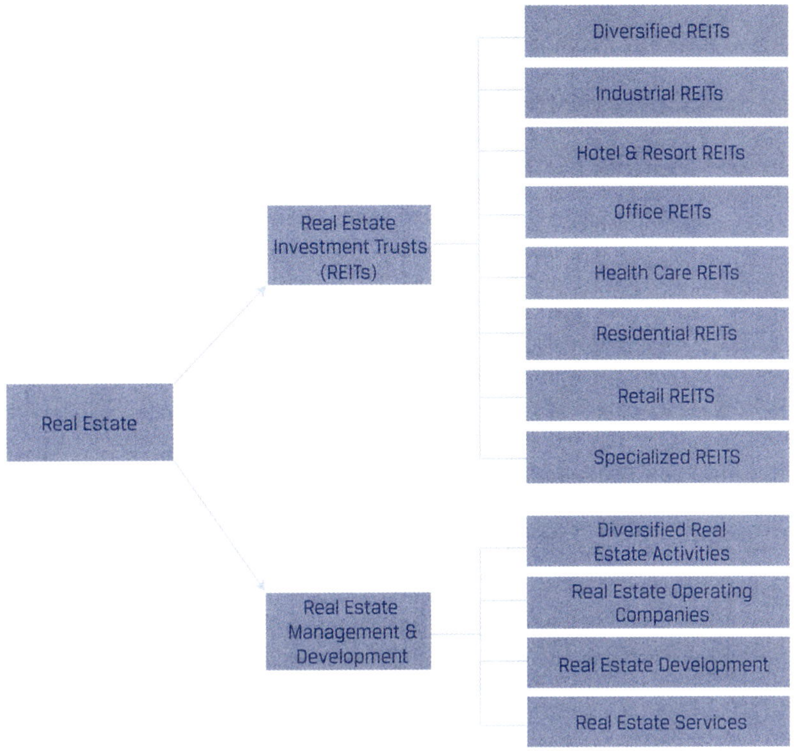

Debt-based real estate investments, such as mortgages, are typically classified as financial industry fixed-income investments. Industry classifications seek to group companies with similar demand characteristics based on similar principal business activities. This assumes that management and development firms have broad exposure to the industry and that REITs have granular property portfolios with geographic diversification. If a real estate management and development company or REIT has a regional focus, investors may conduct more detailed analysis on property-specific characteristics, competitive dynamics in local markets where properties are located, and regional economic trends.

A separate form of classification commonly applied to businesses and industries pertains to their relative sensitivity to the business cycle. Real estate investors focus on the underlying industry or industries in which property lessees operate in order to gauge future performance. For example, health care REITs might be considered a more defensive investment because the demand for medical services typically exhibits less fluctuation over the business cycle. Industrial and office REITs, in contrast, are usually considered more cyclical in nature because underlying lessors experience more volatile demand for their products over the cycle.

Statistical factors broadly relevant to real estate investments offer investors an additional classification approach. One such approach involves the bundling of real estate property features into classes. **Property classes** involve a relative ranking based on a combination of features, such as location, property age, local income levels, recent property appreciation, and relative condition, as shown for the case of multi-family properties in Exhibit 3.

Exhibit 3: Multi-family Property Classes

Property Class A	▪ Built within past 10 years or substantially renovated ▪ Top exterior and interior amenities as compared to market ▪ High quality construction with best materials
Property Class B	▪ Built within past 20 years or renovated older property ▪ Dated exterior and interior amenities as compared to market ▪ Good quality construction with limited deferred maintenance
Property Class C	▪ Built within past 30 years or renovated older property ▪ Limited and dated exterior and interior amenities as compared to market ▪ Aging construction has deferred maintenance
Property Class D	▪ Built over 30 years ago in less desirable location ▪ No exterior or interior amenities ▪ Poor construction quality and condition with limited remaining usability

Expected income versus capital appreciation opportunities usually vary across real estate property classes. For example, properties in the highest class typically command high market prices and the highest rental/lease rates in an area but offer less opportunity for capital appreciation. Lower-class properties are offered at more attractive prices with greater price appreciation potential. Capital expenditures to upgrade a property and improved local economic conditions may be needed to generate higher rental and lease income.

In addition to the quality of construction, materials, and amenities, real estate investors and tenants also increasingly consider the environmental impact of building construction and operation as an important feature for both newly constructed buildings and the renovation of existing properties.

SUSTAINABLE BUILDING CERTIFICATION

Growing demand for environmental building standards led to the establishment of two official property certifications in the 1990s. The first of which, developed in the United Kingdom, is known as BREEAM (Building Research Establishment Environmental Assessment Methodology), and the second is the Leadership in Energy and Environmental Design (LEED) standards, created in the United States. Both involve third-party, rating-based evaluation and certification systems that use rankings to establish the relative sustainability of buildings based on several criteria, including energy and water use efficiency, use of sustainable building materials, the ability for occupants to use alternative or public transportation, and the size of a property's carbon footprint, among others. While the BREEAM approach is prevalent in the United Kingdom and across Europe, LEED certification is a more widely recognized global designation, with such countries as China, Canada, and India pursuing the largest number of LEED projects outside the United States.

While sustainable materials and methods increase new construction and renovation costs, potential benefits include lower operating costs, higher rents, and lower vacancy because green properties are more attractive to tenants, as well as the opportunity to meet an investor's environmental, social, and governance objectives. In addition, many jurisdictions offer tax incentives for buildings that meet the highest certification standards.

The availability of both traditional and non-traditional data sources affecting property values has sparked the use of machine learning techniques to incorporate statistical factors into real estate investment decisions, particularly for owner-occupied homes. For example, supervised machine learning algorithms offer the potential to incorporate large datasets including census data, crime statistics, local pollution levels, and measures of school quality to model and better predict home prices. While these algorithms are most applicable to relatively homogeneous housing markets and newer construction, changes in the real estate cycle pose a greater challenge for models.

Basic Forms

Public and private forms of real estate investment across equity and debt capital alternatives described in an earlier lesson are shown in Exhibit 4.

Exhibit 4: Selected Forms of Real Estate Investment

	Debt	Equity
Private	Mortgage Debt Construction Loans Mezzanine Debt	*Direct Ownership* Sole ownership Joint ventures Limited partnerships *Indirect Ownership* Real estate funds Private REITs
Public	MBS/CMBS/CMOs Covered Bonds Mortgage REITs Mortgage EFTs	*Publicly Traded Shares* Construction Operating Development Public REITs UCITS / Mutual Funds / ETFs

Recall from the industry classification that public real estate equity investments include corporate issuers whose primary activity is in the construction, development, operation, and servicing of real estate, such as **real estate operating companies** (REOCs) and real estate investment trusts. While REOCs are taxable corporations that own, operate, and manage commercial real estate with few restrictions, REITs are restricted to primarily owning and operating rental properties or purchasing mortgages and are required to distribute nearly all or all of their earnings to investors to avoid paying corporate income tax.

First established in the United States, domestic REITs are now available in over 30 countries and are organized either as a corporation under respective country tax laws, as in the United States and much of Europe, or as a trust that holds investment properties and is externally managed, as in Australia.

REITS IN CHINA

The China Securities Regulatory Commission (CSRC) initiated the use of REITs as a part of its financial market structural reforms in order to expand the sources of capital available for commercial and residential real estate. Starting with an initial launch of nine infrastructure REITs on the Shenzhen and Shanghai exchanges in 2021, which raised RMB30 billion, the use of REITs was expanded to the residential sector with the launch of three new rental property REITs the following year.

Whereas net operating income, introduced earlier, provides a measure of income-based returns at the property level, funds from operations (FFO) is a common measure of REIT performance that excludes net gains from property sales:

$$\text{FFO} = \text{Net income} + \text{Depreciation} + \text{Amortization} - \text{Net gains from property sales.} \quad (8)$$

Real estate debt investments range from individual property loans based on a variety of loan terms to portfolios of commercial or residential property loans available to public investors in different investment forms described earlier in the curriculum.

As mentioned previously, property loans are usually long-term secured loans with a first lien and security interest. Loans may be extended at an interest rate that fluctuates based on market reference rates, is fixed, or combines a fixed-rate period with a variable-rate period at a so-called **adjustable rate**. In some cases, such as the US and Japanese markets, mortgage-based debt investors face prepayment risk because borrowers retain the right to repay debt earlier than scheduled, subjecting lenders to reinvestment risk.

Commercial or residential property loans are often bundled and sold to investors in the form of covered bonds or mortgage-backed securities (MBS). In the case of covered bonds, senior debt obligations are issued by financial institutions that retain the segregated real estate loan portfolio on their balance sheet. Investor recourse to both the financial institution and the loan portfolio, strict eligibility criteria, and the ability to substitute collateral if it fails to meet preset criteria reduce the risk and return of covered bonds. Mortgage-backed securities are securitized, with the asset pool removed from the original issuer's balance sheet to a special purpose entity. Mortgage-backed securities distribute interest and principal cash flows to different bond tranches, creating securities with varying exposures to prepayment and other risks.

Our focus in this learning module is how the leverage, debt coverage, and income-producing potential of underlying properties affect debt interest and principal cash flows.

Principal Risks

Real estate investment risks are derived from both economic and competitive factors affecting the economic use of real estate assets, as well as property-specific issues that can affect real estate returns.

Changes in the level and type of economic activity across industries and regions, demographics, the relative supply of commercial and residential real estate, and the cost and availability of capital are all factors that affect market rent and lease rates, occupancy levels, and real estate prices.

Risk issues unique to a particular property that affect individual real estate returns include real estate management, obsolescence, and technological change, as well as environmental, zoning, and other factors. Management issues include properly conducting regularly scheduled or preventative service and repairs to allow full realization of a property's useful life and managing tenants and lease terms to maximize income and minimize vacancy and turnover. Obsolescence may result in extensive renovation and upgrade costs borne by the owner that exceed estimates, while in other cases, it may not be economically viable to upgrade older buildings to comply with modernization requirements or changing user preferences. Environmental factors include increased energy efficiency requirements and exposure to geographic and climate risks, such as floods, earthquakes, and hurricanes.

As the use of machine learning techniques and big data creates new opportunities for real estate investors, overreliance on statistical analysis to predict real estate prices is a source of risk, as shown in the following example.

ZILLOW OFFERS

The COVID-19 pandemic caused many individuals to re-evaluate their living situations, creating many new potential home buyers and sellers. Beginning in 2020, demand for residential properties outpaced sales, driving home prices higher. Zillow, a Seattle-based company historically focused on earning advertising revenue from its online residential property marketplace, expanded its business model at the time to make market-based cash offers to residential homeowners based on a valuation algorithm targeting short-term profits from reselling the homes.

In mid-2021, Zillow's new property purchase business, Zillow Offers, recorded a new high in purchases in the Phoenix area, while other competitors, such as OpenDoor, were slowing their buying activity. As the unpredictability of home price movements created losses in this operation, Zillow sharply cut its purchase activity. The company subsequently reported a net loss of USD328 million for the quarter ending 30 September, attributable principally to its home purchase and sale activities, and its stock price fell by approximately 25% as this information became public.

Ultimately, Zillow found that its algorithm could not successfully capture the many factors necessary to scale their home-buying, renovation, and selling activities. The company was hoping to be a low-risk market maker for home buyers and sellers but ended up as a housing trader unable to deal effectively with market price volatility with losses totaling USD1 billion.

QUESTION SET

1. Assume that in Example 1, Wallonia Transit has multiple tenants.
   If the vacancy rate for the property is 10%, which of the following is closest to the updated estimate of its NOI?

   A. EUR366,075

   B. EUR354,250

   C. EUR459,250

   Solution:

   B is correct. A 10% allowance for vacancies would require a deduction of EUR52,500 (i.e., 10% of gross rent), which would cause both effective gross income and net operating income to decline by EUR52,500, from EUR406,750 to EUR354,250. Response A is simply 90% of EUR406,750. Response C adds EUR52,500 to EUR406,750.

2. In Example 1, which of the following operating strategies would result in a higher NOI for Wallonia Transit?

   A. Negotiate with the taxing authority to lower the property tax bill.

   B. Negotiate for lower insurance rates.

C. Negotiate with vendors for lower rates on service and repairs.

Solution:

C is correct. Service and repair expenses are not fully passed through to the lessee. Wallonia receives a fixed amount of EUR102,500 from the lessee to help offset service and repairs. If Wallonia's management can lower service and repair expenses, then these cost improvements improve the NOI. Responses A and B are incorrect because both property tax and insurance expenses are fully passed through to the lessee.

3. Two similar properties are available to you as an investor at prices of AUD2,000,000 each. You expect both to generate the same NOI. The only significant difference between the two properties is that the value of the first property includes land value of AUD600,000 while the second property's land value is AUD800,000. Which of the following statements is most accurate regarding the difference between the after-tax cash flows of the two properties?

   A. The first property has higher after-tax cash flow compared to the second property.

   B. The first property has lower after-tax cash flow compared to the second property.

   C. The two properties have the same after-tax cash flow.

Solution:

A is correct. The first property will have a higher after-tax cash flow than the second property because its taxes will be lower because of a higher depreciable base resulting from its lower land value. The first property will have annual depreciation expense based on its AUD1.4 million property value, while the second property will have annual depreciation expense based on its AUD1.2 million property value. Looking at Equation 5–Equation 7, the only difference in the two properties is the depreciation expense.

$$\text{Pre-tax cash flow} = \text{Net operating income} - \text{Debt service.}$$

$$\text{After-tax cash flow} = \text{Pre-tax cash flow} - \text{Taxes.}$$

$$\text{Taxes} = t \times (\text{NOI} - \text{Interest expense} - \text{Depreciation expense}).$$

3 ECONOMIC VALUE DRIVERS AND PORTFOLIO CHARACTERISTICS OF REAL ESTATE INVESTMENTS

☐ explain economic value drivers of real estate investments and their role in a portfolio

Economic Value Drivers

Business cycles represent fluctuations in economic activity across broad segments of the economy that drive real estate investment income and capital appreciation overall, as well as in different ways across sectors and regions.

Macroeconomic factors such as GDP growth, job creation, and wage growth tend to have positive effects across the entire real estate sector. Since commercial real estate serves as a significant factor of production in many industries, an increase in goods and services production usually translates to greater demand for industrial, office, and retail space among businesses. Given the relatively long development and construction period associated with these real estate assets, the initial effect of an increase in demand is a rise in market rent and lease rates and a decline in vacancies followed by a slow increase in supply over time.

Job creation and wage growth drive higher personal income, which, combined with positive demographic trends and consumer confidence, leads to rising **household formation**, or the establishment of new residences, leading to an increase in demand for both rental housing and owner-occupied housing. Because residential and commercial properties are heavily financed by debt capital, the real estate sector is highly sensitive to interest rates and the credit cycle. Home purchase and construction activity expands in lower mortgage rate environments and declines as loan rates rise. Prospective homeowners typically weigh the cost of homeownership versus renting when considering a purchase. When housing prices are low relative to household incomes, terms are attractive, and mortgage rates are low, the cost of homeownership falls and the demand for owner-occupied housing versus multi-family rentals increases. Attractive housing market conditions also usually spur an increase in new home construction and an eventual increase in supply.

The so-called **real estate cycle** combines these short-term adjustments in market rent or lease rates and occupancy in response to economic signals of growth versus a slowdown with the long-term decision to develop and build new supply based on current market conditions. The typical lag in construction and development of new properties often means that new supply often does not become fully available until market conditions have changed. Exhibit 5 provides an illustration of the real estate cycle.

Exhibit 5: Real Estate Cycle

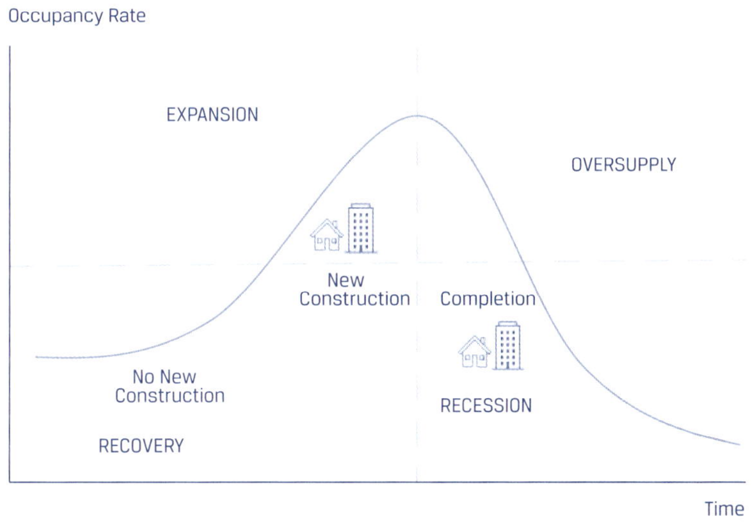

All economic cycles differ in frequency, length, and severity; here, we identify four common phases of the real estate cycle.

- Recovery: This phase is characterized by a business cycle trough, with little or no new construction due to an uncertain economic outlook and tight credit conditions. Weak economic activity reduces commercial occupancy, and property owners may cut leases to retain existing or attract new tenants. In addition to limiting construction, tight credit conditions and limited growth prospects often lead to lower commercial real estate prices. Households facing less certain employment and income prospects and tighter credit conditions often delay household formation and defer plans for new housing, slowing demand for multi-family rental housing units and owner-occupied homes. This places downward pressure on rents and home prices.
- Expansion: Periods of economic growth and easing credit conditions stimulate demand for commercial real estate, driving higher occupancy rates and a greater ability among property owners to raise lease rates as incremental demand exceeds supply. Stronger growth and improved credit conditions cause commercial real estate prices to rise, stimulating new construction and upgrades of existing properties. Consumer confidence rises as unemployment declines and wages rise, stimulating demand for rental and owner-occupied housing and driving rents and home prices higher. As the economic growth cycle reaches its peak, rising interest rates and prices result in maximum occupancy, while higher mortgage rates and prices discourage incremental construction.
- Oversupply: As economic growth softens, construction projects in the pipeline continue to completion, contributing to a property glut that drives a decline in occupancy and lower rents. A less certain outlook and worsening financial conditions cause real estate prices to level off and begin to decline.
- Recession: Economic slowdown and tightening credit accelerate the decline in occupancy due to increased supply. Landlords seek to retain tenants with favorable terms. Construction starts reach lows, and real estate prices decline.

While the performance of various real estate investments may lead or lag the real estate cycle, the expansion phase for income-producing properties with no capital structure changes is typically associated with rising NOI and DSC and falling LTV and may be summarized over the cycle as shown in Exhibit 6.

Exhibit 6: Key Real Estate Financial Metrics over the Cycle

Phase/Measure	Interest Rates	NOI	DSC	LTV
Recovery	Reach a Bottom and Begin to Rise	Reaches Bottom and Begins to Rise	Reaches Bottom and Begins to Rise	Peaks and Begins to Fall
Expansion	Rising	Rising	Increase	Decrease
Oversupply	Peak and Begin to Fall	Peaks and Begins to Fall	Peaks and Begins to Fall	Reaches Bottom and Begins to Rise
Recession	Low	Falling	Decrease	Increase

The macroeconomic effect of this cycle on individual properties will vary based on local factors. As a fixed real asset, the income and capital appreciation potential of commercial and residential properties is inextricably linked to the local economy and market conditions. Factors include the attractiveness of the local business climate, the presence of major firms, industries, and employers, as well as local infrastructure and services, tax policies, and regulatory factors, such as zoning laws. Commercial properties benefit from proximity to suppliers and customers and convenient links to air, water, and land transportation. The attractiveness of a residential property rises with greater availability of employment and recreational opportunities, better transportation access, and the quality of local public schools, public safety, and other services in a local jurisdiction. Prospective property income and real estate prices are adversely impacted in areas with greater exposure to technological change, such as those with declining industries, and areas with a declining population.

Portfolio Characteristics of Real Estate

Sources of real estate investment return include periodic income and asset appreciation, or a combination of the two. Property investments typically generate either recurring bond-like cash flows from leases, or higher-risk, equity-like speculative returns from development projects with no current cash flows, but rather anticipated future income or expected price appreciation.

Key characteristics of real estate investments that affect their role in a portfolio include not only current income and capital appreciation but also inflation-hedging properties, diversification, and tax benefits.

Current Income

Despite the apparent similarity of recurring lease payments to fixed-rate bond coupon cash flows, property leases often incorporate rental terms that differ from fixed rent payments or fixed expense reimbursement, as in the earlier Wallonia Transit example. For example, leases may include **step-up clauses**, which, unlike bond step-up features, are not contingent but, rather, are pre-specified future rent increases. **Indexed rents**, in contrast, specify rent changes based on an observed market variable, such as the consumer price index, while sales-based rental adjustments, or an **overage rent** clause, result in higher rent if a retailer's sales exceed a pre-agreed minimum target or breakeven sales level, as shown in the following example.

EXAMPLE 5

Chandra Shops Overage Rent

Chandra Shops operates several luxury retail stores in central business districts across India. Following the COVID-19 pandemic, Chandra renegotiated the fixed lease on its 500 square foot Chennai store by lowering base rent by 10% from the original INR300 per square foot per month and agreeing to an 8% overage rent on gross monthly sales in excess of INR1,000,000.

1. If Chandra's gross sales were INR1,250,000 under the new lease, calculate the monthly rent and compare it to Chandra's cost under the original lease ignoring other expenses.

   Solution:

   While Chandra's base rent has declined from INR150,000 (= INR300/ $ft^2 \times 500\ ft^2$) to INR135,000 (= INR270/$ft^2 \times 500\ ft^2$), it must pay overage rent of INR20,000 [= $0.08 \times (1{,}250{,}000 - 1{,}000{,}000)$] on sales in excess of

INR1,000,000, for a total of INR155,000, versus INR150,000 under the original lease terms.

Owners may cover all operating expenses under a lease, pass through certain expenses, or charge tenants a share of increases over an operating expense limit. Owners also assess charges on common areas for service and use.

Lease terms vary greatly, and when the investment holding period exceeds the lease term, property income is subject to **rollover risk**, or the likelihood an owner will lose an existing tenant and forgo income until a new one is found.

Capital Appreciation

Increases in estimated property value over time contribute to an investor's holding period return. Given the heterogeneous and illiquid nature of real estate investments, price changes may be precisely measured only in the event of a property sale. Price estimation techniques based on relative value and property price indexes will be addressed later.

Inflation Hedge

Beyond explicit means of capturing price rises, such as indexed rents, rents and property prices tend to rise in an inflationary environment. In contrast to investments with fixed nominal cash flows or firms that lack pricing power in a competitive industry, physical assets such as real estate tend to generate a real return over time despite inflation.

Diversification

Real estate property values have not typically been highly correlated with the performance of other asset classes—such as stocks, bonds, or cash—so adding real estate to a portfolio often lowers the overall risk of the portfolio (that is, the volatility of returns) relative to the expected return. However, liquid public real estate investments, such as mortgage-backed securities and REITs, tend to exhibit higher correlation with public fixed-income and equity markets in the short to medium term.

Tax Benefits

Real estate investments may offer tax advantages for some investors. For example, in such countries as the United States, private real estate may be depreciated for tax purposes over a shorter period than the actual useful property life. In many jurisdictions, REIT structures that distribute income before tax to shareholders on a pass-through basis are favorable from a tax perspective compared to corporations that are taxed twice, that is, subject to both corporate tax and investor income tax.

QUESTION SET

1. Which of the following statements best characterizes the typical changes in key financial metrics over the real estate cycle?

   A. Debt service coverage ratios typically peak during the recovery phase and reach their lows during the oversupply phase.

   B. LTVs typically peak during the oversupply phase and reach lows during the recovery phase.

C. NOI typically peaks during the oversupply phase and reaches a low during the recovery phase.

Solution:

C is correct. NOI rises as rents increase and vacancies decline during real estate market expansion, peaking in an oversupply phase before falling. Response A is incorrect because DSCs typically peak during an oversupply phase and reach a low during a recovery phase. Response B is incorrect because LTVs usually peak during recovery and reach a low in an oversupply phase.

2. An analyst is working on an assessment of the attractiveness of investing in residential homebuilders versus developers of multi-family rental housing. Which of the following combinations of factors is most likely to provide a bullish scenario for residential homebuilders compared to rental housing developers.

A. High job creation and positive demographic trends

B. Low ratio of housing prices to household income and declining mortgage rates

C. Large supply of owner-occupied housing and declining mortgage rates

Solution:

B is correct. When housing prices are low compared to household income, owner-occupied housing becomes more attractive to buyers. Coupled with declining mortgage rates, the conditions are favorable for the residential housing market compared to multi-family rental housing. Response A is consistent with positive environments for both residential and rental markets. Response C is a characteristic of an oversupply phase of the real estate cycle; thus, this situation would likely be negative for both residential and rental markets.

3. In Example 5, Chandra Shops renegotiated new lease terms, including a reduction of its base rent by 10% with an overage rent of 8% of gross monthly sales in excess of INR1,000,000. These new lease terms were shown to be consistent with a monthly total rent of INR155,000 if Chandra Shops generated gross sales of INR1,250,000. The prior lease terms yielded total monthly rent of INR150,000. If this level of sales adequately reflects Chandra's expectations of future monthly gross sales, which of the following base rent reductions and levels of overage rent would cause Chandra to prefer the new lease terms?

A. Base rent reduction by 11.5% and overage rent of 7.2%

B. Base rent reduction by 8.5% and overage rent of 5.2%

C. Base rent reduction by 9.6% and overage rent of 5.6%

Solution:

C is correct. At a base rent reduction of 9.6% and an overage rent of 5.6%, the total monthly rent is INR149,600 (i.e., less than the prior level of INR150,000). The terms associated with both Responses A and B yield total monthly rent greater than INR150,000.

4 COMMERCIAL PROPERTY INVESTMENT CHARACTERISTICS

☐ discuss the distinctive investment characteristics of commercial property types

Given the real estate cycle and the effects of real estate investment features on an investor's portfolio addressed in the prior section, we now turn our attention to specific demand and supply factors affecting the relative risk and return of commercial real estate subsegments, including residential and non-residential (office, industrial and warehouse, retail, and hospitality) properties.

Residential Use Property Investment Characteristics

Residential properties include both single-family detached homes and multi-family properties, such as apartments. While owner-occupied housing dominates most single-family markets, multi-family properties form the bulk of residential properties that are typically included in the commercial real estate category.

Multi-family properties contain multiple residential units, apartments, or flats. A property may be owned by one investor, or units may be owned by separate investors who occupy or rent the unit. Multi-family housing is typically categorized based on location (urban or suburban), structure height (high-rise or garden apartments or townhouses), and amenities (balcony or outdoor space, pool, exercise or other shared facilities, concierge services, etc.).

Beyond key macroeconomic factors such as personal income and job growth, residential demand for rental housing properties is driven by local economic conditions and the availability and affordability of owner-occupied alternatives. Tenants may enjoy such protections as limits on rent increases or evictions, and leases are usually for a much shorter term than for non-residential properties. Residential property cash flow analysis is often based on **gross potential rental income** (GPRI), which is equal to the current market rent at full occupancy:

$$\text{Gross potential rental income} = \text{Market rent} \times \text{Rentable space}. \quad (9)$$

Since properties with multiple tenants are often leased at different times with different rental rates and terms, changing market rents, tenant turnover, and vacancies, as well as rent concessions and other adjustments, all affect net operating income, as shown in the following example.

EXAMPLE 6

Pinebranch Estates

Pinebranch is a multi-family property on the outskirts of a major Australian city consisting of 240 one- and two-bedroom rental units that average 1,200 square feet each and include parking and other resident amenities. Current market rent is AUD2.00 per square foot per month. The following table shows other income sources and expenses for the year, as well as rental income deductions.

Rental Deductions	**AUD**
Loss to Lease (Difference between Market Rents and Current Leases)	128,200
Less: Vacancy & Collection Cost	791,236
Concessions & Adjustments	485,124
	1,404,560
Additional Income	
Other Income	295,211
Expense Recovery from Tenants	525,800
	820,211
Expenses	
Operating & Leasing Expenses	2,753,000
Property Maintenance Allowance	655,000
	3,408,000

1. Calculate Pinebranch's annual GPRI and NOI.

   Solution:

   Per Equation 9, GPRI is equal to market rent at full capacity:

   AUD6,912,000 = 240 units × 1,200 ft^2 × AUD2.00 per ft^2/month × 12 months.

   NOI is equal to GPRI plus additional income less rental deductions and expenses:

   AUD2,919,651
   = AUD6,912,000 + AUD820,211 – AUD1,404,560 – AUD3,408,000.

2. Contrast the NOI drivers of Pinebranch Estates and the Wallonia Transit warehouse facility.

   Solution:

   In contrast to the case of the warehouse facility, Wallonia, where the owner was able to pass through property tax and insurance costs to its single tenant, these costs were absorbed by the owners of Pinebranch. Given multiple tenants and shorter rental terms, rental deductions have a significant impact on Pinebranch's cash flow and NOI. Pinebranch Estates' income statement is shown in the following table.

Pinebranch Estates Cash Flow	**AUD**
Gross Potential Rent Income	6,912,000
Less: Loss to Lease	(128,200)
Gross Rental Income	6,783,800
Less: Vacancy & Collection Cost	(791,236)
Concessions & Adjustments	(485,124)
Net Rental Income	5,507,440
Add: Other Income	295,211

Pinebranch Estates Cash Flow	AUD
Expense Recovery from Tenants	525,800
Total Income	6,327,651
Less: Operating & Leasing Expenses	(2,753,000)
Property Maintenance Allowance	(655,000)
Net Operating Income	2,919,651

Commercial Use Property Investment Characteristics

While tenant demand for residential properties is broadly based on local economic conditions, the income and capital appreciation features of commercial facilities are more closely tied to economic use within a respective industry or area of activity, may exhibit more or less volatility over the real estate cycle, and are often more impacted by structural changes than housing is.

- *Office properties:* Properties range from major multi-tenant office buildings in central business districts to single-tenant office buildings. They are often built for the needs of key tenants, such as a medical office facility near a hospital or the headquarters of a large company. In other cases, new construction begins when an anchor tenant commits to occupy a large portion of the space, reducing development risk. While demand for office space was historically correlated with service industry employment, a shift to remote or hybrid work following the COVID-19 outbreak has reduced demand for office space in industries where in-person work is no longer considered a requirement.
- *Industrial and warehouse properties:* Wholesale and retail distribution centers, combined warehouse/showroom and office facilities, and manufacturing facilities combined with warehouse space are included in this subsegment. The rise of e-commerce caused a structural increase in demand for warehouse facilities among online retailers seeking to meet consumer needs. While many industrial properties are designed for a specific industrial use and are difficult to convert, those in desirable areas are more often adapted to alternative uses.
- *Retail properties:* This category includes regional shopping centers and malls with anchor department stores and many smaller in-line stores, local shopping centers with smaller anchor tenants and in-line tenants, and standalone properties, such as grocery stores or restaurants. The structural shift in the retail business model to web-based sales has reduced shopping center and mall demand, driving conversion to alternative uses. Retail outlets (particularly on lower floors in central business districts) are often combined with office space or residential space. Proximity to local workers and residents is an important feature affecting rents, occupancy, and property values.
- *Hospitality properties:* These facilities and their business drivers vary widely based on size, clientele, and available amenities. Hotels used primarily for business travel range from extended stay units to those for shorter-stay corporate travel concentrated in major business centers and airports to large convention centers whose business largely depends on major trade

shows with multiyear contracts. Business travel is often cyclical; firms cut expenses in a downturn, placing pressure on occupancy and rental rates. While smaller motels and hotels primarily used by households and workers in transit, which offer fewer amenities, are less prone to business fluctuations, those designed for vacationing tourists with more amenities depend on strong consumer confidence and high disposable income. Destination resorts offer the most amenities, can be quite luxurious, and either are located near major recreational attractions or offer all-inclusive experiences that are management intensive, involving many employees and high fixed costs.

Other specialty real estate subsectors include residential units for students or senior citizens and special-use commercial properties, such as hospitals, self-storage facilities, cell towers, data centers, and parking facilities. Each subsegment has its own unique features affecting investment risk and return. For example, self-storage properties have relatively low capital requirements and low operating costs. Units are used by many businesses and households, rather than one lessee as in the Wallonia case, but leases are typically month to month, giving owners greater pricing flexibility but also more exposure to fluctuations in demand. Senior housing facilities range widely from independent living to more management-intensive continuing care facilities. While aging populations have contributed to growing demand in this subsegment in developed markets, rising wealth and longevity among retirees have increased both supply and competition in terms of the range of non-medical amenities and activities offered to residents.

Commercial real estate that combines more than one tenant type and economic use is referred to as **mixed-use development**, commonly combining residential or office space and retail outlets, as in the following example.

EXAMPLE 7

Eastmain Plaza NOI

Eastmain Plaza is a 350,000 square foot multistory mixed-use development in Kuala Lumpur that combines office space on upper floors, a cell tower on the roof, and retail outlets and parking below; 90% of Eastmain's rentable area is dedicated to office tenants at an average annual base rent of MYR100 per ft^2, and the remainder is retail space leased at MYR250 per ft^2 per year. While the office space has some vacancies, the retail area is fully leased, given the lack of nearby retail outlets.

1. Calculate Eastmain's gross rent.

   Solution:

   Recall that gross rent is equal to base rent multiplied by rentable area, which in this case combines office and retail space:

   Gross rent = Base rent (MYR/ft^2) × Rentable area.

   MYR40,250,000
   = ($0.9 \times$ MYR100/$ft^2 \times$ 350,000 ft^2) + ($0.1 \times$ MYR250/$ft^2 \times$ 350,000 ft^2).

2. Given the prospect of significant new retail development close to Eastmain, an analyst is considering a downside scenario under which retail sales decline significantly and retail rent receipts fall by half versus the past year.

Explain the impact on Eastmain's NOI assuming no changes to operating expenses or expense recoveries based on its most recent income statement:

Eastmain Plaza	MYR
Gross Rent	40,250,000
Expense Recoveries from Tenants	3,904,250
Overage Rent	450,800
Cell Tower Rent	354,200
Storage Fees	60,375
Parking	281,750
Less: Vacancy	(2,012,500)
Less: Concessions	(483,000)
Effective Gross Income	42,805,875
Operating Expenses	
Property Taxes	(3,122,709)
Management/Admin./Lease Expenses	(3,358,089)
Insurance	(2,181,189)
Service & Repairs	(3,373,781)
Utilities	(5,915,886)
Janitorial/Cleaning	(2,479,337)
Business & Other Taxes	(580,604)
Total Operating Expenses	(21,011,595)
Property Maintenance Allowance	(8,709,063)
Net Operating Income	13,085,217

Solution:

The downside scenario has an adverse impact on overage rent and retail rent receipts, while possibly affecting parking revenue as well. If overage rent is eliminated and total retail rent is halved (due to rent concessions or vacancies), then Eastmain's NOI would decline by overage rent of MYR450,800 and retail base rent receipts of MYR4,375,000 [= (0.1 × MYR250/ft^2 × 350,000 ft^2)/2], for a total decline of MYR4,825,800, or 37% of NOI, to MYR8,259,417.

Note that while mixed-use properties generally offer income streams spread across different types of revenue or activity, they also tend to be both closely related to local economic conditions and correlated with one another, because other tenants are often the primary customers of retail outlets in the same location.

QUESTION SET

1. An analyst is interviewing for a new job with a real estate investment firm. The interviewer asks about the difference between gross potential rental income and gross rental income for a property. Which of the following is the most correct response that the analyst might provide?

   A. The difference between gross potential rental income and gross rental income reflects the vacancy rate of the property.

   B. The difference between gross potential rental income and gross rental income reflects the difference between market rents on the property and its current rents.

   C. The difference between gross potential rental income and gross rental income reflects rental concessions provided to tenants.

   Solution:

   B is correct. Gross potential rental income is shown in Equation 9 and reflects the product of market rents and rentable space. Gross rental income reflects the product of current rents and rentable space. Responses A and C are incorrect because vacancies and concessions are deducted from gross rental income to obtain net rental income.

2. An analyst working for a real estate investment firm is studying the effects of recent events, such as the evolution of the internet and the COVID-19 pandemic, on different commercial property types. Which of the following commercial property types is least likely to be converted to an alternative use because of structural and technological change?

   A. Retail properties

   B. Office properties

   C. Industrial and warehouse properties

   Solution:

   C is correct. Industrial and warehouse properties are often designed for a specific use, making them less viable for conversion to alternative uses. Response A is incorrect. Retail properties have been significantly affected by the move to internet-based retail, and the COVID-19 pandemic accelerated this shift in the retail environment. As a result, demand for shopping centers and other retail properties has declined, forcing them into alternative uses. Response B is incorrect. The COVID-19 pandemic has significantly driven a trend away from workers commuting to office spaces and has created significant vacancies in the office market.

3. An analyst is considering multiple scenarios of net operating income for a mixed-use development of a 20-story building containing retail, commercial office, and hotel properties for business travelers. The building is in a busy area of the city with considerable pedestrian traffic. Which one of the following events is most likely to lead to a worst-case scenario for the mixed-use development?

   A. One of the major tenants of the office space gives notice that it will not be renewing its lease in six months.

B. A significant construction project is scheduled to begin that will limit sidewalk access to most of the building's entry points.

C. Poor business conditions, likely to result in a national economic recession, which will affect business travel.

Solution:

C is correct. A poor economic environment is likely to affect all the commercial property types negatively. A decline in business travel affects the hotel directly, and retail businesses will suffer from the reduced number of hotel guests. While the office properties may suffer less, the reduced employment situation from a recession is likely to hurt office rents and vacancies going forward. Response A is likely to affect only the office properties, with a possible indirect effect on the building's retailers. Response B is likely to affect only the retail properties directly and possibly make the business hotel less attractive during construction.

5 REAL ESTATE DUE DILIGENCE AND VALUATION APPROACHES

☐ explain the due diligence process and valuation approaches for real estate investments

Unlike public debt or equities for which analysts rely primarily on market prices, audited financial statements, industry and company analysis, and the economic outlook to make investment decisions, the relative lack of transparency and standardization in real estate and the importance of a property's physical attributes and exact location demand more detailed due diligence to estimate income and capital appreciation potential. Once the expected size and variability of future cash flows is established, real estate valuation approaches are similar to those for other financial assets, which we will show in this section.

Real Estate Due Diligence

Key elements of real estate due diligence are summarized in Exhibit 7.

Exhibit 7: Elements of Real Estate Due Diligence

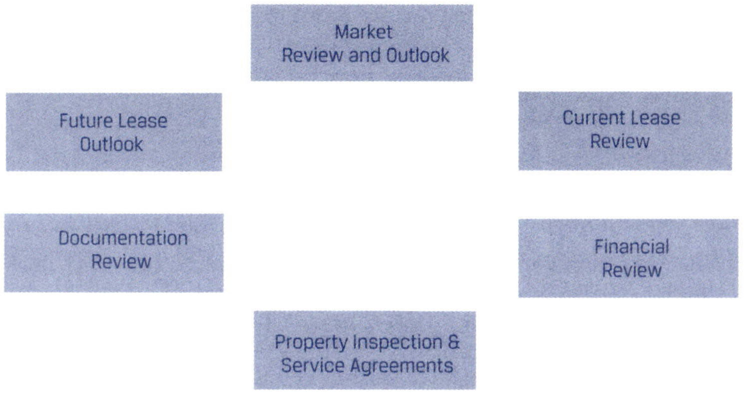

Market Review and Outlook

The heterogeneous, illiquid, and local nature of real estate markets leads participants to use a variety of sources to gather information about current prices and factors affecting future economic uses, demand and supply changes, and other market drivers, which include both macroeconomic forecasts and local business conditions.

Buyers, sellers, lessors, lessees, and brokers often rely on web-based aggregated information regarding current sale and lease offer prices based on standardized criteria, such as floor space, amenities, and precise property location. While such information may help establish a range of expectations for rental income and property prices, the real estate cycle phase often dictates whether properties are purchased or sold above or below the offer price or whether owners offer concessions, expense reductions, or amenities to tenants in exchange for maintaining a higher lease rate. Analysts typically prefer to use actual sale prices when available rather than estimates or offer prices. Environmental factors and impacts are of critical importance in real estate due diligence, especially for new development. For example, vulnerability to wildfires, hurricanes, and flooding impact the cost of insurance, as well as future capital appreciation and income. Investors in older structures must consider the cost of upgrading a property to meet energy efficiency or other environmental standards.

Current Lease Review

Evaluation of a property's current income stream—including current tenant rents versus forecasted market rents for similar properties, vacancies representing potential future income, and current lease length—is an important gauge of value to assess how and when income may change as leases expire. A lease expiration schedule may be used to support a rental income forecast. In addition, rental payment history, late payments, and tenant defaults provide a measure of current tenant creditworthiness.

Future Lease Outlook

A forward-looking view of a property's income must consider both costs and incentives for renewing existing tenants and acquiring new ones, including commissions paid to real estate brokers and downtime between leases. Incentives may involve a period of free rent and allowances for space improvements. These costs are typically not included in annual operating income but, rather, capitalized and amortized over the length of the lease.

The re-lease outlook is also affected by changes in local supply, as in the earlier Eastmain example, as well as local zoning or other legal changes, such as rent caps and stabilization, as shown in the following example.

BERLIN'S RENT CAP (*MIETENDECKEL*) LAW

In response to soaring rents following the privatization of formerly public housing after German reunification, Berlin lawmakers passed a rent cap measure, *Mietendeckel*, in early 2020 preventing owners of residential properties built before 2014 from raising rents above their June 2019 levels and mandating the reduction of any rents that were 20% above fixed levels established according to location and quality. The measure froze rents for five years, after which a modest increase for inflation was allowed.

While the immediate effect was an 11% decline in rent, Berlin's housing shortage became more severe. According to Immunoscout24.com, a leading German online platform for commercial and residential real estate, the immediate effect of the legislation was to reduce the overall supply of rental apartments in Berlin falling under the cap by nearly 59% from October 2019 to October 2020. This effect was almost entirely accounted for by rental apartments built before 2014 (–59.1%), while the supply of units built after 2014 rose by 6.7% over the same period.

In the following year, a German federal court struck down the new law as unconstitutional.

Financial Review

Analysts usually review several years of audited financial statements and operating expenses, such as utility bills and real estate taxes, to establish revenue and expense trends. Historical cash flow statements provide perspective on whether an existing property owner has inflated NOI by underinvesting in property maintenance or overstating occupancy and monthly rent by providing significant tenant incentives.

Documentation Review

Due diligence involves a legal and tax review of ownership history to ensure a property may be acquired free of any outstanding liens or tax obligations. Not only is this important for a new owner, but it is also a key requirement imposed by mortgage lenders in order to secure a claim to the property used as loan collateral. In addition to tax compliance and the lack of liens or other encumbrances, an analyst should verify the property is compliant with zoning laws and environmental regulations, with no restrictions on the anticipated economic use going forward.

Property Inspection and Service Agreements

Prospective buyers typically commission a property survey and a comprehensive physical, engineering, and environmental inspection involving all building systems and structures, including the building's foundation, and examining the adequacy of utilities to identify any property issues. The assessment of the property's manager is an important element to consider if a property is not directly managed by its owners. Existing agreements with service and maintenance providers are reviewed to determine whether recurring problems exist.

Any discrepancies or differences that arise during this review are subject to either remediation or a property price adjustment. A potential investor may negotiate a lower price or seek another investment opportunity.

Real Estate Valuation Approaches

The due diligence process both ensures an owner's claim to a property and provides a basis for estimating potential future cash flows. Despite the different and unique features of real estate, the principles of valuation used are similar to those for other financial assets when these features are taken into consideration. Three primary valuation methods—the income, cost, and sales comparison approaches—are addressed in the following sections.

Income Approach

The income approach corresponds to the discounted cash flow valuation introduced earlier for both public and private companies and is a primary approach for income-producing properties. Exhibit 8 summarizes key areas of focus when this method is applied to real estate properties.

Exhibit 8: Areas of Focus for Real Estate Valuation: Income Approach

1. Conduct Due Diligence to Estimate Property Rental Income and Expenses

   Property Rental Income and Expense

$$\text{Property Value}_t = \sum_{i=1}^{n} \frac{NOI_{t+i}}{(1+r)^i} + \frac{\text{Terminal Value}}{(1+r)^n}$$

2. Capitalization Rate / Rate of Return Estimates

NOI = Effective Gross Income – Operating Expenses – Property Maintenance Allowance

---

Under this method, the numerator consists of a property's actual or estimated NOI, while the denominator involves a discount rate that reflects the unique risk characteristics of the property derived from market comparisons or specific analysis, as shown below. Income approaches used to estimate or appraise a property's value include the **direct capitalization method** and the **discounted cash flow method**. The direct capitalization method estimates the value of an income-producing property based on a single year's net operating income, while the discounted cash flow (DCF) method involves a series of income projections discounted to the present with a terminal value. As for similar valuations based on a single cash flow, the direct capitalization method uses the formula for the present value of a perpetuity:

$$\text{Property value} = \frac{\text{Expected NOI}}{\text{Capitalization rate}}. \quad (10)$$

The **capitalization rate** (or cap rate) used to discount expected NOI in Equation 10 combines the required rate of return on similar properties (r) with an implied constant growth rate (g) assumed to continue indefinitely:

$$\text{Capitalization rate} = r - g. \quad (11)$$

Note that this required rate of return incorporates both the risk-free rate (r_f) and a risk premium unique to the type of property considered. While a higher risk premium will increase r and reduce a property's value, faster NOI growth will increase g, reducing the capitalization rate and resulting in a higher value.

EXAMPLE 8

Wallonia Transit Valuation—Direct Capitalization Method

Recall from an earlier example that Wallonia Transit is a fully rented single tenant warehouse facility with an estimated annual NOI of EUR406,750 per year. An analyst estimates that the required rate of return on similar facilities is 12.5% and expects NOI to grow at a constant 2% per year.

1. Estimate Wallonia Transit's value using the direct capitalization method.

   Solution:

   Using Equation 10 and Equation 11, solve for the property value by dividing expected NOI of EUR406,750 assuming r of 12.5% and g of 2%:

   $$\text{Property value} = \frac{\text{Expected NOI}}{r - g}.$$

   $$\text{EUR}3,873,810 = \frac{\text{EUR}406,750}{0.125 - 0.02}.$$

2. Calculate the estimated property value if Wallonia incurs 20% higher service and repair costs and NOI falls to EUR382,600.

   Solution:

   Using Equation 10 and Equation 11, solve for the property value by dividing expected NOI of EUR382,600 assuming r of 12.5% and g of 2%:

   $$\text{Property value} = \frac{\text{Expected NOI}}{r - g}.$$

   $$\text{EUR}3,643,810 = \frac{\text{EUR}382,600}{0.125 - 0.02}.$$

   The lower NOI due to higher expenses reduces the estimated property value by 6%.

The direct capitalization approach is most appropriate when a property generates consistent NOI and relationships between cash flows, expenses, and other factors are expected to remain constant. In the Wallonia example, this implies the analyst expects the single-year NOI to be representative of future periods with a steady 2% rate of growth. In the alternative case of higher service and repair costs, these should be included in the valuation only if they are expected to be incurred annually going forward. If, however, the investor or appraiser anticipates ongoing changes in rents, expenses, or other factors affecting NOI, then under the direct capitalization method, an analyst should project a normalized or so-called **stabilized NOI** in the numerator instead.

The use of a discounted cash flow methodology is more appropriate when an analyst has greater visibility into NOI dynamics, implying that a series of projected cash flows will result in a more accurate present value for a property. This cash flow projection generally involves the estimation of a terminal value by capitalizing NOI at some future date. Income can be projected either for the entire economic life of a property or for a finite holding period, at the end of which it is assumed that the property will be sold, as shown in Equation 12.

$$\text{Property value} = \sum_{i=1}^{n} \frac{\text{NOI}_{t+i}}{(1+r)^i} + \frac{\text{Terminal value}}{(1+r)^n}. \quad (12)$$

Terminal values used to gauge the potential future selling price of a property may be derived by either capitalizing the NOI of comparable properties or using the final year's projected NOI multiplied by 1 plus the constant growth rate *g* discounted by the cap rate:

$$\text{Terminal value} = \frac{\text{NOI}_n(1+g)}{r-g}. \quad (13)$$

EXAMPLE 9

Eastmain Plaza—Discounted Cash Flow Valuation

Recall from an earlier example that Eastmain Plaza is a multistory mixed-use development combining office and retail space. Given the opening of significant new retail space near Eastmain, retail sales and rent receipts are expected to decline sharply in the coming year while office rentals are expected to remain stable. A prospective investor is considering a five-year holding period over which she plans to upgrade and release the retail space to new tenants. She instructs an analyst to project NOI for the next five years using the downside scenario in the earlier example for the first year, a 50% increase in property maintenance allowance in Year 2 while regaining half of retail rents lost in Year 1, and a steady 3% rise in gross rents with proportional growth in expenses and normalized capital expenditure rising in line with gross rent thereafter starting in Year 3.

Eastmain Five-Year NOI Projections

NOI Components	Year 1	Year 2	Year 3	Year 4	Year 5
Gross Rent	40,250,000	40,250,000	41,457,500	42,701,225	43,982,262
of Which: Office Rent	31,500,000	31,500,000	32,445,000	33,418,350	34,420,901
Retail Rent	8,750,000	8,750,000	9,012,500	9,282,975	9,561,361
Expense Recoveries	3,904,250	3,904,250	4,021,378	4,142,019	4,266,279
Overage Rent	—	—	450,800	464,324	478,254
Other Income	696,325	696,325	717,215	738,731	760,893
Less:					
Vacancies and Concessions	(6,870,500)	(4,683,000)	(2,495,500)	(2,495,500)	(2,495,500)
Effective Gross Income	37,980,075	40,167,575	44,151,392	45,550,759	46,992,188
Total Operating Expenses	(21,011,595)	(21,011,595)	(21,641,943)	(22,291,201)	(22,959,937)
Property Maintenance Allowance	(8,709,063)	(13,063,595)	(8,970,335)	(9,239,445)	(9,516,629)
NOI	8,259,417	6,092,385	13,539,114	14,020,153	14,515,622

1. Assuming a required rate of return of 14% for Eastmain, calculate the present value of NOI over the five-year holding period.

   Solution:

   Calculate the present value of NOI for Years 1–5 using the first expression in Equation 12:

   $$\text{MYR}36{,}911{,}526$$

$$= \frac{8,259,417}{(1.14)} + \frac{6,092,385}{(1.14)^2} + \frac{13,539,114}{(1.14)^3} + \frac{14,020,153}{(1.14)^4} + \frac{14,515,622}{(1.14)^5}.$$

2. Assuming that Eastmain's NOI will grow at a constant 3% after Year 5, calculate Eastmain's terminal value and the expected property value.

Solution:

Solve for Eastmain's terminal value using Equation 13:

$$\text{MYR135,919,006} = \frac{14,515,622(1.03)}{(0.14 - 0.03)}.$$

Substitute the Solution to 1 for the present value expression and the terminal value above into Equation 12 to calculate the estimated property value:

$$\text{Property value} = \sum_{i=1}^{n} \frac{\text{NOI}_{t+i}}{(1+r)^i} + \frac{\text{Terminal value}}{(1+r)^n}.$$

$$\text{MYR107,503,599} = \text{MYR36,911,526} + \frac{\text{MYR135,919,006}}{(1.14)^5}.$$

The use of an appropriate cap rate is important for valuing income-producing real estate property. Rearranging Equation 10, we see that the capitalization rate may be interpreted as the ratio of NOI to property value:

$$\text{Capitalization rate} = \frac{\text{Expected NOI}}{\text{Property value}}. \tag{14}$$

Analysts often derive the cap rate from observations based on the current income and sale price of similar or comparable properties. Since the cap rate represents earnings cash flow for a given asset value, it is often compared to the current yield on a bond or the inverse of the enterprise value (EV) to EBITDA (EV/EBITDA) multiple for a stock as a measure of return that excludes capital gains or losses.

As in the case of other discount rates, the required rate of return (r) for a specific property will depend on a number of factors, including the level of benchmark interest rates, the risks associated with a specific property, and the supply/demand dynamics of the local real estate market. For example, the higher the benchmark rate, the greater the risk of a property, or the greater the oversupply in the real estate market, the higher the r and lower the respective present value of property cash flows. Investors also sometimes assume changing cap rates over the life of a real estate investment. The capitalization rate based on the first year of ownership used for the initial annual cash flow is referred to as the **going-in cap rate**, while the **terminal cap rate** is based on expected income for the period after the anticipated sale of the property. While the assumption of a positive constant growth rate as in the Eastmain example involves future NOI growth, $g < 0$ implies that a property may be approaching the end of its useful life and NOI is expected to decline.

Cost Approach

The cost approach to real estate valuation considers the cost of reproducing or replicating an asset and deducts depreciation and other factors that reduce property value. **Replacement cost** includes the expense of buying the land and constructing a new property on the site that has the same economic use as the property being appraised (referred to as the **subject property**). Adjustments are made if the subject property is older or requires updating, if the location of the property is less ideal for its current use, or if it is not feasible (due to ordinance restrictions, such as building codes and historical protections) to construct a new property in the current market. These adjustments may be higher or lower than the annual depreciation expense.

The cost approach suggests an investor should not pay more for a property than the cost of purchasing vacant land and developing a comparable property. That said, given the time lag and economic risk associated with construction, significant divergence between the replacement cost of a property and its current market price may reflect supply and demand imbalances. For example, one would expect replacement costs to exceed market prices during the oversupply phase of the real estate cycle. The cost includes the developer's expected profit as compensation for development risk, including time, complexity, and the cost of financing, as shown in the following example.

EXAMPLE 10

Wallonia—Cost Approach

An investor considering the purchase of Wallonia obtains the following estimate for constructing an identical facility near the subject property:

Estimate Components	Estimate (EUR)
Excavation and steel framing	150,000
Foundation	225,000
Corrugated steel walls	500,000
Building façade (glass, brick, mortar)	150,000
Floor finishing	150,000
Roofing/ceiling/insulation	175,000
Interior walls and finishing	150,000
Electrical and lighting	150,000
Plumbing	175,000
HVAC (heating, ventilation, and A/C)	200,000
Interior structures and lifts, scales	225,000
Loading stations and transport link	225,000
Parking and paving	200,000
SUBTOTAL	2,675,000
Architect/legal/tax/permits/accounting	300,000
Development period interest	200,000
Contractor profit	425,000
SUBTOTAL	925,000
Comparable land cost	750,000
Cost estimate	4,350,000

As in the earlier Wallonia example, we assume the warehouse has a 30-year useful life and straight-line depreciation is used.

1. If the Wallonia facility is four years old and its value is adjusted to solely reflect depreciation expense, calculate the estimated property value.

   Solution:

   We must first calculate the depreciable base of the newly constructed warehouse under the estimate, which is the capitalized cost less the value of the land, which has an infinite life:

   Depreciable base = EUR3,600,000 = 4,350,000 – 750,000.

   Annual depreciation expense is EUR120,000 (= EUR3,600,000/30), and therefore, the cost estimate should be reduced by EUR480,000 (= 120,000 × 4) to arrive at a comparable property value estimate of EUR3,870,000:

   EUR3,870,000 = 4,350,000 – 480,000.

Sales Comparison Approach

The **sales comparison approach**, sometimes referred to as the market approach, considers what similar or comparable properties (comparables) transacted for in the current market. As in the case of the method of comparables for equity valuation, the validity of this approach hinges on finding sufficient rental or sales prices for properties with similar features. While relative value comparison of public equities is made easier by the availability of market prices and financial statements on similar dates, the illiquidity of both real estate and private companies limits comparability to the use of actual transactions at different times in the past.

Recent property sales serve as the basis for establishing market comparables or **units of comparison**. Price per square meter or square foot of leasable area or total area is the most common measure, while others include price per gross or net rent per square meter or price to revenue. Adjustments are made to reflect comparables' differences from the subject property, such as size, age, location, and condition of the property, and to adjust for differences in market conditions at the times of sale. Recent transactions often carry more weight than prior-period sales. This method is based on the premise that an investor should not pay more than others have for similar properties when these adjustments are considered and transaction costs, such as the expected bid–offer spread, are factored into the price. The following example illustrates this approach for Pinebranch Estates.

EXAMPLE 11

Pinebranch Estates—Sales Comparison Approach

Recall from an earlier example that Pinebranch is a multi-family property near a major Australian city. A potential investor conducts a sales comparison of three comparable properties of a similar design and quality and the same amenities as Pinebranch in the vicinity of the subject property in the past two years:

Measure/Property	Subject Property (Pinebranch)	Comparable Property 1	Comparable Property 2	Comparable Property 3
Sale Date		6 months	1 year	2 years
Sales Price		32,500,000	25,800,000	21,300,000
Gross Annual Rent		9,000,000	6,500,000	6,000,000
Gross Square Feet	288,000	375,000	250,000	220,000
Price/ft^2		86.67	103.20	96.82
Rent/ft^2		24.00	26.00	27.27

Measure/Property	Subject Property (Pinebranch)	Comparable Property 1	Comparable Property 2	Comparable Property 3
Additional distance from city center		5 miles	2 miles	3 miles
Age	5y	3y	2y	3y
Price/ft^2		86.67	103.20	96.82
Adjustments:				
Sale date		0%	3%	5%
Square footage		–4%	1%	2%
Location		10%	5%	8%
Age		–3%	–5%	–3%
Net difference		3%	1%	7%
Adjusted price		33,475,000	26,058,000	22,791,000
Adjusted price/ft^2		89.27	104.23	103.60
Estimated price/ft^2 for subject property		99.03		
Estimated value		28,520,640		

The investor adjusts for factors including sale timing, square footage, location, and property age. For example, sales in past periods when real estate prices were lower should be adjusted upward for comparison to today, while a greater distance from the city center reduces a property's relative value. Newer and/or larger properties trade at a premium. In this case, the sum of these adjustments for Comparable Property 1 is 3% (= 0% – 4% + 10% – 3%), resulting in an upward adjustment in the price per square foot from AUD86.67 to AUD89.27 (= AUD86.67 × 1.03). These adjusted prices are averaged for the three properties to arrive at an estimated AUD99.03 per square foot, or AUD28,521,036, for Pinebranch.

1. Interpret the effect of the adjustments of the comparable properties and their effect on Pinebranch's estimated value for each factor.

Solution:

A negative adjustment reduces the estimated price/ft^2 for the subject property and the estimated value, while a positive adjustment increases the price/ft^2.

Sale date: A greater positive adjustment for sales that occurred further in the past reflects an adjustment for rising real estate prices over time.

Square footage: A negative adjustment for Property 1 and a positive adjustment for Properties 2 and 3 imply a discount for larger multi-family properties.

Location: The greater the distance from the city center, the larger the positive adjustment to the subject property's value versus the comparable property.

Age: Because all the recent transactions involved properties that were newer than Pinebranch, the negative adjustment reflects a discount in Pinebranch's value.

While best practice typically dictates the consideration of more than one valuation method, the income approach tends to be more common among properties for which fewer similar properties are bought and sold and where periodic income carries more weight for the investment decision, such as large office, retail, or other facilities used by businesses. The sales comparison approach tends to be more reliable in real estate markets with a larger number of similar properties changing hands, such as single-family residential units. Independent appraisers often place significant weight on sales comparisons.

QUESTION SET

1. In Example 9, Eastmain Plaza's value is estimated to be MYR107,503,600. Based on this value and Eastmain's first-year NOI of MYR8,259,417, the property's going-in cap rate is equal to 7.68%. How does this going-in cap rate compare to Eastmain's terminal cap rate, and what is the rationale? Select the best response below.

   A. The going-in cap rate is lower than the terminal cap rate of 14% because of lower risk assumed for the first-year NOI.

   B. The going-in cap rate is lower than the terminal cap rate of 11% because of lower risk assumed for the first-year NOI.

   C. The going-in cap rate is lower than the terminal cap rate of 11% because the first two years of the forecast assume low NOI associated with a downside scenario of losing retail tenants before recovering lost revenue in later years.

   Solution:

   C is correct. The going-in cap rate is computed by simply dividing first-year NOI by the property value. When NOI in the first year reflects worse economic conditions (and so NOI is lower than it would be under normal economic conditions), the going-in cap rate is lower to reflect the short-term negative NOI dynamics assumed. The terminal cap rate is the difference between the required rate of return of 14% and the 3% growth rate, so Response B is incorrect. Responses A and B are incorrect because the valuation assumes the same level of risk in all years by using the same required return of 14% across all years.

2. During which phase of the real estate cycle would an analyst expect the replacement cost valuation of a property to exceed its market price?

   A. Oversupply phase

   B. Recovery phase

   C. Expansion phase

   Solution:

   A is correct. During the oversupply phase, NOI peaks and begins to decline, and the oversupply causes market prices of properties to weaken. As construction continues until completion, costs of materials and labor remain high. Response B is incorrect because the recovery phase is characterized by little new construction. As a result, costs are likely to be low. Response C is incorrect because during the expansion phase, property prices are likely to rise faster than costs because a new supply of properties has not come onto the market.

3. Which statement most correctly describes valuation approaches to single-family residential housing properties and large commercial properties?

   A. Single-family residential properties are likely to be valued using the income approach because there are fewer comparable transactions from which to use sales comparisons.

   B. Large commercial properties are likely to be valued using the income approach because there are fewer comparable transactions from which to use sales comparisons.

   C. Both single-family and large commercial properties are likely to be valued using the income approach because there are fewer comparable transactions from which to use sales comparisons.

   Solution:

   B is correct. Because large commercial properties are transacted less frequently, it is more difficult to find sales comparisons. These commercial properties are more likely to be used for investment purposes, so the income generation potential is the driving factor in valuing these properties. Response A is incorrect because the sales comparison approach tends to be more reliable in real estate markets where many similar properties change hands, such as single-family residential units. Response C is incorrect because it implies that the income approach is common for single family residential properties and commercial properties.

4. Which portion of the real estate due diligence process is least likely to provide information used in developing a forecast of NOI for a property?

   A. Market review and outlook

   B. Future lease outlook

   C. Documentation review

   Solution:

   C is correct. Documentation review is focused on ensuring that the property may be acquired free of any outstanding liens or tax obligations. Thus, this portion of the due diligence process is vital; the information from it will not be featured in the NOI forecast. Response A is incorrect because the market outlook will include information on property prices that will be incorporated into the NOI forecast. Response B is incorrect because the information from this portion of the process will include such information as downtime between the end of one lease and the beginning of another.

REAL ESTATE INDEXES 6

☐ discuss real estate investment indexes, including their construction and potential biases

As is true for other asset classes, real estate investment indexes aim to track the broad risk and return of real estate markets, allowing market performance evaluation, benchmarking of individual investments and investment managers, and the creation of index-based investments. Real estate indexes measure such factors as property income performance and total return, investment fund performance, and listed security returns.

Private real estate market indexes generally involve property-based metrics that use either recent appraisals or actual real estate transactions in order to gauge price and market changes over time. Private market indexes are generally not directly investable. Public real estate market indexes, in contrast, are often directly investable and are made up of listed equity or debt securities. Investors typically gain such exposure using mutual funds, exchange traded funds (ETFs), or, for European investors, UCITS (Undertakings for the Collective Investment in Transferable Securities) investments.

Investors should be awareg of how real estate indexes are constructed and the inherent limitations that may result. In some cases, the apparent low correlation of real estate with other asset classes may be due to limitations in real estate index construction, the periodicity of updates to the index, and biases rather than true market differences.

Appraisal- vs. Transaction-Based Indexes

In this section, we examine two main types of real estate indexes: those based on appraisals and those based on transactions.

Appraisal-Based Indexes

Many indexes rely on **appraisals**, or professional estimates of value, to determine changes in the market price of a portfolio of properties or the real estate market in general. Property and private real estate investment indexes often rely on appraisals to estimate values due to a lack of sufficient transactions of the same property to indicate value. Although many real estate transactions may occur in a period, they are not for the same property; differences in the prices at which properties trade can be due to changes in the market or differences in the characteristics of the property, such as size, age, or location. Appraisal-based indexes combine valuation information from individual properties and provide a measure of market movements.

For example, the Global Real Estate Fund Index (GREFI), launched in 2014, is a capitalization-weighted index published quarterly that incorporates local-currency returns. The GREFI combines data from the United States, Europe, and Asia from NCREIF (National Council of Real Estate Investment Fiduciaries), the European Association for Investors in Non-Listed Real Estate Vehicles (INREV), and the Asian Association for Investors in Non-Listed Real Estate Vehicles (ANREV), respectively. Investment managers contribute information on appraised values, along with NOI, capital expenditures, and other data used to create the index, such as occupancy. It provides quarterly and annual returns and may be used on an aggregated or disaggregated basis by property type and region. The **holding period return** for properties is calculated as follows:

$$\text{Holding period return} = \frac{\begin{array}{c}\text{NOI} - \text{Capital expenditures}\\ +(\text{Ending market value} - \text{Beginning market value})\end{array}}{\text{Beginning market value}}. \tag{15}$$

In this calculation, the beginning and ending market values are based on appraisals of similar properties over a period. The holding period return is equivalent to a single-period internal rate of return, or the IRR if the property were purchased at the beginning of the period and sold at the end of the period at its ending market value. Although it is similar to holding period return calculations for stocks and bonds, in those cases, an actual transaction price is typically used. Because this is not possible for real estate, the appraised value is used, as illustrated in the following example.

EXAMPLE 12

Wallonia Holding Period Return

Recall that Wallonia Transit is a warehouse with NOI of EUR406,750 in the most recent year and with EUR100,000 in capital expenditures. Wallonia's owner purchased the facility for EUR3,750,000 two years ago.

1. Estimate the beginning and ending market values for the Wallonia facility for the most recent year if the INREV asset level return for Belgian warehouses was +5.6% in the first year of ownership and +3.2% in the second year.

   Solution:

   Beginning market value = Original purchase price × (1 + First-year return).

   Ending market value = Beginning market value × (1 + Second-year return).

   Beginning market value = EUR3,960,000 = EUR3,750,000 × (1.056).

   Ending market value = EUR4,086,720 = EUR3,960,000 × (1.032).

2. Calculate the estimated holding period return for the most recent year.

   Solution:

   Use Equation 15 to solve for Wallonia's holding period return of 10.95%:

$$\text{Holding period return} = \frac{\begin{array}{c}\text{NOI} - \text{Capital expenditures} \\ +(\text{Ending market value} - \text{Beginning market value})\end{array}}{\text{Beginning market value}}.$$

$$10.95\% = \frac{\begin{array}{c}\text{EUR}406,750 - \text{EUR}100,000 \\ +(\text{EUR}4,086,720 - \text{EUR}3,960,000)\end{array}}{\text{EUR}3,960,000}.$$

An index such as the one described allows us to compare the performance of real estate with other asset classes, such as stocks and bonds. The quarterly returns are also important for measuring risk, which is often measured as the volatility or standard deviation of the quarterly returns. A major drawback, however, is that the income component of real estate returns does not represent distributions to investors in real estate funds or REITs. The total return for equities is based on capital appreciation plus dividends, not on the underlying company's operating income. The index does succeed, however, as a benchmark to compare returns among individual real estate funds.

Transaction-Based Indexes

Some indexes are based on actual transactions rather than appraised values. These indexes have been made possible by companies that collect information on enough transactions to create an index based only on transactions. In fact, both NCREIF and MSCI have transaction information that can be used for this purpose. When creating a transaction-based index, the fact that the same property does not sell very frequently is still an issue. So, to develop an index that measures changes in value on a quarterly basis as discussed for appraisal indexes, data providers must control for the fact that different properties sell every quarter. Econometric techniques, such as regression analysis, are used to address the issue and to create the index in two main ways. One is referred to as a **repeat sales index**, and the other is a so-called **hedonic index**.

A repeat sales index relies on multiple sales of the same property. A particular property may sell only twice during the entire period of the index. That said, if at least some properties have sold each quarter, the repeat sales regression methodology can use this information to create an index. A repeat sales index is more reliable if more transactions occur. When the same property has sold twice, the change in value between the two sale dates indicates how market conditions have changed over time. Property and tenant credit quality, the lease maturity schedule, and market conditions may have changed, depending on the amount of time between sales. The regression methodology allocates this change in value to each period—that is, each quarter based on the information from sales that occurred that quarter. An example of a repeat sales index for commercial real estate in the United States is the suite of RCA Commercial Property Price Indexes.

Hedonic indexes do not require repeat sales. This approach addresses the fact that different properties sell each quarter by including regression variables controlled for differences in property characteristics, such as size, age, quality of construction, and location. These independent variables in the regression reflect how differences in characteristics cause values to differ so that they can be separated from the differences in value due to changes in market conditions from quarter to quarter. The details of these regressions are beyond the scope of this learning module. They require a lot of data and are usually most reliable at the national level for the major property types, but sometimes they are reliable at the regional level within a country if sufficient transactions are available.

Advantages and Disadvantages of Appraisal- and Transaction-Based Indexes

Appraisal-based indexes are often criticized for having appraisal lags, which result from appraised values tending to lag when there are sudden shifts in the market.

Appraisal Lags in Rising and Falling Markets

In a rising market, transaction prices usually start to rise first. As these higher prices are reflected in comparable sales and investor surveys, they are captured in appraised values. Thus, appraisal-based indexes will tend to lag a rising market and may not capture the price increase until a quarter or more after it is reflected in transactions. In a falling market, transaction prices would fall first. Later, these lower prices would be reflected in appraised values. Thus, appraisal-based indexes will tend to lag a falling market.

Infrequent Appraisals

Another cause of appraisal lags is that all properties in an appraisal-based index may not be appraised every quarter. A manager may assume the value has remained constant for several quarters until he or she goes through the appraisal process to estimate a new value. In a pooled fund, a manager may have a subset of properties appraised each quarter with the aim that each will be appraised at least annually, causing a lag in the index.

Impact on Performance Measurement and Asset Allocation

If the investment managers are all using appraised values to measure returns and if the index is based on appraised values, then the comparison is consistent and is less of a concern from a performance measurement perspective. If the index is used for comparison with other asset classes that are publicly traded, however, appraisal lag is more of an issue. Appraisal lag tends to smooth an index and reduce volatility. Thus, appraisal-based indexes may underestimate the volatility of real estate returns.

Because of the lag in appraisal-based real estate indexes, they also tend to have a lower correlation with other asset classes. The smoothing effect will also overstate Sharpe ratios, which is a problem if the index is used in asset allocation models to determine how much of a portfolio should be allocated to real estate versus other asset classes. The appropriate allocation to and benefits from private real estate would likely be overestimated.

Adjustment for Appraisal Lag

Appraisal lag can be adjusted for in two ways. The first is to "unsmooth" the appraisal-based index. The resulting unsmoothed index is seen as a more accurate representation of true market returns., with greater volatility and higher correlation with other asset classes. The second way of adjusting for appraisal lag is to use a transaction-based index when comparing real estate with other asset classes.

Unsmoothing an appraisal-based index requires an assumption regarding how smoothing occurs and may be modeled and then reversing the process. For example, if we assume appraisals take place based on previous transactions or lagged prices, then we can model the current observed price based on a modified autoregressive model approach, or time series regressed on past values, as introduced in earlier learning modules:

$$R_t^* = aR_t + (1 - a)R_{t-1}^*. \quad (16)$$

Equation 16 shows that the appraised index return during period t (R_t^*) is a function of the actual return (R_t) and the prior period's appraisal index return (R_{t-1}^*). The coefficient a (where $0 \leq a \leq 1$) reflects the speed at which actual returns are reflected in appraisal-based returns, with a higher a representing more rapid adjustment. We reverse the smoothing process by solving for R_t in Equation 16:

$$R_t = \frac{R_t^*}{a} + \left(\frac{1-a}{a}\right) R_{t-1}^*. \quad (17)$$

If, for example, $a = 0.5$, then true returns are estimated based on a price change that is double that of the most recently reported returns. The following example illustrates the unsmoothing process.

EXAMPLE 13

Unsmoothing Appraisal Index Returns

An analyst is presented with the following appraisal-based index returns:

Period	Appraisal-Based Index Return
0	2.70%
1	0.50%
2	2.20%
3	7.30%
4	3.20%
5	1.00%
6	−8.70%
7	−1.10%
8	2.40%
9	3.10%
10	4.20%

1. Calculate expected unsmoothed actual returns for Periods 1 through 10 under the assumption that appraisal-based index returns depend on actual returns and one-period lagged returns, with a = 0.6.

Solution:

Using Equation 17, solve for R_t:

$$R_t = \frac{R_t^*}{0.6} + \left(\frac{1-0.6}{0.6}\right)R_{t-1}^*.$$

For Period 1, where $R_t^* = 0.50$ and $R_{t-1}^* = 2.70\%$,

$$R_t = 2.63\% = \frac{0.50\%}{0.6} + \left(\frac{1-0.6}{0.6}\right)2.70\%.$$

Solve for each period's expected unsmoothed actual returns:

Period	Appraisal-Based Index Return	Lagged Appraisal-Based Index Return	Unsmoothed Actual Return
0	2.70%		
1	0.50%	2.70%	2.63%
2	2.20%	0.50%	4.00%
3	7.30%	2.20%	13.97%
4	3.20%	7.30%	8.87%
5	1.00%	3.20%	3.80%
6	−8.70%	1.00%	−13.83%
7	−1.10%	−8.70%	−5.63%
8	2.40%	−1.10%	3.27%
9	3.10%	2.40%	6.77%
10	4.20%	3.10%	9.07%

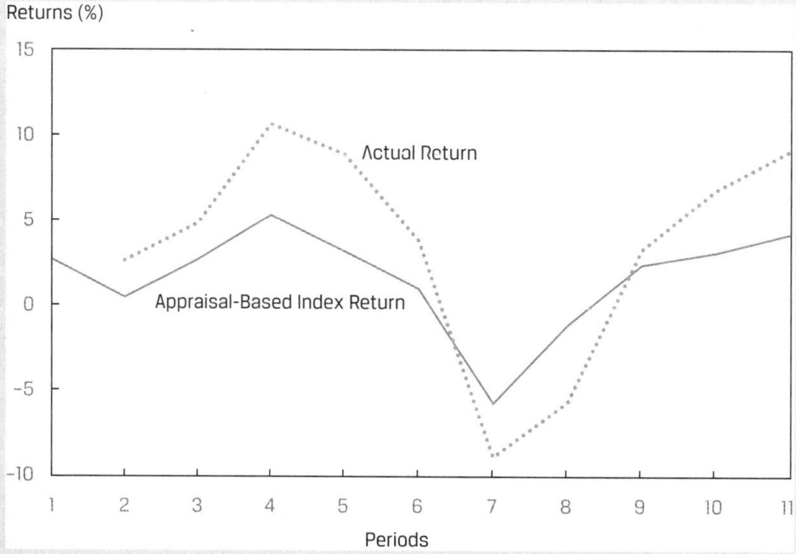

Transaction-based indexes tend to lead appraisal-based indexes for the reasons discussed, but they can include random elements in the observations due to the use of statistical techniques to estimate the index. This may introduce noise in quarter-to-quarter changes, although the index correctly captures market movements over the long term. The challenge for data providers is to minimize such noise using appropriate statistical techniques and collecting as much data as possible.

Public Real Estate Equity Indexes

The most common public equity indexes available to investors are REIT indexes. Recall that REITs are publicly traded entities and are required to distribute nearly all of their earnings to investors, who are taxed based on their respective individual rate. **Equity REITs** are those that primarily own and operate properties, with indexes typically based on industry classification or region, as in Exhibit 9.

Exhibit 9: Asia-Pacific REIT Index

	S&P Asia-Pacific REIT Index (USD) Brief Summary of Inclusion Criteria
Issuers:	Includes eligible publicly traded REITs from developed Asia-Pacific markets, including Australia, Hong Kong SAR, Japan, New Zealand, Singapore, and South Korea.
Eligibility:	Companies must be engaged in real estate ownership, development, and/or management and conform to legal structures that define a REIT in the US or guidelines similar to those that define a REIT in the US within the country or region of their domicile. The index specifically excludes timber REITs, mortgage REITs, tower REITs, and mortgage-backed REITs.
Weighting Method:	Float-adjusted, market-cap weighted
Currencies:	USD, with calculation currencies USD, AUD, CAD, EUR, GBP, JPY, LCL, NZD, and SGD
Rebalancing:	Annually in September with share changes and IPO updates in March, June, and December
Calculation Frequency:	End of day

Note that the float-adjusted market value weighting methodology causes this index to be skewed toward the largest-value markets, such as Singapore, rather than a weighting based on the volume of transactions.

Real Estate Fixed-Income Indexes

Recall from earlier in the curriculum that fixed-income indexes play a role in bond markets similar to the role equity indexes play for stocks, with a number of differences. For example, finite bond maturities and the frequency of new issuance lead to greater turnover and more frequent rebalancing in fixed-income indexes versus equity indexes. In real estate markets, fixed-income indexes include additional features unique to property debt, such as mortgage-backed securities and covered bonds.

Previous fixed-income lessons described how MBS are created based on either residential or commercial mortgages. In contrast to non-callable, non-amortizing bonds, MBS involve **prepayment risk**, or the risk that some or all of the MBS principal is repaid at a different speed than expected, either in the form of **contraction risk** (or earlier repayment than expected) or **extension risk** (later repayment). MBS indexes face prepayment risk similar to that for individual mortgage-backed securities, which is most prevalent in the United States given the lack of prepayment penalties that are common in other countries.

Changes to interest rates and the underlying property values over time are among the key drivers of prepayment risk commonly observed among residential mortgages. For example, when interest rates are relatively low and property values are stable or higher, an increase in borrower prepayments and refinancing activity tends to shorten the effective duration of MBS bonds and indexes. When interest rates increase, actual prepayments are often lower than forecasted because homeowners are less likely to refinance mortgages and may also delay new home purchases. Thus, the maturity of MBS will be longer than anticipated at the time of purchase, which will have the effect of increasing the effective duration of an MBS index.

Covered bonds, introduced earlier in the curriculum, are the simplest securitization structure of mortgage loans. Issuers are primarily European banks, which create a pool of mortgage loans on their balance sheet segregated from other assets. This pool then serves as collateral ("cover") for non-amortizing bonds issued by the bank with a fixed maturity. Given borrower prepayment penalties for such mortgages and the dual recourse of investors to both the issuing bank and the collateral under a default scenario, covered bonds and covered bond indexes offer investors a relatively stable return with low risk compared to other fixed-income investments. The following example illustrates the case of Denmark, home to the largest covered bond market, and its attraction for investors.

DENMARK'S COVERED BOND MARKET

Denmark's covered bond market consists primarily of residential home loans. While the securities are created by mortgage lenders, the homeowner is effectively the bond issuer. In the case of homeowner default, the mortgage lender is able to take over the property quickly. The lender serves as an intermediary between the bond issuer (a homeowner) and the bond investor. Denmark's covered bonds have generated significant market interest among international bond investors because of Denmark's solid economic condition, including its AAA credit rating. By early 2021, approximately 25% of the issued bonds were owned by foreign investors. Furthermore, the mortgages are not limited to long-term fixed-rate securities, because borrowers also issue shorter-term and adjustable-rate bonds as well. As a result, the market for Denmark's covered bonds exhibits considerable liquidity. Thus, borrowers and investors can access the market as credit and interest rate conditions evolve. As interest rates fell during 2019–2021, borrowers were able to easily shift into longer-term fixed-rate loans and then pivot into shorter-term adjustable-rate loans in 2022 as interest rates sharply rose. The liquidity of the market allows for ease of tracking by homeowners and investors, as evidenced by the existence of an S&P Denmark Collateralized Bond Index since February 2017.

QUESTION SET

1. Which of the following statements most accurately describes volatility estimation in real estate indexes?

   A. Volatility of real estate is typically underestimated when using appraisal-based indexes.

   B. Volatility of real estate is typically overestimated in appraisal-based indexes because of the infrequent transactions in real estate markets.

   C. Volatility of appraisal-based indexes creates difficulty in comparing real estate investment performance across different international markets.

   Solution:

   A is correct. The lag and infrequency of real estate appraisals creates a smoothed pattern of real estate returns, thus causing lower estimated volatility than if returns were measured more frequently and with no lag. Response B is an incorrect statement because appraisal-based indexes underestimate volatility and because they do not use transactions. Response C is incorrect because the appraisal lag is less likely to cause problems with comparing real estate investment performance if all indexes are using appraisal data.

2. While real estate indexes allow for comparisons with returns on other asset categories, such as stocks and bonds, which of the following statements best reflects a potential problem in such comparisons?

   A. Real estate indexes based on appraised values likely overstate returns in rising markets and understate returns in falling markets.

   B. Appraisal-based real estate indexes that have been smoothed provide less comparability to stock and bond indexes over longer time frames.

   C. The income component of real estate returns does not necessarily represent cash flow distributions to investors in real estate funds or REITs.

   Solution:

   C is correct. Equation 15 (shown below) illustrates the standard approach to calculating real estate returns:

$$\text{Holding period return} = \frac{\begin{array}{c}\text{NOI} - \text{Capital expenditures}\\ +(\text{Ending market value} - \text{Beginning market value})\end{array}}{\text{Beginning market value}}.$$

   The portion of the holding period return equation that estimates the income portion of returns (NOI – Capital expenditures) does not reflect cash flow distributions to investors, as is the case for stocks and bonds. Response A is an incorrect statement: Appraisal-based indexes understate returns in rising markets and overstate returns in falling markets. Response B is an incorrect statement because appraisal-based real estate indexes that have been smoothed become more comparable with more data observations.

3. Hedonic and repeat sales indexes are based on actual real estate transactions. Which of the following statements is most correct about the construction of hedonic and repeat sales indexes?

   A. Both hedonic and repeat sales indexes require information on sales of the same properties over the time frame of measurement.

   B. Hedonic indexes use sales in each time period and account for differences in properties based on property characteristics.

   C. Repeat sales indexes use all transactions that have occurred over the time frame of measurement.

   Solution:

   B is correct. The hedonic approach controls for the fact that different properties sell each quarter by including regression variables controlled for differences in property characteristics, such as size, age, quality of construction, and location. Response A is incorrect because only the repeat sales index requires information on sales of the same properties. The hedonic approach will use all transactions, but the approach does not require repeat sales of the same property. Response C is incorrect because a repeat sales index uses data only from sales of properties that have sold more than once. One-time transactions are not used in a repeat sales index.

PRACTICE PROBLEMS

The following information relates to questions 1-5

Jane Lee is the new chief investment officer of the Eastland University Endowment Fund (the Fund). Historically, the Fund has invested based on a 60% equity/40% fixed-income allocation. However, Lee is looking to change the fund's allocation to include real estate assets after incorporating data from the appraisal-based Global Real Estate Fund Index. GREFI returns and volatilities imply strong risk-adjusted performance from real estate assets with low correlation with stocks and bonds. Lee is considering the following two asset allocations:

Allocation 1	50% equity/35% fixed income/15% real estate
Allocation 2	55% equity/35% fixed income/10% real estate

Allocation 1 is based on an allocation model incorporating the GREFI data, while Allocation 2 assumes a higher correlation between real estate and other asset classes in an attempt to adjust for smoothing and therefore has a lower real estate market allocation.

Lee recently hired Jon Tarrow as the Fund's new head of real estate. During a recent meeting, Tarrow and Lee concluded that the initial real estate investment strategy would be to acquire stabilized office buildings located in primary markets. Tarrow has been working on the potential acquisition of a 100% occupied Class A office building located in New York City. Tarrow and his junior analyst will conduct a thorough due diligence process for the property. Tarrow has also hired an appraiser to value the building and provide valuation support. The appraiser will use three different approaches to estimate the building's value but will place emphasis on both the direct capitalization and the discounted cash flow methods.

During an internal meeting, the junior analyst makes the following three statements about the appraiser's two primary valuation methods:

Statement 1	The direct capitalization method requires an estimation of a terminal value.
Statement 2	Properties expected to generate faster growth will require a capitalization rate that results in a higher value.
Statement 3	The direct capitalization and discounted cash flow methods both consider growth and property quality.

The appraiser has concluded that net operating income for the New York City office building is expected to be USD15.6 million for the first year, and after that, NOI is expected to increase at 0.50% annually for the foreseeable future. The building's value is also expected to increase by 0.50% annually, and investors expect to achieve a 5.75% required rate of return given the level of risk.

After considering the appraiser's valuation, Lee then tells Tarrow that she can negotiate a purchase price of USD283 million for the building. Furthermore, she can procure a loan with an interest-only 5.25% coupon provided that the loan-to-value ratio does not exceed 65% and the debt service coverage ratio is at least 1.65×, with the loan balance due after 10 years.

1. Which of the following statements is most accurate as to how Lee should decide on Allocation 1 versus Allocation 2?

   A. Lee should prefer Allocation 2 to Allocation 1 because real estate is closely correlated with other asset classes.

   B. Lee should prefer Allocation 1 to Allocation 2 to ensure an optimal Sharpe ratio.

   C. Lee should prefer Allocation 2 to Allocation 1 because the GREFI likely understates the volatility of real estate and its correlation with stocks and bonds.

2. Which of the junior analyst's three statements regarding the appraiser's two primary valuation methods is incorrect?

   A. Statement 1

   B. Statement 2

   C. Statement 3

3. Which of the following phases of the due diligence process is most likely to ensure that the building's NOI projection for the next year is correct?

   A. Documentation review

   B. Current lease review

   C. Future lease outlook

4. Based on the direct capitalization method, the appraiser's current value of the New York City office building is closest to:

   A. USD249,600,000.

   B. USD271,300,000.

   C. USD297,100,000.

5. The maximum loan amount that the Fund can obtain on the New York City office building is closest to:

   A. USD111.5 million.

   B. USD180.1 million.

   C. USD184 million.

The following information relates to questions 6-10

Amanda Rodriguez is an alternative investment analyst for a US investment management firm, Delphinus Brothers. Delphinus's chief investment officer, Michael Tang, has informed Rodriguez that he wants to reduce the amount invested in traditional asset classes and gain exposure to the real estate sector by acquiring commercial property in the United States. Rodriguez is asked to analyze potential commercial real estate investments for Delphinus Brothers. Selected data on three commercial real estate properties are shown in Exhibit 1.

Exhibit 1: Selected Property Data

	Property 1	Property 2	Property 3
Property Type	**Downtown Office Building**	**Grocery-Anchored Retail Center**	**Multi-Family Building**
Location	New York City	Miami	Boston
Age	10 years	7 years	5 years
Occupancy	90.00%	93.00%	95.00%
Square feet or number of units	100,000 sf	205,000 sf	360,000 sf
Gross potential rental income	$4,750,000	$1,800,000	$3,100,000
Loss to lease	($475,000)	($90,000)	$155,000
Gross rental income	$5,225,000	$1,890,000	$2,945,000
Vacancy loss	($564,333)	($156,887)	($157,250)
Net rental income	$4,660,667	$1,733,113	$2,787,750
Expense reimbursement revenue	$333,333	$426,248	$0
Other income (includes % rent)	$560,000	$15,000	$45,000
Effective gross income	$5,554,000	$2,174,361	$2,832,750
Property management fees	($203,160)	($83,374)	($119,510)
Other operating expenses	($2,100,000)	($342,874)	($1,175,000)
Net operating income	$3,250,840	$1,748,113	$1,538,240

Rodriguez asks Tang about the relative magnitudes of operating expenses in determining property NOI. Tang explains that the retail center in Miami is able to be fully reimbursed for its operating expenses but that the office property in New York City and the multi-family property in Boston must absorb considerable unreimbursed operating expenses.

Tang comments to Rodriguez that these three properties may be in different phases of the real estate cycle. He specifically cites the differences between gross potential rental income and gross rental income in making his argument. In response to Tang's comments, Rodriguez makes the two following statements about the office building in New York City:

Statement 1 I believe that the office market in New York City is likely to enter the recovery stage of the real estate cycle within two years.

Statement 2 I believe that the high vacancy rates indicate that the net operating income of the office building has the potential to improve within two years.

Tang continues the conversation by commenting about the relative riskiness of various types of real estate given such developments as the COVID-19 pandemic, the movement toward remote working, and the evolution of internet-based retail.

Rodriguez asks Tang about the appropriateness of various valuation methods on these three properties. Tang suggests that the sales comparison approach is likely to be useful, but he is particularly interested in seeing the valuation results from an income approach for each of the three properties.

6. Which of the following statements is most accurate regarding the effect of unreimbursed operating expenses on the NOI of the New York City and Boston properties?

   A. The NOI of the office property in New York City is more negatively affected by unreimbursed operating expenses than is the NOI of the multi-family property in Boston.

   B. The NOI of the multi-family property in Boston is more negatively affected by unreimbursed operating expenses than is the NOI of the office property in New York City.

   C. The NOIs of both properties are affected similarly by unreimbursed operating expenses.

7. Which of the following properties is least likely to be in the oversupply phase of its real estate cycle, based on Tang's argument?

   A. The office building in New York City

   B. The retail center in Miami

   C. The multi-family complex in Boston

8. Which of the following responses is most accurate regarding Rodriguez's Statement 1 and Statement 2?

   A. Statements 1 and 2 are both accurate statements.

   B. Statement 1 is more accurate than Statement 2.

   C. Statement 2 is more accurate than Statement 1.

9. Which of the three property types faces the lowest level of relative risk factors associated with structural and technological changes in the real estate market?

   A. Office property in New York City

   B. Retail center in Miami

   C. Multi-family property in Boston

10. Given Rodriguez's comment in Statement 1 about office property in New York City, which of the following approaches to estimating property value is most appropriate?

    A. Direct capitalization method using last year's NOI

    B. Sales comparison approach

    C. Direct capitalization method using a normalized NOI forecast.

The following information relates to questions 11-15

Michael Tang, the chief investment officer of Delphinus Brothers, asks an analyst at the firm, Amanda Rodriguez, to focus her analysis on the 100,000 square foot office property in New York City (introduced in the previous question set). Tang believes that Delphinus can purchase the property for USD50 million.

Rodriguez begins her analysis by assembling the data shown in Exhibit 1.

Exhibit 1: Six-Year NOI and DCF Assumptions for New York City Office Property

	Year 1	Year 2	Year 3	Year 4	Year 5	Year 6
NOI	\$3,250,840	\$3,185,823	\$3,217,681	\$3,265,947	\$3,339,430	\$3,439,613
DCF Assumptions						
Investment holding period	5 years					
Going-in cap rate	6.50%					
Terminal cap rate	6.00%					
Discount rate	9.00%					

Using the data from Exhibit 1, Rodriguez is able to compute a value of USD49.9 million for this property using the DCF method. After Rodriguez presents this valuation to Tang, Tang is surprised that the analysis does not demonstrate that the property is underpriced. Tang asks Rodriguez to value the property using the sales comparison method, and she compiles the data shown in Exhibit 2.

Exhibit 2: Sales Comparison Data for Comparable Office Properties

Variable	NYC Office	Sales Comp A	Sales Comp B	Sales Comp C
Age (years)	10	5	12	25
Condition	Good	Excellent	Good	Average
Location	Prime	Secondary	Secondary	Prime
Sale price (per ft^2)		\$415/ft^2	\$395/ft^2	\$400/ft^2
Adjustments:				
Age (years)		–10%	2%	10%
Condition		–10%	0%	10%
Location		15%	15%	0%
Total adjustments		–5%	17%	20%

To conclude her valuation work on the office property, Rodriguez compiles detailed data on the replacement costs of the office building, its land value, and the total depreciation. She finds that the cost of constructing a building identical to the subject property is USD57 million. The land value is USD7 million, and the total depreciation is USD5 million. From these data, she calculates a value of the property using the cost approach.

Rodriguez presents her valuation findings to Tang. After a thorough review of the valuation including consideration of a variety of scenarios, Tang decides to proceed with plans to purchase the office property in New York City. He contacts several potential lenders, ultimately deciding to contract with Rich Life Insurance, a publicly traded company with extensive investments in commercial real estate, to discuss terms on arranging a loan of USD35 million.

11. Which of the following amounts is closest to the undiscounted terminal value of the New York City office property at the end of the five-year investment holding period?

    A. USD57.3 million

    B. USD52.9 million

    C. USD55.7 million

12. Which of the following statements is most correct about cap rates and discount rates used in the discounted cash flow valuation of the New York City office property using the data in Exhibit 1?

    A. The going-in cap rate is used to discount the first-year NOI in the discounted cash flow valuation.

    B. The terminal cap rate equals the difference between the discount rate and the constant growth rate of NOI between Years 5 and 6.

    C. The growth rate of NOI in Years 1 through 5 equals the difference between the discount rate and the going-in cap rate.

13. Which of the following statements is consistent with the results of a sales comparison valuation using the information from Exhibit 2?

    A. The sales comparison approach to valuing the office property is consistent with Tang's belief that the property is underpriced.

    B. The sales comparison approach to valuing the office property suggests that the property is overpriced by approximately 11%.

    C. The sales comparison approach to valuing the office property suggests that the property is overpriced by approximately 19%.

14. Which of the following statements is most accurate regarding Rodriguez's valuation of the office property using the cost approach?

    A. The replacement cost may exceed the market price of the property's building if the real estate cycle for this property is in the oversupply phase.

    B. Rodriguez's valuation of the office property implies that it is overpriced.

    C. Replacement costs include the real estate developer's profits.

15. If Tang purchases the office property in New York City, what are the forms of real estate investment taken by Delphinus Brothers and Rich Life Insurance?

    A. Delphinus invests in public real estate equity and Rich invests in public real estate debt.

B. Delphinus invests in private real estate equity and Rich invests in private real estate debt.

C. Delphinus invests in private real estate equity and Rich invests in public real estate debt.

SOLUTIONS

1. C is correct. The appraisal-based GREFI likely overstates the Sharpe ratio of real estate and underestimates the correlation of real estate returns with those of stocks and bonds. As a result, Allocation 1 likely includes more real estate in the allocation than is optimal. Response A does not provide the correct reason for why a lower real estate allocation makes sense, and Response B ignores the problems associated with appraisal-based indexes.

2. A is the correct choice because Statement 1 is incorrect. The discounted cash flow method (not the direct capitalization method) requires a terminal value by capitalizing NOI at some future date. Responses B and C are not correct, because both Statements 2 and 3 are correct. Properties expected to generate faster growth will use a capitalization rate that results in a higher value, and properties with slower growth will use a capitalization rate that results in a lower value. Both income approaches consider growth and property quality.

3. B is the most likely portion of the due diligence process of the three choices to ensure that the NOI projections are correct. Currently, the building is 100% occupied, so the current lease review would provide information as to whether there will be any leases up for renewal during the next year. Response A is incorrect because documentation review ensures that there are no legal issues that may complicate the purchase of the building. Response C is likely incorrect given that the building is 100% occupied, so the outlook for re-leasing space is not likely to be included in NOI projections.

4. C is correct. The value of a property = NOI/(r – g), where r = the discount rate (required return) and g = the growth rate for income (given constant growth in income, value will grow at the same rate). Therefore, the building's value is calculated as follows:

   15,600,000/(5.75% – 0.50%) = 297,142,857 (= 297,100,000 after rounding).

   Response A is incorrect because a property value of 249,600,000 is incorrectly calculated as follows:

   15,600,000/(5.75% + 0.50%) = 249,600,000.

   Response B is incorrect because a property value of 271,300,000 is incorrectly calculated as follows:

   15,600,000/5.75% = 271,300,000.

5. B is correct. Based on the LTV, the maximum loan amount would be 65% of 283 million, or 183.95 million, with a DSC of 1.62×, which is below the 1.65 minimum. However, with a minimum DSC of 1.65×, the maximum debt service would be 15,600,000/1.65 = 9,454,545. This amount is the mortgage payment that would result in a 1.65× DSC for an interest-only loan. If the loan is interest only, then we can obtain the loan amount by simply dividing the mortgage payment by the interest rate. Therefore, the loan amount would be 9,454,545/0.0525 = 180,086,580 (= 180,100,000 after rounding). Because the loan amount based on the minimum DSC results in a lower loan amount, that would be the maximum amount that could be borrowed.

   Response A is incorrect because USD117,100,000 is incorrectly calculated as follows:

   283,000,000/1.65 = 180,086,580.

180,086,580 × 65% = 111,484,848 (= 111,500,000 after rounding).

C is incorrect because USD184 million is the rounded loan amount based on the maximum LTV of 65%. Because the loan amount based on the minimum DSC results in a lower loan amount, USD180,086,580 ($180,100,000 rounded) would be the maximum loan amount that could be borrowed.

6. B is correct. The multi-family property in Boston has total operating expenses of USD1,294,510 (the sum of its property management fees plus other operating expenses) and zero in expense reimbursement revenue. Dividing this amount by effective gross income creates a ratio of 45.7%. Doing the same for the office property in New York City creates a ratio of 35.5%. Response A is incorrect because although the New York City property has higher expenses, it also has higher income amounts as well. Response C is incorrect because the effect of unreimbursed expenses is clearly different for the two properties.

7. C is correct. The difference between gross potential rental income and gross rental income is represented by the loss to lease figure. A positive loss to lease reflects that current lease rates are lower than potential lease rates. The multi-family complex in Boston is the only property of the three for which gross rental income is lower than potential income. This is likely due to a lack of supply of rental housing. Responses A and B are both incorrect because the negative loss to lease may indicate excess supply and a likelihood that lease rates are decreasing.

8. B is correct. The vacancy rate likely indicates that the New York City office building market is currently in either an oversupply or a recession phase. Rodriguez's first statement implies that the recession phase will be short in duration, followed by recovery. Her Statement 2 implies a movement into the expansion phase of the real estate cycle given her comment about improving NOI. Response A is incorrect because her statements are inconsistent in terms of their implications about the real estate cycle.

9. C is correct, by the process of elimination. Office properties are negatively affected by the structural shift towards remote working, so Response A is incorrect. Retail centers face difficulties in the wake of technological change and the rise of internet-based retail, so Response B is incorrect. Residential housing is more of a necessity than the other two types of properties, so from a relative risk perspective, the multi-family property faces the lowest risk due to these changes.

10. C is correct. The direct capitalization method uses a single-period cash flow in the valuation, so properties subject to significant dynamics in their future NOI projections should use a normalized NOI or the discounted cash flow method. The office property in New York City appears to be subject to short-term NOI disruptions due to the real estate cycle. The sales comparison approach (Response B) is less appropriate in this case due to the continued expectation of a real estate market recovery, while the proposed use of last year's NOI (Response A) does not represent a normalized NOI.

11. A is correct. Terminal value is calculated by dividing the sixth-year NOI by the terminal cap rate of 6% (3,439,613/0.06). Response B is incorrect because this amount is obtained by dividing the sixth-year NOI by the going-in cap rate. Response C incorrectly uses the fifth-year NOI instead of the sixth-year NOI.

12. B is correct. The difference between the discount rate of 9% and the terminal cap rate of 6% equals the constant growth rate of 3%, and the sixth-year NOI of 3,439,613 is 3% greater than the fifth-year NOI of 3,339,340 (3,439,613/3,339,340 = 1.03). Response A is incorrect because each year of NOI is discounted using the discount rate of 9%. Response C is incorrect: If this statement were true, then

NOI growth in Years 1–5 would be 2.5% (9% – 6.5%), but the growth rate observed is closer to 1%. A calculation of the compound annual growth rate of NOI between Year 1 and Year 5 is 1.14%.

13. B is correct. Applying the sum of adjustments to each of the comparable properties yields adjusted per square foot values of 394.25 for Sales Comp A [= 415 × (1 – 0.05)], 462.15 for Sales Comp B [= 395 × (1 + 0.17)], and 480 for Sales Comp C [= 400 × (1 + 0.20)]. The average of these three adjusted per square foot values is 445.47, and multiplying this number by the office property's 100,000 square feet yields an implied property value of USD44.5 million. Comparing this amount to the expected purchase price of USD50 million reflects an approximate 11% difference.

14. A is correct. During an oversupply phase of the real estate cycle, the cost approach may inflate the value estimate because replacement costs of the building are likely higher than the true market value of the building. Response B is incorrect: The value estimate using the data is USD59 million (57 + 7 – 5), and this estimate is higher than the expected purchase price of USD50 million. Response C is incorrect because the developer's profit is a component of the overall costs used to estimate building replacement cost.

15. B is correct. Both parties are investors in private real estate because buying a property directly is a private market transaction. Delphinus takes a private position in real estate equity by investing USD15 million, and Rich takes a private position in real estate debt by lending USD35 million to Delphinus to purchase the property. Responses A and C are incorrect because public investments in real estate revolve around such securities as REITs, MBS, and covered bonds.

LEARNING MODULE

3

Investments in Real Estate through Publicly Traded Securities

by Steven G. Bloom, CFA, Jeffrey D. Fisher, PhD, David Kruth, CFA, Bryan D. MacGregor, PhD, MRICS, MRTPI, Ian Rossa O'Reilly, CFA, and Anthony Paolone, CFA.

Steven G. Bloom, CFA, is at ARC Fiduciary (USA). Jeffery D. Fisher, PhD. David Kruth, CFA. Bryan MacGregor, PhD, MRICS, MRTPI. Ian Rossa O'Reilly, CFA (Canada). Anthony Paolone, CFA.

LEARNING OUTCOMES

Mastery	The candidate should be able to:
☐	discuss types of publicly traded real estate securities
☐	justify the use of net asset value per share (NAVPS) in valuation of publicly traded real estate securities and estimate NAVPS based on forecasted cash net operating income
☐	describe the use of funds from operations (FFO) and adjusted funds from operations (AFFO) in REIT valuation
☐	calculate and interpret the value of a REIT share using the net asset value, relative value (price-to-FFO and price-to-AFFO), and discounted cash flow approaches
☐	explain advantages and disadvantages of investing in real estate through publicly traded securities compared to private vehicles

INTRODUCTION

1

Historically real estate investing was reserved for the wealthy and institutions. REITs were initially conceived of as a way to make real estate investing more accessible to small investors to gain exposure to a professionally managed, diversified real estate portfolio. REITs were viewed as a type of (closed-end) mutual fund and income passthrough vehicle through which the portfolio manager would acquire attractively valued properties, occasionally sell fully valued properties, and distribute property earnings to the trust's investors. Legislation was passed in the United States in 1960 to authorize REITs, and the Netherlands followed suit in 1969. The US model and other types of tax-advantaged real estate investment vehicles have been adopted worldwide. The S&P 500 Index added REITs as a separate Global Industry Classification Standard (GICS) sector in 2016.

Almost 40 countries have REITs or REIT-like structures, and more are considering adopting similar vehicles. REITs are widely held by individuals and institutions alike.

LEARNING MODULE OVERVIEW

- The principal types of publicly traded real estate securities include real estate investment trusts (REITs), real estate operating companies (REOCs), residential mortgage-backed securities (RMBS), and commercial mortgage-backed securities (CMBS).
- Compared with other publicly traded shares, REITs typically offer higher-than-average dividend yields and greater stability of income and returns. They are amenable to a net asset value approach to valuation because of the existence of active private markets for their real estate assets.
- Compared with REOCs, REITs offer higher dividend yields and income tax exemptions but have less operating flexibility to invest in a broad range of real estate activities and less potential for growth from reinvesting their operating cash flows because of their high income-to-payout ratios.
- In assessing the investment merits of REITs, investors analyze the effects of trends in general economic activity, retail sales, job creation, population growth, and new supply and demand for specific types of space. Investors also pay particular attention to occupancies, leasing activity, rental rates, remaining lease terms, in-place rents compared with market rents, costs to maintain space and re-lease space, tenants' financial health and tenant concentration in the portfolio, financial leverage, debt maturities and costs, and the quality of management and governance.
- Analysts adjust the historical cost-based financial statements of REITs and REOCs to obtain better measures of current income and net worth. The three principal figures they calculate and use are (1) funds from operations or accounting net earnings, excluding depreciation, deferred tax charges, and gains or losses on sales of property and debt restructuring; (2) adjusted funds from operations, or funds from operations adjusted to remove straight-line rent and to provide for maintenance-type capital expenditures and leasing costs, including leasing agents' commissions and tenants' improvement allowances; and (3) net asset value or the difference between a real estate company's asset and liability ranking prior to shareholders' equity, all valued at market values instead of accounting book values.
- REITs and some REOCs generally return a significant portion of their income to their investors as required by law and, as a result, tend to pay high dividends. Thus, dividend discount or discounted cash flow models for valuation are also applicable. These valuation approaches are applied in the same manner as they are for shares in other industries. Usually, investors use two- or three-step dividend discount models with near-term, intermediate-term, and/or long-term growth

assumptions. In discounted cash flow models, investors often use intermediate-term cash flow projections and a terminal value based on historical cash flow multiples.

TYPES OF PUBLICLY TRADED REAL ESTATE SECURITIES

2

☐ discuss types of publicly traded real estate securities

Publicly traded real estate securities allow investors to gain indirect exposure to real estate equity and debt by purchasing shares of companies that own real estate, real estate loans, or both. Securitization makes it possible for investors of all sizes to access an asset class that was once available only to the largest investors. Globally, the principal types of publicly traded real estate securities are REITs, REOCs, and MBS.

- **Real estate investment trusts** are companies that own, finance, and—to a limited extent—develop income-producing real estate across a range of property sectors. These companies must meet a number of requirements in order to qualify as REITs. Most REITs are required to distribute 90%–100% of their taxable income to shareholders.
- REITs that own real estate are called **equity REITs**. Those that make or invest in loans secured by real estate are categorized as mortgage REITs. The companies' tax advantages result from being allowed to deduct dividends paid from income, which effectively exempts REITs from corporate income tax in many countries. In many jurisdictions, qualifying REITs are simply exempt from corporate income tax.
- **Real estate operating companies** are ordinary taxable real estate ownership companies. Businesses are organized as REOCs, as opposed to REITs, if the following is true:
  - they are located in countries that do not have a tax-advantaged REIT regime in place,
  - they engage to a large extent in the development of for-sale real estate properties, or
  - they offer other non-qualifying services, such as brokerage and third-party property management.
- Mortgage-backed securities are asset-backed securitized debt obligations that represent rights to receive cash flows from portfolios of mortgage loans—mortgage loans on commercial properties in the case of commercial mortgage-backed securities and mortgage loans on residential properties in the case of residential mortgage-backed securities. Whereas residential mortgage pools often contain thousands of loans, commercial mortgage pools typically range from around 100 loans to as few as one loan when the asset is very large.

The market capitalization of publicly traded real estate equity securities is greatly exceeded by the market value of real estate debt securities—in particular, RMBS. In addition to publicly traded real estate securities, there are privately held real estate securities, including private REITs and REOCs, privately held mortgages, private debt issues, and bank debt. Many real estate private equity partnerships create private REITs to own income-producing properties.

REIT Structures

REITs are tax-efficient conduits for distributing earnings from rental income to shareholders. Most are structured as corporations or trusts. There are numerous requirements for a company to qualify as a REIT. In most countries, REITs are required to

- distribute 90%–100% of their otherwise taxable earnings,
- invest at least 75% of their assets in real estate, and
- derive at least 75% of income from real estate rental income or interest on mortgages.

Countries may specify a minimum number of shareholders, maximum share ownership by a single shareholder, a minimum number of properties/maximum asset concentration, a maximum level of non-rental income, a maximum amount of development, and limits on leverage and types of loans. In the United States, a REIT must have at least 100 shareholders, and no fewer than five shareholders can own more than 50% of the shares (the 5/50 rule). There are numerous other requirements as well. The restrictions effectively bar an individual or small group from creating REITs to own individual real estate assets.

Most REITs in the United States are self-managed and self-advised. Senior executives are company employees who report to trustees or the board of directors, who, in turn, are elected by shareholders. Fully integrated REITs generally have fewer conflicts than REITs that are externally advised or externally managed. Externally managed REITs pay asset management fees to the third-party adviser, which has an inherent incentive to increase the size of the REIT if fees are based on total assets. External managers may require REITs to pay for other services that are provided by affiliates of the manager, such as property management, acquisitions, and debt placement.

Market Size

Details about the market's relative size by geographic area and security type are shown in Exhibit 1.

Exhibit 1: Relative Size and Composition of Publicly Traded Real Estate Equity Security Markets

A. Percentage of market value of publicly traded real estate equity securities (REITs and REOCs) in developed markets as of 30 September 2022

By Region (%)		By Market (%)	
North America	64.9	United States	62.2
Asia Pacific	23.5	Japan	11.1
Europe	11.4	Hong Kong SAR	4.8
Middle East, Africa	0.2	Australia	3.5
		Germany	2.0
		United Kingdom	3.9
		Canada	2.7
		Singapore	3.7

A. Percentage of market value of publicly traded real estate equity securities (REITs and REOCs) in developed markets as of 30 September 2022

By Region (%)		By Market (%)	
		Sweden	1.5
		France	0.9
		Netherlands	0.5
		Other	3.2

B. Percentage of market value of publicly traded real estate equity securities in developed markets by type of structure as of 30 September 2022

	Global	North America	Europe	Asia Pacific
REITs	59	98	41	49
Non-REITs, REOCs	41	2	59	51

Sources: www.ftserussell.com and www.epra.com. Based on data from the FTSE EPRA Nareit Developed Index.

Note that, as evidenced in Panel B of Exhibit 1, REIT structures are relatively more common in North America than in Europe or Asia Pacific, due to the favorable tax structure afforded to REIT structures in North America versus other parts of the world, where REOC structures are relatively more common. As an investment asset class, income-producing real estate offers the advantages of stable income based on its contractual revenue from leases and a measure of long-term inflation protection because, over the long term, rents tend to rise with inflation.

Advantages and Disadvantages of Investing in REITs

The advantages and disadvantages of investing in public real estate companies as compared with private real estate investments include the following:

Advantages of REITs

1. *Liquidity*: Ability to buy and sell shares of almost any amount on major exchanges
2. *Transparency*: Readily available share prices and transaction histories
3. *Diversification of property holdings*: By property type, geography, and underlying tenant credit
4. *High-quality portfolios*: Many companies own high-quality assets in leading markets.
5. *Active professional management*: Most companies have strong executive management overseeing dedicated property management teams with economies of scale.
6. *Potentially stable income*: Well-occupied properties subject to long-term leases generate predictable property income, sometimes with distributions occurring monthly.
7. *Tax efficiency*: REIT and passthrough structures avoid corporate income taxation, leaving only the investor to pay taxes on dividends received (i.e., single taxation).

Disadvantages of REITs

1. *Lack of retained earnings*: As REITs are required to pay 90%+ of earnings to shareholders as dividends, REITs must access capital markets to fund growth. The faster the expansion, the more often the company must raise new capital.
2. *Regulatory costs*: REITs have the cost burden of maintaining a corporate structure of a publicly traded company and complying with regulatory filings.
3. *Reduced portfolio diversification benefits*: Because shares of REITs are publicly traded, the pricing is partially determined by stock market movements and liquidity rather than only by underlying value. This reduces the diversification benefits for the overall portfolio as compared to private real estate.
4. *Limited in types of assets owned*: REITs are also constrained in the types of assets they own. Consequently, many REITs form **taxable REIT subsidiaries** (TRS), which pay income taxes on earnings from non-REIT-qualifying activities, such as merchant development or third-party property management.

3 VALUATION: NET ASSET VALUE APPROACH

☐ justify the use of net asset value per share (NAVPS) in valuation of publicly traded real estate securities and estimate NAVPS based on forecasted cash net operating income

Introduction

The approaches analysts take in valuing equity include those based on the following:

- asset value estimates,
- price multiple comparisons,
- discounted cash flow.

Two possible measures of value that analysts might use are

- book value per share (BVPS), based on reported accounting values, and
- net asset value per share (NAVPS), based on market values for assets.

Note that in this reading, BVPS refers to depreciated real estate value rather than total shareholders' equity per share. NAVPS is the relevant market-based valuation measure for valuing REITs and REOCs.

NAVPS is a fundamental benchmark for the value of a REIT or REOC. In Europe and Asia, the price-to-NAV multiple is the primary measure that analysts use to value real estate companies. (US analysts more commonly report on price multiples of gross cash flow.) Real estate NAV may be viewed as the largest component of the intrinsic value of a REIT or REOC. NAVPS should also include the following:

- assessments of the value of any non-asset-based income streams (e.g., fee or management income);
- the value of non–real estate assets, including cash;
- net of the value of any contingent liabilities; and

- the value added by management of the REIT or REOC.

Shares priced at discounts to NAVPS suggest potential undervaluation, and shares priced at premiums to NAVPS suggest potential overvaluation. However, this discount or premium might be justified by indications of future events, such as a missed property development completion or expected high value creation by a management team. These assessments must be made in the context of the stock market's tendency to be forward looking in its valuations and at times to have different investment criteria from property markets. In addition, the stock price discount or premium to NAVPS may be explained by investors' view of management's added value, leverage, and company governance.

REITs whose shares trade below NAVPS or have high leverage may have a more difficult time raising new capital to fund acquisitions and development, which, in turn, may limit long-term growth, in contrast to REITs that trade at or above NAVPS. Selling equity below NAVPS can be dilutive for investors.

Accounting for Investment Properties

If accounting is on a fair value basis, accounting values may be relevant for asset-based valuation. If historical cost values are used, however, accounting values are generally not relevant and must be adjusted.

Under International Financial Reporting Standards (IFRS), companies are allowed to value investment properties using either a *cost model* or a *fair value model*:

- The cost model is identical to the cost model used for property, plant, and equipment.
- The fair value model assumes all changes in the asset's fair value affect net income. To use the fair value model, a company must be able to reliably determine the property's fair value on a continuing basis. In general, a company must consistently apply its chosen model (cost or fair value) to all its investment property. If a company chooses the fair value model for its investment property, it must continue to use the fair value model until it disposes of the property or changes its use such that it is no longer considered investment property (e.g., it becomes owner-occupied property or part of inventory). The company must continue to use the fair value model for that property even if transactions on comparable properties, used to estimate fair value, become less frequent.

Investment property appears as a separate line item on the balance sheet. Companies are required to disclose whether they use the fair value model or the cost model for their investment property. If the company uses the fair value model, it must make additional disclosures about how it determines fair value and must provide reconciliation between the beginning and ending carrying amounts of the investment property. If the company uses the cost model, it must make additional disclosures—for example, the depreciation method and useful life estimates must be disclosed. In addition, if the company uses the cost model, it must also disclose the fair value of investment property.

In contrast to IFRS, under US GAAP, most US real estate owners use the historical cost accounting model, which values an asset at its original purchase price plus capital investment less historical depreciation. This model does not accurately represent the economic values of assets and liabilities in environments of significant operating income and asset price changes or long-term inflation. US GAAP historical cost accounting practices tend to distort the measure of economic income and asset value by (1) understating carrying values on long-held property assets that are often appreciating in value because of general price inflation or other property-specific reasons and (2) overstating depreciation when companies use accelerated depreciation.

Net Asset Value per Share: Calculation

As a result of shortcomings in accounting reported values, investment analysts and investors use estimates of **net asset value per share**. NAVPS is the difference between a real estate company's assets and its liabilities, *all taken at current market values instead of accounting book values*, divided by the number of shares outstanding.

NAVPS = (Market value of assets – Market value of liabilities)/Number of shares.

NAVPS is a superior measure of a company's net worth compared with historical book value per share.

In valuing a REIT's or REOC's real estate portfolio, analysts will look for the results of existing appraisals if they are available (such as those provided by companies reporting under IFRS). If such appraisals are unavailable or if they disagree with the assumptions or methodology of those appraisals, analysts will often capitalize the rental streams—represented by net operating income—produced by a REIT's or REOC's properties, using a market-required rate of return.

To calculate NAVPS, begin with net operating income (NOI), which is defined as gross rental revenue minus estimated vacancy and collection loss minus operating expenses (which include property insurance, real estate taxes, utilities, general and administrative, and repairs and maintenance expenses but before deducting interest expense, federal and local income taxes, depreciation, and amortization).

NOI = (Gross rental revenue – Estimated vacancy and collections loss – Operating expenses).

NOI is analogous to earnings before interest expense and federal and local income taxes.

These estimated asset values will be substituted for the book values of the properties on the balance sheet and adjustments made to any related accounting assets, such as capitalized leases, to avoid double counting.

Generally, goodwill, deferred financing expenses, and deferred tax assets will be excluded to arrive at a "hard" economic value for total assets. Liabilities will be similarly adjusted to replace the face value of debt with market values if these are significantly different (e.g., because of changes in interest rates), and any such "soft" liabilities as deferred tax liabilities will be removed. The revised net worth of the company divided by the number of shares outstanding is the NAVPS. Although this figure is calculated before provision for any income or capital gains taxes that might be payable on liquidation, the inability to predict how the company or its assets might be sold and the prospect that it might be kept intact in an acquisition make investors look to the pre-tax asset value as their primary net worth benchmark. If a company has held its assets for many years and has a very low remaining depreciable value for its assets for tax purposes, it can affect investors' perspectives on valuation. Quantifying the effects of a low adjusted cost base, however, is impeded by lack of knowledge of the tax circumstances and strategies of a would-be acquirer.

Exhibit 2 provides an example of the calculations involved in estimating NAV based on capitalizing rental streams. Because the book values of assets are based on historical costs, the analyst estimates NAVPS. First, by capitalizing NOI with certain adjustments, the analyst obtains an estimate of the value of rental properties; then, the value of other tangible assets is added, and the total is netted of liabilities. This net amount, NAV, is then divided by the number of shares outstanding to obtain NAVPS.

Exhibit 2: Analyst Adjustments to REIT Financials to Obtain NAVPS

Last-12-month real estate NOI	$270,432
Less: Non-cash rent	7,667
Plus: Adjustment for full impact of acquisitions[a]	4,534
Pro forma cash NOI for last 12 months	$267,299
Plus: Next-12-month growth in NOI[b]	$4,009
Estimated next-12-month cash NOI	$271,308
Assumed cap rate[c]	7.00%
Estimated value of operating real estate	$3,875,829
Plus: Cash and equivalents	65,554
Plus: Land held for future development	34,566
Plus: Accounts receivable	45,667
Plus: Prepaid/other assets[d]	23,456
Estimated gross asset value	$4,045,072
Less: Total debt	1,010,988
Less: Other liabilities	119,886
Net asset value	$2,914,198
Shares outstanding	55,689

[a] *An incremental 50% of the annual expected return on acquisitions that were completed midway through the previous year.*
[b] *Growth is estimated at 1.5%.*
[c] *The cap rate is based on recent comparable transactions in the property market.*
[d] *This figure does not include intangible assets.*

NAVPS is calculated to be $2,914,198 divided by 55,689 shares, which equals $52.33 per share.

The second line in Exhibit 2 shows the adjustment to remove **non-cash rent**; this adjustment is the result of the accounting practice of "straight lining" the rental revenue from long-term leases with contractual step-ups. When the real estate company reports the average contractual rent it expects to receive over the course of each lease, rent received from the tenant is less than the average revenue booked during the early years of the lease, and the tenant pays more rent than the company reports during the latter years of the lease term. (The amount of this deduction is the difference between the average contractual rent over the leases' terms and the cash rent actually paid.) NOI is also increased to reflect a full year's rent for properties acquired during the year, resulting in pro forma "cash NOI" for the previous 12 months of $267,299,000. This amount is then increased to include expected growth for the next 12 months at 1.5%, resulting in expected next-12-month cash NOI of $271,308,000.

An appropriate capitalization rate is then estimated based on recent transactions for comparable properties in the property market. An estimated value for the REIT's operating real estate is obtained by dividing expected next-12-month cash NOI by the decimalized capitalization rate (in this case, 0.07). The book values of the REIT's other tangible assets, including cash, accounts receivable, land for future development, and prepaid expenses, are added to obtain estimated gross asset value. (Land is sometimes taken at market value if this amount can be determined reliably, but because land is often difficult to value and of low liquidity, analysts tend to use book values.) From this figure, debt and other liabilities (but not deferred taxes, because this item is an accounting provision rather than an economic liability) are subtracted to obtain net asset value. Division by the number of shares outstanding produces NAVPS.

Net Asset Value per Share: Application

NAVPS can be reasonably estimated when there are ample market transactions to provide property comparables. Investors can make observations about how such properties trade based on the price per square foot or on the basis of capitalization rate (the rate obtained by dividing net operating income by total value). Broker reports and private real estate research companies also track rental rates by property and other tenant incentives, such as free rent or capital to improve the space, and then apply these valuations to the assets of a public company. As of 2022, 12% of commercial real estate was held by publicly traded REITs in the United States (www.epra.com). In Europe, only 4% of the commercial real estate market was owned by listed real estate companies (REITs and REOCs), and in Singapore, 30% of the commercial market was owned by listed real estate companies

Important Considerations in an NAV-Based Approach to Valuing REITs

Although NAV estimates provide investors with a specific value, several important considerations should be taken into account when using this approach to value REITs and REOCs. First, investors must understand the implications of using a private market valuation tool on a publicly traded security. In this context, it is useful to examine how NAVs are calculated.

The methods most used to calculate NAV are

1. using the cap rate approach to valuing the NOI of a property or portfolio of properties,
2. applying value per square foot (or unit) to a property or portfolio of properties, and
3. using appraised values disclosed in the company's financial statements.

An analyst may adjust these appraised values reported by the company if she does not agree with the underlying assumptions and if there is sufficient information to do so. In the first two instances, the cap rates and values per square foot are derived from observing transactions that have occurred in the marketplace. In contrast, most sophisticated direct purchasers of commercial real estate arrive at a purchase price after performing detailed forecasting of the cash flows they expect to achieve from owning and operating a specific property over their investment time horizon. These cash flows are then discounted to a present value or purchase price.

Whatever that present value or purchase price is, an analyst can estimate value by dividing an estimate of NOI by the cap rate—essentially, the required rate of current return for income streams of that risk. In addition, an analyst can take the present value or purchase price and divide by the property's rentable area for a value per square foot. The point is that cap rates and values per square foot result from a more detailed analysis and discounted cash flow process. The discount rate used by a private owner/operator of commercial real estate could differ from the discount rate used by investors purchasing shares of REITs.

Premium or Discount to NAV

Real estate stocks can trade at either premiums or discounts to NAV. Over time, REITs and REOCs globally have at times traded at premiums to NAV of more than 25% and at other times at discounts to NAV exceeding 25%. Thus, if the NAV of a REIT were $20 per share, the stock might trade as low as $15 per share or as high as $25 per share, depending on a range of factors.

The price-to-NAV ratio will vary by market, sector, outlook, and perceived quality of management and governance. Private property investors may or may not value individual assets the same way public equity investors value listed real estate companies. Property buyers frequently consider the long-term prospects and valuation for an asset when making an investment. Appraisal-based NAV estimates, however, often lag changes in market conditions.

Stock investors tend to focus more on the near-term projected outlook for changes in income and asset value. These factors help explain why share valuation may differ from NAV. As alluded to earlier, it is possible that REITs and REOCs can trade at some premium or discount to NAV until the premium/discount becomes wide enough for market forces to close the arbitrage gap.

Another factor to consider when using an NAV approach to REIT or REOC valuation is that NAV implicitly treats a company as an individual asset or static pool of assets. In practice, such treatment is not consistent with a going-concern assumption. Management teams have different track records and abilities to produce value over time, assets can be purchased and sold, and capital market decisions can add or subtract value. An investor must thus consider how much value a management team can add to (or subtract from) current NAV.

For instance, an investor may be willing to purchase REIT A trading at a 10% premium to NAV versus REIT B trading at a small discount to NAV because the management team of REIT A has a stronger track record and better opportunities to grow the NAV compared with REIT B, thus justifying the premium at which REIT A trades relative to REIT B.

NAV estimates can also become quite subjective when property markets become illiquid and few transactions are observable or when REITs and REOCs own hundreds of properties, making it difficult for an investor to estimate exactly how much the portfolio would be worth if the assets were sold individually. There may also be a large-portfolio premium in good economic environments when prospective strategic purchasers may be willing to pay a premium to acquire a large amount of desired property at once or a large-portfolio discount when there are few buyers for the kind of property in question. In addition, such assets as undeveloped land, very large properties with few comparable assets, properties with specific uses, service businesses, and joint ventures complicate the process of estimating NAV with accuracy and confidence.

Further Observations on NAV

Among institutional investors, the most common view is that if REIT management is performing well in the sense of creating value, REITs and REOCs should trade at premiums to underlying NAVPS. This rationale is based on the following:

1. Investors in the stocks have liquidity on a day-to-day basis, whereas a private investor in real estate does not, thus warranting a lower required rate of return (higher value) in the public market than in the private market for the same assets.
2. The competitive nature of the public markets and the size of the organizations should attract above-average management teams, which should produce better real estate operating performance and lead to better investment decisions than the average private real estate concern.

In conclusion, although NAV is by its nature an absolute valuation metric, in practice it is often more useful as a relative valuation tool. If all REITs are trading above or below NAV, selecting individual REITs could become a relative exercise—that is, purchasing the REIT stock trading at the smallest premium to NAV when REITs are trading above NAV or selling the REIT trading at the smallest discount to NAV when REITs are all trading at a discount to NAV. In practice, NAV is also used as a relative metric by investors looking at implied cap rates. To calculate the implied cap rate of a REIT or REOC, the current price is used in an NAV model to work backward and solve for the cap rate. By doing so, an investor looking at two similar portfolios of real estate could ascertain whether the market is valuing these portfolios differently based on the implied cap rates.

4 VALUATION: RELATIVE VALUE (PRICE MULTIPLE) APPROACH

☐ describe the use of funds from operations (FFO) and adjusted funds from operations (AFFO) in REIT valuation

Conventional equity valuation approaches, including market-based or relative value approaches, are used with some adaptations to value REITs and REOCs. Such multiples as the price-to-funds from operations ratio (P/FFO), the price-to-adjusted funds from operations ratio (P/AFFO), and the enterprise value-to-EBITDA ratio (EV/EBITDA) are used for valuing shares of REITs and REOCs in much the same way as for valuing shares in other industries.

Relative Value Approach to Valuing REIT Stocks

REIT analysts and investors make extensive use of two measures of operating performance that are specific to REITs. **Funds from operations** (FFO) is defined as net income plus depreciation and amortization less gains or losses on the sale of real property.

FFO = (Net income + Depreciation + Amortization) – (Net gains on sale of real property).

FFO is one of the most commonly used metrics in the United States. (In Europe and Asia, NAVPS is more commonly used, as discussed earlier.) Over the past five years, the FFO metric has become more widely used in the Asia-Pacific region as well.

Adjusted funds from operations (AFFO) subtracts from FFO recurring capital expenditure and the difference between reported rents and cash rents:

AFFO = (FFO – Non-cash rent – Recurring capex).

AFFO better approximates a company's sustainable dividend-paying capacity.

The price-to-earnings ratio (P/E) and P multiples are commonly used to value equities. For REITs, the relative value measures used most frequently are P/FFO and P/AFFO. The ratio EV/EBITDA is used to a lesser extent. The use of P/FFO and P/AFFO multiples allows investors to quickly ascertain the value of a given REIT's shares compared with that of other REIT shares or to compare the current valuation level of a REIT's shares with historical levels. Within the REIT sector, P/FFO and P/AFFO multiples are also often compared with the average multiple of companies owning similar properties—for example, comparing the P/FFO multiple of a REIT that owns office properties with the average P/FFO multiple for all REITs owning office properties. These multiples are typically calculated using current stock prices and year-ahead estimated FFO or AFFO.

FFO and AFFO are based on net income available to equity and thus represent levered income. P/FFO multiples are generally lower for companies with higher leverage, all things equal. EBITDA, by definition, measures income before the leveraging effect of debt. Not only do EV/EBITDA multiples facilitate like-for-like valuation comparisons; they also better approximate how investors evaluate real estate. Recall that the inverse of the multiple, EBITDA/EV, closely approximates the real estate capitalization rate formula (NOI/market value).

There are three main drivers that differentiate P/FFO, P/AFFO, and EV/EBITDA multiples among most REITs and REOCs:

1. *Expectation for growth in FFO and AFFO*: The higher the expected growth, the higher the multiple or relative valuation. Growth can be driven by the following:

   - business model (e.g., REITs and REOCs successful in real estate development often generate above-average FFO and AFFO growth over time);
   - geography (e.g., having a concentration of properties in primary, supply-constrained markets, such as New York City or London, can give landlords more pricing power and higher cash flow growth than can be obtained in secondary markets); and
   - other factors (e.g., management skill or lease structure).

2. *Risk associated with the underlying real estate*: Cash flow volatility related to asset type, quality, and age; market conditions; lease types; and submarket location also affect valuation.

   - Example 1: Owning apartments is viewed as having less cash flow variability than owning hotels. As such, apartment-focused REITs tend to trade at relatively high multiples compared with hotel REITs.
   - Example 2: Shares of companies with young, well-maintained portfolios generally trade at higher multiples than stocks of companies with older or out-of-date properties with deferred maintenance that will require higher capital expenditures to sustain rent growth.

3. *Risks associated with the company's capital structures and access to capital*: As financial leverage increases, equities' FFO and AFFO multiples decrease because required return increases as risk increases. Higher leverage constrains a company's incremental borrowing capacity and may create a stock overhang if investors avoid buying shares in anticipation of future equity offerings.

There are many other factors that affect valuation, as with any investment, including investor perceptions of management, asset types or markets being in or out of favor, complexity, quality of financial disclosure, transparency, and governance.

P/FFO is, in essence, the REIT sector equivalent of P/E. Investors can derive a quick "cash flow" multiple by looking at P/AFFO because AFFO makes a variety of adjustments to FFO that result in an approximation of cash earnings.

Funds from Operations and Adjusted Funds from Operations

FFO has long been the standard measure of REIT performance. The National Association of Real Estate Investment Trusts (Nareit) took steps to standardize and promote the definition. FFO is an SEC-accepted non-GAAP financial measure (as is EBITDA), which, according to the SEC and as specified in updated guidance from Nareit (2018), must be reconciled with GAAP net income. The SEC also recommends that companies that report adjustments to FFO reconcile those figures with the Nareit-defined FFO, sometimes referred to as Nareit FFO.

FFO attempts to approximate continuing operating performance. A more complete definition of FFO is as follows:

> net income (computed in accordance with GAAP) plus losses (minus gains) from sales of properties, plus depreciation and amortization related to real estate, plus real estate impairments and write-downs unrelated to depreciation.

Why is depreciation added back to net income? Investors believe that real estate maintains its value to a greater extent than other business assets, often appreciating in value over the long term, and that depreciation deductions under IFRS and US GAAP do not represent economic reality. A taxable REOC that uses a moderate degree of leverage and regularly chooses to reinvest most of its income in its business usually will be able to defer a large part of its annual tax liability; that is, its cash income taxes will be low because of the accelerated depreciation rates for tax purposes permitted in most countries, and reinvesting continues to add to the depreciable real estate base.

Net income is adjusted for gains and losses from sales of previously depreciated operating properties on the grounds that they do not represent sustainable, normal income. The amortization add-back includes amortization of leasing commissions, tenant improvements, and tenant allowances.

Like cash flow from operations, FFO is not a measure of cash flow. It does not include investment and spending necessary to sustain cash flow growth or cash flow related to financing activities. FFO also includes FFO from unconsolidated businesses.

Adjusted funds from operations, also known as **funds available for distribution** (FAD) or **cash available for distribution**, is a refinement of FFO that is designed to be a more accurate measure of current economic income. AFFO is most often defined as FFO adjusted to remove any non-cash rent and to subtract maintenance-type capital expenditures and leasing costs (including leasing agents' commissions and tenants' improvement allowances). So-called **straight-line rent** is the average contractual rent over a lease term, and this figure is recognized as revenue under IFRS and US GAAP. The difference between this figure and the cash rent paid during the period is the amount of the non-cash rent, or **straight-line rent adjustment**. Because most long-term leases contain escalating rental rates, this difference in rental revenue recognition can be significant. Also, deductions from FFO for capital expenditures related to maintenance and for leasing the space in properties reflect costs that need to be incurred to maintain the value of properties.

The purpose of the adjustments to net earnings made in computing FFO and AFFO is to obtain a more tangible, cash-focused measure of sustainable economic income that reduces reliance on non-cash accounting estimates and excludes non-economic, non-cash charges.

AFFO is superior to FFO as a measure of economic income and thus economic return because it considers the capital expenditures necessary to maintain the economic income of a property portfolio. AFFO is also more reflective of a REIT's dividend-paying ability than FFO. It is open, however, to more variation and error in estimation than FFO.

The precise annual provision required to maintain and lease the space in a property is difficult to predict, and the actual expense in any single year may be significantly more or less than the norm because of the timing of capital expenditure programs and the uneven expiration schedule of leases. Consequently, estimates of FFO are more frequently referenced measures, although analysts and investors will tend to base their investment judgments to a significant degree on their AFFO estimates. Although many REITs and REOCs compute and refer to AFFO in their disclosures, their methods of computation and their assumptions vary. Firms that compile statistics and estimates of publicly traded enterprises for publications, such as Bloomberg and Refinitiv, tend not to gather AFFO estimates because of the absence of a universally accepted methodology for computing AFFO and inconsistent corporate reporting of actual AFFO figures, which hinder corroboration of analysts' estimates.

Exhibit 3 illustrates the most straightforward, convenient way of calculating FFO and AFFO for a hypothetical firm, Office Equity REIT Inc.

Exhibit 3: Calculation of FFO and AFFO for Office Equity REIT Inc. (SGD thousands, except per-share data)

A. Calculation of funds from operations	
Net income	160,638
Add: Depreciation and amortization	76,100
Add: (Gains)/losses from sale of depreciable real estate	25,000
Funds from operations	261,738
FFO per share (55,689 shares outstanding)	4.70
B. Calculation of adjusted funds from operations	
Funds from operations	261,738
Less: Non-cash (straight-line) rent adjustment	21,103
Less: Recurring maintenance-type capital expenditures and leasing commissions	55,765
Adjusted funds from operations	184,870
AFFO per share (55,689 shares outstanding)	3.32

P/FFO and P/AFFO Multiples: Advantages and Disadvantages

The key advantages and disadvantages of using P/FFO and P/AFFO multiples in the valuation of REITs and REOCs are as follows:

Advantages

1. Multiples of earnings measures of this kind are widely accepted in evaluating shares across global stock markets and industries.
2. In light of this acceptance, portfolio managers can put the valuation of REITs and REOCs into context with other investment alternatives.
3. FFO estimates are readily available through market data providers, such as Bloomberg and Refinitiv, which facilitates calculating P/FFO multiples.

4. Multiples can be used in conjunction with such items as expected growth and leverage levels to deepen the relative analysis among REITs and REOCs. Because FFO and AFFO do not consider differences in leverage, leverage ratios can be used to adjust for leverage differences among REITs when using these multiples to compare valuations.

Disadvantages

1. Applying a multiple to FFO or AFFO may not capture the intrinsic value of all real estate assets held by the REIT or REOC, such as non-income-producing assets (for example, land held for development, vacant buildings, and properties under development), underused assets (current use may not represent highest and best use), or assets with below-market rents.
2. P/FFO does not adjust for the impact of recurring capital expenditures needed to keep properties operating smoothly. Although P/AFFO should do so, wide variations in estimates and assumptions are incorporated into the calculation of AFFO.
3. An increased level of such one-time items as gains and accounting charges, as well as new revenue recognition rules, has affected the income statement, thus making P/FFO and P/AFFO more difficult to compute and complicating comparisons between companies.

5 REIT MINI CASE STUDY: EXAMPLE OF DISCLOSURES AND VALUATION ANALYSIS

☐ calculate and interpret the value of a REIT share using the net asset value, relative value (price-to-FFO and price-to-AFFO), and discounted cash flow approaches

In this section, we undertake the valuation of a REIT by using the previously outlined approaches for valuation. The REIT in our example is Capitol Shopping Center REIT Inc. (CSC), a fictitious company that owns and operates retail shopping centers primarily in the Washington, DC, metropolitan area. Exhibit 4 shows CSC's income statements, balance sheets, and cash flow statements for Year 1 and Year 2.

Exhibit 4: Capitol Shopping Center REIT Inc. Financial Statements (USD thousands, except per-share data)

A. Income statements

	Three Months Ending 31 December		Year Ending 31 December	
	Year 2	Year 1	Year 2	Year 1
Rental revenue	133,700	130,300	517,546	501,600
Other property income	3,600	2,100	14,850	13,450

A. Income statements

	Three Months Ending 31 December		Year Ending 31 December	
	Year 2	Year 1	Year 2	Year 1
Total property revenue	137,300	132,400	532,396	515,050
Rental expenses	29,813	28,725	112,571	109,775
Property taxes	15,050	14,850	57,418	55,375
Total property expenses	44,863	43,575	169,989	165,150
Property net operating income	92,437	88,825	362,407	349,900
Other income	450	385	1,840	1,675
General and administrative expenses	6,150	7,280	23,860	26,415
EBITDA	86,737	81,930	340,387	325,160
Depreciation and amortization	28,460	27,316	115,110	111,020
Net interest expense	25,867	25,015	100,823	99,173
Net income available to common shareholders	32,410	29,599	124,454	114,967
Weighted average common shares	61,100	60,100	60,600	60,100
Earnings per share	0.53	0.49	2.05	1.91

B. Balance sheets

	Year Ending 31 December	
	Year 2	Year 1
Assets		
Real estate, at cost		
Operating real estate	3,627,576	3,496,370
Land held for future development	133,785	133,785
	3,761,361	3,630,155
Less accumulated depreciation	(938,097)	(822,987)
Net real estate	2,823,264	2,807,168
Cash and equivalents	85,736	23,856
Accounts receivable, net	72,191	73,699

B. Balance sheets

	Year Ending 31 December	
	Year 2	**Year 1**
Deferred rent receivable, net	38,165	33,053
Prepaid expenses and other assets	106,913	101,604
Total assets	3,126,269	3,039,380
Liabilities and shareholders' equity		
Liabilities		
Mortgages payable	701,884	647,253
Notes payable	1,090,745	1,090,745
Accounts payable and other liabilities	219,498	200,439
Total liabilities	2,012,127	1,938,437
Common shares and equity	1,114,142	1,100,943
Total liabilities and shareholders' equity	3,126,269	3,039,380

C. Cash flow statements

	Year Ending 31 December	
	Year 2	Year 1
Operating activities		
Net income	124,454	114,967
Depreciation and amortization	115,110	111,020
Change in accounts receivable	1,508	452
Change in deferred rents	(5,112)	(4,981)
Change in prepaid expenses and other assets	(5,309)	1,237
Change in accounts payable and other liabilities	19,059	(11,584)
Net cash provided by operating activities	249,710	211,111
Investing activities		
Acquisition of real estate	(111,200)	(22,846)
Capital expenditures on operating real estate	(20,006)	(18,965)
Net cash used in investing activities	(131,206)	(41,811)
Financing activities		
Issuance of mortgages	54,631	14,213

C. Cash flow statements		
Issuance of common shares	58,425	0
Dividends paid to common shareholders	(169,680)	(165,275)
Net cash used in financing activities	(56,624)	(151,062)
Increase (decrease) in cash and equivalents	61,880	18,238
Cash and cash equivalents, beginning of year	23,856	5,618
Cash and cash equivalents, end of year	85,736	23,856

CSC also publishes a supplemental investor packet that provides further disclosures used by the investment community to analyze the company. Exhibit 5 shows its adjustments to arrive at FFO and AFFO, as well as its calculation of dividend payouts based on dividends paid.

Exhibit 5: Capitol Shopping Center REIT Inc. FFO, AFFO, and Dividend Payouts (USD thousands, except per-share data)

	Three Months Ending 31 December		Year Ending 31 December	
	Year 2	Year 1	Year 2	Year 1
Funds from operations				
Net income	32,410	29,599	124,454	114,967
Depreciation and amortization	28,460	27,316	115,110	111,020
Funds from operations	60,870	56,915	239,564	225,987
FFO/share	1.00	0.95	3.95	3.76
Adjusted funds from operations				
Funds from operations	60,870	56,915	239,564	225,987
Less non-cash rents[a]	(1,469)	(1,325)	(5,112)	(4,981)
Less recurring capital expenditures[b]	(5,638)	(5,101)	(20,006)	(18,965)
Adjusted funds from operations	53,763	50,489	214,446	202,041
AFFO/share	0.88	0.84	3.54	3.36
Dividends/share	0.70	0.69	2.80	2.75
Dividend payout ratios				
On FFO	70.0%	72.6%	70.9%	73.1%

	Three Months Ending 31 December		Year Ending 31 December	
	Year 2	Year 1	Year 2	Year 1
On AFFO	79.6%	82.1%	79.1%	81.8%
Weighted average common shares	61,100	60,100	60,600	60,100

[a]*Non-cash rents include the impact of straight-lining contractual rent increases in leases, per accounting rules. The change in deferred rents can often provide the impact of this accounting on rental revenues.*
[b]*Recurring capital expenditures include those costs needed to maintain the revenue-producing ability of existing assets, such as leasing commissions to keep or attract new tenants, such maintenance items as roofs and parking lot repairs, and basic buildouts of space as an inducement to attract tenants.*

The historical stock price and the company's financial statements, including disclosures, are used to complete a simple analysis of the balance sheet, as shown in Exhibit 6.

Exhibit 6: Capitol Shopping Center REIT Inc. Balance Sheet Analysis (USD thousands, except per-share data)

	Year Ending 31 December	
	Year 2	Year 1
Ending debt	1,792,629	1,737,998
Ending stock price	72.36	61.50
Ending shares	61,100	60,100
Ending market capitalization	4,421,196	3,696,150
Debt/total market capitalization	*40.5%*	*47.0%*
Peer group debt/total market capitalization	47.1%	56.7%
All REITs debt/total market capitalization	42.8%	49.6%
EBITDA	340,387	325,160
Interest expense	100,823	99,173
Interest coverage	*3.38×*	*3.28×*
Peer group interest coverage	2.35×	2.16×
All REITs interest coverage	2.58×	2.27×
Ending net debt	1,706,893	1,714,142
EBITDA	340,387	325,160
Net debt-to-EBITDA	*5.01×*	*5.27×*
Peer group net debt-to-EBITDA	7.10×	8.60×
All REITs net debt-to-EBITDA	6.70×	7.80×
Ending net debt	1,706,893	1,714,142
Ending gross real estate	3,761,361	3,630,155

	Year Ending 31 December	
	Year 2	Year 1
Net debt/gross real estate (book)	*45.4%*	*47.2%*
Peer group net debt/ gross real estate (book)	52.8%	55.1%
All REITs net debt/gross real estate (book)	49.6%	52.6%

The previous exhibits provide a historical picture of CCS's financial performance and balance sheet. Some key points about the company's properties, operations, dividend policy, recent business activity, and historical trading attributes follow.

- CSC owns properties that are generally considered defensive in the commercial real estate sector because many of its properties are tenanted by basic necessity goods retailers, such as grocery stores and drug stores.
- CSC's location in the Washington, DC, metropolitan area is generally viewed as favorable for two key reasons: (1) Washington, DC, is the capital of the United States, and the government is the largest driver of employment and has historically provided more stability than the private sector, and (2) the city is a fairly dense area with strict zoning restrictions that make new construction of shopping centers difficult, which limits competing new supply.
- CSC has been able to increase its rents and net operating income by 2%–3% each year, on average, in the past decade.
- The past two reported years (Year 1 and Year 2) were difficult for the broader commercial real estate markets. CSC was able to achieve positive growth while many of its peers saw FFO and AFFO decline. Because forecasts now call for improving fundamental property-level conditions, CSC's portfolio may not have as much "upside" because it did not experience the decline in occupancy and rents that other REITs did.
- In the middle of Year 2, the company purchased a portfolio of three shopping centers from a local developer for a total price of $111.2 million. The return on these assets in the first year is an estimated 6.75%. The company was able to achieve a better going-in cap rate on this acquisition than the market averages of 6.0%–6.25% because of its strong relationships and reputation with tenants, commercial property brokers, and competitors, as well as its ability to act quickly because of its strong balance sheet. In addition, the property is not fully leased, leaving the potential to increase net operating income if CSC can attract additional tenants. CSC funded the purchase with a $54.6 million mortgage at a 6% interest rate and cash from a common stock offering of 1 million shares and from cash on hand.
- The company intends to make additional acquisitions in the future as part of its growth plan. It intends to use a combination of debt, common equity, and internally generated cash to make these purchases. It typically requires the properties it acquires to generate an unleveraged internal rate of return of 9.5% in the form of current yield and capital appreciation over time.
- CSC's balance sheet strategy is to operate at less than 50% debt/market capitalization, with a preference for leverage to be closer to 40%. At year-end 2018, CSC's debt/market capitalization was 40.5% and its interest coverage

was 3.38×. The company's current in-place average debt cost is 5.7%. In comparison, CSC's peers operate at an average leverage level of 47.1% and have an interest coverage ratio of 2.35×.

- CSC's board has chosen a dividend policy that provides an approximate 80% payout of cash flow, or AFFO. This level allows the company to pay an attractive dividend to shareholders, retain some cash flow, provide a cushion in the event of a downturn, and remain in compliance with REIT payout requirements in the United States. It is easily able to meet these REIT payout requirements because the requirements are based on taxable net income, which is calculated after deducting depreciation. In fact, CSC's dividend level has run well in excess of taxable net income, according to comments made by its management.
- Over the last decade, CSC has traded between 9× and 19× FFO, while its peers have traded between 8× and 18×, and all REITs have traded between 7× and 20×. On an AFFO basis, CSC's historical multiple has been 10×–21×, with its peers trading between 9× and 19× and all REITs being in the 9×–24× range.
- Currently, shopping center REITs are estimated to be trading at 7.6% above analyst estimates of NAV. The overall REIT sector is estimated to be trading at a 14.8% premium to estimated NAV.
- CSC's historical beta to the broader equity market is 0.80. The current risk-free rate of return is 4.0%, and the market risk premium is estimated at 5.0%.

Investors and analysts who cover CSC have published estimates for its FFO per share, AFFO per share, and dividends per share for the next three years. Putting the average, or "consensus," of these estimates together with the company's reported results reveals the FFO/AFFO and dividend snapshot shown in Exhibit 7.

Exhibit 7: Capitol Shopping Center REIT Inc. Actual and Estimated Earnings and Dividends (all amounts are per share)

	Year Ending 31 December				
	Yr1A	Yr2A	Yr3E	Yr4E	Yr5E
CSC's FFO/share	$3.76	$3.95	$4.23	$4.59	$4.80
Growth		5.1%	7.1%	8.5%	4.6%
Peer group FFO/share growth		3.4%	6.8%	8.2%	4.2%
All REITs FFO/share growth		1.2%	7.9%	9.8%	10.2%
CSC's AFFO/share	$3.36	$3.54	$3.76	$4.09	$4.31
Growth		5.4%	6.2%	8.8%	5.4%
Peer group AFFO/share growth		−1.0%	6.2%	9.1%	4.8%
All REITs AFFO/share growth		−3.0%	8.1%	9.7%	10.8%
CSC's dividends/share	$2.75	$2.80	$2.98	$3.25	$3.40
Growth		1.8%	6.4%	9.1%	4.6%

	Year Ending 31 December				
	Yr1A	Yr2A	Yr3E	Yr4E	Yr5E
Peer group dividends/ share growth		−2.0%	5.6%	7.9%	5.1%
All REITs dividends/ share growth		−5.0%	7.8%	8.9%	6.0%
CSC's dividend pay-out on AFFO	81.8%	79.1%	79.3%	79.5%	78.9%

Taking the recent stock price of $69.85 per share and focusing on the next two years (as most analysts looking at multiples do), we can determine comparative FFO and AFFO multiples for CSC. Exhibit 8 also includes the multiples of its direct peers and the entire REIT industry.

Exhibit 8: Comparative Multiple Analysis

	P/FFO		P/AFFO	
	Yr3E	Yr4E	Yr3E	Yr4E
Capitol Shopping Center REIT Inc. (CSC)[a]	16.5×	15.2×	18.6×	17.1×
Shopping center–oriented REITs	14.5×	13.3×	16.1×	14.5×
All REITs	14.2×	12.8×	16.5×	14.6×
CSC's premium/(discount) to:				
Shopping center REITs	13.8%	14.3%	15.5%	17.9%
All REITs	16.2%	18.8%	12.7%	17.1%

[a]*Based on a current stock price of $69.85.*

Selection of Valuation Methods

As this discussion demonstrates, different valuation methods can yield different results. Under such circumstances, an analyst should re-examine the assumptions made to investigate why the approaches are generating such different results. The methods selected by an analyst may depend on which ones the analyst believes use the most reliable assumptions, which ones the analyst believes will be used by other investors, or which ones best reflect the analyst's own investment philosophy or view of value. The analyst may choose to use a single valuation approach, a midpoint in the range of values obtained by using several approaches, or a weighted average of the values obtained based on the analyst's view of the relative reliability of the models used to arrive at the values.

6 PRIVATE VS. PUBLIC: A COMPARISON

☐ explain advantages and disadvantages of investing in real estate through publicly traded securities compared to private vehicles

Large institutional and high-net-worth investors have historically pursued private real estate investments through direct ownership, joint ventures, and private fund investments, whereas individual investors, without the resources to invest directly, typically invested in listed property companies. As more real estate companies went public and continued to issue equity to fund acquisitions, developments, and mergers, the market cap of the publicly listed real estate sector rose significantly. This larger market float and liquidity permitted institutional investors to add to their real estate exposure by creating allocations to public real estate companies.

Should investors with the ability to pursue both public *and* private real estate investments choose one over the other? The answer depends on investor objectives, including total return requirements, volatility (risk) tolerance, diversification goals, and the expected returns from each investment. Many institutional investors, such as pension funds and endowments, have chosen to allocate to both.

Both public and private real estate equity investments provide exposure to real estate properties, potentially hedge inflation, deliver attractive risk-adjusted returns, and provide some diversification benefits to stock and bond portfolios.

Listed real estate can play a complementary role in private real estate. Listed real estate's liquidity makes it easier to express a short-term view, such as when markets become too negative on retail and drive shares of public companies below net asset value. When there are sustained valuation differences between public and private real estate, fund and company managers can capture opportunities. If public companies trade well below net asset value, the public companies may choose to go private or sell to private real estate funds. When real estate values are high, public companies can sell real estate to realize gains and private funds may seek exits through the IPO market.

Private real estate investors can pursue a variety of strategies, such as merchant (for sale) development, which is highly restricted for REITs. In some countries, REITs were early movers in specialty sectors, such as self-storage and data centers. Investors wanting exposure to some of these niches had to seek out listed company exposure until the private funds moved into these sectors, often in the search for higher yield.

Private and public real estate investments both have something to offer investors, and each has its drawbacks. Exhibit 9 summarizes some of the key differences, advantages, and disadvantages of public and private real estate investing.

Exhibit 9: Advantages and Disadvantages of Private and Public Real Estate

Private Real Estate (Direct Investment)	Public Real Estate (Equity REITs and Real Estate Operating Companies)
Advantages	
▪ Direct exposure to real estate fundamentals ▪ Stable returns/low volatility ▪ Property performance drives returns ▪ Low correlations with other asset classes ▪ Potential inflation hedge ▪ Control (direct real estate and separate accounts) ▪ Potential to earn illiquidity premium ▪ Wide variety of strategies/few restrictions ▪ Tax benefits (e.g., accelerated depreciation, deferred taxes in some markets when sales are reinvested in other real estate)	▪ Tracks real estate fundamentals over the long term ▪ Liquidity ▪ Access to professional management ▪ Potential inflation hedge ▪ Potential for strong alignment of interests ▪ Tax-efficient structure avoids double taxation (REITs only) ▪ Potential for exposure to diversified portfolios ▪ Access to diverse sectors, including data centers, medical offices, and self-storage ▪ Low investment requirements ▪ Low entry/exit costs ▪ No special investor qualifications beyond equity investing generally ▪ Limited liability ▪ Greater regulation and investor protections ▪ High transparency
Disadvantages	
▪ Low liquidity ▪ Difficult-to-exit funds' redemption activity is high ▪ High fees and expenses ▪ Appraisal valuations commonly lag changes in market conditions ▪ Fewer regulations to protect investors ▪ Some managers focus on asset gathering over high profitability ▪ High investment minimums and high-net-worth requirements ▪ Low transparency ▪ High returns often derived from leverage	▪ High volatility (compared with private real estate) ▪ Equity market correlation is high in short term ▪ REIT structure limits possible activities ▪ Stock prices may not reflect underlying property values (i.e., trade at discount to NAV) ▪ Dividends taxed at high current income tax rates ▪ Regulatory compliance costs are prohibitive for small companies ▪ Poor governance/mis-aligned interests can penalize stock performance ▪ Equity markets often penalize companies with high leverage

QUESTION SET

1. Which of the following assets requires the *most* expertise in real estate on the part of the investor?

   A. An REOC share

   B. An equity REIT share

   C. A direct investment in a single property

   Solution:

   C is correct. Direct investment in a single property requires a high level of real estate expertise. Investment in publicly traded equity investments (in REITs or REOCs) requires much less expertise because investors benefit from having their property interests actively managed on their behalf by professional managers and from having their business interests overseen and guided by boards of directors, as in the case of all public corporations.

2. Which of the following has the *most* operating and financial flexibility?

   A. An REOC

   B. An equity REIT

   C. A direct investment in a single property

   Solution:

   A is correct. REOCs are free to invest in any kind of real estate or related activity without limitation. This freedom gives management the opportunity to create more value in development activity and in trading real estate and to retain as much of their income as they believe is appropriate. A wider range of capital structures and degrees of financial leverage may be used in the process. In contrast to REOCs, REITs face restrictions on the amount of income and assets accounted for by activities other than collecting rent and interest payments. Direct investment is less liquid and divisible than REOC and REIT shares, which limits the operational flexibility of such investment.

3. Investors seeking broad diversification would invest in the securities of which of the following companies?

   A. A company that owns multi-family rental properties in Hong Kong SAR

   B. A company that owns large office properties in New York City, San Francisco, Los Angeles, and Chicago

   C. A company with a mix of office and retail properties in urban and suburban markets

   Solution:

   C is correct. It should be clear that a company with a mix of assets—office and retail—with exposure to urban and suburban markets offers the best diversification. A is incorrect because the company has only one type of asset, multi-family rentals, in one market, Hong Kong SAR. The systematic risk is high for that portfolio. B is incorrect because the company owns only one asset type, office properties, and the economic activity correlation may be high among urban cities with exposure to global trade and the financial sector.

Alternatively, investors looking for property and market diversification might, instead of the solutions provided, consider investing in a few large companies that own different asset types in multiple cities or several pure-play companies, each of which concentrates on a single asset type in its given region, if the companies' regions and product type do not overlap to a large extent.

4. Which of the following best represents an advantage of REITs over a direct investment in an income-producing property?

   A. Diversification—of property holdings

   B. Operating flexibility

   C. Diversification—of overall portfolio

   Solution:

   A is correct. REITs provide diversification of property holdings. B is incorrect because REITs do face restrictions on the amount of income and assets accounted for by activities other than collecting rent and interest payments; these restrictions can prevent a REIT from maximizing its returns. C is incorrect because as shares of REITs are publicly traded, their price is partly determined by stock market movements and market liquidity, reducing the diversification benefits to an overall portfolio as compared with private real estate.

The following information relates to questions 5-6

Two real estate investors are each choosing from among the following investment types: an REOC, an equity REIT, and a direct investment in an income-producing property. Investor A's primary objective is liquidity, and Investor B's primary objective is maximum growth/capital gain potential. State and explain which real estate investment type best suits:

5. Investor A.

   Solution:

   For Investor A, with a liquidity objective, REOC and REIT investments are most appropriate because REOCs and REITs are traded on stock exchanges and are more liquid. Direct investments in income-producing property are generally less liquid.

6. Investor B.

   Solution:

   For Investor B, with a maximum growth objective, REOCs and direct property investment are most appropriate because REOCs and direct investors are free to invest in any kind of real estate or related activity without limitation and to reinvest as much of their income as they believe is appropriate for their objectives. This freedom gives them the opportunity to create more value in development activity and in trading real estate. REITs' constraints prevent them from retaining earnings to reinvest, so their growth opportunities are more limited.

   There are several caveats to note for each generalized solution. Shares of closely held listed companies with low market float that trade infrequently may not offer the desired liquidity. Management quality, corporate governance, balance-sheet capacity and leverage, attractive investment and reinvestment opportunities, and many other considerations matter greatly when it comes to selecting the vehicle and company that are best at delivering growth and value to shareholders.

7. Which of the following is the *best* measure of a REIT's current economic return to shareholders?

   A. FFO

   B. AFFO

   C. Net income

   Solution:

   B is correct. AFFO is calculated from FFO by deducting non-cash rent, capital expenditures for maintenance, and leasing costs.

   A is incorrect because it does not account for non-cash rent, capital expenditures for maintenance, and leasing costs. C is incorrect because it includes non-cash depreciation and amortization expense and does not account for non-cash rent, capital expenditures, and capitalized leasing costs, which are appropriate adjustments to net income in calculating current economic return.

8. An analyst gathers the following information for a REIT:

Net operating income	$115 million
Book value of properties	$1,005 million
Market value of debt outstanding	$505 million
Market cap rate	7%
Shares outstanding	100 million

   The REIT's NAV per share is *closest* to:

   A. $10.05.

   B. $11.38.

   C. $16.42.

   Solution:

   B is correct. NAVPS estimates real estate values by capitalizing NOI. Valuing $115 million of NOI with a capitalization rate of 7% yields a value for the properties of $1,642,857,000. After deducting $505 million of debt at market value, NAV is $1,137,857,000; NAVPS equals NAV divided by 100 million shares outstanding, or $11.38.

   A is incorrect because it is the book value of the assets (not the net assets) per share: $1,005 million divided by 100 million shares = $10.05 per share. It does not take into account the market value of the assets and does not deduct debt. C is incorrect because it is the market value of the real estate—that is, NOI capitalized at 7%, divided by 100 million shares: $1,642,857,000/100,000,000 = $16.42. This calculation excludes the liabilities of the entity.

9. All else equal, estimated NAV per share will decrease with an increase in the:

   A. capitalization rate.

   B. estimated growth rate.

C. deferred tax liabilities.

Solution:

A is correct. The capitalization rate is used to calculate the estimated value of operating real estate because it is the NOI as a percentage of the value of operating real estate: NOI/Capitalization rate = Estimated value. As the capitalization rate increases, the estimated value of operating real estate and thus NAV will decrease.

B is incorrect because an increase in the estimated growth rate would increase the estimated NOI and the estimated value of operating income. C is incorrect because deferred liabilities are not counted as "hard" liabilities and are not subtracted from the NAV.

10. An increase in the capitalization rate will *most likely* decrease a REIT's:

A. cost of debt.

B. estimated NOI.

C. estimated NAV.

Solution:

C is correct. The capitalization rate is used to estimate the market value of real estate, which is then used to calculate NAV.

A is incorrect because a higher capitalization rate does not decrease the REIT's cost of debt. B is incorrect because the estimated NOI is based on income growth, not the capitalization rate.

11. An analyst gathers the following information for a REIT:

Non-cash (straight-line) rent	€207,430
Depreciation	€611,900
Recurring maintenance-type capital expenditures and leasing commissions	€550,750
Adjusted funds from operations	€3,320,000
AFFO per share	€3.32

The REIT's FFO per share is *closest* to:

A. €3.93.

B. €4.08.

C. €4.48.

Solution:

B is correct. FFO = AFFO + Non-cash (straight-line) rent + Recurring maintenance-type capital expenditures and leasing commissions = 3,320,000 + 550,750 + 207,430 = €4,078,180. The number of shares outstanding = 3,320,000/3.32 = 1,000,000. FFO per share = 4,078,180/1,000,000 ≈ €4.08.

A is incorrect because it adds depreciation to AFFO (3,320,000 + 611,900 = €3,931,900; 3,931,900/1,000,000 ≈ €3.93 per share). C is incorrect because it also adds depreciation to AFFO + Non-cash (straight-line) rent + Recurring maintenance-type capital expenditures and leasing commissions.

12. Which of the following estimates is *least likely* to be compiled by firms that publish REIT analysts' estimates?

A. FFO

B. AFFO

C. NAV

Solution:

B is correct. Firms that compile statistics and estimates of REITs tend not to gather AFFO estimates because of the absence of a universally accepted methodology for computing AFFO and inconsistent corporate reporting of actual AFFO figures. FFO is commonly tracked in the United States, and NAV is the standard measure in Europe and Asia.

13. If the outlook for economic growth turns negative and property market transaction volumes decline, it is *least likely* that CSC's:

A. P/FFO and P/AFFO would be lower.

B. relative P/FFO and P/AFFO multiples would be higher than those of peers.

C. NAV would become the most useful valuation method.

Solution:

C is correct. NAV becomes more subjective in a negative and less liquid market with fewer observable transactions, and thus this basis of valuation becomes less useful and reliable.

A and B are incorrect because P/FFO and P/AFFO are likely to fall in a negative economic environment, but investors may be willing to pay a relative premium for CSC's stock based on its superior stability in economically challenging times. Thus, P/FFO and P/AFFO are likely to be higher than those of peers.

14. If other REITs have no land on their balance sheets, how is CSC's "Land held for future development" *best* factored into a relative P/FFO or P/AFFO multiple valuation?

A. There should be no impact on multiples as a result of land value.

B. CSC would warrant lower multiples to account for land value.

C. CSC would warrant higher multiples to account for land value.

Solution:

C is correct. Although it may not produce income that contributes to FFO or AFFO, the land has value and represents a source of greater internal growth potential. For that reason, A and B are incorrect.

15. An analyst speaks with private market real estate investors and learns that because interest rates have just increased 200 bps, buyers will require future property acquisitions to have going-in cap rates that are 100 bps to 200 bps higher than those on recent property market transactions. The analyst's estimate of NAV for CSC *most likely*:

A. increases as cap rates are higher.

B. decreases as cap rates are higher.

C. remains the same unless CSC has debt maturing in the near term.

Solution:

B is correct. Estimated real estate value decreases as the cap rate increases. Because NAV is derived directly from estimated real estate value, it also decreases. For this reason, A is incorrect. C is incorrect because an increase in cap rates decreases asset values. The fact that CSC has debt maturing in the near term is not a key factor influencing NAV.

16. An analyst determines that CSC purchased its "Land held for future development" 15 years ago and that on average, land values at that time were one-third of what they are today. Which of the following *best* adjusts NAV to reflect this consideration?

A. The cap rate on operating assets should be changed.

B. Land value and thus NAV should be adjusted higher to reflect today's valuations.

C. NAV is still mainly a representation of book values; thus, there should be no adjustments.

Solution:

B is correct. An analyst tries to attribute market values to real property owned.

A is incorrect because the cap rate used by analysts in calculating NAVs represents the return on only the income-producing asset portfolio and does not relate to land holdings that are not currently producing any income. C is incorrect because NAV is not a representation of book values, which rely on accounting methodology rather than market values.

17. Zoning in CSC's real estate markets has changed to allow more new space in the future, dampening CSC's long-term FFO growth by about 0.5%. The effect on CSC's valuation using a dividend discount model is *most likely* that the present value of the dividend stream:

A. decreases because of lower growth.

B. remains the same.

C. increases because of the new supply.

Solution:

A is correct. Lower growth affects the projected dividend stream, decreasing its present value. For that reason, B and C are incorrect.

18. An analyst gathers the following information for two REITs:

	Price/NAV	Capitalization Rate Used in NAV
REIT A	100%	6%
REIT B	99%	8%

If the REITs have similar property portfolio values, interest expense, and corporate overhead, which REIT *most likely* has the higher price/FFO?

A. REIT A

B. REIT B

C. They will have similar levels of P/FFO because their ratios of price to NAV are almost identical.

Solution:

A is correct. If both companies have similar portfolio values as indicated in the text and by the similar P/NAV, then the company with the lower capitalization rate is more expensive, which results in lower FFO and hence a higher P/FFO. If each company were worth ¥100, then REIT A, which is valued at a 6% cap rate, would have ¥6 of NOI and REIT B would have ¥8 of NOI. Because interest expense and overhead are similar for both companies, REIT A would also have lower FFO and a correspondingly higher P/FFO multiple.

B is incorrect because A has a lower capitalization rate, implying a lower FFO and hence a higher P/FFO if P/NAV for each company is similar, which is the case here.

C is incorrect because it neglects the effect of the lower capitalization rate of REIT A.

PRACTICE PROBLEMS

The following information relates to questions 1-4

Maitha Smith is the chief investment officer of the Westland Pension Fund (the "Fund"). Smith and her junior analyst are analyzing Bay Realty Corp. ("Bay"), a publicly traded REIT based in San Francisco, for a potential investment. Bay currently owns and operates 40 office buildings totaling 8 million square feet. These properties exhibit an average LTV (loan-to-value) ratio of 40%. Bay owns no other real estate–related assets. Bay's senior executives are company employees who report to the board of directors, whose members are elected by shareholders.

Smith first instructs her junior analyst to conduct an NAVPS (net asset value per share) analysis on Bay. The junior analyst makes the following three statements:

Statement 1: NAVPS should not include investors' assessments of the value of any non-asset-based income streams, the value of non–real estate assets, or the value added by management.

Statement 2: REITs whose shares trade below NAVPS or have high leverage might have a more difficult time raising new capital to fund acquisitions and development, which could limit long-term growth.

Statement 3: Shares priced at discounts to NAVPS are interpreted as indications of potential overvaluation.

To complement the NAVPS, Smith instructs her junior analyst to also calculate FFO and AFFO measures for Bay. The junior analyst then makes the following three statements as part of the ongoing discussion:

Statement 4: AFFO better approximates a company's sustainable dividend-paying capacity than FFO.

Statement 5: FFO and AFFO are based on net income available to equity and thus represent levered income.

Statement 6: FFO is superior to AFFO as a measure of economic income and thus economic return because it takes into account the capital expenditures necessary to maintain the economic income of a property portfolio.

After the discussion, the junior analyst obtains selected information on Bay, which is shown in Exhibit 1:

Exhibit 1

Non-cash (straight-line) rent	$215,000
Recurring maintenance–type capital expenditures and leasing commissions	$700,000
Adjusted funds from operations	$4,000,000
AFFO per share	$5.00
Current stock price	$80.00

1. Which of the following *best* describes Bay?

   A. Mortgage REIT

B. Internally managed REIT

C. Real estate operating company (REOC)

2. Which of the junior analyst's three statements regarding NAVPS is correct?

   A. Statement 1

   B. Statement 2

   C. Statement 3

3. Which of the junior analyst's three statements regarding FFO and AFFO is *incorrect*?

   A. Statement 4

   B. Statement 5

   C. Statement 6

4. Based on Exhibit 1, Bay's P/FFO is *closest* to:

   A. 14.3×.

   B. 13.0×.

   C. 20.7×.

The following information relates to questions 5-10

Hui Lin, CFA, is an investment manager looking to diversify his portfolio by adding equity real estate investments. Lin and his investment analyst, Maria Nowak, are discussing whether they should invest in publicly traded real estate investment trusts or public real estate operating companies. Nowak expresses a strong preference for investing in public REITs in taxable accounts.

Lin schedules a meeting to discuss this matter, and for the meeting, Lin asks Nowak to gather data on three specific REITs and come prepared to explain her preference for public REITs over public REOCs. At the meeting, Lin asks Nowak, "Why do you prefer to invest in public REITs over public REOCs for taxable accounts?"

Nowak provides Lin with an explanation for her preference of public REITs and provides Lin with data on the three REITs shown in Exhibit 1 and Exhibit 2.

The meeting concludes with Lin directing Nowak to identify the key investment characteristics along with the principal risks of each REIT and to investigate the valuation of the three REITs. Specifically, Lin asks Nowak to value each REIT using four different methodologies:

Valuation Method 1: Net asset value

Valuation Method 2: Discounted cash flow valuation using a two-step dividend model

Valuation Method 3: Relative valuation using property subsector average P/FFO multiple

Valuation Method 4: Relative valuation using property subsector average P/

AFFO multiple

Exhibit 1: Select REIT Financial Information

	REIT A	REIT B	REIT C
Property subsector	Office	Storage	Health Care
Estimated 12-month cash net operating income	$350,000	$267,000	$425,000
Funds from operations	$316,965	$290,612	$368,007
Cash and equivalents	$308,700	$230,850	$341,000
Accounts receivable	$205,800	$282,150	$279,000
Debt and other liabilities	$2,014,000	$2,013,500	$2,010,000
Non-cash rents	$25,991	$24,702	$29,808
Recurring maintenance–type capital expenditures	$63,769	$60,852	$80,961
Shares outstanding	56,100	67,900	72,300

Exhibit 2: REIT Dividend Forecasts and Average Price Multiples

	REIT A	REIT B	REIT C
Expected annual dividend next year	$3.80	$2.25	$4.00
Dividend growth rate in Years 2 and 3	4.0%	5.0%	4.5%
Dividend growth rate (after Year 3 into perpetuity)	3.5%	4.5%	4.0%
Assumed cap rate	7.0%	6.25%	6.5%
Property subsector average P/FFO multiple	14.4×	13.5×	15.1×
Property subsector average P/AFFO multiple	18.3×	17.1×	18.9×

Note: Nowak estimates an 8% cost of equity capital for all REITs and a risk-free rate of 4.0%.

5. Nowak's *most likely* response to Lin's question is that the type of real estate security she prefers:

   A. offers a high degree of operating flexibility.

   B. provides dividend income that is exempt from double taxation.

   C. has below-average correlations with overall stock market returns.

6. Based on Exhibit 1 and Exhibit 2, the value per share for REIT A using valuation Method 1 is *closest* to:
   A. $51.26.
   B. $62.40.
   C. $98.30.

7. Based on Exhibit 1 and Exhibit 2, the value per share of REIT B using Valuation Method 3 is *closest* to:
   A. $40.77.
   B. $57.78.
   C. $73.19.

8. Based on Exhibit 2, the value per share of REIT C using Valuation Method 2 is *closest* to:
   A. $55.83.
   B. $97.57.
   C. $100.91.

9. Based on Exhibit 1 and Exhibit 2, the value per share of REIT A using Valuation Method 4 is *closest* to:
   A. $58.32.
   B. $74.12.
   C. $103.40.

10. The risk factor *most likely* to adversely affect an investment in REIT B is:
    A. new competitive facilities.
    B. tenants' sales per square foot.
    C. obsolescence of existing space.

The following information relates to questions 11-16

Tim Wang is a financial adviser specializing in commercial real estate investing. He is meeting with Mark Caudill, a new client who is looking to diversify his investment portfolio by adding real estate investments. Caudill has heard about various investment vehicles related to real estate from his friends and is seeking a more in-depth understanding of these investments from Wang.

Wang begins the meeting by advising Caudill of four options that are available when investing in real estate, including the following:

Option 1. Direct ownership in real estate

Option 2. Publicly traded real estate investment trusts

Option 3. Publicly traded real estate operating companies

Option 4. Publicly traded residential mortgage-backed securities

Wang next asks Caudill about his investment preferences. Caudill responds by telling Wang that he prefers to invest in equity securities that are highly liquid, provide high income, and are not subject to double taxation.

Caudill asks Wang how the economic performance of REITs and REOCs is evaluated and how their shares are valued. Wang advises Caudill there are multiple measures of economic performance for REITs and REOCs, including the following:

Measure 1. Net operating income

Measure 2. Funds from operations

Measure 3. Adjusted funds from operations

In response, Caudill asks Wang,

"Which of the three measures is the best measure of a REIT's current economic return to shareholders?"

To help Caudill's understanding of valuation, Wang presents Caudill with data on Baldwin, a health care REIT that primarily invests in independent and assisted senior housing communities in large cities across the United States. Selected financial data on Baldwin for the past two years are provided in Exhibit 1.

Exhibit 1: Baldwin REIT Summarized Income Statement (USD thousands, except per-share data)

	Year Ending 31 December	
	2019	2018
Rental income	339,009	296,777
Other property income	6,112	4,033
Total income	345,121	300,810
Rental expenses		
Property operating expenses	19,195	14,273
Property taxes	3,610	3,327
Total property expenses	22,805	17,600
Net operating income	322,316	283,210
Other income (gains on sale of properties)	2,162	1,003
General and administrative expenses	21,865	19,899
Depreciation and amortization	90,409	78,583
Net interest expenses	70,017	56,404
Net income	142,187	129,327
Weighted average shares outstanding	121,944	121,863
Earnings per share	1.17	1.06

	Year Ending 31 December	
	2019	**2018**
Dividend per share	0.93	0.85
Price/FFO, based on year-end stock price	11.5×	12.7×

Before the meeting, Wang had put together some valuation assumptions for Baldwin in anticipation of discussing valuation with Caudill. Wang explains the process of valuing a REIT share using discounted cash flow analysis, and he proceeds to estimate the value of Baldwin on a per-share basis using a two-step dividend discount model using the data provided in Exhibit 2.

Exhibit 2: Baldwin Valuation Projections and Assumptions

Current risk-free rate	4.0%
Baldwin beta	0.90
Market risk premium	5.0%
Appropriate discount rate (CAPM)	8.5%
Expected dividend per share, 1 year from today	$1.00
Expected dividend per share, 2 years from today	$1.06
Long-term growth rate in dividends, starting in Year 3	5.0%

11. Based on Caudill's investment preferences, the type of real estate investment Wang is *most likely* to recommend to Caudill is:

    A. Option 2.

    B. Option 3.

    C. Option 4.

12. Relative to Option 2 and Option 3, an advantage of investing in Option 1 is:

    A. greater liquidity.

    B. lower investment requirements.

    C. greater control over property-level investment decisions.

13. The Baldwin REIT is *least likely* to experience long-run negative effects from:

    A. an economic recession.

    B. an unfavorable change in population demographics.

    C. a major reduction in government funding of health care.

14. The *most appropriate* response to Caudill's question is:

    A. Measure 1.

B. Measure 2.

C. Measure 3.

15. Based on Exhibit 1, the 2019 year-end share price of Baldwin was *closest* to:

A. \$13.23.

B. \$21.73.

C. \$30.36.

16. Based on Exhibit 2, the intrinsic value of the Baldwin REIT on a per share basis using the two-step dividend discount model is *closest* to:

A. \$26.72.

B. \$27.59.

C. \$28.76.

SOLUTIONS

1. B is correct. Bay is internally managed, or self-managed. Bay's senior executives are company employees who report to the board of directors, whose members are elected by shareholders. Fully integrated REITs, such as Bay, generally have fewer conflicts than REITs that are externally advised or externally managed.

   A is incorrect because Bay is an equity REIT, not a mortgage REIT. Bay currently owns and operates 40 office buildings totaling 8 million square feet.

   C is incorrect because REOCs are ordinary taxable real estate ownership companies, which are different from REITs. Businesses are organized as REOCs, as opposed to REITs, if they are located in countries that do not have a tax-advantaged REIT regime in place, if they engage to a large extent in the development of for-sale real estate properties, or if they offer other non-qualifying services, such as brokerage and third-party property management.

2. B is correct. REITs whose shares trade below NAVPS or have high leverage might have a more difficult time raising new capital to fund acquisitions and development, which in turn could limit long-term growth, in contrast to REITs that trade at or above NAVPS.

   A is incorrect because NAVPS should include investors' assessments of the value of any non-asset-based income streams, the value of non–real estate assets, and the value added by management.

   C is incorrect because shares priced at discounts to NAVPS are interpreted as indications of potential undervaluation.

3. C is the correct choice because Statement 6 is incorrect. AFFO is superior to FFO (not the other way around) as a measure of economic income and thus economic return because it takes into account the capital expenditures necessary to maintain the economic income of a property portfolio.

   A is not the correct choice because Statement 4 is true. AFFO better approximates a company's sustainable dividend-paying capacity than FFO.

   B is not the correct choice because Statement 5 is true. Both FFO and AFFO are based on net income available to equity and thus represent levered income.

4. B is correct. FFO = AFFO + Non-cash (straight-line) rent + Recurring maintenance–type capital expenditures and leasing commissions = \$4,000,000 + \$215,000 + \$700,000 = \$4,915,000. The number of shares outstanding = 4,000,000/5.00 = 800,000. FFO per share = \$4,915,000/800,000 = \$6.14.

   Current stock price = \$80.00 per share.

   P/FFO = \$80.00/\$6.14 = 13.0×.

   A is incorrect because 14.3× is incorrectly calculated as follows:

   \$4,000,000 – \$215,000 + \$700,000 = \$4,485,000. The number of shares outstanding = 4,000,000/5.00 = 800,000. FFO per share = \$4,485,000/800,000 = \$5.61.

   Current stock price = \$80.00 per share.

   P/FFO = \$80.00/\$5.61 = 14.3×.

   C is incorrect because 20.7× is incorrectly calculated as follows:

   \$4,000,000 – \$215,000 – \$700,000 = \$3,085,000. The number of shares outstanding = 4,000,000/5.00 = 800,000. FFO per share = \$3,085,000/800,000 = \$3.86.

   Current stock price = \$80.00 per share.

   P/FFO = \$80.00/\$3.86 = 20.7×.

5. B is correct. REITs are tax-advantaged entities, whereas REOC securities are not

typically tax-advantaged entities. More specifically, REITs are typically exempt from the double taxation of income that comes from taxes being due at the corporate level and again when dividends or distributions are made to shareholders in some jurisdictions, such as the United States.

6. B is correct. The NAV is $62.40.

Estimated cash NOI	350,000
Assumed cap rate	0.07
Estimated value of operating real estate (350,000/0.07)	5,000,000
Plus: Cash + accounts receivable	514,500
Less: Debt and other liabilities	2,014,000
Net asset value	3,500,500
Shares outstanding	56,100
NAV/share	**$62.40**

7. B is correct. The value per share is $57.78, calculated as follows:

   Funds from operations = $290,612.

   Shares outstanding = 67,900 shares.

   FFO/share = $290,612/67,900 shares = $4.28.

   Applying the property subsector average P/FFO multiple of 13.5× yields a value per share of

   $4.28 × 13.5 = $57.78.

8. C is correct. The value per share for REIT C is $100.91.

		Step 1		Step 2
	Year 1	Year 2	Year 3	Year 4
Dividends per share	$4.00	$4.18	$4.37	$4.54
Value of stock at end of 2013[a]			$113.57	
			$117.94	
Discount rate: 8.00%				
Net present value of all dividends:[b] $100.91				

[a]*Calculated as* $\$4.54/(0.08 - 0.04) = \$113.57$.
[b]*Calculated as* $\$4.00/(1.08) + \$4.18/(1.08)^2 + \$117.94/(1.08)^3 = \$100.91$.

9. B is correct. The value per share is $74.11, calculated as follows:

   Funds from operations (FFO) = $316,965.

   Less: Non-cash rents: $25,991

   Less: Recurring maintenance–type capital expenditures: $63,769

   Equals AFFO: $227,205

   Shares outstanding = 56,100 shares.

AFFO/share = $227,205/56,100 shares = $4.05.

Applying the property subsector average P/AFFO multiple of 18.3× yields a value per share of

$4.05 × 18.3 = $74.12.

10. A is correct. As a storage REIT, this investment faces competitive pressures because the ease of entry into the field of self-storage properties can lead to periods of overbuilding.

11. A is correct. Option 2 (publicly traded REITs) best satisfies Caudill's investment preferences. REITs are equity investments that, in general, are income tax exempt at the corporate/trust level, so there is no double income taxation. To qualify for the income tax exemption, REITs are legally obligated to pay out a high percentage of taxable income to their shareholders, which typically results in relatively high dividend income for investors. Lastly, public REITs are generally liquid because they are traded in stock exchanges.

12. C is correct. Direct property ownership offers greater control over property-level investment decisions compared with the level of control exhibited by shareholders in REITs and REOCs.

13. A is correct. Baldwin, a health care REIT, is largely resistant to economic recessions but is exposed to changes in population demographics and changes in government funding for health care.

14. C is correct. Measure 3, adjusted funds from operations, is a refinement of FFO that is designed to be a more accurate measure of current economic income. In essence, FFO is adjusted to remove any non-cash rent and to include a provision for maintenance-type capital expenditures and leasing costs. Maintenance expenses are required for a business to continue as a going concern.

15. B is correct. Baldwin's FFO per share in 2019 was $1.89, and the resulting share price was $21.73. First, calculate FFO per share in 2019, and then apply the year-end P/FFO multiple of 11.5×.

    FFO = accounting net earnings, excluding (a) depreciation charges on real estate, (b) deferred tax charges, and (c) gains or losses from sales of property and debt restructuring.

    2019 accounting net income: $142,187

    2019 depreciation charges: $90,409

    2019 deferred tax charges: na

    2019 gains on sale of properties (other income): $2,162

    2019 shares outstanding: 121,944

    2019 year-end price/FFO = 11.5×.

    2019 Baldwin FFO per share = ($142,187 + $90,409 – $2,162)/121,944 shares = $1.89. At the given 2019 year-end price/FFO multiple of 11.5×, this results in a share price for Baldwin of $1.89 × 11.5

    = $21.73.

16. C is correct. The estimated value per share for the Baldwin REIT using a two-step

dividend discount model is \$28.76, calculated as follows:

	Step 1		Step 2
	Year 1	Year 2	Year 3
Dividends per share	\$1.00	\$1.06	\$1.11
Value of stock at end of Year 2[a]		\$31.71	
		\$32.77	
Discount rate: 8.50%			
Net present value of all dividends:[b] \$28.76			

[a]*Calculated as \$1.11/(0.085 – 0.05) = \$31.71.*
[b]*Calculated as \$1.00/(1.085) + \$32.77/(1.085)^2 = \$28.76.*

LEARNING MODULE

4

Hedge Fund Strategies

by Barclay T. Leib, CFE, CAIA, Kathryn M. Kaminski, PhD, CAIA, and Mila Getmansky Sherman, PhD.

Barclay T. Leib, CFE, CAIA, is at Sand Spring Advisors LLC (USA). Kathryn M. Kaminski, PhD, CAIA, is at Alpha Simplex Group, LLC (USA). Mila Getmansky Sherman, PhD, is at Isenberg School of Management, UMASS Amherst (USA).

LEARNING OUTCOMES

Mastery	*The candidate should be able to:*
☐	discuss how hedge fund strategies may be classified
☐	discuss investment characteristics, strategy implementation, and role in a portfolio of equity-related hedge fund strategies
☐	discuss investment characteristics, strategy implementation, and role in a portfolio of event-driven hedge fund strategies
☐	discuss investment characteristics, strategy implementation, and role in a portfolio of relative value hedge fund strategies
☐	discuss investment characteristics, strategy implementation, and role in a portfolio of opportunistic hedge fund strategies
☐	discuss investment characteristics, strategy implementation, and role in a portfolio of specialist hedge fund strategies
☐	discuss investment characteristics, strategy implementation, and role in a portfolio of multi-manager hedge fund strategies
☐	describe how factor models may be used to understand hedge fund risk exposures
☐	evaluate the impact of an allocation to a hedge fund strategy in a traditional investment portfolio

INTRODUCTION AND CLASSIFICATION OF HEDGE FUND STRATEGIES — 1

☐	discuss how hedge fund strategies may be classified

Hedge funds form an important subset of the alternative investments opportunity set, but they come with many pros and cons in their use and application across different asset classes and investment approaches. The basic tradeoff is whether the added fees typically involved with hedge fund investing result in sufficient additional alpha and portfolio diversification benefits to justify the high fee levels. This is an ongoing industry debate.

Some argue that investing in hedge funds is a key way to access the very best investment talent—those individuals who can adroitly navigate investment opportunities across a potentially wider universe of markets. Others argue that hedge funds are important because the alpha that may be produced in down markets is hard to source elsewhere.

The arguments against hedge funds are also non-trivial. In addition to the high fee levels, the complex offering memorandum documentation needs to be understood by investors (i.e., the limited partners). Other issues include lack of full underlying investment transparency/attribution, higher cost allocations associated with the establishment and maintenance of the fund investment structures, and generally longer–lived investment commitment periods with limited redemption availability.

In addition, each hedge fund strategy area tends to introduce different types of added portfolio risks. For example, to achieve meaningful return objectives, arbitrage-oriented hedge fund strategies tend to utilize significant leverage that can be dangerous to limited partner investors, especially during periods of market stress. Long/short equity and event-driven strategies may have less beta exposure than simple, long-only beta allocations, but the higher hedge fund fees effectively result in a particularly expensive form of embedded beta. Such strategies as managed futures or global macro investing may introduce natural benefits of asset class and investment approach diversification, but they come with naturally higher volatility in the return profiles typically delivered. Extreme tail risk in portfolios may be managed with the inclusion of relative value volatility or long volatility strategies, but it comes at the cost of a return drag during more normal market periods. In other words, some hedge fund strategies may have higher portfolio diversification benefits, while others may simply be return enhancers rather than true portfolio diversifiers. Many hedge fund strategies employ leverage to amplify their asset base and to increase their returns, through the combination of margin, highly levered derivatives, and other highly leveraged investment strategies.

Also, the hedge fund industry continues to evolve in its overall structure. Over the past decade, traditional limited partnership formats have been supplemented by offerings of liquid alternatives (liquid alts)—which are mutual fund, closed-end fund, and ETF-type vehicles that invest in various hedge fund-like strategies. Liquid alts are meant to provide daily liquidity, transparency, and lower fees while opening hedge fund investing to a wider range of investors. However, empirical evidence shows that liquid alts significantly underperform similar strategy hedge funds, which suggests that traditional hedge funds may be benefiting from an illiquidity premium phenomenon that cannot be easily transported into a mutual fund format. Since these liquid alternatives are often subjected to meeting certain regulatory criteria, their inherent structures restrict the use of highly risky, illiquid investment strategies and alternatives.

Investors must understand the various subtleties involved with investing in hedge funds. Notably, as demonstrated by the endowment model of investing, placing hedge funds as a core allocation can increase net returns and reduce risk.

This learning module presents the investment characteristics and implementation for the major categories of hedge fund strategies. It also provides a framework for classifying and evaluating these strategies based on their risk profiles. Section 1 summarizes some distinctive regulatory and investment characteristics of hedge funds and discusses ways to classify hedge fund strategies. Sections 2 through 12 present investment characteristics and strategy implementation for each of the following hedge fund strategy categories: equity-related; event-driven; relative value; opportunistic; specialist; and multi-manager strategies. Section 13 introduces a conditional factor model as a unifying framework for understanding and analyzing the risk exposures of these strategies. Section 16 evaluates the contributions of each hedge fund strategy to the return and risk profile of a traditional portfolio of stocks and bonds. The reading concludes with a summary.

Classification of Hedge Funds and Strategies

The most important characteristics of hedge funds are summarized as follows:

1. **Legal/Regulatory Overview:** Different countries have varying requirements for investor eligibility to access hedge fund investments. These regulations are typically intended to limit access to traditional hedge funds to sophisticated investors with a minimum income or net-worth requirement, and they allow hedge fund managers to accept only a limited number of investment subscriptions. Most traditional hedge funds in the United States are offered effectively as private placement offerings. Whether the underlying fund manager must register with regulatory authorities depends on assets under management (AUM); however, regardless of AUM, all US hedge funds are subject to regulatory oversight against fraudulent conduct. Hedge funds offered in other jurisdictions—attractive, tax-neutral locales like the Cayman Islands, the British Virgin Islands, or Bermuda—are typically presented to investors as stand-alone corporate entities subject to the rules and regulations of the particular locality.

   From a regulatory perspective, the advent of liquid alts has likely caused the greatest shift in the industry over the past decade. Some of the more liquid hedge fund strategies that meet certain liquidity and diversification requirements (generally long/short equity and managed futures strategies) are offered by many fund sponsors in mutual fund-type structures in the United States and in the undertakings for collective investment in transferable securities (UCITs) format in Europe and Asia. By law, these liquid alts vehicles can be more widely marketed to retail investors. Whereas traditional hedge funds typically offer only limited periodic liquidity, liquid alts funds may be redeemed by investors on a daily basis. Also, traditional hedge funds typically involve both a management fee and an incentive fee; however, liquid alts in most countries are prohibited from charging an incentive fee.

   Finally, the overall regulatory constraints for hedge funds are far less than those for regulated investment vehicles—except for the liquid alts versions, which have much higher constraints to provide liquidity to investors.
2. **Flexible Mandates—Few Investment Constraints:** Given the relatively low legal and regulatory constraints faced by hedge funds, their mandates are flexible; thus, they are relatively unhindered in their trading and investment activities in terms of investable asset classes and securities, risk exposures, and collateral. The fund prospectus (i.e., offering memorandum) will specify the hedge fund's mandate and objectives and will include constraints, if any, on investment in certain asset classes as well as in the use of leverage, shorting, and derivatives.
3. **Large Investment Universe:** Lower regulatory constraints and flexible mandates give hedge funds access to a wide range of assets outside the normal set of traditional investments. Examples include private securities, non-investment-grade debt, distressed securities, derivatives, and more-esoteric contracts, such as life insurance contracts and even music or film royalties.

4. **Aggressive Investment Styles:** Hedge funds may use their typically flexible investment mandates to undertake strategies deemed too risky for traditional investment funds. These strategies may involve significant shorting and/or concentrated positions in domestic and foreign securities that offer exposure to credit, volatility, and liquidity risk premiums.
5. **Relatively Liberal Use of Leverage:** Hedge funds generally use leverage more extensively than regulated investment funds. Their leveraged positions are implemented either by borrowing securities from a prime broker or by using implied leverage via derivatives. In many instances, such leverage is necessary to make the return profile of the strategy meaningful. In other instances, derivatives utilized to hedge away unwanted risks (e.g., interest rate or credit risk) may create high "notional leverage" but result in a less risky portfolio. Within long/short equity trading, leverage is most often applied to quantitative approaches in which small statistical valuation aberrations—typically over short windows of time—are identified by a manager or an algorithm. Such quant managers will typically endeavor to be market neutral but will apply high leverage levels to make the opportunities they identify meaningful from a return perspective.
6. **Hedge Fund Liquidity Constraints:** Limited partnership-format hedge funds involve initial lock-up periods, liquidity gates, and exit windows. These provide hedge fund managers with a greater ability to take and maintain positions than vehicles that allow investors to withdraw their investment essentially at will. It is thus not surprising that empirical evidence shows that such privately-placed hedge funds significantly outperform similar-strategy liquid alts products by approximately 100 bps–200 bps, on average, per year.
7. **Relatively High Fee Structures:** Hedge funds have traditionally imposed relatively high investment fees on investors, including both management fees and incentive fees. These have historically been 1% or more of AUM for management fees and 10%–20% of annual returns for incentive fees. The incentive fee structure is meant to align the interests of the hedge fund manager with those of the fund's investors.

With this background, we now address how hedge funds are classified. One distinction is between single manager hedge funds and multi-manager hedge funds. A **single-manager fund** is a fund in which one portfolio manager or team of portfolio managers invests in one strategy or style. A **multi-manager fund** can be of two types. One type is a **multi-strategy fund**, in which teams of portfolio managers trade and invest in multiple different strategies within the same fund. The second type, a fund-of-hedge funds, often simply called a **fund-of-funds** (FoF), is a fund in which the fund-of-funds manager allocates capital to separate, underlying hedge funds (e.g., single manager and/or multi-manager funds) that themselves run a range of different strategies.

At the single manager and single strategy level, hedge fund strategies can be classified in various ways. The taxonomy is often based on some combination of:

1. the instruments in which the managers invest (e.g., equities, commodities, foreign exchange, convertible bonds);
2. the trading philosophy followed by the managers (e.g., systematic, discretionary); and
3. the types of risk the managers assume (e.g., directional, event driven, relative value).

Most prominent hedge fund data vendors use a combination of these criteria to classify hedge fund strategies. For example, Hedge Fund Research, Inc. (HFR) reports manager performance statistics on more than 30 strategies and divides funds into six single strategy groupings that are widely used in the hedge fund industry. HFR's seven main single strategy groupings are

1. equity hedge;
2. event driven;
3. fund-of-funds;
4. macro;
5. relative value;
6. risk parity; and
7. Blockchain.

Refinitive Lipper, another well-known data vendor, classifies funds into the following ten categories:

1. dedicated short bias;
2. equity market neutral;
3. long/short equity hedge;
4. event driven;
5. convertible arbitrage;
6. fixed-income arbitrage;
7. global macro;
8. managed futures;
9. fund-of-funds; and
10. multi-strategy.

Morningstar CISDM goes even further and separates hedge funds in its database into finer categories, like merger arbitrage and systematic futures, among others. In addition, the Morningstar CISDM Database separates fund-of-funds strategies into several different sub-categories, such as debt, equity, event driven, macro/systematic, multi-strategy, and relative value.

Eurekahedge, an important index provider with its roots in Asia, has grown to include many smaller hedge fund managers globally. Its main strategy indexes include nine categories:

1. arbitrage;
2. commodity trading adviser (CTA)/managed futures;
3. distressed debt;
4. event driven;
5. fixed income;
6. long/short equities;
7. macro;
8. multi-strategy; and
9. relative value.

A final example of a prominent hedge fund data vendor is Credit Suisse. Its Credit Suisse Hedge Fund Index is an asset-weighted index that monitors approximately 9,000 funds and consists of funds with a minimum of US$50 million AUM, a 12-month track record, and audited financial statements. The index is calculated and rebalanced monthly, and it reflects performance net of all performance fees and expenses. Credit Suisse also subdivides managers into nine main sub-indexes for strategy areas:

1. convertible arbitrage;
2. emerging markets;
3. equity market neutral;
4. event driven;
5. fixed income;
6. global macro;
7. long/short equity;
8. managed futures; and
9. multi-strategy.

These different data providers use different methodologies for index calculation. HFR produces both the HFRX Index of equally weighted hedge funds, which includes those that are open or closed to new investment, and its HFRI index series, which tracks only hedge funds open to new investment. Because managers who have closed their funds to new investment are typically superior managers who are limited in their capacity to manage additional funds, the HFRX series regularly outperforms the HFRI series. However, the mix of managers represented by the HFRX Index would obviously not be replicable in real-time by an investor, thus limiting its usefulness. Meanwhile, the Credit Suisse Hedge Fund Index is weighted by fund size (i.e., AUM), so its overall performance is more reflective of the performance of the larger hedge funds, such as the multi-strategy managers.

Notably, less overlap exists in manager reporting to the different index providers than one might expect or is likely optimal. In fact, less than 1% of hedge fund managers self-report to all the index service providers mentioned. Clearly, no single index is all-encompassing.

Generally consistent with the above data vendor groupings and with a practice-based risk factor perspective, this reading groups single hedge fund strategies into the following six categories: 1) equity; 2) event-driven; 3) relative value; 4) opportunistic; 5) specialist; and 6) multi-manager.

- **Equity-related hedge fund strategies** focus primarily on the equity markets, and the majority of their risk profiles involve equity-oriented risk. Within this equity-related bucket, long/short equity, dedicated short bias, and equity market neutral are the main strategies that will be discussed further.
- **Event-driven hedge fund strategies** focus on corporate events, such as governance events, mergers and acquisitions, bankruptcy, and other key events for corporations. The primary risk for these strategies is event risk, the possibility that an unexpected event will negatively affect a company or security. Unexpected events include unforeseen corporate reorganization, a failed merger, credit rating downgrades, or company bankruptcy. The most common event-driven hedge fund strategies, merger arbitrage and distressed securities, will be discussed in detail.
- **Relative value hedge fund strategies** focus on the relative valuation between two or more securities. These strategies are often exposed to credit and liquidity risks because the valuation differences from which these strategies seek to benefit often are due to differences in credit quality and/

or liquidity across different securities. The two common relative value hedge fund strategies to be covered further are fixed-income arbitrage and convertible bond arbitrage.

- **Opportunistic hedge fund strategies** take a top-down approach, focusing on a multi-asset (often macro-oriented) opportunity set. The risks for opportunistic hedge fund strategies depend on the opportunity set involved and can vary across time and asset classes. The two common opportunistic hedge fund strategies that are discussed in further detail are global macro and managed futures.
- **Specialist hedge fund strategies** focus on special or niche opportunities that often require a specialized skill or knowledge of a specific market. These strategies can be exposed to unique risks that stem from particular market sectors, niche securities, and/or esoteric instruments. We will explore two specialist strategies in further detail: volatility strategies involving options and reinsurance strategies.
- **Multi-manager hedge fund strategies** focus on building a portfolio of diversified hedge fund strategies. Managers in this strategy bucket use their skills to combine diverse strategies and dynamically re-allocate among them over time. The two most common types of multi-manager hedge funds are multi-strategy funds and funds-of-funds, which we will discuss in further detail.

Exhibit 1 shows the five single strategy hedge fund buckets that will be covered individually. Multi-strategy funds and funds-of-funds—two types of multi-manager strategies—will also be covered. A discussion of each strategy's contributions to portfolio risk and return will follow.

Exhibit 1: Hedge Fund Strategies by Category

Equity	Event-Driven	Relative Value	Opportunistic	Specialist	Multi-Manager
• Long/Short Equity • Dedicated Short Bias • Equity Market Neutral	• Merger Arbitrage • Distressed Securities	• Fixed Income Arbitrage • Convertible Bond Arbitrage	• Global Macro • Managed Futures	• Volatility Strategies • Reinsurance Strategies	• Multi-Strategy • Fund-of-Funds

2 EQUITY STRATEGIES: LONG/SHORT EQUITY

☐ discuss investment characteristics, strategy implementation, and role in a portfolio of equity-related hedge fund strategies

Equity hedge fund strategies invest primarily in equity and equity-related instruments. As mentioned previously, the alpha related to equity strategies tends to derive from the wide variety of equity investments available globally combined with astute long and short stock picking. The size and sign of equity market exposure often dictate the classification of equity hedge fund strategies. As the name suggests, long-only equity hedge fund strategies focus on holding only long positions in equities, and they sometimes use leverage. Long/short equity hedge fund strategies hold both long and short positions in equities that typically result in more-hedged, less-volatile overall portfolios. Short-biased strategies focus on strategic short selling of companies that are expected to lose value in the future (sometimes with an activist inclination, sometimes with long positions in other securities as an offset). Equity market-neutral strategies hold balanced long and short equity exposures to maintain zero (or close to zero) net exposure to the equity market and such factors as sector and size (i.e., market cap). They then focus on, for example, pairs of long and short securities whose prices are out of historical alignment and are expected to experience mean reversion. The following sections discuss long/short equity, dedicated short bias, and equity market-neutral hedge fund strategies.

Long/Short Equity

Long/short (L/S) equity managers buy equities of companies they expect will rise in value (i.e., they take long positions in undervalued companies) and sell short equities of companies they think will fall in value (i.e., they take short positions in overvalued companies). The objective of long/short equity strategies is to be flexible in finding attractive opportunities on both the long and short sides of the market and to size them within a portfolio. Depending on their specific mandates, long/short equity strategies can shift between industry sectors (e.g., from technology to consumer goods), factors (e.g., from value to growth), and geographic regions (e.g., from Europe to Asia). In practice, however, managers tend to maintain their philosophical biases and areas of focus, typically with a heavy emphasis on fundamental research.

Although market timing using "beta tilts" can play a factor in manager performance, studies have shown that most fundamental long/short equity managers offer little added alpha from such adjustments. They are typically either too net long at market highs or not net long enough at market lows. Most L/S equity managers are not known for their portfolio-level market-timing abilities, but those with such market-timing skills may be particularly valuable from a portfolio allocation perspective.

L/S equity managers also are typically able to take concentrated positions in high conviction buys or sells and can readily apply leverage to increase these positions (although higher levels of leverage are used mostly by quantitatively-oriented managers, not fundamental managers). As a result, stock selection defines manager skill for most L/S equity managers—with market-timing ability being an additive, but generally secondary, consideration. L/S equity is one of the most prevalent hedge fund strategies. It accounts for about 30% of all hedge funds.

Investment Characteristics

Because manager skill derives mainly from stock selection, it is not surprising that individual long/short equity managers tend to have a focus based on their own unique skill sets. As a result, many long/short equity managers specialize in either a specific geographic region, sector, or investment style. However, several key characteristics define long/short equity managers: their strategy focus, their flexibility in holding long and short positions over time, and their use of leverage. Given the specific mandate for a long/short equity manager, his/her exposures to various equity factors can be very different from other long/short equity managers. For example, a manager focusing on small-cap growth stocks would have a positive exposure to the size factor and a negative exposure to the value factor. Conversely, a manager with a focus on large-cap value stocks would have a negative exposure to the size factor and a positive exposure to the value factor.

Given that equity markets tend to rise over the long run, most long/short equity managers typically hold net long equity positions. Some managers maintain their short positions as a hedge against unexpected market downturns. Other managers are more opportunistic; they tend to take on more short positions after uncovering negative issues with a company's management, strategies, and/or financial statements or whenever their valuation models suggest selling opportunities in certain stocks or sectors. As a result, performance during market crisis periods is important for differentiating between hedge fund managers. Given that hedge funds typically carry high fees, it is important to avoid paying such added fees just for embedded beta exposure that could be achieved more cheaply by investing in traditional long-only strategies. The goal in long/short equity investing is generally to find more sources of idiosyncratic alpha (primarily via stock picking and secondarily by market timing) rather than embedded systematic beta. Exhibit 2 presents some key aspects of this important strategy area.

Exhibit 2: Long/Short Equity—Risk, Liquidity, Leverage, and Benchmarking

Risk Profile and Liquidity

- Diverse opportunities globally create a wide universe from which to create alpha through astute stock picking.
- Diverse investment styles include value/growth, large cap/small cap, discretionary/quantitative, and industry specialized.
- They typically have average exposures of 40%–60% net long, composed of gross exposures of 70%–90% long, vs. 20%–50% short, but they can vary widely. Long/short strategies are typically designed to achieve average annual returns roughly equivalent to a long-only approach but with a standard deviation 50% lower than a long-only approach.
- Some managers use index-based short hedges to reduce market risk, but most search for single-name shorts for portfolio alpha and added absolute return.
- Some managers are able to add alpha via market timing of portfolio beta tilt, but evidence suggests that most L/S managers do this poorly.
- This strategy can typically be handled by both limited partner and mutual fund-type vehicles.
- Attractiveness: Liquid, diverse, with transparent mark-to-market pricing driven by public market quotes; added short-side exposure typically reduces beta risk and provides an additional source of potential alpha and reduced portfolio volatility.

Leverage Usage

- Variable: The more market-neutral or quantitative the strategy approach, the more levered the strategy application tends to be to achieve a meaningful return profile.

Benchmarking

- L/S equity benchmarks include HFRX and HFRI Equity Hedge Indices; Lipper L/S Equity Hedge; Morningstar/CISDM Equity L/S Index; and Credit Suisse L/S Equity Index.

Strategy Implementation

When long and short stock positions are placed together into a portfolio, the market exposure is the net of the beta-adjusted long and short exposures. For example, with many strong sells and a relatively large short position, the strategy could be net short for brief periods of time. Typically, most long/short equity managers end up with modest net long exposures averaging between 40%–60% net long. Many long/short equity managers are naturally sector-specific, often designing their funds around their industry specialization. Such specialist L/S fund managers analyze fundamental situations that they know well from both a top-down and bottom-up analytical perspective. Natural areas of specialization include potentially more complex sectors, such as telecom/media/technology (TMT), financial, consumer, health care, and biotechnology sectors, where the portfolio managers can meaningfully add value to their investors through their sector-specific knowledge. Conversely, generalist L/S managers search further afield, thus having flexibility to invest across multiple industry groups. Typically, these generalists avoid complex sectors; for example, they may avoid biotechnology because corporate outcomes may be deemed too binary depending on the success or failure of drug trials. Although generalist managers do take a more balanced and flexible approach, they may miss detailed industry subtleties that are increasingly important to understand in a world where news flows 24/7 and is increasingly nuanced.

Overall, long/short equity investing in most instances is a mix of extracting alpha on the long and short sides from single-name stock selection combined with some naturally net long embedded beta.

EXAMPLE 1

Long/Short Equity Investing Dilemma

The Larson family office views L/S equity investing as a significant portion of the hedge fund universe and would like to access managers talented not only at long investing but also at short selling. However, it does not want to pay high hedge fund fees just for long-biased beta because it has access to long-biased beta at lower fees elsewhere in its portfolio. But, Larson will pay hedge fund fees for strategies that can produce strong risk-adjusted performance in a unique and differentiated fashion.

1. Discuss some potential hedge fund strategies the Larson family office should consider adding to its existing portfolio.

Solution:

The Larson family office should consider managers focused on an L/S equity strategy with a sector-specialization as opposed to a generalist fundamental L/S strategy. Generalist L/S managers can benefit from the flexibility to scan a wide universe of stocks to find investments, but they may not be able to develop a sufficient information edge in their analysis to dependably deliver sufficient alpha relative to their fees and natural long beta positioning. However, managers running specialist L/S equity strategies—especially in such complex sectors as technology, finance, and biotechnology/health care—are more likely to have the specialized capabilities to perform the "deep-dive" differentiated analysis required to develop more original views and stronger portfolio performance.

2. Discuss some of the problems and risks that it may encounter.

Solution:

A key problem with selecting sector-specialist L/S equity hedge funds is that they are more difficult to analyze and assess. There are also fewer to choose from compared to generalist L/S hedge funds. Sectors can fall out of favor, risking an allocation to a good fund but in the wrong area given dynamic macroeconomic and financial market conditions. Moreover, generalist L/S strategies, by definition, can readily reallocate capital more efficiently as opportunities emerge in different sectors. Put another way, the Larson family office could potentially find itself with too much single sector, short-sided, or idiosyncratic exposure at the wrong time if it chooses a sector-specialist L/S equity fund.

EQUITY STRATEGIES: DEDICATED SHORT SELLING AND SHORT-BIASED 3

☐ discuss investment characteristics, strategy implementation, and role in a portfolio of equity-related hedge fund strategies

Dedicated short-selling hedge fund managers take short-only positions in equities deemed to be expensively priced versus their deteriorating fundamental situations. Such managers may vary their short exposures only in terms of portfolio sizing by, at times, holding higher levels of cash. **Short-biased** hedge fund managers use a less extreme version of this approach. They also search for opportunities to sell expensively priced equities, but they may balance short exposure with some modest value-oriented, or possibly index-oriented, long exposure. This latter approach can potentially help short-biased hedge funds cope with long bull market periods in equities. Both types of short sellers actively aim to create an uncorrelated or negatively correlated source of return by seeking out failing business models, fraudulent accounting, corporate mismanagement, or other factors that may sour the market's perception of a given equity. Because of the overall secular up-trend in global equity markets, especially across the past several decades, it has been very difficult to be a successful short seller. As a result, fewer such managers are in existence today than in the 1990s. However, with the market volatility and global economic disruption in the aftermath of the Covid-19 pandemic, short-selling opportunities have increased.

Activist short selling is a strategy whereby managers take a short position in a given security and then publicly present their research backing the short thesis. Typically, if the hedge fund manager has a solid reputation from its past activist short-selling forays, the release of such research causes a significant stock price plunge into which the activist short seller might cover a portion of its short position. In the United States, this practice has not been deemed to be market manipulation by securities regulators as long as the activist short seller is not publishing erroneous information, is not charging for such information (which might create potential conflicts of interest between subscribers and investors), and is acting only in the best interests of its limited partner investors.

Investment Characteristics

Short-selling managers focus on situations involving overvalued equities of companies facing deteriorating fundamentals that typically have not yet been perceived by the market. They also attempt to maximize returns during periods of market declines. If these short-selling managers can achieve success with their approaches, they can provide a unique and useful source of negatively correlated returns compared to many other strategy areas.

Short selling involves borrowing securities, selling them "high," and then after prices have declined, buying the same securities back "low" and returning them to the lender. To borrow the securities to short sell, the manager must post collateral with the securities lender to cover potential losses. The manager must also pay interest on the securities loan, which can be high if the securities are difficult for the lender to locate. One key risk is that the lender may want the securities back at an inopportune time—such as before the expected price decline has materialized, which could be disadvantageous for the hedge fund manager.

Short selling in general is a difficult investment practice to master in terms of risk management because of the natural phenomenon that positions will grow if prices advance against the short seller but will shrink if prices decline. This is the opposite of what occurs with long-only investing, and it is more difficult to manage. Additionally, access to company management for research purposes can be blocked for fund managers who become known as active short sellers.

From a regulatory perspective, many countries limit or impose stringent rules on short selling. In the United States, the "alternative uptick rule" states that when a stock decreases by 10% or more from its prior closing price, a short sale order can be executed only at a price higher than the current best (i.e., highest) bid. This means the stock's price must be rising to execute the short sale. Although many emerging markets have allowed short selling, particularly to enhance market liquidity (e.g., the Saudi Stock Exchange allowed short sales beginning in 2016), there is always concern that limits could be placed on short selling during extreme market environments or that regulations could change. For example, for a brief period during the global financial crisis of 2007–2009, new short sales on a designated list of financial stocks were banned by the US SEC to lessen systematic market stress.

Given the difficult operational aspects of short selling, and because equity markets tend to secularly rise over time, successful short-selling managers typically have something of a short-term "attack and retreat" style. The return profile for a successful short-biased manager might best be characterized by increasingly positive returns as the market declines and the risk-free return when the market rises. In some idealized short-selling world, this would entail being short the market during down periods and investing in low-risk government debt when the market is not declining. But, the actual goal of a short seller is to pick short-sale stocks that can still generate positive returns even when the general market trend is up. Skillful, dedicated short-biased managers look for possible short-selling targets among companies that are overvalued, that are experiencing declining revenues and/or earnings, or that have internal management conflicts, weak corporate governance, or even potential accounting frauds. Other possible short-sale candidates are companies that may have single products under development that the short seller believes will ultimately be either unsuccessful or non-repeatable. Exhibit 3 shows some important aspects of this strategy area.

Exhibit 3: Dedicated Short Sellers and Short-Biased—Risk, Liquidity, Leverage, and Benchmarking

Risk Profile and Liquidity

- Dedicated short sellers: They only trade with short-side exposure, although they may moderate short beta by also holding cash.
- Short-biased managers: They are focused on good short-side stock picking, but they may moderate short beta with some value-oriented long exposure or index-oriented long exposure as well as cash.
- Dedicated short sellers tend to be 60%–120% short at all times. Short-biased managers are typically around 30%–60% net short. The focus in both cases tends to be on single equity stock picking as opposed to index shorting.
- Return goals are typically less than those for most other hedge fund strategies but with a negative correlation benefit. They are more volatile than a typical L/S equity hedge fund given short beta exposure.
- This strategy is typically handled best in a limited partnership because of difficult operational aspects of short selling.
- Attractiveness: Liquid, negatively correlated alpha to that of most other strategies, with mark-to-market pricing from public prices. Historic returns have been lumpy and generally disappointing.

Leverage Usage

- Low: There is typically sufficient natural volatility that short-selling managers do not need to add much leverage.

Benchmarking

- Short-biased indexes include Eurekahedge Equity Short Bias Hedge Fund Index and Lipper Dedicated Short-Bias Index. Some investors also compare short-biased funds' returns to the inverse of returns on related stock indexes.

Note: Each index has different methodologies for fund inclusion. Because there are fewer short-selling managers, the construction of an acceptably diverse index is particularly difficult. The Lipper Dedicated Short-Bias Index, for example, includes just four managers.

Strategy Implementation

Because finding strategic selling opportunities is key to dedicated short-biased strategies, stock selection is an important part of the investment process. Short-selling managers typically take a bottom-up approach by scanning the universe of potential sell targets to uncover and sell short those companies whose shares are most likely to substantially decline in value over the relevant time horizon. Managers search for, among other factors, inherently flawed business models, unsustainable levels of corporate leverage, and indications of poor corporate governance and/or accounting gimmickry. Tools that may be helpful to dedicated short-biased managers in finding potential sell candidates include monitoring single name credit default swap spreads, corporate bond yield spreads, and/or implied volatility of exchange-traded put options. Traditional technical analysis and/or pattern recognition techniques may assist the manager in the market timing of short sales. Various accounting ratios and measures, such as the Altman *Z*-score for judging a company's bankruptcy potential and the Beneish *M*-score for identifying potentially fraudulent financial statements, may also be useful. Because of the inherent difficulty and dangers of short selling, most successful short sellers do significant "deep-dive" forensic work on their short-portfolio candidates. As such, short sellers serve as a valuable resource in creating more overall pricing efficiency in the market.

EXAMPLE 2

Candidate for Short-Biased Hedge Fund Strategy

Kit Stone, a short-biased hedge fund manager, is researching Generic Inc. (GI) for possible addition to his portfolio. GI was once a drug industry leader, but for the past 10 years its R&D budgets have declined. Its drug patents have all expired, so it now operates in the competitive generic drug business. GI has staked its future on a new treatment for gastro-intestinal disease. R&D was financed by debt, so GI's leverage ratio is twice the industry average. Early clinical trials were inconclusive. Final clinical trial results for GI's new drug are to be revealed within one month. Although the market is constructive, many medical experts remain doubtful of the new drug's efficacy. Without any further insights into the trial results, Stone reviews the following information.

Generic Inc. (GI)			Industry Average		
PE (X)	PB (X)	T12M EPS Growth	PE (X)	PB (X)	T12M EPS Growth
30	3.5	3%	20	2.5	18%

Additionally, Stone notes that GI shares are very thinly traded, with a high short-interest ratio of 60%. Stone's broker has informed him that it is expensive to borrow GI shares for shorting; they are on "special" (i.e., difficult to borrow), with a high borrowing cost of 20% per year. Moreover, there is an active market for exchange-traded options on GI's shares. Prices of one-month GI options appear to reflect a positive view of the company.

1. Discuss whether Stone should add GI shares to his short-biased portfolio.

Solution:

Generic Inc. appears to be substantially overvalued. Its main business relies on the competitive generic drug market; it has taken on substantial debt to fund R&D; and skepticism surrounds its new drug. GI's P/Es and P/Bs are higher than industry averages by 50% and 40%, respectively, and its trailing 12-month EPS growth is meager (3% vs. 18% industry average). However, although Stone would normally decide to add GI to his short-biased portfolio, the stock's high short-interest ratio and high cost to borrow (for shorting) are very concerning. Both factors suggest significant potential that a dangerous short-squeeze situation could develop if clinical results really do show efficacy of GI's new drug. So, based on the negative demand/supply dynamics for the stock, Stone decides not to add GI to his portfolio.

2. Discuss how Stone might instead take advantage of the situation using GI options.

Solution:

Stone might instead consider expressing his negative view on GI by simply purchasing put options. Alternatively, Stone could purchase a long put calendar spread, where he would buy a put with expiry beyond and sell a put with expiry before the expected release date of the clinical trial results. In that case, the premium received from writing the shorter tenor put would finance, in part, the cost of buying the longer tenor put. As a third possibility, Stone might even consider buying GI shares and then lending them at the attractive 20% rate. In that case, he would need to hedge this long stock position with the purchase of out-of-the-money puts, thereby creating a protective put position. As a final possibility, if out-of-the-money calls are deemed to be expensive because of positive sentiment, Stone could sell such calls to finance the purchase of out-of-the-money puts, creating a short risk reversal that provides synthetic short exposure.

EQUITY STRATEGIES: EQUITY MARKET NEUTRAL 4

☐ discuss investment characteristics, strategy implementation, and role in a portfolio of equity-related hedge fund strategies

Equity market-neutral (EMN) hedge fund strategies take opposite (i.e., long and short) positions in similar or related equities that have divergent valuations, and they also attempt to maintain a near net zero portfolio exposure to the market. EMN managers neutralize market risk by constructing their portfolios such that the expected portfolio beta is approximately equal to zero. Moreover, managers often choose to set the betas for sectors or industries as well as for such common risk factors as market size, price-to-earnings ratio, or book-to-market ratio, which are also equal to zero. Because these portfolios do not take beta risk and attempt to neutralize so many other factor risks, they typically must apply leverage to the long and short positions to achieve a meaningful expected return from their individual stock selections. Approaches vary, but equity market-neutral portfolios are often constructed using highly quantitative methodologies; the portfolios end up being diverse in their holdings; and the portfolios are typically modified and adjusted over shorter time horizons. The condition of zero market beta can also be achieved with the use of derivatives, including stock index futures and options. Whichever way they are constructed, the overall goal of equity market-neutral portfolios is to capture alpha while minimizing portfolio beta exposure.

Although **pairs trading** is just one subset of equity market-neutral investing, it is an intuitively easy example to consider. With this strategy, pairs are identified of similar under- and overvalued equities, divergently valued shares of a holding company and its subsidiaries, or different share classes of the same company (multi-class stocks typically having different voting rights) in which their prices are out of alignment.

In whatever manner they are created, the pairs are monitored for their typical trading patterns relative to each other—conceptually, the degree of co-integration of the two securities' price changes. Positions are established when unusually divergent spread pricing between the two paired securities is observed. Underpinning such a strategy is the expectation that the differential valuations or trading relationships will revert to their long-term mean values or their fundamentally-correct trading relationships, with the long position rising and the short position declining in value. Situations will obviously vary, but strictly quantitative EMN pairs trading, while attempting to minimize overall beta exposure, may still have effective short volatility "tail risk" exposure to abnormal market situations of extreme stress. This is less the case if a fundamental pricing discrepancy is being exploited in anticipation of a possible event that would cause that discrepancy to correct.

Another type of EMN trading is **stub trading**, which entails buying and selling stock of a parent company and its subsidiaries, typically weighted by the percentage ownership of the parent company in the subsidiaries. Assume parent company A owns 90% and 75% of subsidiaries B and C, respectively, and shares of A are determined to be overvalued while shares of B and C are deemed undervalued, all relative to their historical mean valuations. Then, for each share of A sold short, the EMN fund would buy 0.90 and 0.75 shares of B and C, respectively.

Yet another type of EMN approach may involve **multi-class trading**, which involves buying and selling different classes of shares of the same company, such as voting and non-voting shares. As with pairs trading, the degree of co-integration of returns and the valuation metrics for the multi-class shares are determined. If/when prices move outside of their normal ranges, the overvalued shares are sold short while the undervalued shares are purchased. The goal is to gain on the change in relative pricing on the two securities as market pricing reverts to more normal ranges.

Fundamental trade setups—although not per se "equity market neutral" but still designed to be market neutral—may be created that are long or short equity hedged against offsetting bond exposures if relative pricing between the stocks and bonds is deemed to be out of alignment. Such pairs trading is referred to as capital structure arbitrage and will be discussed in the event-driven strategies section. In these situations, attractive expected outcomes are often created from relative security mispricings designed to exploit potential event situations (e.g., a potential merger or bankruptcy) that would have an impact on relative pricing. Moreover, when two bonds are positioned relative to each other (e.g., to exploit a misunderstood difference in bond covenants or a potential differential asset recovery), a market-neutral strategy can also be employed.

When building market-neutral portfolios, sometimes large numbers of securities are traded and positions are adjusted on a daily or even an hourly basis using algorithm-based models. Managers following this approach are referred to as **quantitative market-neutral** managers. The frequent adjustments implemented by such managers are driven by the fact that market prices change faster than company fundamental factors. This price movement triggers a rebalancing of the EMN portfolio back to a market neutrality. When the time horizon of EMN trading shrinks to even shorter intervals and mean reversion and relative momentum characteristics of market behavior are emphasized, quantitative market-neutral trading becomes what is known as statistical arbitrage trading. With EMN and statistical arbitrage trading, a natural push/pull occurs between maintaining an optimal beta-neutral portfolio and the market impacts and brokerage costs of nearly continuous adjusting of the portfolio. So, many EMN managers use trading-cost hurdle models to determine if and when they should rebalance a portfolio.

Overall, the main source of skill for an EMN manager is in security selection, with market timing being of secondary importance. Sector exposure also tends to be constrained, although this can vary by the individual manager's approach. Managers that are overall beta neutral and specialize in sector rotation exposure as their source of alpha are known as market-neutral tactical asset allocators or macro-oriented market-neutral managers.

Investment Characteristics

Equity market-neutral fund managers seek to insulate their portfolios from movements in the overall market, and they can take advantage of divergent valuations by trading specific securities. As discussed, this is often a quantitatively driven process that uses a substantial amount of leverage to generate meaningful return objectives. However, many discretionary EMN managers implement their positions with significantly less leverage.

Overall, EMN managers generally are more useful for portfolio allocation during periods of non-trending or declining markets because they typically deliver returns that are steadier and less volatile than those of many other hedge strategy areas. Over time, their conservative and constrained approach typically results in less-volatile overall returns than those of managers who accept beta exposure. The exception to this norm is when the use of significant leverage may cause forced portfolio downsizing. By using portfolio margining techniques offered by prime brokers, market-neutral managers may run portfolios with up to 300% long versus 300% short exposures. Prime broker portfolio margining rules generally allow managers to maintain such levered positioning until a portfolio loss of a specified magnitude (i.e., excess drawdown) is incurred. At the time of such excess drawdown, the prime broker can force the manager to downsize his/her overall portfolio exposure. This is a key strategy risk, particularly for quantitative market-neutral managers.

Despite the use of substantial leverage and because of their more standard and overall steady risk/return profiles, equity market-neutral managers are often considered as preferred replacements for (or at least a complement to) fixed-income managers during periods when fixed-income returns are unattractively low and/or the yield curve is flat. EMN managers are, of course, sourcing a very different type of alpha with very different risks than in fixed-income investing. EMN managers must deal with leverage risk, including the issues of availability of leverage and at what cost, and tail risk, particularly the performance of levered portfolios during periods of market stress. Exhibit 4 presents important aspects of this strategy area.

Exhibit 4: Equity Market Neutral—Risk, Liquidity, Leverage, and Benchmarking

Risk Profile and Liquidity

- They have relatively modest return profiles, with portfolios aimed to be market neutral, and differing constraints to other factors and sector exposures are allowed.
- They generally have high levels of diversification and liquidity and lower standard deviation of returns than many other strategies across normal market conditions.
- Many different types of EMN managers exist, but many are purely quantitative managers (vs. discretionary managers).
- Time horizons vary, but EMN strategies are typically oriented toward mean reversion, with shorter horizons than other strategies and more active trading.
- Because of often high leverage, EMN strategies typically do not meet regulatory leverage limits for mutual fund vehicles. So, limited partnerships are the preferred vehicle.
- Attractiveness: EMN strategies typically take advantage of idiosyncratic short-term mispricing between securities whose prices should otherwise be co-integrated. Their sources of return and alpha, unlike

those of many other strategies, do not require accepting beta risk. So, EMN strategies are especially attractive during periods of market vulnerability and weakness.

Leverage Usage

- High: As many beta risks (e.g., market, sector) are hedged away, it is generally deemed acceptable for EMN managers to apply higher levels of leverage while striving for meaningful return targets.

Benchmarking

- Market-neutral indexes include HFRX and HFRI Equity Market Neutral Indices; Lipper Equity Market Neutral Index; Morningstar/CISDM Equity Market Neutral Index; and Credit Suisse Equity Market Neutral Index.

Strategy Implementation

Equity market-neutral portfolios are constructed in four main steps. First, the investment universe is evaluated to include only tradable securities with sufficient liquidity and adequate short-selling potential. Second, securities are analyzed for buy and sell opportunities using fundamental models (which use company, industry, and economic data as inputs for valuation) and/or statistical and momentum-based models. Third, a portfolio is constructed with constraints to maintain market risk neutrality, whereby the portfolio's market value-weighted beta is approximately zero and there is often dollar (i.e., money), sector, or other factor risk neutrality. Fourth, the availability and cost of leverage are considered in terms of desired return profile and acceptable potential portfolio drawdown risk. The execution costs of the strategy rebalancing are also introduced as a filter for decision making as to how often the portfolio should be rebalanced. Markets are dynamic because volatility and leverage are always changing; therefore, the exposure to the market is always changing. Consequently, EMN managers must actively manage their funds' exposures to remain neutral over time. However, costs are incurred every time the portfolio is rebalanced. So, EMN managers must be very careful to not allow such costs to overwhelm the security-selection alpha that they are attempting to capture.

Note that the following is a simplified example. In reality, most EMN managers would likely not hedge beta on a stock-by-stock basis but rather would hedge beta on an overall portfolio basis. They would also likely consider other security factor attributes.

EXAMPLE 3

Equity Market-Neutral Pairs Trading:

1. Ling Chang, a Hong Kong-based EMN manager, has been monitoring PepsiCo Inc. (PEP) and Coca-Cola Co. (KO), two global beverage industry giants. After examining the Asia marketing strategy for a new PEP drink, Chang feels the marketing campaign is too controversial and the overall market is too narrow. Although PEP has relatively weak earnings prospects compared to KO, 3-month valuation metrics show PEP shares are substantially overvalued versus KO shares (relative valuations have moved beyond their historical ranges). As part of a larger portfolio, Chang wants to allocate $1

million to the PEP versus KO trade and notes the historical betas and S&P 500 Index weights, as shown in the following table.

Stock	Beta	S&P 500 Index Weight
PEP	0.65	0.663
KO	0.55	0.718

Discuss how Chang might implement an EMN pairs trading strategy.

Solution:

Chang should take a short position in PEP and a long position in KO with equal beta-weighted exposures. Given Chang wants to allocate $1 million to the trade, she would take on a long KO position of $1 million. Assuming realized betas will be similar to historical betas, to achieve an equal beta-weighted exposure for the short PEP position, Chang needs to short $846,154 worth of PEP shares [= –$1,000,000 / (0.65/0.55)]. Only the overall difference in performance between PEP and KO shares would affect the performance of the strategy because it will be insulated from the effect of market fluctuations. If over the next 3 months the valuations of PEP and KO revert to within normal ranges, then this pairs trading EMN strategy should reap profits.

Note: The S&P 500 Index weights are not needed to answer this question.

EVENT-DRIVEN STRATEGIES: MERGER ARBITRAGE 5

☐ discuss investment characteristics, strategy implementation, and role in a portfolio of event-driven hedge fund strategies

Event-driven (ED) hedge fund strategies take positions in corporate securities and derivatives that are attempting to profit from the outcome of mergers and acquisitions, bankruptcies, share issuances, buybacks, capital restructurings, re-organizations, accounting changes, and similar events. ED hedge fund managers analyze companies' financial statements and regulatory filings and closely examine corporate governance issues (e.g., management structure, board composition, issues for shareholder consideration, proxy voting) as well as firms' strategic objectives, competitive position, and other firm-specific issues. Either investments can be made proactively in anticipation of an event that has yet to occur (i.e., a **soft-catalyst event-driven approach**), or investments can be made in reaction to an already announced corporate event in which security prices related to the event have yet to fully converge (i.e., a **hard-catalyst event-driven approach**). The hard approach is generally less volatile and less risky than soft-catalyst investing. Merger arbitrage and distressed securities are among the most common ED strategies.

Merger Arbitrage

Mergers and acquisitions can be classified by the method of purchase: cash-for-stock or stock-for-stock. In a cash-for-stock acquisition, the acquiring company (A) offers the target company (T) a cash price per share to acquire T. For example, assume T's share price is $30 and A decides to purchase T for $40 per share (i.e., A is offering a 33% premium to purchase T's shares). In a stock-for-stock acquisition, A offers a specific number of its shares in exchange for 1 T share. So, if A's share price is $20 and it offers 2 of its shares in exchange for 1 T share, then T's shareholders would receive a value of $40 per T share, assuming A's share price is constant until the merger is completed. Although merger deals are structured in different ways for many reasons (e.g., tax implications, corporate structure, or provisions to dissuade a merger, such as a "poison pill"[1]), acquiring companies are generally more likely to offer cash for their target companies when cash surpluses are high. However, if the stock prices are high and acquiring companies' shares are considered richly valued by management, then stock-for-stock acquisitions can take advantage of potentially overvalued shares as a "currency" to acquire target companies.

Investment Characteristics

In a cash-for-stock acquisition, the merger-arb manager may choose to buy just the target company (T), expecting it to increase in value once the acquisition is completed. In a stock-for-stock deal, the fund manager typically buys T and sells the acquiring company (A) in the same ratio as the offer, hoping to earn the spread on successful deal completion. If the acquisition is unsuccessful, the manager faces losses if the price of T (A) has already risen (fallen) in anticipation of the acquisition. Less often, managers take the view that the acquisition will fail—usually due to anti-competition or other regulatory concerns. In this case, he/she would sell T and buy A.

For most acquisitions, the initial announcement of a deal will cause the target company's stock price to rise toward the acquisition price and the acquirer's stock price to fall (either because of the potential dilution of its outstanding shares or the use of cash for purposes other than a dividend payment). The considerable lag time between deal announcement and closing means that proposed merger deals can always fail for any variety of reasons, including lack of financing, regulatory hurdles, and not passing financial due diligence. Hostile takeover bids, where the target company's management has not already agreed to the terms of a merger, are typically less likely to be successfully completed than friendly takeovers, where the target's management has already agreed to merger terms.

Approximately 70%–90% of announced mergers in the United States eventually close successfully. Given the probability that some mergers will not close for whatever reason as well as the costs of establishing a merger arbitrage position (e.g., borrowing the acquiring stock, commissions) and the risk that merger terms might be changed because of market conditions (especially in stressed market environments), merger arbitrage typically offers a 3%–7% return spread depending on the deal-specific risks. Of course, a particularly risky deal might carry an even larger spread. If the average time for merger deal completion is 3-4 months—with managers recycling capital into new deals several times a year and typically applying some leverage to their portfolio positions—then attractive return/risk profiles can be created, earning net annualized returns in the range of 7%–12%, with little correlation to non-deal-specific factors. Diversifying across a variety of mergers, deals, and industries can further help hedge the risk of any one deal failing. So overall, this strategy can be a good uncorrelated source of alpha.

1 A poison pill is a pre-offer takeover defense mechanism that gives target company bondholders the right to sell their bonds back to the target at a pre-specified redemption price, typically at or above par; this defense increases the acquirer's need for cash and raises the cost of the acquisition.

When merger deals do fail, the initial price rise (fall) of the target (acquirer) company is typically reversed. Arbitrageurs who jumped into the merger situation after its initial announcement stand to incur substantial losses on their long (short) position in the target (acquirer)—often as large as negative 20% to 40%. So, the strategy thus does have left-tail risk associated with it.

Corporate events are typically binary: An acquisition either succeeds or fails. The merger arbitrage strategy can be viewed as selling insurance on the acquisition. If the acquisition succeeds (no adverse event occurs), then the hedge fund manager collects the spread (like the premium an insurance company receives for selling insurance) for taking on event risk. If the acquisition fails (an adverse event occurs), then he/she faces the losses on the long and short positions (similar to an insurance company paying out a policy benefit after an insured event has occurred). Thus, the payoff profile of the merger arbitrage strategy resembles that of a riskless bond and a short put option. The merger arbitrage investor also can be viewed as owning an additional call option that becomes valuable if/when another interested acquirer (i.e., White Knight) makes a higher bid for the target company before the initial merger proposal is completed. Exhibit 5 shows risk and return attributes of merger arbitrage investing.

Exhibit 5: Event-Driven Merger Arbitrage—Risk, Liquidity, Leverage, and Benchmarking

Risk Profile and Liquidity

- Merger arbitrage is a relatively liquid strategy—with defined gains from idiosyncratic single security takeover situations but occasional downside shocks when merger deals unexpectedly fail.
- To the extent that deals are more likely to fail in market stress periods, this strategy has market sensitivity and left-tail risk attributes. Its return profile is similar to a bond plus a short put option.
- Because cross-border merger and acquisition (M&A) usually involve two sets of governmental approvals and M&A deals involving vertical integration often face anti-trust scrutiny, these situations carry higher risks and offer wider merger spread returns.
- Some merger arbitrage managers invest only in friendly deals trading at relatively tight spreads, while others embrace riskier hostile takeovers trading at wider spreads. In the latter case, there may be expectations of a higher bid from a White Knight.
- The preferred vehicle is limited partnership because of merger arbitrage's use of significant leverage, but some low-leverage, low-volatility liquid alts merger arbitrage funds do exist.
- Attractiveness: Relatively high Sharpe ratios with typically low double-digit returns and mid-single-digit standard deviation (depending on specific levels of leverage applied), but left-tail risk is associated with an otherwise steady return profile.

Leverage Usage

- Moderate to high: Managers typically apply 3 to 5 times leverage to this strategy to generate meaningful target return levels.

Benchmarking

- Sub-indexes include HFRX or HFRI Merger Arbitrage Index; CISDM Hedge Fund Merger Arbitrage Index; and Credit Suisse Merger Arbitrage Index.

Strategy Implementation

Merger arbitrage strategies are typically established using common equities; however, a range of other corporate securities, including preferred stock, senior and junior debt, convertible securities, options, and other derivatives, may also be used for positioning and hedging purposes. Often for a cash-for-stock acquisition, a hedge fund manager may choose to use leverage to buy the target firm. For a stock-for-stock acquisition, leverage may also often be used, but short selling the acquiring firm may be difficult due to liquidity issues or short-selling constraints, especially in emerging markets. Merger arbitrage strategies can utilize derivatives to overcome some short-sale constraints or to manage risks if the deal were to fail. For example, the manager could buy out-of-the money (O-T-M) puts on T and/or buy O-T-M call options on A (to cover the short position).

Convertible securities also provide exposure with asymmetrical payoffs. For example, the convertible bonds of T would also rise in value as T's shares rise because of the acquisition; the convertibles' bond value would provide a cushion if the deal fails and T's shares fall. When the acquiring company's credit is superior to the target company's credit, trades may be implemented using credit default swaps (CDS). In this case, protection would be sold (i.e., shorting the CDS) on the target company to benefit from its improved credit quality (and decline in price of protection and the CDS) once a merger is completed. If the pricing is sufficiently cheap, buying protection (i.e., going long the CDS) on the target may also be used as a partial hedge against a merger deal failing. Overall market risk (that could potentially disrupt a merger's consummation) might also be hedged by using added short equity index ETFs/futures or long equity index put positions.

In sum, the true source of return alpha for a merger arbitrage hedge fund manager is in the initial decision as to which deals to embrace and which to avoid. However, once involved with a given merger situation, there may be multiple ways to implement a position depending on the manager's deal-specific perspectives.

EXAMPLE 4

Merger Arbitrage Strategy Payoffs

1. An acquiring firm (A) is trading at $45/share and has offered to buy target firm (T) in a stock-for-stock deal. The offer ratio is 1 share of A in exchange for 2 shares of T. Target firm T was trading at $15 per share just prior to the announcement of the offer. Shortly thereafter, T's share price jumps up to $19 while A's share price falls to $42 in anticipation of the merger receiving required approvals and the deal closing successfully. A hedge fund manager is confident this deal will be completed, so he buys 20,000 shares of T and sells short 10,000 shares of A.

   What are the payoffs of the merger arbitrage strategy if the deal is successfully completed or if the merger fails?

Solution:

At current prices it costs $380,000 to buy 20,000 shares of T, and $420,000 would be received for short selling 10,000 shares of A. This provides a net spread of $40,000 to the hedge fund manager if the merger is successfully completed. If the merger fails, then prices should revert to their pre-merger announcement levels. The manager would need to buy back 10,000 shares of A at $45 (costing $450,000) to close the short position, while the long position in 20,000 shares of T would fall to $15 per share (value at $300,000). This would cause a total loss of $110,000 [= (A: +$420,000 – $450,000) + (T: –$380,000 + $300,000)]. In sum, this merger strategy is equivalent to holding a riskless bond with a face value of $40,000 (the payoff for a successful deal) and a short binary put option, which expires worthless if the merger succeeds but pays out $110,000 if the merger fails.

EVENT-DRIVEN STRATEGIES: DISTRESSED SECURITIES 6

☐ discuss investment characteristics, strategy implementation, and role in a portfolio of event-driven hedge fund strategies

Distressed securities strategies focus on firms that either are in bankruptcy, facing potential bankruptcy, or under financial stress. Firms face these circumstances for a wide variety of reasons, including waning competitiveness, excessive leverage, poor governance, accounting irregularities, or outright fraud. Often the securities of such companies have been sold out of long-only portfolios and may be trading at a significant discount to their eventual work-out value under proper stewardship and guidance. Because hedge funds are not constrained by institutional requirements on minimum credit quality, hedge fund managers are often natural candidates to take positions in such situations. Hedge funds, generally, also provide their investors only periodic liquidity (typically quarterly or sometimes only annually), making the illiquid nature of such securities less problematic than if such positions were held within a mutual fund. Hedge fund managers may find inefficiently priced securities before, during, or after the bankruptcy process, but typically they will be looking to realize their returns somewhat faster than the longer-term orientation of private equity firms. However, this is not always the case; for example, managers that invest in some distressed sovereign debt (e.g., Sri Lanka, Venezuela) often must face long time horizons to collect their payouts.

At times, distressed hedge fund managers may seek to own the majority or all of a certain class of securities within the capital structure, which enables them to exert creditor control in the corporate bankruptcy or reorganization process. Such securities will vary by country depending on individual bankruptcy laws and procedures. Some managers are active in their distressed investing by building concentrated positions and placing representatives on the boards of the companies they are seeking to turn around. Other distressed managers may be more "passive" in their orientation, relying on others to bear the often substantial legal costs of a corporate capital structure reorganization that may at times involve expensive proxy contests.

By nature, distressed debt and other illiquid assets may take several years to resolve, and they are generally difficult to value. Therefore, hedge fund managers running portfolios of distressed securities typically require relatively long initial lock-up periods (e.g., no redemptions allowed for the first two years) from their investors. Distressed investment managers may also impose fund-level or investor-level redemption gates that are meant to limit the amount of money that investors (i.e., limited partners) may withdraw from a partnership during any given quarter. As for valuing distressed securities, external valuation specialists may be needed to provide an independent estimate of fair value. Valuations of distressed securities with little or no liquidity (e.g., those deemed Level 3 assets according to various accounting and financial standards) are subject to the smoothing effect of "mark-to-model" price determination.

The bankruptcy process typically results in one or two outcomes: liquidation or firm re-organization. In a liquidation, the firm's assets are sold off over some time period; then, based on the priority of their claim, debt- and equity-holders are paid off sequentially. In this case, claimants on the firm's assets are paid in order of priority from senior secured debt, junior secured debt, unsecured debt, convertible debt, preferred stock, and finally common stock. In a re-organization, a firm's capital structure is re-organized and the terms for current claims are negotiated and revised. Current debtholders may agree to extend the maturity of their debt contracts or even to exchange their debt for new equity shares. In this case, existing equity would be canceled (so existing shareholders would be left with nothing) and new equity issued, which would also be sold to new investors to raise funds to improve the firm's financial condition.

Investment Characteristics

Distressed securities present new sets of risks and opportunities and thus require special skills and increased monitoring. As previously mentioned, many institutional investors, like banks and insurance companies, by their mandates cannot hold non-investment-grade securities in their portfolios. As a result, many such investors must sell off investments in firms facing financial distress. This situation may result in illiquidity and significant price discounting when trades do occur, but it also creates potentially attractive opportunities for hedge funds. Moreover, the movement from financial distress to bankruptcy can unfold over long periods and because of the complexities of legal proceedings, informational inefficiencies cause securities to be improperly valued.

To successfully invest in distressed securities, hedge fund managers require specific skills for analyzing complicated legal proceedings, bankruptcy processes, creditor committee discussions, and re-organization scenarios. They also must be able to anticipate market reactions to these actions. At times, and depending on relative pricing, managers may establish "capital structure arbitrage" positions: For the same distressed entity, they may be long securities where they expect to receive acceptable recoveries but short other securities (including equity) where the value-recovery prospects are dim.

Current market conditions also affect the success of distressed securities strategies. In liquidation, assets may need to be sold quickly, and discounted selling prices will lower the total recovery rate. When illiquid assets must be sold quickly, forced sales and liquidity spirals may lead to fire-sale prices. For re-organizations, current market conditions partly determine whether (and how much) a firm can raise capital from asset sales and/or from the issuance of new equity. Exhibit 6 provides some key attributes of distressed securities investing.

Exhibit 6: Distressed Securities—Risk, Liquidity, Leverage, and Benchmarking

Risk Profile and Liquidity

- The return profile for distressed securities investing is typically at the higher end of event-driven strategies but with more variability.

- Outright shorts or hedged positions are possible, but distressed securities investing is usually long-biased. It is subject to security-specific outcomes but still impacted by the health of the macro-economy.
- Distressed securities investing typically entails relatively high levels of illiquidity, especially if using a concentrated activist approach. Pricing may involve "mark-to-model" with return smoothing. Ultimate results are generally binary: either very good or very bad.
- Attractiveness: Returns tend to be "lumpy" and somewhat cyclical. Distressed investing is particularly attractive in the early stages of an economic recovery after a period of market dislocation.

Leverage Usage

- Moderate to low: Because of the inherent volatility and long-biased nature of distressed securities investing, hedge fund managers utilize modest levels of leverage, typically with 1.2 to 1.7 times NAV invested, and with some of the nominal leverage from derivatives hedging.

Benchmarking

- Hedge fund sub-indexes include HFRX and HFRI Distressed Indices; CISDM Distressed Securities Index; Lipper Event-Driven Index; and Credit Suisse Event Driven Distressed Hedge Fund Index.

Note: Alpha produced by distressed securities managers tends to be idiosyncratic. Also, the strategy capitalizes on information inefficiencies and structural inabilities of traditional managers to hold such securities.

Strategy Implementation

Hedge fund managers take several approaches when investing in distressed securities. In a liquidation situation, the focus is on determining the recovery value for different classes of claimants. If the fund manager's estimate of recovery value is higher than market expectations, perhaps due to illiquidity issues, then he/she can buy the undervalued debt securities in hopes of realizing the higher recovery rate. For example, assume bankrupt company X's senior secured debt is priced at 50% of par. By conducting research on the quality of the collateral and by estimating potential cash flows (and their timing) in liquidation, the hedge fund manager estimates a recovery rate of 75%. He/she can buy the senior secured debt and expect to realize the positive difference in recovery rates. It is also important to assess, with the help of experienced bankruptcy counsel and other legal advisors, the estimated timing for the conclusion of the legal process. Such process may be lengthy—in some cases, up to several years. However, even assuming the manager is correct, if the liquidation process drags on and/or market conditions deteriorate, then this premium may be only partly realized, if at all.

In a reorganization situation, the hedge fund manager's focus is on how the firm's finances will be restructured and on assessing the value of the business enterprise and the future value of different classes of claims. There are various avenues for investing in a re-organization. The manager will evaluate the different securities of the company in question and purchase those deemed to be undervalued given the likely re-organization outcome. The selection of security will also depend on whether the manager seeks a control position or not. If so, he/she will be active in the negotiating process and will seek to identify fulcrum securities that provide leverage (or even liquidation) in the reorganization. **Fulcrum securities** are partially-in-the-money claims (not expected to be repaid in full) whose holders end up owning the reorganized company. Assuming the re-organization is caused by excessive financial leverage but the company's operating prospects are still good, a financial restructuring may be implemented whereby senior unsecured debt purchased by the hedge fund manager is swapped for new shares (existing debt and equity are cancelled) and new equity investors inject fresh capital into the company. As financial distress passes and the intrinsic value of the reorganized company rises, an initial public offering (IPO) would likely be undertaken. The hedge fund manager could then exit and earn the difference between what was paid for the undervalued senior unsecured debt and the proceeds received from selling the new shares of the revitalized company in the IPO.

EXAMPLE 5

Capital Structure Arbitrage in the Energy Crisis of 2015–2016

With a sudden structural increase in US energy reserves caused by modern fracking techniques, oil prices tumbled dramatically from more than $60/barrel in mid-2015 to less than $30/barrel in early 2016. Debt investors suddenly became concerned about the very survivability of the smaller, highly levered exploration and production (E&P) companies if such low energy prices were to persist. Prices of many energy-related, junior, unsecured, non-investment-grade debt securities fell dramatically. However, retail equity investors generally reacted more benignly. As a result, the shares of several such E&P companies still carried significant implied enterprise value while their debt securities traded as if bankruptcy was imminent.

1. Discuss why such a divergence in the valuation of the debt and equity securities of these E&P companies might have occurred.

Solution:

This divergence in valuation occurred because of structural differences between the natural holders of debt and equity securities. Institutional holders of the debt likely felt more compelled, or in some cases were required by investment policy, to sell these securities as credit ratings on these bonds were slashed. Retail equity investors were likely less informed as to the potential seriousness of the impact of such a sharp energy price decline on corporate survivability. With equity markets overall still moving broadly higher, retail equityholders may have been expressing a "buy the dip" mentality. Such cross-asset arbitrage situations represent a significant opportunity for nimble and flexible hedge fund managers that are unrestrained by a single asset class perspective or other institutional constraints.

2. Discuss how a hedge fund manager specializing in distressed securities might take advantage of this situation.

Solution:

An astute hedge fund manager would have realized three key points: 1) the junior unsecured debt securities were temporarily undervalued; 2) although bankruptcy in certain specific companies was indeed possible (depending on how long energy prices stayed low), detailed research could uncover those E&P companies for which bankruptcy was less likely; and 3) the unsecured debt securities could be purchased with some safety by shorting the still overvalued equities (or buying put options on those equities) as a hedge.

If energy prices subsequently remained low for too long and bankruptcy was indeed encountered, the equities would become worthless. However, the unsecured debt might still have some recovery value from corporate asset sales, or these securities might become the fulcrum securities that would be converted in a bankruptcy reorganization into new equity in an ongoing enterprise. Alternatively, if oil prices were to recover (as indeed transpired; oil prices closed 2017 at more than $60/barrel), the unsecured debt securities of many of these companies would rebound far more substantially than their equity shares would rise.

In sum, a distressed securities hedge fund arbitrageur willing to take a position in the unsecured debt hedged against short equity (or long puts on the equity) could make money under a variety of possible outcomes.

RELATIVE VALUE STRATEGIES: FIXED-INCOME ARBITRAGE

7

☐ discuss investment characteristics, strategy implementation, and role in a portfolio of relative value hedge fund strategies

We have previously described equity market-neutral investing as one specific equity-oriented relative value hedge fund approach, but other types of relative value strategies are common for hedge funds involving fixed-income securities and hybrid convertible debt. Like equity market-neutral trading, many of these strategies involve the significant use of leverage. Changes in credit quality, liquidity, and implied volatility (for securities with embedded options) are some of the causes of relative valuation differences. During normal market conditions, successful relative value strategies can earn credit, liquidity, or volatility premiums over time. But, in crisis periods—when excessive leverage, deteriorating credit quality, illiquidity, and volatility spikes come to the fore—relative value strategies can result in losses. Fixed-income arbitrage and convertible bond arbitrage are among the most common relative value strategies.

Fixed-Income Arbitrage

Fixed-income arbitrage strategies attempt to exploit pricing inefficiencies by taking long and short positions across a range of debt securities, including sovereign and corporate bonds, bank loans, and consumer debt (e.g., credit card loans, student loans, mortgage-backed securities). Arbitrage opportunities between fixed-income instruments may develop because of variations in duration, credit quality, liquidity, and optionality.

Investment Characteristics

In its simplest form, fixed-income arbitrage involves buying the relatively undervalued securities and short selling the relatively overvalued securities with the expectation that the mispricing will resolve itself (reversion back to normal valuations) within the specified investment horizon. Valuation differences beyond normal historical ranges can result from differences in credit quality (investment-grade versus non-investment-grade securities), differences in liquidity (on-the-run versus off-the-run securities), differences in volatility expectations (especially for securities with embedded options), and even differences in issue sizes. More generally, fixed-income arbitrage can be characterized as exploiting price differences relative to expected future price relationships, with mean reversion being one important aspect. In many instances, realizing a net positive relative carry over time may also be the goal of the relative security positioning, which may involve exploiting kinks in a yield curve or an expected shift in the shape of a yield curve.

Where positioning may involve the acceptance of certain relative credit risks across different security issuers, fixed-income arbitrage morphs into what is more broadly referred to as L/S credit trading. This version of trading tends to be naturally more volatile than the exploitation of small pricing differences within sovereign debt alone.

Unless trading a price discrepancy directly involves establishing a desired yield curve exposure, fixed-income arbitrageurs will typically immunize their strategies, which involve both long and short positions, from interest rate risk by taking duration-neutral positions. However, duration neutrality provides a hedge against only small shifts in the yield curve. To hedge against large yield changes and/or non-parallel yield curve movements (i.e., steepening or flattening), the manager might employ a range of fixed-income derivatives, including futures, forwards, swaps, and swaptions (i.e., options on a swap). Moreover, fixed-income securities also vary in their complexity. For example, in addition to interest rate risk, straight government debt is exposed to sovereign risk (and potentially currency risk), which can be substantial in many countries, while asset-backed and mortgaged-backed securities are subject to credit risk and pre-payment risk. Derivatives are also useful for hedging such risks.

Fixed-income security pricing inefficiencies are often quite small, especially in the more-efficient developed capital markets, but the correlation aspects across different securities is typically quite high. Consequently, it may be necessary and acceptable to utilize substantial amounts of leverage to exploit these inefficiencies. Typical leverage ratios in fixed-income arbitrage strategies can be 4 to 5 times (assets to equity). In the case of some market-neutral multi-strategy funds, where fixed-income arbitrage may form just a portion of total risk, fixed-income arbitrage leverage levels can sometimes be as high as 12 to 15 times assets to equity. Of course, leverage will magnify the myriad risks to which fixed-income strategies are exposed, especially during stressed market conditions.

Another factor that has compounded the risks of fixed-income arbitrage strategies has been the inclination of financial engineers to create tranched, structured products around certain fixed-income cash flows—particularly involving residential mortgages—to isolate certain aspects of credit risk and prepayment risk. For example, within a pool of mortgages, cash flows may be divided such that some credit tranche holders have seniority over others or so that interest-only income payments flow to one set of holders and principal-only payoffs flow to another set of holders. The risks of relative value strategies involving mortgage-related securities, which are especially relevant during periods of market stress, include negative convexity aspects of many mortgage-backed securities and some of the structured products built around them; underlying default rates potentially exceeding expectations and resulting in a high-volatility environment; balance sheet leverage of hedge funds; and hedge fund investor redemption pressures.

Globally, fixed-income markets are substantially larger in total issuance size and scale than equity markets and come in a myriad of different securities types. Away from on-the-run government securities and other sovereign-backed debt securities, which in most developed financial markets are generally very liquid, the liquidity aspects of many fixed-income securities are typically poor. This creates relative value arbitrage opportunities for hedge fund managers, but it also entails positioning and liquidity risks in portfolio management. Natural price opaqueness must often be overcome—particularly for "off-the-run" securities that may trade only occasionally. Liquidity in certain municipal bond markets and corporate debt markets, for example, can be particularly thin. Some key points of fixed-income arbitrage appear in Exhibit 7.

Exhibit 7: Fixed-Income Arbitrage—Risk, Liquidity, Leverage, and Benchmarking

Risk Profile and Liquidity

- The risk/return profile of fixed-income arbitrage trading derives from the high correlations found across different securities, the yield spread pick-up to be captured, and the sheer number of different types of debt securities across different markets with different credit quality and convexity aspects in their pricing. Structured products built around debt securities introduce added complexity that may result in mispricing opportunities.
- Yield curve and carry trades within the US government universe tend to be very liquid but typically have the fewest mispricing opportunities. Liquidity for relative value positions generally decreases in other sovereign markets, in mortgage-related markets, and especially across corporate debt markets.
- Attractiveness: A function of correlations between different securities, the yield spread available, and the high number and wide diversity of debt securities across different markets.

Leverage Usage

- High: This strategy has high leverage usage, but leverage availability typically diminishes with product complexity. To achieve the desired leverage, prime brokers offer collateralized repurchase agreements with associated leverage "haircuts" depending on the types of securities being traded. The haircut is the prime broker's cushion against market volatility and illiquidity if posted collateral ever needs to be liquidated.

Benchmarking

- This is a broad category that encompasses the following sub-indexes: HFRX and HFRI Fixed Income Relative Value Indices; Lipper Fixed Income Arbitrage Index; CISDM Debt Arbitrage Index; and Credit Suisse Fixed Income Arbitrage Index.

Note: HFRX and HFRI also offer more granular hedge fund fixed-income, relative value indexes related to sovereign bonds trading, credit trading, and asset-backed trading.

Strategy Implementation

The most common types of fixed-income arbitrage strategies include yield curve trades and carry trades. Considering yield curve trades, the prevalent calendar spread strategy involves taking long and short positions at different points on the yield curve where the relative mispricing of securities offers the best opportunities, such as in a curve flattening or steepening, to profit. Perceptions and forecasts of macroeconomic conditions are the backdrop for these types of trades. The positions can be in fixed-income securities of the same issuer; in that case, most credit and liquidity risks would likely be hedged, making interest rate risk the main concern. Alternatively, longs and shorts can be taken in the securities of different issuers—but typically ones operating in the same industry or sector. In this case, differences in credit quality, liquidity, volatility, and issue-specific characteristics would likely drive the relative mispricing. In either case, the hedge fund manager aims to profit as the mispricing reverses (mean reversion occurs) and the longs rise and shorts fall in value within the targeted time frame.

Carry trades involve going long a higher yielding security and shorting a lower yielding security with the expectation of receiving the positive carry and of profiting on long and short sides of the trade when the temporary relative mispricing reverts to normal. A classic example of a fixed-income arbitrage trade involves buying lower liquidity, off-the-run government securities and selling higher liquidity, duration matched, on-the-run government securities. Interest rate and credit risks are hedged because long and short positions have the same duration and credit exposure. So, the key concern is liquidity risk. Under normal conditions, as time passes the more (less) expensive on- (off-) the-run securities will decrease (increase) in price as the current on-the-runs are replaced by a more liquid issue of new on-the-run bonds that then become off-the-run bonds.

The payoff profile of this fixed-income arbitrage strategy resembles a short put option. If the strategy unfolds as expected, it returns a positive carry plus a profit from spread narrowing. But, if the spread unexpectedly widens, then the payoff becomes negative. Mispricing of government securities is generally small, so substantial leverage would typically be used to magnify potential profits. But, with highly levered positions, even a temporary negative price shock can be sufficient to set off a wave of margin calls that force fund managers to sell at significant losses. It is important to note that there are far more complex relative value fixed-income strategies beyond just yield curve trades, carry trades, or relative credit trades.

EXAMPLE 6

Fixed-Income Arbitrage: Treasuries vs. Inflation Swap + TIPS

1. Guernsey Shore Hedge Fund closely monitors government bond markets and looks for valuation discrepancies among the different issues.

   Portfolio manager Nick Landers knows that Treasury Inflation-Protected Securities (TIPS) pay a coupon (i.e., real yield) while accruing inflation into the principal, which is paid at maturity. This insulates the TIPS owner from inflation risk.

   Landers also understands that because the US government issues both TIPS and Treasuries that have the same maturity, they should trade at similar yields after adjusting for inflation. Landers knows that by using OTC inflation swaps, the inflation-linked components of TIPS can be locked in, thereby fixing all payments to be similar to those of a Treasury bond.

   After accounting for expected inflation in normal periods, global investors often prefer Treasuries to inflation-indexed bonds. This may be because market participants do not fully trust the way inflation may be measured over time. As such, inflation-hedged TIPS (as a package with the associated offsetting inflation swap) have typically yielded about 25 bps to 35 bps more than similar maturity Treasuries.

During a period of extreme market distress, in November 2XXX, Landers keenly observed that TIPS were particularly mispriced. Their yields, adjusted for inflation, were substantially higher than straight Treasuries, while inflation swaps were priced as if outright deflation was imminent. Landers notes the information on the relative pricing of these different products and considers whether to implement the following trade:

November 2XXX	Fixed Rate	Inflation Rate	Cost
Buy 5-year TIPS	Receive 3.74%	Receive inflation	–1,000,000
Short 5-year Treasuries	Pay 2.56%	—	+1,000,000
Inflation swap: receive fixed rate and pay inflation index	Receive 1.36%	Pay inflation	0
Net of three trades	Receive 2.54%	—	0

Discuss whether Landers has uncovered a risk-free arbitrage, and if so, discuss some of the risks he may still face with its execution.

Solution:

The situation observed by Landers occurred during a period of extreme market stress. In such turbulent times, instances of very attractive, near risk-free arbitrage can occur, as in this case. Often these periods are characterized by a fear of deflation, so straight Treasury bonds are in high demand for flight-to-quality reasons. But there would be some operational hurdles to overcome. For Landers to short the expensive Treasuries and buy the more attractive TIPS, Guernsey Shore would need access as a counterparty to the interbank repurchase market to borrow the Treasury bonds. Bank credit approval would also be required for accessing the inflation swap market for yield enhancement and to lock in the inflation hedge. Unfortunately, during periods of extreme market distress, credit lines to hedge funds typically shrink (or are withdrawn), not expand. Moreover, there is potential for "losing the borrow" on the short Treasuries (i.e., the lender demanding return of his/her Treasuries), which makes the trade potentially difficult to maintain. Assuming Guernsey Shore met these operational requirements, Landers would need to act quickly to capture the fixed-income arbitrage profit of 2.54%. Such extreme levels of arbitrage rarely persist for very long.

RELATIVE VALUE STRATEGIES: CONVERTIBLE BOND ARBITRAGE 8

- [ ] discuss investment characteristics, strategy implementation, and role in a portfolio of relative value hedge fund strategies

Convertible bonds are hybrid securities that can be viewed as a combination of straight debt plus a long equity call option with an exercise price equal to the strike price times the conversion ratio. The conversion ratio is the number of shares for which the bond can be exchanged. The bond's conversion value is the current stock price times the conversion ratio. The conversion price is the current convertible bond price divided by the conversion ratio. If the current conversion value is significantly below the convertible bond price (or equivalently, the current share price is significantly below the conversion price), the call is out-of-the-money and the convertible bond will behave more like a straight bond. Conversely, if the conversion value is significantly above the convertible bond price (or equivalently, the current share price is significantly above the conversion price), the call is in-the-money and the convertible bond will behave more like the underlying equity.

Investment Characteristics

Convertible securities are naturally complex and thus generally not well understood. They are impacted by numerous factors, including overall interest rate levels, corporate credit spreads, bond coupon and principal cash flows, and the value of the embedded stock option (which itself is influenced by dividend payments, stock price movements, and equity volatility). Convertibles are often issued sporadically by companies in relatively small sizes compared to straight debt issuances, and thus they are typically thinly-traded securities. Moreover, most convertibles are non-rated and typically have fewer covenants than straight bonds. Because the equity option value is embedded within such thinly-traded, complex securities, the embedded options within convertibles tend to trade at relatively low implied volatility levels compared to the historical volatility level of the underlying equity. Convertibles also trade cyclically relative to the amount of new issuance of such securities in the overall market. The higher the new convertible issuance that the market must absorb, the cheaper their pricing and the more attractive the arbitrage opportunities for a hedge fund manager.

The key problem for the convertible arbitrage manager is that to access and extract the relatively cheap embedded optionality of the convertible, he/she must accept or hedge away other risks that are embedded in the convertible security. These include interest rate risk, credit risk of the corporate issuer, and market risk (i.e., the risk that the stock price will decline and thus render the embedded call option less valuable). Should the convertible manager desire, all these risks can be hedged using a combination of interest rate derivatives, credit default swaps, and short sales of an appropriate delta-adjusted amount of the underlying stock. The purchase of put options can also be a stock-sale substitute. The use of any such hedging tools may also erode the very attractiveness of the targeted convertible holding.

Convertible managers who are more willing to accept credit risk may choose to not hedge the credit default risk of the corporate issuer; instead, they will take on the convertible position more from a credit risk perspective. Such managers are known as credit-oriented convertible managers. Other managers may hedge the credit risk but will take a more long-biased, directional view of the underlying stock and then underhedge the convertible's equity exposure. Yet other managers may overhedge the equity risk to create a bearish tilt with respect to the underlying stock, thus providing a more focused exposure to increased volatility. These managers are referred to as volatility-oriented convertible managers. In sum, several different ways and styles can be utilized to set up convertible arbitrage exposures. Exhibit 8 presents some key aspects of convertible bond arbitrage.

Exhibit 8: Convertible Bond Arbitrage—Risk, Liquidity, Leverage, and Benchmarking

Risk Profile and Liquidity

- Convertible arbitrage managers strive to extract and benefit from this structurally cheap source of implied volatility by delta hedging and gamma trading short equity hedges against their long convertible holdings (this is discussed further in the next section).
- Liquidity issues surface for convertible arbitrage strategies in two ways: 1) naturally less-liquid securities because of their relatively small issue sizes and inherent complexities; 2) availability and cost to borrow underlying equity for short selling.
- Attractiveness: Convertible arbitrage works best during periods of high convertible issuance, moderate volatility, and reasonable market liquidity. It fares less well in periods of acute credit weakness and general illiquidity, when the pricing of convertible securities is unduly impacted by supply/demand imbalances.

Leverage Usage

- High: Because of many legs needed to implement convertible arbitrage trades (e.g., short sale, CDS transaction, interest rate hedge), relatively high levels of leverage are used to extract a modest ultimate gain from delta hedging. Managers typically run convertible portfolios at 300% long vs. 200% short, the lower short exposure being a function of the delta-adjusted equity exposure needed from short sales to balance the long convertible.

Benchmarking

- Sub-indexes include HFRX and HFRI FI-Convertible Arbitrage Indices; Lipper Convertible Arbitrage Index; CISDM Convertible Arbitrage Index; and Credit Suisse Convertible Arbitrage Index.

Note: Convertible bond arbitrage is a core hedge fund strategy area that is run within many multi-strategy hedge funds together with L/S equity, merger arbitrage, and other event-driven distressed strategies.

Strategy Implementation

A classic convertible bond arbitrage strategy is to buy the relatively undervalued convertible bond and take a short position in the relatively overvalued underlying stock. The number of shares to sell short to achieve a delta neutral overall position is determined by the delta of the convertible bond. For convertible bonds with low conversion prices relative to the current stock price (i.e., the long call is I-T-M), the delta will be close to 1. For convertibles with high conversion prices relative to the current stock price (i.e., the long call is O-T-M), the delta will be closer to 0. The combination of a long convertible and short equity delta exposure would create a situation where for small changes in the equity price, the portfolio will remain essentially balanced. As the underlying stock price moves further, however, the delta hedge of the convertible will change because the convertible is an instrument with the natural positive convexity attributes of positive gamma. Because stock gamma is always zero, the convertible arbitrage strategy will leave the convertible arbitrageur "synthetically" longer in total equity exposure as the underlying security price rises and synthetically less long as the equity price falls. This added gamma-driven exposure can then be hedged at favorable levels with appropriate sizing adjustments of the underlying short stock hedge—selling more stock at higher levels and buying more stock at lower levels. The convertible arbitrage strategy will be profitable given sufficiently large stock price swings and proper periodic rebalancing (assuming all else equal). If realized equity volatility exceeds the implied volatility of the convertible's embedded option (net of hedging costs), an overall gain is achieved by the arbitrageur.

Several circumstances can create concerns for a convertible arbitrage strategy. First, when short selling, shares must be located and borrowed; as a result, the stock owner may subsequently want his/her shares returned at a potentially inopportune time, such as during stock price run-ups or more generally when supply for the stock is low or demand for the stock is high. This situation, particularly a short squeeze, can lead to substantial losses and a suddenly unbalanced exposure if borrowing the underlying equity shares becomes too difficult or too costly for the arbitrageur (of course, initially locking in a "borrow" over a "term period" can help the arbitrageur avoid short squeezes, but this may be costly to execute). Second, credit issues may complicate valuation given that bonds have exposure to credit risk; so when credit spreads widen or narrow, there would be a mismatch in the values of the stock and convertible bond positions that the convertible manager may or may not have attempted to hedge away. Third, the strategy can lose money because of time decay of the convertible bond's embedded call option during periods of reduced realized equity volatility and/or from a general compression of market implied volatility levels.

Convertible arbitrage strategies have performed best when convertible issuance is high (implying a wider choice among convertible securities and generally cheaper prices), general market volatility levels are moderate, and the liquidity to trade and adjust positions is ample. On the other hand, extreme market volatility also typically implies heightened credit risks; given that convertibles are naturally less-liquid securities, convertible managers generally do not fare well during such periods. The fact that hedge funds have become the natural market makers for convertibles and they typically face significant redemption pressures from investors during crises implies further unattractive left-tail risk attributes to the strategy during periods of market stress.

EXAMPLE 7

Convertible Arbitrage Strategy

Cleopatra Partners is a Dubai-based hedge fund engaging in convertible bond arbitrage. Portfolio manager Shamsa Khan is considering a trade involving the euro-denominated convertible bonds and stock of QXR Corporation. She has assembled the following information:

QXR Convertible Bond		
Price (% of par)	120	—
Coupon (%)	5.0	—
Remaining maturity (years)	1.0	
Conversion ratio	50	—
S&P Rating	BBB	—

QXR Inc.		Industry Average
Price (per share)	30	—
P/E (x)	30	20

QXR Inc.		Industry Average
P/BV (x)	2.25	1.5
P/CF (x)	15	10

Additional Information:

- It costs €2 to borrow each QXR share (paid to the stock lender) to carry the short position for a year.
- The stock pays a €1 dividend.

1. Discuss (using only the information in the table) the basic trade setup that Khan should implement.

Solution:

QXR's convertible bond price is €1,200 [= €1,000 × (120/100)], and its conversion ratio is 50; so, the conversion price is €24 (€1,200/50). This compares with QXR's current share price of €30. QXR's share valuation metrics are all 50% higher than its industry's averages. It can be concluded that in relative terms, QXR's shares are overvalued and its convertible bonds are undervalued. Thus, Khan should buy the convertibles and short sell the shares.

2. Demonstrate (without using the additional information) that potential profits earned are the same whether QXR's share price falls to €24, rises to €36, or remains flat at €30.

Solution:

By implementing this trade and buying the bond at €1,200, exercising the bond's conversion option, and selling her shares at the current market price, Khan can lock in a profit of €6 per share under any of the scenarios mentioned, as shown in the following table:

	Profit on:		
QXR Share Price	Long Stock via Convertible Bond	Short Stock	Total Profit
24	0	6	6
36	12	−6	6
30	6	0	6

3. Discuss (using also the additional information) how the results of the trade will change.

Solution:

The €2 per share borrowing costs and the €1 dividend payable to the lender together represent a €3 per share outflow that Khan must pay. But, the convertible bond pays a 5% coupon or €50, which equates to an inflow of €1 per share equivalent (€50 coupon/50 shares per bond). Therefore, the total profit outcomes, as indicated in the table, would each be reduced by €2. In sum, Khan would realize a total profit of €4 per each QXR share.

9 OPPORTUNISTIC STRATEGIES: GLOBAL MACRO STRATEGIES

☐ discuss investment characteristics, strategy implementation, and role in a portfolio of opportunistic hedge fund strategies

Opportunistic hedge fund strategies seek to profit from investment opportunities across a wide range of markets and securities using a variety of techniques. They invest primarily in asset classes, sectors and regions, and across macro themes and multi-asset relationships on a global basis (as opposed to focusing on the individual security level). So, broad themes, global relationships, market trends, and cycles affect their returns.

Although opportunistic hedge funds can sometimes be difficult to categorize and may use a variety of techniques, they can generally be divided by

1. the type of analysis and approach that drives the trading strategy (technical or fundamental),
2. how trading decisions are implemented (discretionary or systematic), and
3. the types of instruments and/markets in which they trade.

Fundamental-based strategies use economic data as inputs and focus on fair valuation of securities, sectors, markets, and intra-market relationships. Technical analysis utilizes statistical methods to predict relative price movements based on past price trends.

Discretionary implementation relies on manager skills to interpret new information and make investment decisions, and it may be subject to such behavioral biases as overconfidence and loss aversion. Systematic implementation is rules-based and executed by computer algorithms with little or no human intervention; however, it may encounter difficulty coping with new, complex situations (not seen historically). As the absolute size of systematic trend-following funds has increased in significance, so too has the issue of negative execution slippage caused by the simultaneous reversal of multiple trend-following models that sometimes creates a "herding effect." Such effects can temporarily overwhelm normal market liquidity and at times temporarily distort fundamental market pricing of assets (i.e., trend-following "overshoots" caused by momentum-signal triggers). We now discuss the two most common hedge fund strategies: global macro and managed futures.

Global Macro Strategies

Global macro strategies focus on global relationships across a wide range of asset classes and investment instruments, including derivative contracts (e.g., futures, forwards, swaps, and options) on commodities, currencies, precious and base metals, and fixed-income and equity indexes—as well as on sovereign debt securities, corporate bonds, and individual stocks. Given the wide range of possibilities to express a global macro view, these strategies tend to focus on certain themes (e.g., trading undervalued emerging market currencies versus overvalued US dollar using OTC currency swaps), regions (e.g., trading stock index futures on Italy's FTSE MIB versus Germany's DAX to capitalize on differences in eurozone equity valuations), or styles (e.g., systematic versus discretionary spread trading in energy futures). Global macro managers typically hold views on the relative economic health and central bank policies of different countries, global yield curve relationships, trends in inflation and relative purchasing power parity, and capital trade flow aspects of different countries (typically expressed through relative currency or rate-curve positioning).

Global macro managers tend to be anticipatory and sometimes contrarian in setting their strategies. Some macro managers may try to extract carry gains or ride momentum waves, but most have a tendency to be early in their positioning and then benefit when some rationality eventually returns to relative market pricing. This can make an allocation to global macro strategies particularly useful when a sudden potential reversal in markets is feared. For example, many global macro managers sensed the developing subprime mortgage crisis in the United States as early as 2006. They took on long positions in credit default swaps (CDS) (i.e., they purchased protection) on mortgage bonds, on tranches of mortgage structured products, or simply on broader credit indexes that they deemed particularly vulnerable to weakening credit conditions. Although they had to wait until 2007–2008 for these CDS positions to pay off, some global macro managers performed spectacularly well as market conditions morphed into the global financial crisis. Including global macro managers with significant subprime mortgage-focused CDS positions within a larger portfolio turned out to be a very valuable allocation.

It is important to note that because global macro managers trade a wide variety of instruments and markets and typically do so by different methods, these managers are fairly heterogeneous as a group. Thus, global macro funds are not as consistently dependable as a source of short alpha when compared to pure systematic, trend-following managed futures funds that typically attempt to capture any significant market trend. But, as noted earlier, global macro managers tend to be more anticipatory (compared to managed futures managers), which can be a useful attribute.

Investment Characteristics

Global macro managers use fundamental and technical analysis to value markets, and they use discretionary and systematic modes of implementation. The view taken by global macro portfolio managers can be directional (e.g., buy bonds of banks expected to benefit from "normalization" of US interest rates) or thematic (e.g., buy the "winning" companies and short sell the "losing" companies from Brexit). Because of their heterogeneity, added due diligence and close attention to the current portfolio of a macro manager may be required by an allocator to correctly anticipate the factor risks that a given global macro manager will deliver.

Despite their heterogeneity, a common feature among most global macro managers is the use of leverage, often obtained through the use of derivatives, to magnify potential profits. A margin-to-equity ratio typically of 15% to 25% posted against futures or forward positions allows a manager to control face amounts of assets up to 6 to 7 times a fund's assets. The use of such embedded leverage naturally allows the global macro manager ease and flexibility in relative value and directional positioning.

Generally, the key source of returns in global macro strategies revolves around correctly discerning and capitalizing on trends in global markets. As such, mean-reverting low volatility markets are the natural bane of this strategy area. Conversely, steep equity market sell-offs, interest rate regime changes, currency devaluations, volatility spikes, and geopolitical shocks caused by such events as trade wars and terrorism are examples of global macro risks; however, they can also provide some of the opportunities that global macro managers often attempt to exploit. Of course, the exposures selected in any global macro strategy may not react to the global risks as expected because of either unforeseen contrary factors or global risks that simply do not materialize. Thus, macro managers tend to produce somewhat lumpier and uneven return streams than other hedge fund strategies, and generally higher levels of volatility are associated with their returns.

Notably, the prevalence of quantitative easing since the global financial crisis of 2007–2009 resulted in generally benign market conditions for most of the subsequent decade, which was an especially imperfect environment for global macro managers. Although equity and fixed-income markets generally trended higher during this period, overall volatility levels across these and many other markets, such as currencies and commodities, were relatively low. In some cases, central bankers intervened to curtail undesirable market outcomes, thereby preventing certain global macro trends from fully materializing. Because such intervention substantially moderates the trendiness and the volatility of markets, which are the lifeblood of global macro strategies, some hedge fund allocators began avoiding these strategies. This may be shortsighted, however, because such opportunistic strategies as global macro can be very useful over a full market cycle in terms of portfolio diversification and alpha generation. Indeed, global economic conditions and the sudden and sharp reversal of monetary policy in the aftermath of the Covid-19 pandemic demonstrate opportunities for global macro strategies.

Strategy Implementation

Global macro strategies are typically top-down and employ a range of macroeconomic and fundamental models to express a view regarding the direction or relative value of an asset or asset class. Positions may comprise a mix of individual securities, baskets of securities, index futures, foreign exchange futures/forwards, precious or base metals futures, agricultural futures, fixed-income products or futures, and derivatives or options on any of these. If the hedge fund manager is making a directional bet, then directional models will use fundamental data regarding a specific market or asset to determine if it is undervalued or overvalued relative to history and the expected macro trend. Conversely, if the manager's proclivity is toward relative value positioning, then that manager will consider which assets are under- or overvalued relative to each other given historical and expected macro conditions.

For example, if currencies of the major ASEAN block countries (i.e., Indonesia, Malaysia, Philippines, Singapore, and Thailand) are depreciating against the US dollar, a directional model might conclude that the shares of their key exporting companies are undervalued and thus should be purchased. However, further investigation might signal that the public bonds of these exporters are cheap relative to their shares, so the bonds should be bought and the shares sold short. This situation might occur in the likely scenario that the share prices react quickly to the currency depreciation and bond prices take longer to react to the trend.

Successful global macro trading requires the manager to have both a correct fundamental view of the selected market(s) and the proper methodology and timing to express tactical views. Managers who repeatedly implement a position too early/unwind one too late or who choose an inappropriate method for implementation will likely face redemptions from their investors. Given the natural leverage used in global macro strategies, managers may be tempted to carry many (possibly too many) positions simultaneously; however, the diversification benefits of doing so are typically less than those derived from more idiosyncratic long/short equity strategies. This is because of the nature of "risk-on" or "risk-off" market conditions (often caused by central bank policies) that impact a variety of asset classes in a correlated manner.

EXAMPLE 8

Global Macro Strategy

1. Consider the following (hypothetical) macroeconomic scenario: Emerging market (EM) countries have been growing rapidly (in fact, overheating) and accumulating both historically large government budget deficits and trade deficits as expanding populations demand more public services and foreign goods. EM central banks have been intervening to support their currencies for some time, and electoral support for candidates promoting exorbitant business taxes and vast social welfare schemes in many EM countries has risen dramatically. These trends are expected to continue.

   Melvin Chu, portfolio manager at Bermuda-based Global Macro Advisers (GMA), has been considering how to position his global macro hedge fund. After careful review of the central bank's financial reports of a leading EM country, it appears this central bank may run out of foreign exchange reserves soon and thus may be unable to continue its supportive currency intervention.

   Discuss a global macro strategy Chu might implement to profit from these trends by using options.

Solution:

Assuming this key EM country runs out of foreign currency reserves, then it is likely its currency will need to be devalued. This initial devaluation might reasonably be expected to trigger a wave of devaluations and economic and financial market turbulence in other EM countries in similar circumstances. So, Chu should consider trades based on anticipated EM currency depreciation (maybe even devaluation) as well as trades benefitting from rising interest rates, downward pressure on equities, and spikes in volatility in the EM space.

A reasonable way for Chu to proceed would be to buy put options. If his expectations fail to materialize, his losses would then be capped at the total of the premiums paid for the options. Chu should consider buying puts on the following: a variety of EM currencies, EM government bond futures, and EM equity market indexes. He should buy in-the-money puts to implement his high conviction trades and out-of-the money puts for trades where he has a lower degree of confidence. Moreover, to take advantage of a possible flight-to-safety, Chu should consider buying call options on developed market (DM) reserve currencies as well as call options on bond futures for highly-rated DM government issuers.

OPPORTUNISTIC STRATEGIES: MANAGED FUTURES 10

☐ discuss investment characteristics, strategy implementation, and role in a portfolio of opportunistic hedge fund strategies

Managed futures, which gained its first major academic backing in a classic paper by John Lintner in 1983, is a hedge fund strategy that focuses on investments using futures, options on futures, and sometimes forwards and swaps (primarily on stock and fixed-income indexes) and commodities and currencies. As futures markets have evolved over time and in different countries—gaining in size (i.e., open interest) and liquidity—some managers have also engaged in trading sector and industry index futures as well as more exotic contracts, such as futures on weather (e.g., temperature, rainfall) and derivatives contracts on carbon emissions.

Investment Characteristics

The uncorrelated nature of managed futures with stocks and bonds generally makes them a potentially attractive addition to traditional portfolios for improved risk-adjusted return profiles (i.e., improved efficient frontiers in a mean–variance framework). The value added from managed futures has typically been demonstrated during periods of market stress; for example, in 2007–2009 managers using this strategy benefitted from short positions in equity futures and long positions in fixed-income futures at a time when equity indexes were falling and fixed-income indexes were rising. Put another way, managed futures demonstrated natural positive skewness that has been useful in balancing negatively-skewed strategies.

The return profile of managed futures tends to be very cyclical. Between 2011 and 2018, the trendiness (i.e., directionality) of foreign exchange and fixed-income markets deteriorated, volatility levels in many markets dissipated, and periods of acute market stress temporarily disappeared. Except for equity markets in some developed countries, many markets became range-bound or mean-reverting, which hurt managed futures performance. The diversification benefit of trend following strong equity markets is also (by definition) less diversifying to traditional portfolios than if such trends existed in other non-equity markets.

In a world where sovereign bonds have approached the zero-yield boundary, the correlation benefit of managed futures has also changed. The past practice of trend following the fixed-income markets as they get higher may likely not be as repeatable going forward. Assuming managed futures managers begin to trend follow fixed-income markets as they get lower (i.e., as developed market interest rates "normalize"), then positive returns may still be realized—although with a very different type of correlation behavior to equity markets (i.e., not as valuable). Also, given the upward sloping nature of most global yield curves, less natural fixed-income "carry" contribution may occur from trend following the fixed-income markets to the downside (i.e., higher interest rates and lower prices).

Managed futures strategies are typically characterized as highly liquid, active across a wide range of asset classes, and able to go long or short with relative ease. High liquidity results from futures markets being among the most actively traded markets in the world. For example, the E-mini S&P 500 futures contract on the Chicago Mercantile Exchange has 3 to 4 times the daily dollar volume of the SPDR S&P 500 ETF (SPY), the world's most actively traded equity index fund. Futures contracts also provide highly liquid exposures to a wide range of asset classes that can be traded across the globe 24 hours a day. Because futures contracts require relatively little collateral to take positions as a result of the exchanges' central clearinghouse management of margin and risk, it is easier to take long and short positions with higher leverage than traditional instruments.

For example, futures contracts require margin from 0.1% to 10% of notional value for both long and short positions, as compared to standard equity market margin levels in the United States of 50%. This introduces inherent leverage into the strategies. Thus, the capital efficiency of futures contracts makes it easier for managed futures managers to be dynamic in both their long and short exposures. A traditional long-only portfolio is levered by borrowing funds to purchase additional assets. Futures portfolios do not own assets; they acquire asset exposures based on the notional value of the futures contracts held. The majority (typically 85% to 90%) of capital in a managed futures account is invested in short-term government debt (or other highly liquid collateral acceptable to the futures clearing house). The remainder (10% to 15%) is used to collateralize long and short futures contracts.

Strategy Implementation

Highly liquid contracts allow managed futures funds the flexibility to incorporate a wide range of investment strategies. Most managed futures strategies involve some "pattern recognition" trigger that is either momentum/trend driven or based on a volatility signal. Managers trade these signals across different time horizons, often with short-term mean reversion filters imposed on top of their core longer-term models. For example, a manager might have traded using a long-term horizon model that suggested gold prices would trend lower; as a result, the manager established a short position in gold futures some time ago. A short-term moving average of gold prices crossing below a longer-term moving average could have triggered this view. But later, that manager might also trade using a second, shorter time horizon model, which suggests that the downside momentum in gold prices has temporarily subsided and a mean-reverting bounce is likely. The results of these two models would be weighted and combined into an adjusted net position, typically with the longer-term model weighted more heavily than the shorter-term filter.

Such fundamental factors as carry relationships or volatility factors are often added to the core momentum and breakout signal methodologies, and they can be particularly useful regarding position sizing. Many managed futures managers implement their portfolios' relative position sizing by assessing both the volatility of each underlying futures position as well as the correlation of their return behaviors against one another. Generally, the greater the volatility of an asset, the smaller its portfolio sizing; and the greater its correlation to other futures being positioned, the smaller its portfolio sizing. Being attentive to correlation aspects between different futures contracts would then become a second step of analysis for most managed futures traders as a portfolio sizing risk constraint.

Besides core position sizing and sizing adjustments for volatility and correlation, managed futures managers will have

- a price target exit methodology,
- a momentum reversal exit methodology,
- a time-based exit methodology,
- a trailing stop-loss exit methodology,
- or some combination thereof.

A key to successful managed futures strategies is to have a consistent approach and to avoid overfitting of a model when backtesting performance across different markets and time periods. The goal is to have a model that performs well in a future "out of sample" period. Of course, trading models have a natural tendency to degrade in effectiveness over time as more and more managers use similar signals and the market opportunity being exploited consequently diminishes. Managed futures traders are thus constantly searching for new and differentiated trading signals. In today's world, many new signals are increasingly being developed using nontraditional, unstructured data and other types of "big data" analysis.

Apart from this accelerating search for more unique nonprice signals, the most common type of managed futures approach is typically referred to as **time-series momentum** (TSM) trend following. Momentum trading strategies are driven by the past returns of the individual assets. Simply put, managers go long assets that are rising in price and go short assets that are falling in price. TSM strategies are traded on an absolute basis, meaning the manager can be net long or net short depending on the current price trend of an asset. Such TSM strategies work best when an asset's (or market's) own past returns are a good predictor of its future returns.

A second, less common approach is using **cross-sectional momentum** (CSM) strategies, which are implemented with a cross-section of assets (generally within an asset class) by going long those that are rising in price the most and by shorting those that are falling the most. Such CSM strategies generally result in holding a net zero or market-neutral position. CSM strategies work well when a market's out- or underperformance relative to other markets is a reliable predictor of its future performance. However, CSM may be constrained by limited futures contracts available for a cross section of assets at the asset class level.

Global macro strategies and managed futures strategies often involve trading the same subset of markets but in different ways. It is important to understand the respective attributes of these two strategies. Exhibit 9 provides such a comparison.

Exhibit 9: Managed Futures and Global Macro Strategies—Comparison of Risk, Liquidity, Leverage, and Benchmarking

Risk Profile and Liquidity

- Both global macro and managed futures strategies are highly liquid but with some crowding aspects and execution slippage in managed futures as AUM have grown rapidly. Being more heterogeneous in approaches used, global macro strategies face less significant execution crowding effects.
- Typically, managed futures managers tend to take a more systematic approach to implementation than global macro managers, who are generally more discretionary in their application of models and tools.
- Returns of managed futures strategies typically exhibit positive right-tail skewness in periods of market stress, which is very useful for portfolio diversification. Global macro strategies have delivered similar diversification in such stress periods but with more heterogeneous outcomes.
- Despite positive skewness, managed futures and global macro managers are somewhat cyclical and at the more volatile end of the spectrum of hedge fund strategies (with volatility positively related to the strategy's time horizon). In addition, macro managers can also be early and overly anticipatory in their positioning.

Leverage Usage

- High: High leverage is embedded in futures contracts. Notional amounts up to 6 to 7 times fund assets can be controlled with initial margin-to-equity of just 10%–20% (with individual futures margin levels being a function of the volatility of the underlying assets). Active use of options by many global macro managers adds natural elements of leverage and positive convexity.

Benchmarking

- Managed futures are best tracked by such sub-indexes as HFRX and HFRI Macro Systematic Indices; CISDM CTA Equal-Weighted Index; Lipper Managed Futures Index; and Credit Suisse Managed Futures Index.
- Global macro strategies are best tracked by HFRX and HFRI Macro Discretionary Indices; CISDM Hedge Fund Global Macro Index; Lipper Global Macro Index; and Credit Suisse Global Macro Index.

EXAMPLE 9

Cross-Sectional and Time-Series Momentum

1. An institutional investor is considering adding an allocation to a managed futures strategy that focuses on medium-term momentum trading involving precious metals. This investor is evaluating two different managed futures funds that both trade precious metals futures, including gold, silver, platinum, and palladium futures. Of the two funds being considered, one is run using a cross-sectional momentum (CSM) strategy, and the other is managed using a time-series momentum (TSM) strategy. Both funds use trailing 6-month returns for developing their buy/sell signals, and they both volatility-weight their futures positions to have equal impact on their overall portfolios.

   Explain how the CSM and TSM strategies would work and compare their risk profiles.

Solution:

For the CSM strategy, each day the manager will examine the returns for the four metals in question and then take a long position in the two metals futures with the best performance (i.e., the top 50%) in terms of trailing 6-month risk-adjusted returns and a short position in the two metals contracts with the worst performance (i.e., the bottom 50%) of returns. According to this strategy, the top (bottom) 50% will continue their relative value out- (under-) performance. Note that it is possible for metals contracts (or markets more generally) in the top (bottom) 50% to have negative (positive) absolute returns—for example, during bear (bull) markets. The CSM strategy is very much a relative momentum strategy, with the established positions acting as a quasi-hedge relative to each other in terms of total sector exposure. This CSM-run fund would likely deliver an overall return profile with somewhat less volatility than the TSM strategy.

For the TSM strategy, each day the manager will take a long position in the precious metals futures with positive trailing 6-month returns and sell short those metals contracts with negative trailing 6-month returns. According to this TSM strategy, the metals futures (or markets, more generally) with positive (negative) returns will continue to rise (fall) in absolute value, resulting in an expected profit on both long and short positions. However, by utilizing a TSM strategy, the fund might potentially end up with long positions in all four metals contracts or short positions in all these precious metals futures at the same time.

Consequently, the CSM strategy typically results in a net zero market exposure during normal periods, while the TSM strategy can be net long or net short depending on how many metals (or markets, generally) have positive and negative absolute returns. The return profile of the TSM managed fund is thus likely to be more volatile than that of the CSM managed fund and also far more sensitive to periods when the precious metals sector is experiencing strong trends (i.e., directionality).

11 SPECIALIST STRATEGIES

- [ ] discuss investment characteristics, strategy implementation, and role in a portfolio of specialist hedge fund strategies

Specialist hedge fund strategies require highly specialized skill sets for trading in niche markets. Two such typical specialist strategies are volatility trading and reinsurance/life settlements.

Volatility Trading

Over the past several decades, volatility trading has become an asset class unto itself. Niche hedge fund managers specialize in trading relative volatility strategies globally across different geographies and asset classes. For example, given the plethora of structured product offerings in Asia with inexpensive embedded options that can be stripped out and resold (usually by investment banks), volatility pricing in Asia is often relatively cheap compared to the more expensive implied volatility of options traded in North American and European markets. In these latter markets, there is a proclivity to buy out-of-the-money options as a protective hedge (i.e., insurance). The goal of **relative value volatility arbitrage** strategies is to source and buy cheap volatility and sell more expensive volatility while netting out the time decay aspects normally associated with options portfolios. Depending on the instruments used (e.g., puts and calls or variance swaps), these strategies may also attempt to extract value from active gamma trading adjustments when markets move.

Investment Characteristics and Strategy Implementation

The easiest way to understand relative value volatility trading is through a few examples. Throughout the 1980s and 1990s, options on the Japanese yen consistently traded at lower volatility levels within Asian time zones than similar options were traded in London, New York, or Chicago (i.e., IMM futures market). Capturing the volatility spread between these options is a type of relative value volatility trading known as time-zone arbitrage—in this case of a single underlying fungible global asset, the Japanese yen. As a second arbitrage example, managers in today's markets may periodically source Nikkei 225 implied volatility in Asia at cheaper levels than S&P 500 implied volatility is being traded in New York, even though the Nikkei 225 typically has realized volatility higher than that of the S&P 500. This type of relative value volatility trading is known as cross-asset volatility trading, which may often involve idiosyncratic, macro-oriented risks.

Of course, another simpler type of volatility trading involves outright long volatility traders who may trade against consistent volatility sellers. Equity volatility is approximately 80% *negatively* correlated with equity market returns. Otherwise stated, volatility levels tend to go up when equity markets fall, with options pricing skew reflecting such a tendency. Clearly, this makes the long volatility strategy a useful potential diversifier for long equity investments, albeit at the cost to the option premium paid by the volatility buyer. Selling volatility provides a volatility risk premium or compensation for taking on the risk of providing insurance against crises for holders of equities and other securities.

In the United States, the most liquid volatility contracts are short-term VIX Index futures contracts, which track the 30-day implied volatility of S&P 500 Index options as traded on the Chicago Board Options Exchange (CBOE). Because volatility is non-constant but high levels of volatility are difficult to perpetuate over long periods of time (markets eventually calm down after sudden jump shifts), VIX futures are often prone to mean reversion. Given this fact and the fact that VIX futures prices typically slide down a positively sloped implied volatility curve as expiration approaches, many practitioners prefer trading simple exchange-traded options, over-the-counter (OTC) options, variance swaps, and volatility swaps. The general mean-reverting nature of volatility still impacts these products, but it does so in a less explicit fashion than with the futures.

Multiple paths can be taken to implement a volatility trading strategy. If a trader uses simple exchange-traded options, then the maturity of such options typically extends out to no more than approximately two years. In terms of expiry, the longer-dated options will have more absolute exposure to volatility levels (i.e., vega exposure) than shorter-dated options, but the shorter-dated options will exhibit more delta sensitivity to price changes (i.e., gamma exposure). Traders need to monitor the following: the term structure of volatility, which is typically upward sloping but can invert during periods of crisis; the volatility smile across different strike prices, whereby out-of-the-money options will typically trade at higher implied volatility levels than at-the-money options; and the volatility skew, whereby out-of-the-money puts may trade at higher volatility levels than out-of-the-money calls. Volatility traders strive to capture relative timing and strike pricing opportunities using various types of option spreads, such as bull and bear spreads, straddles, and calendar spreads.

To extract an outright long volatility view, options are purchased and delta hedging of the gamma exposure is required. How the embedded gamma of the long options position is managed is also important. For example, one could have a positive view of a volatility expansion but then fail to capture gains in a volatility spike during an adverse market move by poorly managing gamma exposure. Conversely, some managers may use options to extract a more intermediate-term, directional insurance protection-type view of both price and volatility and not engage in active delta hedging.

A second, similar path might be to implement the volatility trading strategy using OTC options. Then the tenor and strike prices of the options can be customized, and the tenor of expiry dates can be extended beyond what is available with exchange-traded options. However, by utilizing OTC options, the strategy is subject to counterparty credit risk as well as added illiquidity risk.

Migrating to the use of VIX Index futures (or options on VIX futures) can more explicitly express a pure volatility view without the need for constant delta hedging of an equity put or call for isolating the volatility exposure. However, as just mentioned, volatility pricing tends to be notoriously mean reverting. Also, an abundant supply of traders and investors typically are looking to sell volatility to capture the volatility premium and the volatility roll down payoff. Roll down refers to the fact that the term structure of volatility tends to be positively sloped, so the passage of time causes added option price decay. In other words, the theta of a long option position is always negative, and if shorter-dated options have a lower implied volatility, then the passage of time increases the rate of natural theta decay.

A fourth path for implementing a volatility trading strategy would be to purchase an OTC volatility swap or a variance swap from a creditworthy counterparty. A volatility swap is a forward contract on future realized price volatility. Similarly, a variance swap is a forward contract on future realized price variance, where variance is the square of volatility. In both cases, at inception of the trade the strike is typically chosen such that the fair value of the swap is zero. This strike is then referred to as fair volatility or fair variance, respectively. At expiry of the swaps, the receiver of the floating leg pays the difference between the realized volatility (or variance) and the agreed-on strike times some prespecified notional amount that is not initially exchanged. Both volatility and variance swaps provide "pure" exposure to volatility alone—unlike standardized options in which the volatility exposure depends on the price of the underlying asset and must be isolated and extracted via delta hedging. These swaps can thus be used to take a view on future realized volatility, to trade the spread between realized and implied volatility, or to hedge the volatility exposure of other positions. These OTC products also offer the advantage of longer-dated, tailored maturities and strikes.

A long volatility strategy utilizing OTC volatility or variance swaps, options, or swaptions requires finding undervalued instruments. This is accomplished by being in frequent contact with options dealers around the world in a variety of asset classes. Once implemented, positions are held until they either are exercised, are sold during a volatility event, are actively delta hedged (in the case of a long options position), or expire. A long volatility strategy is a convex strategy because the movement of volatility pricing is typically asymmetric and skewed to the right. Also, strike prices of options may be set such that the cost of the options is small, but their potential payoffs are often many multiples of the premiums paid for the options.

Long volatility strategies are potentially attractive but also come with key challenges and risks for implementation. Given that OTC options, as well as volatility and variance swaps, are not exchange-traded, they must be negotiated. These contracts are typically structured under ISDA documentation; they are subject to bilateral margin agreements (as negotiated within an ISDA Credit Support Annex document), but they still carry more counterparty risk and liquidity risk to both establish and liquidate than instruments traded on an exchange. Also, smaller hedge funds may not even be able to access ISDA-backed OTC derivatives with banking counterparts until surpassing a minimum AUM threshold, generally $100 million. Above all, although the purchase of volatility assets provides positively convex outcomes, it almost always involves some volatility curve roll down risk and premium expense. Key aspects of volatility trading are presented in Exhibit 10.

Exhibit 10: Volatility Trading Strategies—Risk, Liquidity, Leverage, and Benchmarking

Risk Profile and Liquidity

- Long volatility positioning exhibits positive convexity, which can be particularly useful for hedging purposes. On the short side, option premium sellers generally extract steadier returns in normal market environments.
- Relative value volatility trading may be a useful source of portfolio return alpha across different geographies and asset classes.
- Liquidity varies across the different instruments used for implementation. VIX Index futures and options are very liquid; exchange-traded index options are generally liquid, but with the longest tenors of about two years (with liquidity decreasing as tenor increases); OTC contracts can be customized with longer maturities but are less liquid and less fungible between different counterparties.

Leverage Usage

- The natural convexity of volatility instruments typically means that outsized gains may be earned at times with very little up-front risk. Although notional values appear nominally levered, the asymmetric nature of long optionality is an attractive aspect of this strategy.

Benchmarking

- Volatility trading is a niche strategy that is difficult to benchmark.
- CBOE Eurekahedge has the following indexes:

  Long Volatility Index (composed of 15 managers); Short Volatility Index (composed of 5 managers); Relative Value Volatility Index (composed of 11 managers); and Tail Risk Index (composed of 11 managers).

EXAMPLE 10

Long Volatility Strategy Payoff

Consider the following scenario: Economic growth has been good, equity markets have been rising, and interest rates have been low. However, consumer debt (e.g., subprime mortgages, credit card debt, personal loans) has been rising rapidly, surpassing historic levels. In mid-January, Serena Ortiz, a long volatility hedge fund manager, purchased a basket of long-dated (one-year), 10% out-of-the money put options on a major stock index for $100 per contract at an implied volatility level of 12%.

As of mid-April, consumer debt is still at seemingly dangerous levels and financial markets appear ripe for a major correction. However, the stock index has risen another 20% above its mid-January levels, and volatility is low. So, Ortiz's options are priced even more cheaply than before, at $50 per contract.

Now jump forward in time by another three months to mid-July, when a crisis—unexpected by many participants—has finally occurred. Volatility has spiked, and the stock index has fallen to 25% below its April level and 10% below its starting January level. Ortiz's put options are now trading at an implied volatility pricing of 30%.

1. Discuss the time, volatility, and price impact on Ortiz's long volatility exposure in put options as of mid-July.

Solution:

Despite an initial 50% mark-to-market loss on her put exposure as of mid-April, Ortiz likely has substantial unrealized profits by mid-July. As six months passed (other things being equal), Ortiz would have suffered some time decay loss in her long put position, but her options have also gone from being 10% out-of-the-money to now being at-the-money. Implied volatility has increased 2.5 times (from 12% to 30%), which on a six-month, at-the-money put will have a significant positive impact on the option's pricing (the closer an option is to being at-the-money, the greater the impact that changes in implied volatility will have on its price). So, as of mid-July, Ortiz will likely have a significant mark-to-market gain.

2. Discuss what happens if the market subsequently moves broadly sideways between July and the January of the next year.

Solution:

If the market subsequently moves broadly sideways until January of the next year, Ortiz's at-the-money option premium will slowly erode because of time decay. Assuming the puts remain at-the-money, their volatility value will eventually dissipate; Ortiz will ultimately lose all of her original $100 investment per contract unless she has nimbly traded against the position with active delta hedging of the underlying stock index futures. This would entail buying and selling the index futures over time to capture small profitable movements to offset the time decay and volatility erosion in the puts.

Reinsurance/Life Settlements

Although still somewhat nascent, hedge funds have also entered the world of insurance, reinsurance, life settlements, and catastrophe reinsurance. Underlying insurance contracts provide a payout to the policyholder (or their beneficiaries) on the occurrence of a specific insured event in exchange for a stream of cash flows (periodic premiums) paid by the policyholder. Common types of insurance contracts sold by insurance providers include vehicle and home insurance, life insurance, and catastrophe insurance, which covers damage from such events as floods, hurricanes, or earthquakes. The insurance market encompasses a wide range of often highly specific and detailed contracts that are less standardized than other financial contracts. As a result, insurance contracts are generally not liquid and are difficult to sell or purchase after contract initiation.

Although the primary market for insurance has existed for centuries, the secondary market for insurance has grown substantially in the last several decades. Individuals who purchased whole or universal life policies and who no longer want or need the insurance can surrender their policies to the original insurance issuer. However, such policyholders are increasingly finding that higher cash values (i.e., significantly above surrender value) are being paid for their policies by third-party brokers, who, in turn, offer these policies as investments to hedge funds. Hedge funds may formulate a differentiated view of individual or group life expectancy; if correct, investment in such life policies can provide attractive uncorrelated returns.

Reinsurance of catastrophe risk has also increasingly attracted hedge fund capital. These new secondary markets have improved liquidity and enhanced the value of existing insurance contracts. For insurance companies, the reinsurance market allows for risk transfer, capital management, and solvency management. For hedge funds, the reinsurance market offers a source of uncorrelated return alpha.

Investment Characteristics and Strategy Implementation

Life insurance protects the policyholder's dependents in the case of his/her death. The secondary market for life insurance involves the sale of a life insurance contract to a third party—a **life settlement**. The valuation of a life settlement typically requires detailed biometric analysis of the individual policyholder and an understanding of actuarial analysis. So, a hedge fund manager specialized in investing in life settlements would require such expert knowledge and skills or would need to source such knowledge from a trusted partner/actuarial adviser.

A hedge fund strategy focusing on life settlements involves analyzing pools of life insurance contracts being offered for sale, typically being sold by a third-party broker who purchased the insurance contracts from the original policyholders. The hedge fund would look for the following policy characteristics:

1. the surrender value being offered to an insured individual is relatively low;
2. the ongoing premium payments to keep the policy active are also relatively low; and yet,
3. the probability is relatively high that the designated insured person is indeed likely to die within a certain period of time (i.e., earlier than predicted by standard actuarial methods).

On finding the appropriate policy (or, more typically, a pool of policies), the hedge fund manager pays a lump sum (via a broker) to the policyholder(s), who transfers the right to the eventual policy benefit to the hedge fund. The hedge fund is then responsible for making ongoing premium payments on the policy in return for receiving the future death benefit. This strategy is successful when the present value of the future benefit payment received by the hedge fund exceeds the present value of intervening payments made by the hedge fund. The two key inputs in the hedge fund manager's analysis are the expected policy cash flows (i.e., up-front, lump-sum payment to buy the policy; ongoing premium payments to the insurance company; and the eventual death benefit to be received) and the time to mortality. Neither of these factors has anything to do with the overall behavior of financial markets. Thus, this strategy area is unrelated and uncorrelated with other hedge fund strategies.

Catastrophe insurance protects the policyholder in case of such events as floods, hurricanes, and earthquakes, which are highly idiosyncratic and also unrelated and uncorrelated with financial market behavior. Insurance companies effectively reinsure portions of their exposure (typically above a given threshold and for a limited amount) with reinsurance companies, who, in turn, deal with hedge funds as a source of capital. An attractive and uncorrelated return profile may be achieved if by making such reinsurance investments a hedge fund can do the following: 1) obtain sufficient policy diversity in terms of geographic exposure and type of insurance being offered; 2) receive a sufficient buffer in terms of loan loss reserves from the insurance company; and 3) receive enough premium income.

Valuation methods for catastrophe insurance may require the hedge fund manager to consider global weather patterns and make forecasts using sophisticated prediction models that involve a wide range of geophysical inputs. But, more generally, assumptions are made as to typical weather patterns; the worst-case loss potentials are made from different reinsurance structures. These assumptions are then weighed against the reinsurance income to be received. If a catastrophic event does occur, then hedge fund managers hope to have enough geographic diversity that they are not financially harmed by a single event, thereby continuing to benefit when insurance premiums are inevitably increased to cover future catastrophic events.

Organized markets for catastrophe bonds and catastrophe risk futures continue to develop. These bonds and financial futures can be used to take long positions or to hedge catastrophe risk in a portfolio of insurance contracts. Their issuance and performance tend to be seasonal. Many such catastrophe bonds are issued before the annual North American hurricane season begins (May/June) and may perform particularly well if a given hurricane season is benign.

EXAMPLE 11

Investing in Life Settlements

1. Mikki Tan runs specialty hedge fund SingStar Pte. Ltd. (SingStar), based in Singapore, that focuses on life settlements. SingStar is staffed with biometric and actuarial science experts who perform valuation analysis on pools of life insurance policies offered for sale by insurance broker firms. These intermediaries buy the policies from individuals who no longer need the insurance and who want an up-front cash payment that is higher than the surrender value offered by their insurance companies.

   Tan knows that Warwick Direct has been buying many individuals' life insurance policies that were underwritten by NextLife, an insurance company with a reputation in industry circles for relatively weak underwriting procedures (i.e., charging low premiums for insuring its many relatively unhealthy policyholders) and for paying low surrender values. Tan is notified that Warwick Direct is selling a pool of life settlements heavily weighted with policies that were originated by NextLife. Parties wishing to bid will be provided with data covering a random sample of the life insurance policies in the pool.

   Tan asks SingStar's experts to analyze the data, and they report that many of the policies in the pool were written on individuals who have now developed early-onset Alzheimer's and other debilitating diseases and thus required the up-front cash for assisted living facilities and other special care. Moreover, the analysts indicate that early-onset Alzheimer's patients have a life expectancy, on average, that is 10 years shorter than persons without the disease.

   Discuss how Tan and SingStar's team might proceed given this potential investment.

Solution:

SingStar's financial, biometric, and actuarial experts need to work together to forecast expected cash flows from this potential investment and then value it using an appropriate risk-adjusted discount rate. The cash flows would include the following:

- The ongoing premium payments that SingStar would need to make to the originating insurance companies (in this case, mainly to NextLife) to keep the policies active. The low premiums NextLife is known to charge as well as the shorter average life expectancy of many individuals represented in the pool are important factors to consider in making this forecast.
- The timing of future benefit payments to be received by SingStar on the demise of the individuals (the formerly insured). The prevalence of early-onset Alzheimer's disease and other debilitating diseases as well as the shorter average life expectancy of many individuals in the pool are key factors to consider in formulating this forecast.

Once an appropriate discount rate is decided on—one that compensates for the risks of the investment—then its present value can be determined. The difference between the PV and any minimum bid price set by Warwick

Direct, as well as Tan's perceptions of the competition in bidding, will determine Tan's proposed purchase price. If SingStar ultimately buys the pool of life settlement policies and the forecasts (e.g., biometric, actuarial, and financial) of Tan's team are met or exceeded, then this investment should yield attractive returns to SingStar that are uncorrelated to other financial markets.

MULTI-MANAGER STRATEGIES

12

☐ discuss investment characteristics, strategy implementation, and role in a portfolio of multi-manager hedge fund strategies

The previous sections examined individual hedge fund strategies. In practice, most investors invest in a range of hedge fund strategies. Three main approaches are used to combine individual hedge fund strategies into a portfolio: 1) *creating one's own mix of managers* by investing directly into individual hedge funds running different strategies; 2) *fund-of-funds,* which involves investing in a single fund-of-funds manager who then allocates across a set of individual hedge fund managers running different strategies; and 3) *multi-strategy funds,* which entails investing in a single fund that includes multiple internal management teams running different strategies under the same roof. Of course, approaches (1) and (2) are not specific to combinations of strategies; they apply to individual strategies too.

Fund-of-Funds

Fund-of-funds (FoF) managers aggregate investors' capital and allocate it to a portfolio of separate, individual hedge funds following different, less correlated strategies. The main roles of the FoF manager are to provide diversification across hedge fund strategies; to make occasional tactical, sector-based reallocation decisions; to engage in underlying manager selection and due diligence; and to perform ongoing portfolio management, risk assessment, and consolidated reporting. FoF managers can provide investors with access to certain closed hedge funds, economies of scale for monitoring, currency hedging capabilities, the ability to obtain and manage leverage at the portfolio level, and such other practical advantages as better liquidity terms than would be offered by an individual hedge fund manager.

Disadvantages of the FoF approach include a double layer of fees the investor must pay; a lack of transparency into individual hedge fund manager processes and returns; the inability to net performance fees on individual managers; and an additional principal–agent relationship. Regarding fees, in addition to management and incentive fees charged by the individual hedge funds (with historical norms of 1%–2% and 10%–20%, respectively) in which the FoF invests, investors in a fund-of-funds historically paid an additional 1% management fee and 10% incentive fee (again, historical norms) on the performance of the total FoF portfolio. As the performance of funds of funds has generally waned, fees have become more negotiable; management fees of 50 bps and incentive fees of 5% (or simply just a 1% flat total management fee) are becoming increasingly prevalent.

Occasionally, liquidity management of FoFs can result in liquidity squeezes for FoF managers. Most FoFs require an initial one-year lock-up period, and then they offer investors monthly or quarterly liquidity thereafter, typically with a 30- to 60-day redemption notice also being required. However, the underlying investments made by the FoF may not fit well with such liquidity needs. Some underlying managers or newer underlying investments may have their own lock-up provisions or liquidity (i.e., redemption) gates. So, the FoF manager must stagger his/her underlying portfolio investments to create a conservative liquidity profile while carefully assessing the probability and potential magnitude of any FoF-level redemptions that he/she might face. FoFs may also arrange a reserve line of credit as an added liquidity backstop to deal with the potential mismatch between cash flows available from underlying investments and cash flows required to meet redemptions.

Investment Characteristics

FoFs are important hedge fund "access vehicles" for smaller high-net-worth investors and smaller institutions. Most hedge funds require minimum initial investments that range from \$500,000 to \$5,000,000 (with \$1,000,000 being the most typical threshold). To create a reasonably diversified portfolio of 15–20 managers, \$15–20 million would be required, which is a large amount even for most wealthy families and many small institutions. Selecting the 15–20 different hedge fund managers would itself require substantial time and resources that most such investors may lack. In addition, investors may potentially face substantial tax reporting requirements for each separate hedge fund investment owned. By comparison, a high-net-worth investor or small institution can typically start FoF investments with just \$100,000, effectively achieving a portfolio that includes a diversified mix of talented hedge fund managers. Through their network of relationships and their large scale, FoFs may also provide access to successful managers whose funds are otherwise closed to new investment. Overall, FoFs may thus be considered convenient for access, diversification, liquidity, and operational tax reporting reasons.

But FoFs are also designed to provide other attractive features, even for such institutional investors as endowments, foundations, and pension plans. Such institutional clients may initially turn to FoFs as their preferred path to navigate their way into the hedge fund space. FoFs offer expertise not only in individual manager selection and due diligence but also in strategic allocation, tactical allocation, and style allocation into individual hedge fund strategies. The FoF strategic allocation is the long-term allocation to different hedge fund styles. For example, a FoF may have a strategic allocation of 20% to long/short equity strategies, 30% to event-driven strategies, 30% to relative value strategies, and 20% to global macro strategies. Tactical allocations include periodically overweighting and underweighting different hedge fund styles across different market environments depending on the level of conviction of the FoF manager. The overall capital or risk exposure can also be geared up or down to reflect the opportunity set in different market conditions.

Through their prime brokerage services, commercial banks provide levered capital to FoFs. Such leverage is typically collateralized by the existing hedge fund assets held in custody by these banks. Because hedge funds often deliver full funds back to redeeming investors with some substantial time lag (a 10% holdback of the total redemption amount until audit completion is typical), access to leverage can often be useful from a bridge loan point of view. In this way, capital not yet returned can be efficiently redeployed for the benefit of remaining investors.

Another attractive aspect of larger FoFs is that by pooling smaller investor assets into a larger single investment commitment, the FoF may be able to extract certain fee breaks, improved liquidity terms, future capacity rights, and/or added transparency provisions from an underlying hedge fund. The FoF may also be able to secure a commitment from the underlying fund to receive the best terms that might subsequently be offered to any future investor. These can all be valuable concessions that a smaller investor would most likely be unable to obtain by investing directly. Some FoFs have argued that these concessions made at the underlying fund manager level can be worth more than the added layering of fees by the FoF.

Overall, by combining different and ideally less correlated strategies, a FoF portfolio should provide more diversification, less extreme risk exposures, lower realized volatility, and generally less single manager tail risk than direct investing in individual hedge fund strategies. FoFs may also achieve economies of scale, manager access, research expertise, potential liquidity efficiencies, useful portfolio leverage opportunities, and potentially valuable concessions from the underlying funds.

Strategy Implementation

Implementing a FoF portfolio is typically a multi-step process that transpires over several months. First, FoF managers will become acquainted with different hedge fund managers via the use of various databases and introductions at prime broker-sponsored capital introduction events, where hedge fund managers present their perceived opportunity sets and qualifications to potential investors. Then, the FoF manager must decide the desired strategic allocation of the portfolio across the different hedge fund strategy groupings.

Next, with both quantitative and qualitative top-down and bottom-up approaches, the formal manager selection process is initiated. For each strategy grouping, the FoF manager screens the available universe of hedge funds with the goal to formulate a select "peer group" of potential investment candidates. This is followed by direct interviews of each hedge fund manager as well as a review of their relevant materials, such as presentation booklets, Alternative Investment Management Association Due Diligence Questionnaires (AIMA DDQs), recent quarterly letters and risk reports, as well as past audits. Typically, FoF managers will meet with prospective hedge fund managers on several different occasions (with at least one onsite visit at their offices). FoF managers will have an increasingly granular focus not only on the hedge fund managers' investment philosophy and portfolio construction but also on the firms' personnel, operational, and risk management processes.

Once an individual hedge fund is deemed a true candidate for investment, the fund's Offering Memorandum and Limited Partnership Agreement will be fully reviewed. The fund's service providers (e.g., auditor, legal adviser, custodian bank, prime broker) will be verified and other background checks and references obtained. At some larger FoF firms, these more operational aspects of the due diligence process will be performed by a dedicated team of specialists who validate the original FoF team's investment conclusions or cite concerns that may need to be addressed prior to an allocation. At this point, the FoF manager may endeavor to obtain certain concessions, agreed to in "side letters," from the hedge fund manager entitling the FoF to reduced fees, added transparency provisions, capacity rights to build an investment in the future, and/or improved redemption liquidity provisions. The larger the potential investment, the greater the FoF's negotiation advantage.

After a hedge fund is approved and the strategy is included in the FoF portfolio, then the process moves into the ongoing monitoring and review phases. The main concerns are monitoring for performance consistency with investment objectives and for any style drift, personnel changes, regulatory issues, or other correlation/return shifts that may transpire when compared to other managers both within the portfolio and when compared to similar hedge fund peers.

Multi-Strategy Hedge Funds

Multi-strategy hedge funds combine multiple hedge fund strategies under the same hedge fund structure. Teams of managers dedicated to running different hedge fund strategies share operational and risk management systems under the same roof.

Investment Characteristics

A key advantage to this approach is that the multi-strategy manager can reallocate capital into different strategy areas more quickly and efficiently than would be possible by the FoF manager. The multi-strategy manager has full transparency and a better picture of the interactions of the different teams' portfolio risks than would ever be possible for the FoF manager to achieve. Consequently, the multi-strategy manager can react faster to different real-time market impacts—for example, by rapidly increasing or decreasing leverage within different strategies depending on the perceived riskiness of available opportunities. Teams within a multi-strategy manager also can be fully focused on their respective portfolios because the business, operational, and regulatory aspects of running the hedge fund are handled by other administrative professionals. Many talented portfolio managers decide to join a multi-strategy firm for this reason.

The fees paid by investors in a multi-strategy fund can be structured in many ways, some of which can be very attractive when compared to the FoF added fee layering and netting risk attributes. Conceptually, the FoF investor always faces netting risk, whereby he/she is responsible for paying performance (i.e., incentive) fees due to winning underlying funds while suffering return drag from the performance of losing underlying funds. Even if the FoF's overall performance (aggregated across all funds) is flat or down, FoF investors must still pay incentive fees due to the managers of the winning underlying funds.

The fee structure is more investor-friendly at multi-strategy hedge funds where the general partner absorbs the netting risk arising from the divergent performances of his/her fund's different strategy teams. This is an attractive outcome for the multi-strategy fund investor because 1) the GP is responsible for netting risk and 2) the only investor-level incentive fees paid are those due on the total fund performance after netting the positive and negative performances of the various strategy teams. Although beneficial to investors, this structure can at times cause discord within a multi-strategy fund. Because the GP is responsible for netting risk, the multi-strategy fund's overall bonus pool may shrink; thus, high-performing strategy teams will be disaffected if they do not receive their full incentive amounts, which ultimately results in personnel losses.

However, some multi-strategy hedge fund firms operate with a "pass-through" fee model. Using this model, they may charge no management fee but instead pass through the costs of paying individual teams (inclusive of salary and incentive fees earned by each team) before an added manager level incentive fee is charged to the investor on total fund performance. In this instance, the investor does implicitly pay for a portion of netting risk between the different teams (in place of a management fee), while the multi-strategy fund's GP bears a portion of that netting risk (via the risk that the total fund-level incentive fee may not cover contractual obligations that the GP is required to pay individual teams).

The main risk of multi-strategy funds is that they are generally quite levered: Position transparency is closely monitored in-house, and fee structures are typically tilted toward performance (due to high costs of the infrastructure requirements). Leverage applied to tight risk management is usually benign, but in market stress periods, risk management miscalibrations can certainly matter. The left-tail, risk-induced implosions of prominent multi-strategy funds, such as Ritchie Capital (2005), are somewhat legendary. Moreover, the operational risks of a multi-strategy firm, by definition, are not well diversified because all operational processes are performed under the same fund structure. Finally, multi-strategy funds can be somewhat limited in the scope of strategies offered because they are constrained by the available pool of in-house manager talent and skills (and are often staffed by managers with similar investment styles and philosophies).

Strategy Implementation

Multi-strategy funds invest in a range of individual hedge fund strategies. As mentioned, the breadth of strategies they can access is a function of the portfolio management skills available within the particular multi-strategy fund. Similar to a FoF manager, a multi-strategy fund will engage in both strategic and tactical allocations to individual hedge fund strategies. Given that multi-strategy fund teams manage each strategy directly and operate under the same fund roof, compared with FoF managers, they are more likely to be well informed about when to tactically reallocate to a particular strategy and more capable of shifting capital between strategies quickly. Conversely, multi-strategy funds may also be less willing to exit strategies in which core expertise is in-house. Common risk management systems and processes are also more likely to reveal interactions and correlations between the different strategies run by the various portfolio management teams. Such nuanced aspects of risk might be far harder to detect within a FoF structure.

Exhibit 11 compares some key attributes of funds-of-funds and multi-strategy funds that investors must consider when deciding which of these two multi-manager types best fits their needs.

Exhibit 11: Funds-of-Funds and Multi-Strategy Funds—Comparison of Risk, Liquidity, Leverage, and Benchmarking

Risk Profile and Liquidity

- FoFs and multi-strategy funds are designed to offer steady, low-volatility returns via their strategy diversification. Multi-strategy funds have generally outperformed FoFs but with more variance and occasional large losses often related to their higher leverage.
- Multi-strategy funds offer potentially faster tactical asset allocation and improved fee structure (netting risk handled at strategy level) but with higher manager-specific operational risks. FoFs offer a potentially more diverse strategy mix but with less transparency and slower tactical reaction time.
- Both groups typically have similar initial lock-up and redemption periods, but multi-strategy funds also often impose investor-level or fund-level gates on maximum redemptions allowed per quarter.

Leverage Usage

- Multi-strategy funds tend to use significantly more leverage than most FoFs, which gravitate to modest leverage usage. Thus, multi-strategy funds are somewhat more prone to left-tail blow-up risk in stress periods. Still, better strategy transparency and shorter tactical reaction time make multi-strategy funds overall more resilient than FoFs in preserving capital.

Benchmarking

- FoFs can be tracked using such sub-indexes as HFRX and HFRI Fund of Funds Composite Indices; Lipper Fund-of-Funds Index; CISDM Fund-of-Funds Multi-Strategy Index; and the broad Credit Suisse Hedge Fund Index as a general proxy for a diversified pool of managers.

- Multi-strategy managers can be tracked via HFRX and HFRI Multi-Strategy Indices; Lipper Multi-Strategy Index; CISDM Multi-Strategy Index; and Multi-Strategy Hedge Fund Index.

Note: The FoF business model has been under significant pressure since 2008 because of fee compression and increased investor interest in passive, long-only investing and the advent of liquid alternatives for retail investors. Conversely, multi-strategy funds have grown as many institutional investors prefer to invest directly in such funds and avoid FoF fee layering.

EXAMPLE 12

Fund-of-Funds: Net-of-Fee Returns

Squaw Valley Fund of Funds (SVFOF) charges a 1% management fee and 10% incentive fee and invests an equal amount of its assets into two individual hedge funds: Pyrenees Fund (PF) and Ural Fund (UF), each charging a 2% management fee and a 20% incentive fee. For simplicity in answering the following questions, please ignore fee compounding and assume that all fees are paid at year-end.

1. If the managers of both PF and UF generate 20% gross annual returns, what is the net-of-fee return for an investor in SVFOF?

Solution:

Incentive fees are deducted only from gross gains net of management fees and expenses. Thus, the answer becomes:

Net of Fees Return for PF and UF Investor = (20% – 2% – 3.6%) = 14.4%, where 3.6%

= 20% x (20% – 2%);

Net of Fees Return for SVFOF Investor = (14.4% – 1% – 1.34%) = **12.06%**, where 1.34%

= 10% x (14.4% – 1%).

2. If PF's manager earns a gross return of 20% but UF's manager loses 5%, what is the net-of-fee return for an investor in SVFOF?

Solution:

Net of Fees Return for PF Investor = (20% – 2% – 3.6%) = 14.4%;

Net of Fees Return for UF Investor = (–5% – 2% – 0%) = –7.0%;

Gross Return for SVFOF Investor = (0.5 x 14.4% + 0.5 x – 7.0%) = 3.7%;

Net of Fees Return for SVFOF Investor = (3.7% – 1% – 0.27%) = **2.43%**, where 0.27%

= 10% x (3.7% – 1%).

In conclusion, if both PF and UF managers generate gross returns of 20%, then the net-of-fee return for SVFOF's investor is 12.06%, with fees taking up 39.7% of the total gross investment return [(2% + 3.6% + 1% + 1.34%)/20% = 39.7%] and the remainder going to the SVFOF investor.

But, if PF's manager earns a 20% gross return and UF's manager loses 5%, then the net-of-fee return for the SVFOF investor is a meager 2.43%. In this case, most (67.6%) of the original gross return of 7.5% [= 20% x 0.50 + (–5% x 0.50)] goes to PF, UF, and SVFOF managers as fees. Note that {[0.50 x (2% + 3.6% + 2% + 0%)] + (1% + 0.27%)}/7.5% equals 67.6%. This is an example of fee netting risk that comes with investing in FoFs.

EXAMPLE 13

Funds-of-Funds or Multi-Strategy Funds—Which to Choose?

1. The Leonardo family office in Milan manages the €435 million fortune of the Da Vinci family. Mona, the family's matriarch, trained as an economist and worked at Banca d'Italia for many years. She is now retired but still monitors global financial markets. The portfolio that Leonardo manages for the Da Vinci family consists of traditional long-only stocks and bonds, real estate, private equity, and single manager hedge funds following distressed securities and merger arbitrage strategies.

   Mona believes global financial markets are about to enter a prolonged period of heightened volatility, so she asks Leonardo's senior portfolio manager to sell some long-only stocks and the merger arbitrage hedge fund and then buy a multi-manager hedge fund. Mona's objectives are to increase the portfolio's diversification, flexibility, and transparency while maximizing net-of-fees returns during the volatile period ahead.

   Discuss advantages and disadvantages that Leonardo's portfolio manager should consider in choosing between a FoF and a multi-strategy fund.

Solution:

Leonardo's portfolio manager understands that both multi-strategy funds and FoFs are designed to offer steady, low-volatility returns via their strategy diversification.

However, digging deeper he sees that multi-strategy funds have generally outperformed FoFs. This may be because of such key advantages as their enhanced flexibility and the fast pace of tactical asset allocation (important in dynamic, volatile markets) given that the different strategies are executed within the same fund structure. Another advantage of this set-up of multi-strategy funds is increased transparency regarding overall positions and exposures being carried. Moreover, many multi-strategy funds have an investor-friendly fee structure, in which fee netting risk is handled at the strategy level and absorbed (or partially absorbed) by the general partner of the multi-strategy fund. As for disadvantages, Leonardo's portfolio manager should consider that multi-strategy funds entail higher manager-specific operational risks, so detailed due diligence is important; moreover, they tend to use relatively high leverage, which may increase the variance of returns. The main advantages of FoFs are that they offer a potentially more diverse strategy mix with lower leverage (and somewhat less return variance), and they have less operational risk (i.e., each separate underlying hedge fund is responsible for its own risk management). Leonardo's portfolio manager realizes that FoFs also entail reduced transparency into the portfolio decisions made at the underlying hedge funds as well as a slower tactical reaction time. Another key disadvantage is that FoFs require a double layer of fees to be paid, with netting risk borne by the investor, which imposes a substantial drag on net-of-fees returns.

13 ANALYSIS OF HEDGE FUND STRATEGIES USING A CONDITIONAL FACTOR RISK MODEL

☐ describe how factor models may be used to understand hedge fund risk exposures

From the foregoing discussion, it is reasonable to conclude the following: L/S equity and event-driven managers tend to be exposed to some natural equity market beta risk; arbitrage managers often are exposed to credit spread risk and market volatility tail risk; opportunistic managers tend to have risk exposures to the trendiness (or directionality) of markets; and relative value managers do not expect trendiness but are typically counting on mean reversion. Each strategy has unique sources of factor exposures and resulting vulnerabilities. Moreover, risk factor exposures in many strategies arise from simply holding financial instruments whose prices are directly impacted by those risk factors. That is, long and short exposures to a given risk factor in different securities are not equal, thereby giving rise to a non-zero *net* exposure. Following a practice-based risk factor perspective, this reading uses a conditional linear factor model to uncover and analyze hedge fund strategy risk exposures. While this is just one way to go about explaining hedge fund strategies' risks and returns, it is representative of the widely used risk factor approach.

One may ask why it is necessary to use such a model to investigate hedge fund strategies. It is because a linear factor model can provide insights into the intrinsic characteristics and risks in a hedge fund investment. Moreover, given the dynamic nature of hedge fund strategies, a conditional model allows for the analysis in a specific market environment to determine, for example, whether hedge fund strategies are exposed to certain risks under abnormal market conditions. A conditional model can show whether hedge fund risk exposures (e.g., to credit or volatility) that are insignificant during calm market periods may become significant during turbulent market periods. The importance of using a conditional factor model is underscored by the fact that the hedge fund industry is dynamic; for example, it experienced a huge decline in AUM during the global financial crisis. Specifically, after recording more than a 25% CAGR (compound annual growth rate) in assets between 2000 and 2007, the global hedge fund industry's aggregate AUM declined by 17% CAGR between 2007 and 2009 (the period of the global financial crisis) from a high of more than $2.6 trillion. Moreover, global AUM did not surpass the 2007 high until 2014. In short, thousands of hedge funds were shuttered during this time as performance plunged when many managers were caught off guard by their funds' actual risk exposures during the crisis period and in its aftermath.

Conditional Factor Risk Model

A simple conditional linear factor model applied to a hedge fund strategy's returns can be represented as:

$$\begin{aligned}(\text{Return on HF}_i)_t = {} & \alpha_i + \beta_{i,1}(\text{Factor 1})_t + \beta_{i,2}(\text{Factor 2})_t + \ldots + \beta_{i,K}(\text{Factor } K)_t + \\ & D_t\beta_{i,1}(\text{Factor 1})_t + \text{D}_t\beta_{i,2}(\text{Factor 2})_t + \ldots + D_t\beta_{i,K}(\text{Factor } K)_t + \\ & (\text{error})_{i,t}, \text{ where}\end{aligned}$$

- $(\text{Return on HF}_i)_t$ is the return of hedge fund i in period t;
- $\beta_{i,1}(\text{Factor 1})_t$ represents the exposure to risk factor 1 (up to risk factor K) for hedge fund i in period t during normal times;
- $D_t\beta_{i,1}(\text{Factor 1})_t$ represents the *incremental* exposure to risk factor 1 (up to risk factor K) for hedge fund i in period t during financial crisis periods, where D_t is a dummy variable that equals 1 during financial crisis periods (i.e., June 2007 to February 2009) and 0 otherwise;
- α_i is the intercept for hedge fund i; and
- $(\text{error})_{i,t}$ is random error with zero mean and standard deviation of σ_i.

Each factor beta represents the expected change in hedge fund returns for a one-unit increase in the specific risk factor, holding all other factors (independent variables) constant. The portion of hedge fund returns not explained by the risk factors is attributable to three sources: 1) alpha, the hedge fund manager's unique investment skills; 2) omitted factors; and 3) random errors. The starting point for building this model is the identification of a comprehensive set of asset class and macro-oriented, market-based risks, including the behavior of stocks, bonds, currencies, commodities, credit spreads, and volatility. Following Hasanhodzic and Lo (2007) and practice, the model starts with the following six factors:

- **Equity risk (SNP500):** monthly total return of the S&P 500 Index, including dividends.
- **Interest rate risk (BOND):** monthly return of the Bloomberg Barclays Corporate AA Intermediate Bond Index.
- **Currency risk (USD):** monthly return of the US Dollar Index.
- **Commodity risk (CMDTY):** monthly total return of the Goldman Sachs Commodity Index (GSCI).
- **Credit risk (CREDIT):** difference between monthly seasoned Baa and Aaa corporate bond yields provided by Moody's.
- **Volatility risk (VIX):** first-difference of the end-of-month value of the CBOE Volatility Index (VIX).

Once these potentially relevant macro risk factors were identified for analysis, the next consideration was the appropriateness of using them together in the model. To address the issue of highly correlated risk factors and to avoid potential multi-collinearity problems, a four-step "stepwise regression" process was used to build a conditional linear factor model that is less likely to include highly correlated risk factors. This process is described briefly in the accompanying sidebar.

PRACTICAL STEPS FOR BUILDING HEDGE FUND RISK FACTOR MODELS

The following four-step procedure describes a stepwise regression process that can help build linear conditional factor models that are less likely to include highly correlated risk factors, thereby avoiding multi-collinearity issues.

Step 1 Identify potentially important risk factors.

Step 2 Calculate pairwise correlations across all risk factors. If two-state conditional models are used, calculate correlations across all risk factors for both states—for example, during normal market conditions (state 1) and during market crisis conditions (state 2). For illustration purposes, risk factors A and B can be assumed to be highly correlated if the correlation coefficient between them exceeds 60%.

Step 3 For highly correlated risk factors A and B, regress the return series of interest (e.g., hedge fund returns) on all risk factors excluding factor A. Then, regress the same returns on all the risk factors, but this time exclude factor B. Given the adjusted R^2 for regressions without A and without B, keep the risk factor that results in the highest adjusted R^2.

Step 4 Repeat step 3 for all other highly correlated factor pairs, with the aim of eliminating the least useful (in terms of explanatory power) factors and thereby avoiding multi-collinearity issues.

To address the multi-collinearity problem, the stepwise regression procedure was implemented using two of the hedge fund databases mentioned previously: Lipper TASS (TASS) and Morningstar Hedge/CISDM (CISDM). The accompanying sidebar provides useful background for practitioners on these two important sources of hedge fund information.

HEDGE FUND DATABASES

The analysis in this reading uses two well-known hedge fund databases to evaluate hedge fund strategies: Lipper TASS (TASS) and Morningstar Hedge/CISDM (CISDM) databases. These databases are among the ones most widely used for hedge fund research.

The analysis covers the period of 2000–2016. Each database is separated into "live" (operating/open), "defunct" (non-operating/shut down or operating/closed to new investment or operating/delisted and relisted with another database), and "all" funds (live + defunct) groups. Hedge fund return data are filtered to exclude funds that 1) do not report net-of-fee returns; 2) report returns in currencies other than the US dollar; 3) report returns less frequently than monthly; 4) do not provide AUM or estimates; and 5) have less than 36 months of return data. TASS and CISDM databases have a total of 6,352 and 7,756 funds, respectively. Importantly, 82% (18%) and 80% (20%) of all TASS and CISDM funds, respectively, are defunct (live). This is consistent with the relatively high attrition rate of hedge funds and the relatively short life of a typical hedge fund.

Databases that include defunct funds can be highly useful for asset allocators because the historical track record of managers that may be starting new funds might be found to include defunct funds. Then, further analysis could be conducted to determine if such funds became defunct because of the managers' poor performance and/or excessive redemptions, so they were shut down, or because of the managers' initial success, such that an overabundance of inflows caused subsequent investment capacity issues. From a data analysis point of view, including defunct funds also helps to appropriately adjust for database survivorship bias that might otherwise yield incorrect analytical conclusions.

Live, Defunct, and All Funds in TASS Database from 2000–2016

Grouping	TASS Primary Categories	Number of Live Funds	Number of Defunct Funds	Total Number of Funds
Equity	Dedicated short bias	4	38	42
Equity	Equity market neutral	38	270	308
Equity	Long/short equity hedge	350	1,705	2,055
Event driven	Event driven	87	465	552
Relative value	Convertible arbitrage	17	162	179
Relative value	Fixed income arbitrage	42	167	209
Opportunistic	Global macro	59	266	325
Opportunistic	Managed futures	1	2	3
Multi-manager	Fund of funds	454	1,711	2,165
Multi-manager	Multi-strategy	100	414	514
Total		1,152	5,200	6,352

Live, Defunct, and All Funds in CISDM Database from 2000–2016

Grouping	CISDM Categories	Number of Live Funds	Number of Defunct Funds	Total Number of Funds
Equity	Asia/Pacific long/short equity	31	203	234
Equity	Bear market equity	2	36	38
Equity	Equity market neutral	40	272	312
Equity	Europe long/short equity	47	161	208
Equity	Global long/short equity	86	406	492
Equity	US long/short equity	218	849	1,067
Equity	US small-cap long/short equity	67	171	238
Event driven	Merger arbitrage	22	16	38
Event driven	Distressed securities	46	159	205
Event driven	Event driven	63	228	291
Relative value	Convertible arbitrage	25	125	150
Relative value	Debt arbitrage	32	141	173
Opportunistic	Global macro	84	380	464
Opportunistic	Systematic futures	182	518	700
Multi-manager	Fund of funds – debt	20	97	117

Grouping	CISDM Categories	Number of Live Funds	Number of Defunct Funds	Total Number of Funds
Multi-manager	Fund of funds – equity	104	592	696
Multi-manager	Fund of funds – event	10	124	134
Multi-manager	Fund of funds – macro/systematic	30	163	193
Multi-manager	Fund of funds – multi-strategy	164	789	953
Multi-manager	Fund of funds – relative value	12	83	95
Multi-manager	Multi-strategy	111	395	506
Specialist	Volatility	28	30	58
Specialist	Long/short debt	115	279	394
Total		1,539	6,217	7,756

Using TASS and CISDM datasets, the stepwise regression procedure resulted in both BOND and CMDTY factors being dropped from the final conditional linear risk model because of multi-collinearity issues. This is because retaining CREDIT and SNP500 factors produced higher adjusted R^2s compared to retaining BOND and CMDTY factors.

Exhibit 12 provides useful information for interpreting the effects of the factor exposures included in the conditional risk model on hedge fund strategy returns. For both normal and crisis periods, it shows the four risk factors, the typical market trend during these periods, the hedge fund manager's desired position (long or short), and the desired factor exposure for benefitting from a particular market trend.

Exhibit 12: Interpretation of Conditional Risk Factor Exposures

Period/Risk Factor	Typical Market Trend	Desired Position	Desired Factor Exposure	Comments
Normal				
SNP500	Equities Rising	Long	Positive	Aims to add risk, increase return
CREDIT	Spreads Flat/Narrowing	Long	Positive	Aims to add risk, increase return
USD	USD Flat/Depreciating	Short	Negative	Sells USD to boost returns
VIX	Volatility Falling	Short	Negative	Sells volatility to boost returns
Crisis				
DSNP500	Equities Falling Sharply	Short	Negative	Aims to reduce risk
DCREDIT	Spreads Widening	Short	Negative	Aims to reduce risk

Period/Risk Factor	Typical Market Trend	Desired Position	Desired Factor Exposure	Comments
DUSD	USD Appreciating	Long	Positive	USD is haven in crisis periods
DVIX	Volatility Rising	Long	Positive	Negative correlation with equities

14 EVALUATING EQUITY HEDGE FUND STRATEGIES: APPLICATION

Using data from the CISDM and TASS databases from 2000 to 2016, this section discusses key return and risk characteristics for hedge funds pursuing equity-related strategies. More specifically, the conditional factor model is used to assess average risk exposures (during both normal and crisis market periods) for all "live" funds in each of the equity-related categories in these databases. Finally, the heterogeneity among funds, which is masked in the average exposures, is then revealed in an analysis showing the percentage of all hedge funds in each category that have significant factor exposures (positive and negative) during normal and crisis periods.

Note that the results of such a risk factor analysis may vary somewhat based on the hedge fund database used, the time period examined, and the specification of the factor model. However, the key takeaway is that such an analysis can uncover unintended adverse risk exposures to a hedge fund—stemming from the strategy it pursues—that may assert themselves only during turbulent market periods. As mentioned previously, unintended adverse risk exposures that revealed themselves during the global financial crisis resulted in the demise of literally thousands of hedge funds worldwide. Thus, understanding how to interpret the results of such a risk factor analysis is a key practical competency for any practitioner involved in advising on the strategies followed by hedge funds or in managing or owning the hedge funds themselves. First, we describe how the factor model can be used to understand risk exposures of equity-related hedge fund strategies. Then, we turn to understanding risks of multi-manager strategies.

The key return characteristics are shown for equity-related hedge fund strategies by category in Exhibit 13. In addition to the Sharpe ratio, we calculate the Sortino ratio.[2] The Sortino ratio replaces standard deviation in the Sharpe ratio with downside deviation, so it concentrates on returns below a specified threshold. For example, if the threshold return is zero, then the Sortino ratio uses downside deviation based on losses. Because hedge funds potentially invest in illiquid securities (which artificially smooth returns, thus lowering the measured standard deviation), besides measuring risk and return one should also investigate the autocorrelation of returns. Rho is a measure of first order serial autocorrelation, the correlation between a fund's return and its own lagged returns. High Rho signals smoothed returns and thus is an indicator of potential liquidity issues (specifically, illiquidity and infrequent trading) in the underlying securities.

Exhibit 13 shows that L/S Equity Hedge (TASS) has the highest mean return (11.30%) but also the highest standard deviation (22.86%). Among categories with more than four funds, EMN (TASS) has the highest Sharpe ratio; notably, despite

2 In addition to Sharpe and Sortino ratios, other performance measures can be used, such as the Treynor ratio, information ratio, return on VaR, Jensen's alpha, M^2, maximum drawdown, and gain-to-loss ratio.

having the highest standard deviation, L/S Equity Hedge (TASS) also has the highest Sortino ratio; and Global L/S Equity (CISDM) shows the largest Rho. Overall, these results indicate that by accepting some beta and illiquidity exposure, L/S equity managers generally outperform equity market-neutral managers in terms of total returns delivered. Returns of L/S equity managers, however, are also more volatile than those of EMN managers and so produce lower Sharpe ratios. Intuitively, these results are in line with expectations.

Exhibit 13: Key Return Characteristics for Equity Hedge Fund Strategies (2000–2016)

			Annualized Mean (%)		Annualized Sharpe Ratio		Annualized Sortino Ratio		Rho (%)	
Database	**Category**	**Sample Size**	**Mean**	**SD**	**Mean**	**SD**	**Mean**	**SD**	**Mean**	**SD**
TASS	Dedicated short bias	4	2.91	14.75	2.27	4.36	1.35	1.07	20.0	45.7
CISDM	Bear market equity	2	2.04	7.37	0.29	1.18	0.70	1.47	9.15	1.79
TASS	Equity market neutral	38	7.81	10.20	0.83	0.56	0.80	0.53	9.3	15.8
CISDM	Equity market neutral	40	7.48	8.82	0.79	0.81	0.65	0.92	16.29	8.88
TASS	Long/short equity hedge	350	11.30	22.86	0.62	0.64	1.33	1.04	11.0	13.5
CISDM	Global long/short equity	86	8.83	16.93	0.44	0.57	0.76	1.09	17.43	15.63
CISDM	Asia/Pacific long/short equity	31	8.87	20.27	0.45	0.36	0.73	0.57	16.72	10.49
CISDM	Europe long/short equity	47	7.05	11.59	0.56	0.37	0.69	1.08	13.92	10.53
CISDM	US long/short equity	218	9.41	17.50	0.62	0.46	0.60	0.55	12.76	8.98
CISDM	US small cap long/short equity	67	9.88	19.60	0.65	0.48	1.14	0.86	11.71	7.44

Taking a more granular view of factor risks, Exhibit 14 presents average risk exposures (equity, credit, currency, and volatility) for equity-related hedge fund strategies using the conditional risk factor model from 2000 to 2016. The crisis period is from June 2007 to February 2009, and crisis period factors are preceded by the letter "D" (e.g., the crisis period equity factor is DSNP500). Light (dark) shaded coefficients have *t*-statistics greater than 1.96 (1.67) and are significant at the 5% (10%) level.

Exhibit 14: Risk Exposures for Equity Hedge Funds Using the Conditional Risk Factor Model (2000–2016)

Strategy	Dedicated Short Bias	Bear Market Equity	Equity Market Neutral	Equity Market Neutral	Asia/ Pacific Long/ Short Equity	Europe Long/ Short Equity	Global Long/ Short Equity	US Long/ Short Equity	US Small Cap Long/ Short Equity	Long/ Short Equity Hedge
Database	TASS	CISDM	TASS	CISDM	CISDM	CISDM	CISDM	CISDM	CISDM	TASS
Sample Size	4	2	38	40	31	47	86	218	67	350
Normal Times Exposures										
Intercept	−0.02	0.00	0.01	0.01	0.01	0.01	0.02	−0.01	0.01	0.01
SNP500	−0.28	−0.46	0.11	0.09	0.42	0.24	0.52	0.58	0.58	0.41
USD	−0.13	−0.07	−0.02	0.00	−0.02	0.06	−0.01	−0.03	−0.01	−0.04
CREDIT	1.24	0.22	−0.12	−0.07	−0.26	−0.23	−0.77	0.63	−0.09	−0.20
VIX	0.04	−0.05	0.01	0.00	−0.01	0.02	−0.01	−0.03	0.03	0.07
Crisis Times Exposures (Incremental)										
DSNP500	0.04	0.11	0.04	0.05	−0.02	−0.14	−0.04	0.03	−0.02	−0.03
DUSD	−0.08	−0.06	−0.17	−0.02	0.15	−0.42	−0.07	−0.07	−0.09	−0.17
DCREDIT	0.02	0.05	0.06	0.10	−0.01	0.07	0.16	0.03	−0.20	0.07
DVIX	0.00	−0.02	−0.06	−0.04	−0.04	−0.09	−0.04	0.02	−0.02	−0.02

On average, funds following EMN strategies maintain low exposure to equity market risk (0.11, significant at 10%) as well as a neutral exposure to the other risk factors in the model in both normal and crisis periods. L/S equity strategies maintain significant (at the 5% level) average beta loadings to equity risk during normal periods. The equity risk betas range from 0.24 for Europe L/S Equity to 0.58 for both US and US Small Cap L/S Equity strategies. Although there are no significant incremental (i.e., additional) exposures to equity risk (DSNP500) during crisis periods, total exposures during crisis periods (normal + crisis) are positive and significant for all L/S equity strategies. For example, the total equity exposure in crisis times for US L/S Equity is 0.61 (= 0.58 + 0.03). Because they show average exposures across all live funds in the given strategy category, these results mask significant heterogeneity between funds in their exposures to the four risk factors.

Exhibit 15 highlights this heterogeneity by presenting the percentage of funds experiencing significant (at the 10% level or better) factor exposures within each strategy category. The (T) indicates funds from the TASS database, and all other funds are from CISDM; gray (white) bars signify positive (negative) factor exposures. The y-axis indicates the percentage of funds within each strategy category that experienced the significant risk exposures.

Exhibit 15: Significant Positive and Negative Factor Exposures for Funds by Equity Hedge Strategy during Normal and Crisis Periods (2000–2016)

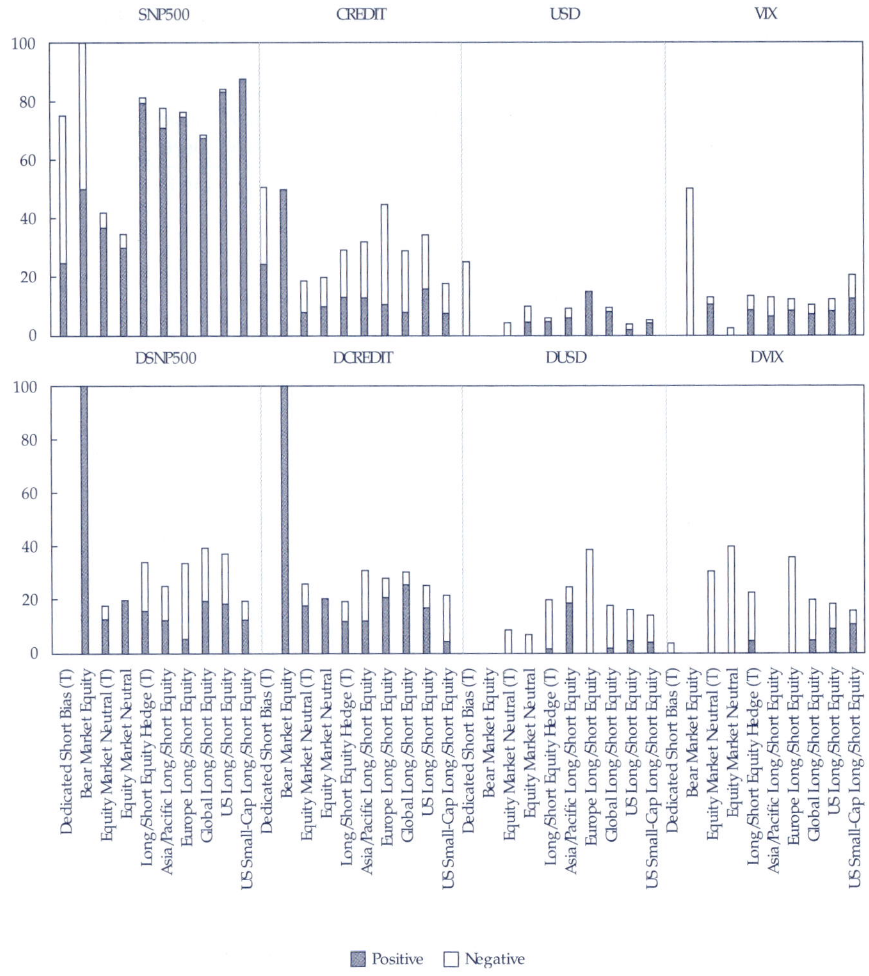

For example, with the exception of dedicated short-biased funds, most equity-related hedge funds have significant positive exposure to equity risk during normal market periods (30%+ for EMN funds and 70%+ for L/S equity funds). However, during crisis periods, less than 40% of L/S equity funds have any significant incremental equity exposure; for those that do, their added exposure is mixed (negative and positive). This suggests that managers were able to decrease adverse crisis period effects on their returns—likely by deleveraging, outright selling of stock (short sales, too) and equity index futures, and/or buying index put options. This also indicates that although they did not reduce long beta tilting by much, on average L/S equity managers did not make things worse by trying to aggressively "bottom pick" the market. Finally, these results are consistent with the average incremental equity exposure during crisis periods of approximately zero, as seen in the previous exhibit.

As one might intuitively expect, most L/S equity managers do not have significant exposure to CREDIT. Only about one-third of L/S equity funds have significant exposure to CREDIT—mainly negative exposure, indicating that they are unlikely to benefit from moderating credit risk (spreads narrowing, credit upgrades). Interestingly, for the 25% of funds with significant incremental crisis period CREDIT exposure, these exposures become more positive, which would tend to hurt returns as spreads widen and credit downgrades accelerate during market sell-offs. Similarly, exposures to USD and VIX for L/S equity funds are marginal during normal times, with few funds having any significant exposures. However, in most cases during crisis periods, any significant additional exposures are mainly negative. For example, about 40% of Europe L/S Equity funds show significant negative exposure to USD—perhaps expecting a crisis-induced flight to quality into the euro or Japanese yen as opposed to USD. Again, nearly 40% of these funds show negative added VIX exposure (i.e., short volatility) during crisis times. Returns of some high-profile hedge funds have been hurt by being unexpectedly short volatility during crisis periods, which underscores why understanding the heterogeneity of factor exposures is important to understanding risk profiles of hedge funds.

EXAMPLE 14

Dedicated Short-Biased Hedge Fund

1. Bearish Asset Management (BAM) manages a short-biased hedge fund that varies its portfolio's short tilt depending on perceived opportunities. Using the fund's monthly returns for the past 10 years, which include periods of financial market crisis, a conditional risk factor model was estimated. The following table provides factor beta estimates with corresponding *t*-statistics [dark (light) shaded are significant at the 5% (10%) level].

   Interpret the factor loadings. Also, what can you infer about BAM's overall risk exposure during crisis periods?

Coefficient	Estimate	*t*-Statistic
Normal Times Exposures		
Intercept	0.005	1.10
USD	0.072	0.72
CREDIT	−0.017	−0.07
SNP500	−0.572	−9.65
VIX	−0.164	−2.19
Crisis Times Exposures (Incremental)		
DUSD	0.456	1.31
DCREDIT	−0.099	−0.40
DSNP500	0.236	1.74
DVIX	0.105	1.03

Solution:

BAM's fund has highly significant negative loadings on equity risk (SNP500) and volatility risk (VIX). The negative equity risk exposure is as expected for a short-biased strategy. But the negative VIX loading is consistent with short volatility exposure. This suggests that BAM's manager may be selling puts against some of its short exposures, thereby attempting to also capture a volatility premium. During crisis periods, the equity beta rises from −0.572 to −0.336 (= −0.572 + 0.236 = −0.336). This negative exposure is still significant and suggests that despite being a short-biased fund, BAM had less negative equity risk exposure during crisis periods. In this case, the manager may be purposefully harvesting some of its short exposure into market weakness.

15 EVALUATING MULTI-MANAGER HEDGE FUND STRATEGIES: APPLICATION

It is important to understand the risks of multi-manager hedge fund strategies. Exhibit 16 shows that multi-strategy hedge funds outperform funds-of-funds: They have higher mean returns (7.85%/TASS and 8.52%/CISDM) and among the highest Sharpe ratios and Sortino ratios. Multi-strategy funds have higher Rho (more than 20%) compared to FoF, indicating relatively high serial autocorrelation. This is reasonable because multi-strategy funds may be simultaneously running strategies using less liquid instruments, such as convertible arbitrage, fixed-income arbitrage, and other relative value strategies. That is why, unlike FoFs, they often impose investor-level or fund-level gates on maximum quarterly redemptions.

Exhibit 16: Key Return Characteristics for Multi-Manager Hedge Fund Strategies (2000–2016)

			Annualized Mean (%)		Annualized Sharpe Ratio		Annualized Sortino Ratio		Rho (%)	
Database	**Category**	**Sample Size**	**Mean**	**SD**	**Mean**	**SD**	**Mean**	**SD**	**Mean**	**SD**
CISDM	Fund of funds – debt	20	6.52	7.94	0.89	0.66	0.68	1.17	13.89	4.24
CISDM	Fund of funds – equity	104	4.69	9.15	0.41	0.28	0.44	0.91	12.27	10.61
CISDM	Fund of funds – event	10	4.59	4.99	0.75	0.51	0.56	1.19	13.76	6.71
CISDM	Fund of funds – macro/ systematic	30	5.09	10.16	0.39	0.39	0.57	0.60	8.15	3.52
CISDM	Fund of funds – multi-strategy	164	4.47	7.18	0.54	1.84	1.34	1.43	12.43	9.31
CISDM	Fund of funds – relative value	12	5.31	8.58	0.70	0.42	1.31	0.63	15.86	13.77
TASS	Fund of funds	454	5.73	10.03	0.38	0.71	0.52	0.62	19.9	18.1
CISDM	Multi-strategy	111	8.52	11.01	0.89	1.36	1.32	1.58	20.09	16.24
TASS	Multi-strategy	100	7.85	11.51	0.86	1.40	1.00	1.05	22.7	24.3

Exhibit 17 presents average risk exposures for multi-manager hedge fund strategies using the conditional risk factor model. The crisis period is from June 2007 to February 2009, and light (dark) shaded betas have t-statistics of more than 1.96 (1.67).

Exhibit 17: Risk Exposures for Multi-Manager Hedge Funds Using the Conditional Risk Factor Model (2000–2016)

Strategy	Fund of Funds – Debt	Fund of Funds – Equity	Fund of Funds – Event	Fund of Funds – Macro/ Systematic	Fund of Funds – Multi-Strategy	Fund of Funds – Relative Value	Fund of Funds	Multi-Strategy	Multi-Strategy
Database	CISDM	CISDM	CISDM	CISDM	CISDM	CISDM	TASS	CISDM	TASS
Sample Size	20	104	10	30	163	12	454	111	100
Normal Times Exposures									
Intercept	0.01	0.01	0.01	0.01	0.01	0.01	0.01	0.10	0.01
SNP500	0.16	0.33	0.14	−0.02	0.21	0.12	0.24	−0.14	0.22
USD	−0.01	0.01	0.01	−0.07	0.00	0.01	0.01	−0.41	−0.01
CREDIT	−0.36	−0.43	−0.22	−0.10	−0.28	−0.14	−0.45	−5.71	−0.03
VIX	0.00	0.03	0.00	0.04	0.01	0.02	0.01	−0.03	0.01
Crisis Times Exposures (Incremental)									
DSNP500	−0.02	0.02	−0.01	−0.01	0.00	0.02	0.00	0.05	0.06
DUSD	0.03	−0.09	−0.19	−0.21	−0.20	−0.27	−0.05	−0.05	−0.05
DCREDIT	−0.10	0.09	−0.13	0.01	0.03	−0.10	0.09	0.07	−0.05
DVIX	0.03	−0.09	−0.03	−0.05	−0.07	−0.06	−0.05	−0.02	−0.05

Results show that all FoF strategies (except macro/systematic) have significant positive exposure to equity risk (ranging from 0.14 to 0.33) for the full period. The finding for macro/systematic is consistent with results presented earlier for opportunistic hedge funds, which show they tend not to be exposed to equity risks in aggregate. Interestingly, multi-strategy funds have significant equity exposure but differing signs—negative (positive) for CISDM (TASS)—which highlights the heterogeneity between the two databases.

Multi-manager funds as a group do not appear to provide significant hedging benefits (via diversification) in crisis times. If they did, then significant negative exposures to DSNP500 would be observed. This is consistent with the research findings that in the 2007–2009 global financial crisis, diversification across hedge fund strategies did not decrease total portfolio risk. These researchers conclude that during crises, simple diversification is insufficient; rather, it is important to focus on such other risks as liquidity, volatility, and credit—particularly because these risks may be magnified by the application of leverage.

Exhibit 18 tells a different story when individual funds are studied. The majority of multi-manager funds have significant positive exposure to the equity factor, but around 30% of funds show a mix of negative and positive incremental exposures (DSNP 500) to equities during the crisis period. This suggests that at least some funds (ones with negative loadings) were able to shield their investors from substantial market declines by deleveraging, selling equity pre-crisis, and/or short selling. About 40% of all multi-manager funds have significant, mostly negative, exposure to CREDIT, indicating that they generally were not positioned to benefit from improving credit spreads. In crisis times, they took on additional (mostly negative) CREDIT exposure. For example, about 50% of FoF-Debt and FoF-Relative Value funds experienced incremental negative CREDIT exposure during turbulent periods, which hedged them from deteriorating credit conditions.

Exhibit 18: Significant Positive and Negative Factor Exposures for Multi-Manager Hedge Funds during Normal and Crisis Periods (2000–2016)

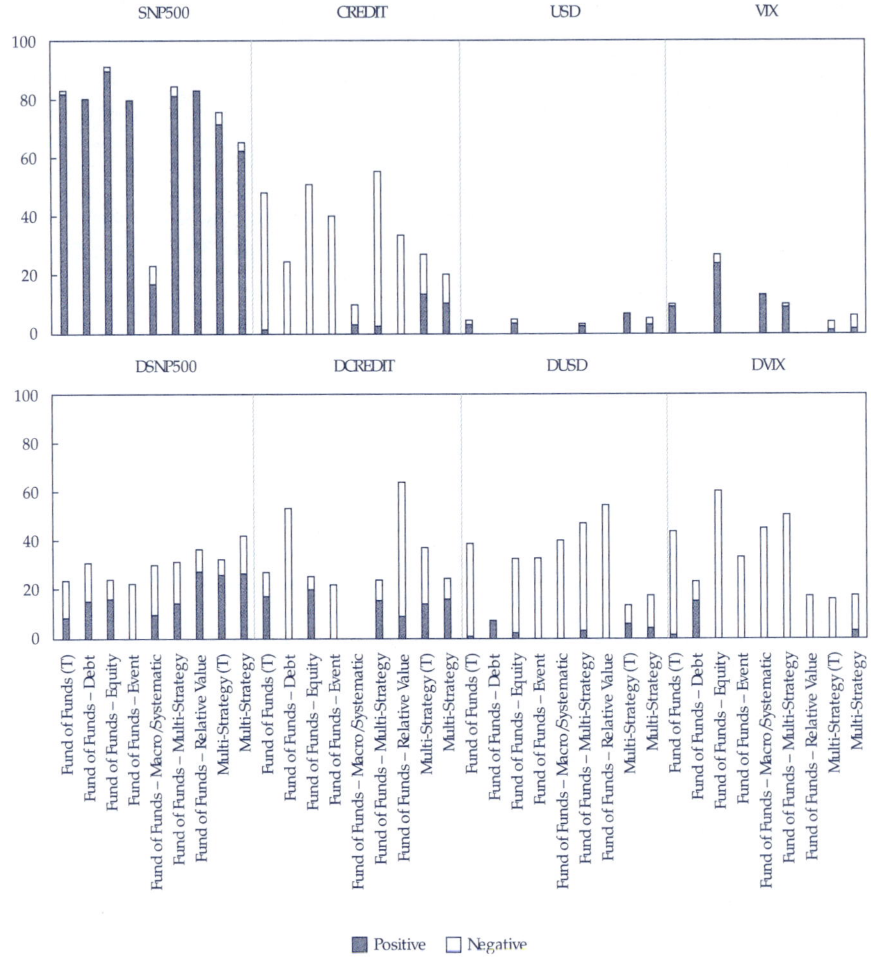

For the full period, multi-manager funds have minimal exposures to USD and VIX. Notably, these exposures increase dramatically, becoming significantly negative during financial crises. For example, only 2% of FoF-Equity have negative exposure to VIX overall. But, 60% of these funds show additional significant negative VIX exposure in crisis times. A similar pattern is revealed for USD exposure. Such negative exposures would seem undesirable during times when volatility is spiking and the USD is likely appreciating. Natural embedded leverage may be a partial explanation for these seemingly undesirable exposures during crisis times. In sum, as crisis periods generate potentially unexpected exposures to systematic risks, it is essential to use conditional factor models to understand risks of hedge fund strategies.

PORTFOLIO CONTRIBUTION OF HEDGE FUND STRATEGIES

16

☐ evaluate the impact of an allocation to a hedge fund strategy in a traditional investment portfolio

This section examines the return and risk contributions of the hedge fund strategies previously covered when added to a traditional 60% stock/40% bond investment portfolio.

Performance Contribution to a 60/40 Portfolio

For each hedge fund strategy category that has been discussed, we now consider an equal-weighted portfolio of the individual funds in that category. We examine the impact of a 20% allocation to such a hedge fund strategy portfolio when combined with a traditional investment portfolio consisting of 60% stocks and 40% bonds. The S&P 500 Total Return Index and the Bloomberg Barclays Corporate AA Intermediate Bond Index are used to proxy the 60%/40% portfolio. When the hedge fund strategy portfolio is added to the traditional portfolio, the resulting allocations for the combined portfolio are 48% stocks, 32% bonds, and 20% in the particular hedge fund strategy portfolio. Please note this exercise is for illustrating the portfolio performance contribution of hedge fund strategies; practically speaking, it is unlikely an investor would hold an allocation (here 20%) that included an equal weighting of all live funds in one particular hedge fund strategy category.

Exhibit 19 provides performance and risk metrics for the combined portfolios from 2000 to 2016. It shows that when added to a traditional 60%/40% portfolio (with a mean return of 6.96%), a 20% allocation to the US Small Cap L/S Equity strategy generates the highest mean return (7.53%) of all the combined portfolios—an improvement of 57 bps. Adding a 20% allocation of an equal-weighted portfolio of funds in any of the following hedge fund categories to the traditional portfolio produces average annual returns of more than 7.30%: fixed-income arbitrage, distressed securities, or systematic futures. Adding a 20% allocation of any of the hedge fund strategies shown in Exhibit 19 to the traditional portfolio almost always decreases total portfolio standard deviation while increasing Sharpe and Sortino ratios (and also decreasing maximum drawdown in about one-third of the combined portfolios). These results demonstrate that hedge funds act as both risk-adjusted return enhancers and diversifiers for the traditional stock/bond portfolio.

Exhibit 19: Performance and Risk of 48/32/20 Portfolio, Where 20% Allocation Is to an Equal-Weighted Portfolio for Each Hedge Fund Strategy Category (2000–2016)

Category	Type	Database	Mean Return (%)	SD (%)	Sharpe Ratio	Sortino Ratio	Maximum Drawdown (%)
60% Stocks/40% Bonds	*Traditional Portfolio*	—	*6.96*	*8.66*	*0.62*	*1.13*	*14.42*
Long/Short Equity Hedge	Equity	TASS	7.22	8.29	0.68	1.45	21.34
Global Long/Short Equity	Equity	CISDM	7.06	8.17	0.67	1.22	22.51
U.S. Long/Short Equity	Equity	CISDM	7.17	8.22	0.68	1.24	16.77

Category	Type	Database	Mean Return (%)	SD (%)	Sharpe Ratio	Sortino Ratio	Maximum Drawdown (%)
U.S. Small Cap Long/Short Equity	Equity	CISDM	7.53	8.75	0.68	1.23	27.02
Asia/Pacific Long/Short Equity	Equity	CISDM	6.44	8.12	0.60	1.07	21.74
Europe Long/Short Equity	Equity	CISDM	6.79	7.69	0.67	1.24	15.20
Dedicated Short Bias	Equity	TASS	6.02	5.59	0.79	1.02	16.06
Bear Market Equity	Equity	CISDM	5.97	5.68	0.77	1.43	16.62
Equity Market Neutral	Equity	TASS	6.81	7.17	0.73	1.80	10.72
Equity Market Neutral	Equity	CISDM	6.79	7.13	0.73	1.36	4.99
Event Driven	Event Driven	TASS	7.13	7.76	0.71	1.44	20.96
Event Driven	Event Driven	CISDM	7.19	7.83	0.71	1.31	20.57
Distressed Securities	Event Driven	CISDM	7.40	7.67	0.75	1.38	20.00
Merger Arbitrage	Event Driven	CISDM	6.85	7.22	0.73	1.35	5.60
Convertible Arbitrage	Relative Value	TASS	6.76	7.75	0.66	1.27	31.81
Fixed-Income Arbitrage	Relative Value	TASS	7.50	7.82	0.75	1.39	12.68
Convertible Arbitrage	Relative Value	CISDM	6.91	7.68	0.69	1.25	27.91
Global Macro	Opportunistic	TASS	6.96	7.36	0.73	1.29	5.14
Global Macro	Opportunistic	CISDM	6.97	7.29	0.74	1.38	5.19
Systematic Futures	Opportunistic	CISDM	7.34	6.94	0.83	1.68	8.04
Fund of Funds	Multi-Manager	TASS	6.43	7.53	0.64	1.23	18.92
Multi-Strategy	Multi-Manager	TASS	6.98	7.57	0.71	1.13	17.35
Fund of Funds – Debt	Multi-Manager	CISDM	6.56	7.40	0.67	1.22	17.77
Fund of Funds – Equity	Multi-Manager	CISDM	6.39	7.76	0.62	1.11	21.63
Fund of Funds – Event	Multi-Manager	CISDM	6.35	7.48	0.63	1.15	21.37
Fund of Funds – Macro/Systematic	Multi-Manager	CISDM	6.47	7.05	0.69	1.31	10.65
Fund of Funds – Multi-Strategy	Multi-Manager	CISDM	6.36	7.41	0.64	1.17	18.17
Fund of Funds – Relative Value	Multi-Manager	CISDM	6.46	7.22	0.67	1.23	17.16
Multi-Strategy	Multi-Manager	CISDM	7.00	7.47	0.72	1.34	13.83

The Sharpe ratio measures risk-adjusted performance, where risk is defined as standard deviation, so it penalizes both upside and downside variability. The Sortino ratio measures risk-adjusted performance, where risk is defined as downside deviation, so it penalizes only downside variability below a minimum target return. For hedge fund strategies with large negative events, the Sortino ratio is considered a better performance measure. The combined portfolio with the highest Sharpe ratio (0.83) includes a 20% allocation to systematic futures hedge funds. High Sharpe ratios are also achieved from allocations to distressed securities, fixed-income arbitrage, and global macro or equity market-neutral strategies. Adding allocations of 20% consisting of hedge funds from equity market-neutral (TASS), systematic futures, L/S equity hedge, or event-driven (TASS) categories to the traditional portfolio produces combined portfolios with by far the best Sortino ratios.

Exhibit 20 plots the Sharpe and Sortino ratios for 48/32/20 portfolios, where the 20% allocation is to an equal-weighted portfolio of the funds in each hedge fund strategy category. As a point of reference, the Sharpe and Sortino ratios for the 60/40 portfolio are 0.62 and 1.13, respectively. This graphic visually demonstrates that adding allocations of systematic futures, equity market-neutral, global macro, or event-driven hedge fund strategies, among others, to the traditional portfolio is effective in generating superior risk-adjusted performance—as evidenced by their relatively high Sharpe and Sortino ratios. Moreover, the implication is that despite the flexibility to invest in a wide range of strategies, funds-of-funds and multi-manager funds do not enhance risk-adjusted performance very much.

Exhibit 20: Sharpe and Sortino Ratios for 48/32/20 Portfolios, Where 20% Allocation Is to an Equal-Weighted Portfolio for Each Hedge Fund Strategy Category

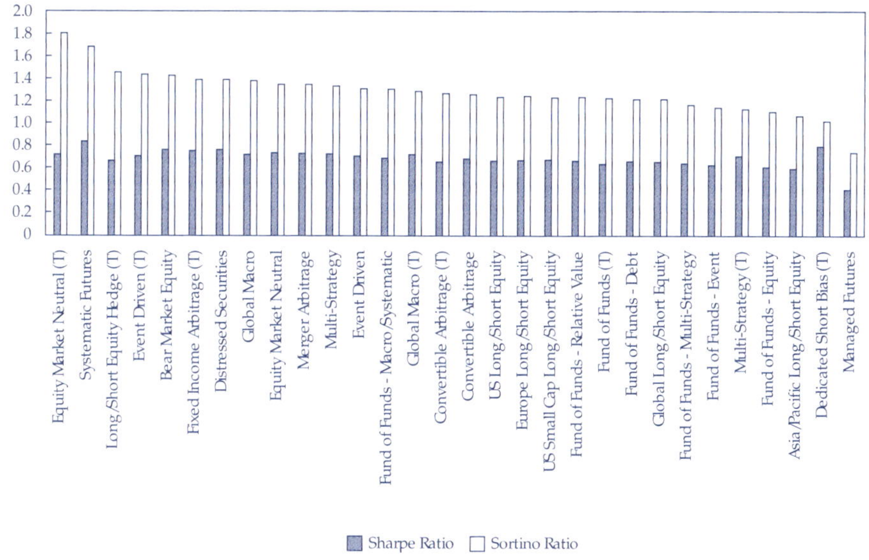

Risk Metrics

Considering the different risk exposures and investments that hedge fund strategies entail, many investors consider these strategies for portfolio risk reduction or risk mitigation. Exhibit 21 illustrates which strategies may be most effective in reducing risk in a traditional portfolio (with standard deviation of 8.66%). The exhibit presents the standard deviation of returns for 48/32/20 portfolios, where the 20% allocation is to an equal-weighted portfolio for each hedge fund strategy category.

Exhibit 21: Standard Deviations for 48/32/20 Portfolios, Where 20% Allocation Is to an Equal-Weighted Portfolio for Each Hedge Fund Strategy Category

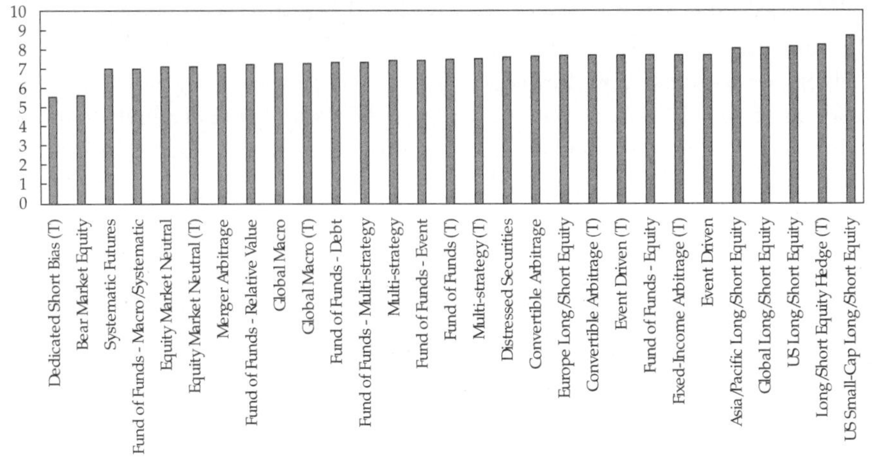

Besides dedicated short-biased and bear market-neutral strategies—for which there are only 6 live funds in total—it can be seen that among the hedge fund strategies that produce the lowest standard deviations of returns in the combined portfolios are systematic futures (6.94%) and FoF-macro/systematic and equity market neutral (a little more than 7.0%). These strategies appear to provide significant risk-reducing diversification benefits; and as discussed previously, they are also the same categories of hedge funds that enhance risk-adjusted returns when added to the traditional 60/40 portfolio. It is evident that standard deviations are relatively high for combined portfolios with event-driven/distressed securities and relative value/convertible arbitrage strategies, indicating they provide little in the way of risk-reduction benefits. This may be attributed to the binary, long-biased nature of most event-driven/distressed securities investing and the typical leverage downsizing/liquidity issues of relative value/convertible arbitrage during periods of market stress.

A drawdown is the difference between a portfolio's highest value (i.e., high-water mark) for a period and any subsequent low point until a new high-water mark is reached. Maximum drawdown is the *largest* difference between a high-water mark and a subsequent low point. The results for maximum drawdown for the 48/32/20 portfolios are shown in Exhibit 22.

Exhibit 22: Maximum Drawdowns for 48/32/20 Portfolios, Where 20% Allocation Is to an Equal-Weighted Portfolio for Each Hedge Fund Strategy Category

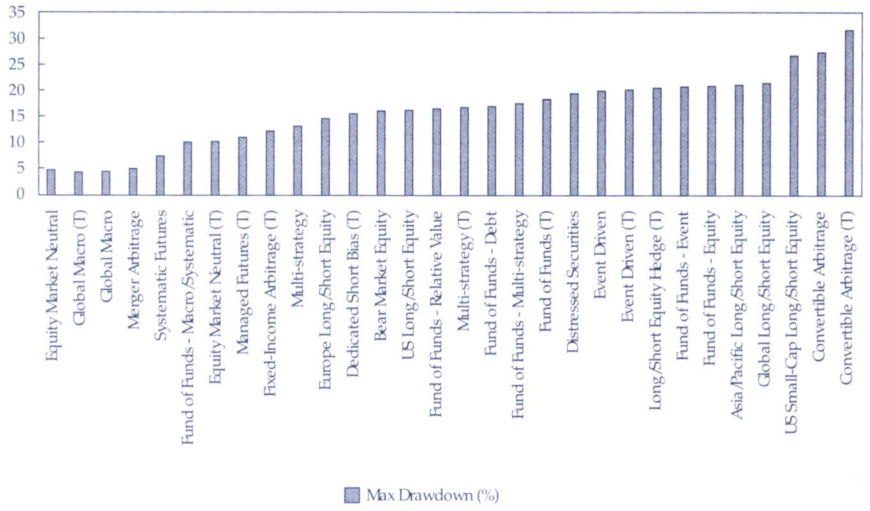

The graphic shows that when combined with the traditional stock and bond portfolio (with a maximum drawdown of 14.42%), the hedge fund strategy portfolios that generate the smallest maximum drawdowns are the opportunistic strategies—specifically, global macro and systematic futures as well as merger arbitrage and equity market-neutral strategies. Notably, the conditional risk model showed that these strategies did not have much exposure to high equity or credit risk during crisis periods. In addition, they also tend to be the strategies with the lowest serial autocorrelation, signaling good liquidity. This suggests that these types of strategies provide risk mitigation for traditional assets because they are not exposed to the same risks, are relatively opportunistic, and are liquid even during periods of market stress. On the other side of the spectrum, L/S equity strategies, event-driven/distressed securities strategies, and relative value/convertible arbitrage strategies show high maximum drawdowns when combined with the traditional portfolio. This is unsurprising because the conditional risk model showed that these event-driven and relative value strategies tended to hold equity risk and that their credit risk also became significant during crisis periods.

EXAMPLE 15

Combining a Hedge Fund Strategy with a Traditional Portfolio

DIY Investment Advisors is a "CIO in a box." Its clients are mainly small institutions and local college endowments. Evergreen Tech, a private 4-year college, is a client with a $150 million endowment and an enrollment of 3,000 students. The endowment's portfolio, which supports 5% of Evergreen's current annual spending needs, has a traditional asset allocation of 60% stocks/40% bonds. Evergreen plans to dramatically increase enrollment to 4,000 students over the next 5 years.

Patricia Chong, principal of DIY, wants to recommend to Evergreen's investment committee (IC) that it add alternative investments to the endowment's portfolio, specifically a 20% allocation to a hedge fund strategy. The IC has indicated to Chong that Evergreen's main considerations for the combined portfolio are that any hedge fund strategy allocation should a) maximize risk-adjusted returns; b) limit downside risk; and c) not impair portfolio liquidity. The IC is also sensitive to fees and considers it important to avoid layering of fees for any hedge fund allocation.

At Chong's request, DIY's hedge fund analysts perform due diligence on numerous hedge funds and assemble the following information on several short-listed funds, showing their past performance contribution to a 48% stocks/32% bonds/20% hedge fund strategy portfolio. Finally, Chong believes historical returns are good proxies for future returns.

Category	Type	Mean Return (%)	SD (%)	Sharpe Ratio	Sortino Ratio	Maximum Draw-down (%)
60% Stocks/40% Bonds	Traditional Portfolio	6.96	8.66	0.62	1.13	14.42
US small-cap long/short equity	Equity	7.53	8.75	0.68	1.23	27.02
Event driven	Event driven	7.19	7.83	0.71	1.31	20.57
Sovereign debt fixed-income arbitrage	Relative value	7.50	7.82	0.75	1.39	12.68
Fund-of-funds – equity	Multi-manager	6.39	7.76	0.62	1.11	21.63

Use the information provided to answer the following questions.

1. Discuss which hedge fund strategy Chong should view as *least* suitable for meeting the considerations expressed by Evergreen's IC.

Solution:

Based on the IC's considerations, Chong should view a 20% allocation to the fund-of-funds equity hedge fund strategy as least suitable for Evergreen's endowment portfolio. Such an allocation offers no improvements in the combined portfolio's Sharpe and Sortino ratios (to 0.62 and 1.11, respectively). The substantially higher maximum drawdown (50% higher at 21.63%) indicates much more downside risk would be in the combined portfolio. Portfolio liquidity may also be impaired due to two levels of redemption lock-ups and liquidity gates. Finally, given the FoF structure for this strategy allocation, Evergreen would need to pay two layers of fees and would also likely face fee netting risk.

2. Discuss which hedge fund strategy Chong should view as *most* suitable for meeting the considerations expressed by Evergreen's IC.

Solution:

Based on the IC's considerations, Chong should view a 20% allocation to the sovereign debt fixed-income arbitrage hedge fund strategy as most suitable for Evergreen's endowment portfolio. Such an allocation would result in significant increases in the combined portfolio's Sharpe and Sortino ratios (to 0.75 and 1.39, respectively), the highest such ratios among the strategies presented. Besides the improvement in Sortino ratio, the lower maximum drawdown (12.68%) indicates less downside risk in the combined portfolio than with any of the other strategy choices. Portfolio liquidity would also likely not be impaired as this strategy focuses on sovereign debt, which typically has good liquidity for most developed market issuers. Finally, similar to the other non-FoF strategies shown, Evergreen would pay only one layer of fees and would also not face any fee netting risk.

SUMMARY

- Hedge funds are an important subset of the alternative investments space. Key characteristics distinguishing hedge funds and their strategies from traditional investments include the following: 1) lower legal and regulatory constraints; 2) flexible mandates permitting use of shorting and derivatives; 3) a larger investment universe on which to focus; 4) aggressive investment styles that allow concentrated positions in securities offering exposure to credit, volatility, and liquidity risk premiums; 5) relatively liberal use of leverage; 6) liquidity constraints that include lock-ups and liquidity gates; and 7) relatively high fee structures involving management and incentive fees.
- Hedge fund strategies are classified by a combination of the instruments in which they are invested, the trading philosophy followed, and the types of risks assumed. Some leading hedge fund strategy index providers are Hedge Fund Research; Lipper TASS; Morningstar Hedge/CISDM; Eurekahedge; and Credit Suisse. There is much heterogeneity in the classification and indexes they provide, so no one index group is all-encompassing.
- This reading classifies hedge fund strategies by the following categories: equity-related strategies; event-driven strategies; relative value strategies; opportunistic strategies; specialist strategies; and multi-manager strategies.
- Equity L/S strategies take advantage of diverse opportunities globally to create alpha via managers' skillful stock picking. Diverse investment styles include value/growth, large cap/small cap, discretionary/quantitative, and industry specialization. Some equity L/S strategies may use index-based short hedges to reduce market risk, but most involve single name shorts for portfolio alpha and added absolute return.
- Equity L/S strategies are typically liquid and generally net long, with gross exposures at 70%–90% long vs. 20%–50% short (but they can vary).
- Equity L/S return profiles are typically aimed to achieve average annual returns roughly equivalent to a long-only approach but with standard deviations that are 50% lower. The more market-neutral or quantitative the strategy approach, the more levered the strategy application to achieve a meaningful return profile.
- Dedicated short sellers only trade with short-side exposure, but they may moderate short beta by also holding cash. Short-biased managers are focused on short-side stock picking, but they typically moderate short beta with some value-oriented long exposure and cash.
- Dedicated short strategies tend to be 60%–120% short at all times, while short-biased strategies are typically around 30%–60% net short. The focus in both cases is usually on single equity stock picking, as opposed to index shorting, and using little if any leverage.

- Dedicated short-selling and short-biased strategies have return goals that are typically less than most other hedge fund strategies but with a negative correlation benefit. Returns are more volatile than a typical L/S equity hedge fund given short beta exposure.
- Equity market-neutral (EMN) strategies take advantage of idiosyncratic short-term mispricing between securities. Their sources of return and alpha do not require accepting beta risk, so EMN strategies are especially attractive in periods of market vulnerability/weakness. There are many types of EMN managers, but most are purely quantitative managers (vs. discretionary managers).
- As many beta risks (e.g., market, sector) are hedged away, EMN strategies generally apply relatively high levels of leverage in striving for meaningful return targets.
- Equity market-neutral strategies exhibit relatively modest return profiles. Portfolios are aimed at market neutrality and with differing constraints to other factor/sector exposures. Generally high levels of diversification and liquidity with lower standard deviation of returns are typical due to an orientation toward mean reversion.
- Merger arbitrage is a relatively liquid strategy. Defined gains come from idiosyncratic, single security takeover situations, but occasional downside shocks can occur when merger deals unexpectedly fail.
- Cross-border M&A usually involves two sets of governmental approvals. M&A deals involving vertical integration often face antitrust scrutiny and thus carry higher risks and offer wider merger spread returns.
- Merger arbitrage strategies have return profiles that are insurance-like, plus a short put option, with relatively high Sharpe ratios; however, left-tail risk is associated with otherwise steady returns. Merger arbitrage managers typically apply moderate to high leverage to generate meaningful target return levels.
- Distressed securities strategies focus on firms in bankruptcy, facing potential bankruptcy, or under financial stress. Hedge fund managers seek inefficiently priced securities before, during, or after the bankruptcy process, which results in either liquidation or reorganization.
- In liquidation, the firm's assets are sold off and securities holders are paid sequentially based on priority of their claims—from senior secured debt, junior secured debt, unsecured debt, convertible debt, preferred stock, and finally common stock.
- In re-organization, a firm's capital structure is re-organized and terms for current claims are negotiated and revised. Debtholders may agree either to maturity extensions or to exchanging their debt for new equity shares (existing shares are canceled) that are sold to new investors to improve the firm's financial condition.
- Outright shorts or hedged positions are possible, but distressed securities investing is usually long-biased, entails relatively high levels of illiquidity, and has moderate to low leverage. The return profile is typically at the higher end of event-driven strategies, but it is more discrete and cyclical.
- For fixed-income arbitrage, the attractiveness of returns is a function of the correlations between different securities, the yield spread pick-up available, and the high number and wide diversity of debt securities across different markets, each having different credit quality and convexity aspects in their pricing.

- Yield curve and carry trades within the US government space are very liquid but have the fewest mispricing opportunities. Liquidity for relative value positions generally decreases in other sovereign markets, in mortgage-related markets, and across corporate debt markets.
- Fixed-income arbitrage involves high leverage usage, but leverage availability diminishes with trade and underlying instrument complexity.
- Convertible arbitrage strategies strive to extract "underpriced" implied volatility from long convertible bond holdings. To do this, managers will delta hedge and gamma trade short equity positions against their convertible positions. Convertible arbitrage works best in periods of high convertible issuance, moderate volatility, and reasonable market liquidity.
- Liquidity issues may arise from convertible bonds being naturally less-liquid securities due to their relatively small issue sizes and inherent complexities as well as the availability and cost to borrow underlying equity for short selling.
- Convertible arbitrage managers typically run convertible portfolios at 300% long vs. 200% short. The lower short exposure is a function of the delta-adjusted exposure needed from short sales to balance the long convertibles.
- Global macro strategies focus on correctly discerning and capitalizing on trends in global financial markets using a wide range of instruments. Managed futures strategies have a similar aim but focus on investments using mainly futures and options on futures, on stock and fixed-income indexes, as well as on commodities and currencies.
- Managed futures strategies typically are implemented via more systematic approaches, while global macro strategies tend to use more discretionary approaches. Both strategies are highly liquid and use high leverage.
- Returns of managed futures strategies typically exhibit positive right-tail skewness during market stress. Global macro strategies generally deliver similar diversification in stress periods but with more heterogeneous outcomes.
- Specialist hedge fund strategies require highly specialized skill sets for trading in niche markets. Two such typical specialist strategies—which are aimed at generating uncorrelated, attractive risk-adjusted returns—are volatility trading and reinsurance/life settlements.
- Volatility traders strive to capture relative timing and strike pricing opportunities due to changes in the term structure of volatility. They try to capture volatility smile and skew by using various types of option spreads, such as bull and bear spreads, straddles, and calendar spreads. In addition to using exchange-listed and OTC options, VIX futures, volatility swaps, and variance swaps can be used to implement volatility trading strategies.
- Life settlements strategies involve analyzing pools of life insurance contracts offered by third-party brokers, where the hedge fund purchases the pool and effectively becomes the beneficiary. The hedge fund manager looks for policies with the following traits: 1) The surrender value being offered to the insured individual is relatively low; 2) the ongoing premium payments are also relatively low; and 3) the probability is relatively high that the insured person will die sooner than predicted by standard actuarial methods.

- Funds-of-funds and multi-strategy funds typically offer steady, low-volatility returns via their strategy diversification. Multi-strategy funds have generally outperformed FoFs, but they have more variance due to using relatively high leverage.
- Multi-strategy funds offer potentially faster tactical asset allocation and generally improved fee structure (netting risk between strategies is often at least partially absorbed by the general partner), but they have higher manager-specific operational risks. FoFs offer a potentially more diverse strategy mix, but they have less transparency, have slower tactical reaction time, and contribute netting risk to the FoF investor.
- Conditional linear factor models can be useful for uncovering and analyzing hedge fund strategy risk exposures. This reading uses such a model that incorporates four factors for assessing risk exposures in both normal periods and market stress/crisis periods: equity risk, credit risk, currency risk, and volatility risk.
- Adding a 20% allocation of a hedge fund strategy group to a traditional 60%/40% portfolio (for a 48% stocks/32% bonds/20% hedge funds portfolio) typically decreases total portfolio standard deviation while it increases Sharpe and Sortino ratios (and also often decreases maximum drawdown) in the combined portfolios. This demonstrates that hedge funds act as both risk-adjusted return enhancers and diversifiers for the traditional stock/bond portfolio.

REFERENCES

Hasanhodzic, Jasmina and Andrew Lo. 2007. "Can Hedge-Fund Returns Be Replicated?: The Linear Case." *Journal of Investment Management* 5 (2): 5–45.

PRACTICE PROBLEMS

1. Bern Zang is the chief investment officer of the Janson University Endowment Investment Office. The Janson University Endowment Fund (the "Fund") is based in the United States and has current assets under management of $10 billion, with minimal exposure to alternative investments. Zang currently seeks to increase the Fund's allocation to hedge funds and considers four strategies: dedicated short bias, merger arbitrage, convertible bond arbitrage, and global macro.

   At a meeting with the Fund's board of directors, the board mandates Zang to invest only in event-driven and relative value hedge fund strategies.

   Determine, among the four strategies under consideration by Zang, the two that are permitted given the board's mandate. **Justify** your response.

   i. Dedicated short bias
   ii. Merger arbitrage
   iii. Convertible bond arbitrage
   iv. Global macro

Determine, among the four strategies under consideration by Zang, the two that are permitted given the board's mandate. (circle two)	Justify your response.
Dedicated short bias	
Merger arbitrage	
Convertible bond arbitrage	
Global macro strategies	

The following information relates to questions 2-9

Snohomish Mukilteo is a portfolio analyst for the Puyallup-Wenatchee Pension Fund (PWPF). PWPF's investment committee (IC) asks Mukilteo to research adding hedge funds to the PWPF portfolio.

A member of the IC meets with Mukilteo to discuss hedge fund strategies. During the meeting, the IC member admits that her knowledge of hedge fund strategies is fairly limited but tells Mukilteo she believes the following:

Statement 1	Equity market-neutral strategies use a relative value approach.
Statement 2	Event-driven strategies are not exposed to equity market beta risk.
Statement 3	Opportunistic strategies have risk exposure to market directionality.

The IC member also informs Mukilteo that for equity-related strategies, the IC considers low volatility to be more important than negative correlation.

Mukilteo researches various hedge fund strategies. First, Mukilteo analyzes an event-driven strategy involving two companies, Algona Applications (AA) and

Tukwila Technologies (TT). AA's management, believing that its own shares are overvalued, uses its shares to acquire TT. The IC has expressed concern about this type of strategy because of the potential for loss if the acquisition unexpectedly fails. Mukilteo's research reveals a way to use derivatives to protect against this loss, and he believes that such protection will satisfy the IC's concern.

Next, while researching relative value strategies, Mukilteo considers a government bond strategy that involves buying lower-liquidity, off-the-run bonds and selling higher-liquidity, duration-matched, on-the-run bonds.

Mukilteo examines an opportunistic strategy implemented by one of the hedge funds under consideration. The hedge fund manager selects 12 AAA rated corporate bonds with actively traded futures contracts and approximately equal durations. For each corporate bond, the manager calculates the 30-day change in the yield spread over a constant risk-free rate. He then ranks the bonds according to this spread change. For the bonds that show the greatest spread narrowing (widening), the hedge fund will take long (short) positions in their futures contracts. The net holding for this strategy is market neutral.

Mukilteo also plans to recommend a specialist hedge fund strategy that would allow PWPF to maintain a high Sharpe ratio even during a financial crisis when equity markets fall.

The IC has been considering the benefits of allocating to a fund of funds (FoF) or to a multi-strategy fund (MSF). Mukilteo receives the following email from a member of the IC:

"From my perspective, an FoF is superior even though it entails higher manager-specific operational risk and will require us to pay a double layer of fees without being able to net performance fees on individual managers. I especially like the tactical allocation advantage of FoFs—that they are more likely to be well informed about when to tactically reallocate to a particular strategy and more capable of shifting capital between strategies quickly."

Finally, Mukilteo creates a model to simulate adding selected individual hedge fund strategies to the current portfolio with a 20% allocation. The IC's primary considerations for a combined portfolio are (1) that the variance of the combined portfolio must be less than 90% of that of the current portfolio and (2) that the combined portfolio maximize the risk-adjusted return with the expectation of large negative events. Exhibit 1 provides historical performance and risk metrics for three simulated portfolios.

Exhibit 1: Performance of Various Combined Portfolios

Hedge Fund Strategy	Standard Deviation (%)	Sharpe Ratio	Sortino Ratio	Maximum Drawdown (%)
Current Portfolio				
NA	7.95	0.58	1.24	14.18
Three Potential Portfolios with a 20% Hedge Fund Allocation				
Merger arbitrage	7.22	0.73	1.35	5.60
Systematic futures	6.94	0.83	1.68	8.04
Equity market neutral	7.17	0.73	1.80	10.72

2. Which of the IC member's statements regarding hedge fund strategies is

incorrect?

A. Statement 1

B. Statement 2

C. Statement 3

3. Based on what the IC considers important for equity-related strategies, which strategy should Mukilteo *most likely* avoid?

   A. Long/short equity

   B. Equity market neutral

   C. Dedicated short selling and short biased

4. Which of the following set of derivative positions will *most likely* satisfy the IC's concern about the event-driven strategy involving AA and TT?

   A. Long out-of-the-money puts on AA shares and long out-of-the-money calls on TT shares

   B. Long out-of-the-money calls on AA shares and long out-of-the-money puts on TT shares

   C. Long risk-free bonds, short out-of-the-money puts on AA shares, and long out-of-the-money calls on TT shares

5. The government bond strategy that Mukilteo considers is *best* described as a:

   A. carry trade.

   B. yield curve trade.

   C. long/short credit trade.

6. The opportunistic strategy that Mukilteo considers is *most likely* to be described as a:

   A. global macro strategy.

   B. time-series momentum strategy.

   C. cross-sectional momentum strategy.

7. The specialist hedge fund strategy that Mukilteo plans to recommend is *most likely*:

   A. cross-asset volatility trading between the US and Japanese markets.

   B. selling equity volatility and collecting the volatility risk premium.

   C. buying longer-dated out-of-the-money options on VIX index futures.

8. Based on the email that Mukilteo received, the IC member's perspective is correct with regard to:

   A. layering and netting of fees.

   B. tactical allocation capabilities.

C. manager-specific operational risks.

9. Based on the IC's primary considerations for a combined portfolio, which simulated hedge fund strategy portfolio in Exhibit 1 creates the *most suitable* combined portfolio?

   A. Merger arbitrage

   B. Systematic futures

   C. Equity market neutral

The following information relates to questions 10-15

Lynet Xu is the Chief Investment Officer for the North University Endowment Fund (the Fund), which is based in Europe. The Fund's investment committee recently made the decision to add hedge funds to the Fund's portfolio to increase diversification. Xu meets with Yolanda Anderson, a junior analyst, to discuss various hedge fund strategies that might be suitable for the Fund. Anderson tells Xu the following:

Statement 1	Relative value strategies tend to use minimal leverage.
Statement 2	Long/short equity strategies are typically not exposed to equity market beta risk.
Statement 3	Global macro strategies come with naturally higher volatility in the return profiles typically delivered.

Xu tells Anderson that while she is open to using all hedge fund strategies, she is particularly interested in opportunistic hedge fund strategies. Xu states that she prefers opportunistic hedge fund strategies that use high leverage, have high liquidity, and exhibit right-tail skewness.

Xu asks Anderson to research an event-driven strategy involving a potential merger between Aqua Company and Taurus, Inc. Aqua has offered to buy Taurus in a stock-for-stock deal: The offer ratio is two shares of Aqua for three shares of Taurus. Aqua was trading at €50 per share prior to the merger announcement, and it fell to €45 per share after the merger announcement. Taurus was trading at €15 per share prior to the announcement, and it rose to €20 per share in anticipation of the merger deal receiving required approvals and closing successfully. Xu decides to enter into a merger arbitrage trade: She buys 22,500 shares of Taurus at €20 per share and sells short 15,000 shares of Aqua at €45 per share.

Xu and Anderson discuss an equity strategy involving two large European car companies, ZMD and Tarreras. Anderson recently attended a trade show where she inspected ZMD's newest model car. Based on information from the trade show and other analysis conducted by Anderson, Xu concludes that ZMD will not meet its revenue expectations. Current valuation metrics indicate that ZMD shares are overvalued relative to shares of Tarreras. Xu decides to take a short position in ZMD and a long position in Tarreras with equal beta-weighted exposure.

Xu next reviews a convertible arbitrage strategy and analyzes a trade involving the euro-denominated stock and convertible bonds of AVC Corporation, a European utility company. Anderson gathers selected data for AVC Corporation, which is presented in Exhibit 1.

Exhibit 1: Selected Data for AVC Corporation

AVC Convertible Bond		AVC Stock	
Price (% of par)	115	Current price (per share)	€28
Coupon (%)	6	P/E	25
Remaining maturity (years)	2	P/BV	2.25
Conversion ratio	50	P/CF	15

Based on comparisons with industry ratios, Xu believes that AVC's shares are overvalued in relative terms and the convertible bonds are undervalued. Anderson analyzes the potential profit outcomes of a long position in the convertible bond combined with a short stock position, assuming small changes in the share price and ignoring dividends and borrowing costs. She offers the following conclusion to Xu:

"The profit earned on the convertible arbitrage trade will be the same regardless of whether the share price of AVC decreases or increases."

Finally, Xu and Anderson consider a hedge fund that specializes in reinsurance and life settlements. Xu tells Anderson about three characteristics that hedge fund managers look for when investing in life settlements:

Characteristic 1	The surrender value offered to the insured individual is relatively high.
Characteristic 2	The ongoing premium payments to keep the policy active are relatively low.
Characteristic 3	There is a high probability that the designated insured person is likely to die within the period predicted by standard actuarial methods.

10. Which of Anderson's three statements regarding hedge fund strategies is correct?

   A. Statement 1

   B. Statement 2

   C. Statement 3

11. Which opportunistic hedge fund strategy meets Xu's preferences?

   A. Only global macro

   B. Only managed futures

   C. Both global macro and managed futures

12. Assuming the merger between Aqua and Taurus successfully closes, the payoff on Xu's merger arbitrage trade will be:

   A. –€187,500.

   B. €225,000.

   C. €412,500.

13. Which equity hedge fund strategy *best* describes the ZMD and Tarreras positions taken by Xu?

    A. Short bias

    B. Long/short equity

    C. Equity market neutral

14. Anderson's conclusion about the profitability of the AVC convertible arbitrage trade is:

    A. correct.

    B. incorrect, because the profit will be higher if the share price decreases.

    C. incorrect, because the profit will be higher if the share price increases.

15. Which of the three characteristics of life settlements noted by Anderson is correct?

    A. Characteristic 1

    B. Characteristic 2

    C. Characteristic 3

The following information relates to questions 16-17

Jane Shaindy is the chief investment officer of a large pension fund. The pension fund is based in the United States and currently has minimal exposure to hedge funds. The pension fund's board has recently approved an additional investment in a long/short equity strategy. As part of Shaindy's due diligence on a hedge fund that implements a long/short equity strategy, she uses a conditional linear factor model to uncover and analyze the hedge fund's risk exposures. She is interested in analyzing several risk factors, but she is specifically concerned about whether the hedge fund's long (positive) exposure to equities increases during turbulent market periods.

16. **Describe** how the conditional linear factor model can be used to address Shaindy's concern.

17. During a monthly board meeting, Shaindy discusses her updated market forecast for equity markets. Due to a recent large increase in interest rates and geopolitical tensions, her forecast has changed from one of modestly rising equities to several periods of non-trending markets. Given this new market view, Shaindy concludes that a long/short strategy will not be optimal at this time and seeks another equity-related strategy. The Fund has the capacity to use a substantial amount of leverage.

    Determine the *most appropriate* equity-related hedge fund strategy that Shaindy should employ. **Justify** your response.

---

18. Gunnar Patel is an event-driven hedge fund manager for Senson Fund, which

focuses on merger arbitrage strategies. Patel has been monitoring the potential acquisition of Meura Inc. by Sellshom, Inc. Sellshom has offered to buy Meura in a stock-for-stock deal. Sellshom was trading at $60 per share just prior to the announcement of the acquisition, and Meura was trading at $18 per share.

The offer ratio is 1 share of Sellshom in exchange for 2 shares of Meura. Soon after the announcement, Meura's share price jumps to $22 while Sellshom's falls to $55 in anticipation of the merger receiving required approvals and the deal closing successfully.

At the current share prices of $55 for Sellshom and $22 for Meura, Patel attempts to profit from the merger announcement. He buys 40,000 shares of Meura and sells short 20,000 shares of Sellshom.

Calculate the payoffs of the merger arbitrage under the following two scenarios:

i. The merger is successfully completed.

ii. The merger fails.

19. Yankel Stein is the chief investment officer of a large charitable foundation based in the United States. Although the foundation has significant exposure to alternative investments and hedge funds, Stein proposes to increase the foundation's exposure to relative value hedge fund strategies. As part of Stein's due diligence on a hedge fund engaging in convertible bond arbitrage, Stein asks his investment analyst to summarize different risks associated with the strategy.

Describe how each of the following circumstances can create concerns for Stein's proposed hedge fund strategy:

i. Short selling

ii. Credit issues

iii. Time decay of call option

iv. Extreme market volatility

	Describe how each of the following circumstances can create concerns for Stein's proposed hedge fund strategy:
Short selling	
Credit issues	
Time decay of call option	
Extreme market volatility	

20. John Puten is the chief investment officer of the Markus University Endowment Investment Office. Puten seeks to increase the diversification of the endowment by investing in hedge funds. He recently met with several hedge fund managers that employ different investment strategies. In selecting a hedge fund manager, Puten prefers to hire a manager that uses the following:

- Fundamental and technical analysis to value markets
- Discretionary and systematic modes of implementation
- Top-down strategies
- A range of macroeconomic and fundamental models to express a view regarding the direction or relative value of a particular asset

Puten's staff prepares a brief summary of two potential hedge fund investments:

Hedge Fund 1: A relative value strategy fund focusing only on convertible arbitrage.

Hedge Fund 2: An opportunistic strategy fund focusing only on global macro strategies.

Determine which hedge fund would be *most appropriate* for Puten. **Justify** your response.

The following information relates to questions 21-22

Sushil Wallace is the chief investment officer of a large pension fund. Wallace wants to increase the pension fund's allocation to hedge funds and recently met with three hedge fund managers. These hedge funds focus on the following strategies:

Hedge Fund A: Specialist—Follows relative value volatility arbitrage

Hedge Fund B: Multi-Manager—Multi-strategy fund

Hedge Fund C: Multi-Manager—Fund-of-funds

21. **Describe** three paths for implementing the strategy of Hedge Fund A.

22. After a significant amount of internal discussion, Wallace concludes that the pension fund should invest in either Hedge Fund B or C for the diversification benefits from the different strategies employed. However, after final due diligence is completed, Wallace recommends investing only in Hedge Fund B, noting its many advantages over Hedge Fund C.

    Discuss *two* advantages of Hedge Fund B relative to Hedge Fund C with respect to investment characteristics.

---

23. Kloss Investments is an investment adviser whose clients are small institutional investors. Muskogh Charitable Foundation (the "Foundation") is a client with $70 million of assets under management. The Foundation has a traditional asset allocation of 65% stocks/35% bonds. Risk and return characteristics for the Foundation's current portfolio are presented in Panel A of Exhibit 1.

    Kloss' CIO, Christine Singh, recommends to Muskogh's investment committee that it should add a 10% allocation to hedge funds. The investment committee indicates to Singh that Muskogh's primary considerations for the Foundation's portfolio are that any hedge fund strategy allocation should: a) limit volatility, b) maximize risk-adjusted returns, and c) limit downside risk.

    Singh's associate prepares expected risk and return characteristics for three portfolios that have allocations of 60% stocks, 30% bonds, and 10% hedge funds, where the 10% hedge fund allocation follows either an equity market-neutral, global macro, or convertible arbitrage strategy. The risk and return characteristics of the three portfolios are presented in Panel B of Exhibit 1.

Exhibit 1

Hedge Fund Strategy	SD (%)	Sharpe Ratio	Sortino Ratio	Maximum Drawdown (%)
Panel A: Current Portfolio				
N/A	8.75	0.82	1.25	16.2
Panel B: Three Potential Portfolios with a 10% Hedge Fund Allocation				
Equity market neutral	8.72	0.80	1.21	15.1
Global macro	8.55	0.95	1.35	15.0
Convertible arbitrage	8.98	0.83	1.27	20.2

Discuss which hedge fund strategy Singh should view as most suitable for meeting the considerations expressed by Muskogh's investment committee.

SOLUTIONS

1.

Determine, among the four strategies under consideration by Zang, the two that are permitted given the board's mandate. (circle two)	Justify your response.
Dedicated short bias	A dedicated short bias hedge fund strategy is an example of an equity hedge fund strategy, not an event-driven or relative value strategy. Equity hedge fund strategies focus primarily on the equity markets, and the majority of their risk profiles contain equity-oriented risk. Dedicated short bias managers look for possible short selling targets among companies that are overvalued, that are experiencing declining revenues and/or earnings, or that have internal management conflicts, weak corporate governance, or even potential accounting frauds.
Merger arbitrage	A merger arbitrage hedge fund strategy is an example of an event-driven strategy, which is permitted under the board's mandate. Event-driven hedge fund strategies focus on corporate events, such as governance events, mergers and acquisitions, bankruptcy, and other key events for corporations. Merger arbitrage involves simultaneously purchasing and selling the stocks of two merging companies to create "riskless" profits.
Convertible bond arbitrage	A convertible bond arbitrage hedge fund strategy is an example of a relative value strategy, which is permitted under the board's mandate. Relative value hedge fund strategies focus on the relative valuation between two or more securities. Relative value strategies are often exposed to credit and liquidity risks because the valuation differences from which these strategies seek to benefit are often due to differences in credit quality and/or liquidity across different securities. A classic convertible bond arbitrage strategy is to buy the relatively undervalued convertible bond and take a short position in the relatively overvalued underlying stock.
Global macro	A global macro hedge fund strategy is an example of an opportunistic hedge fund strategy, not an event-driven or relative value strategy. Opportunistic hedge fund strategies take a top-down approach, focus on a multi-asset opportunity set, and include global macro strategies. Global macro managers use both fundamental and technical analysis to value markets as well as discretionary and systematic modes of implementation.

2. B is correct. Statement 2 is incorrect: Event-driven strategies, such as merger arbitrage, tend to be exposed to some natural equity market beta risk. Overall market risk can potentially disrupt a merger's consummation (though hedging may be possible). To the extent that deals are more likely to fail in market stress periods, event-driven merger arbitrage strategies have market sensitivity and left-tail risk attributes. Also, while event-driven strategies may have less beta exposure than simple, long-only beta allocations, the higher hedge fund fees effectively result in a particularly expensive form of embedded beta. Equity market-neutral strategies do use a relative value approach, because such strategies hold balanced long and short equity exposures to maintain zero (or close to zero) net exposure to the equity market and such factors as sector and size. Also, opportunistic strat-

egies do have risk exposure to market directionality, also called trendiness.

A is incorrect because equity market-neutral strategies do use a relative value approach. Equity market-neutral strategies hold balanced long and short equity exposures to maintain zero (or close to zero) net exposure to the equity market and such factors as sector and size (i.e., market cap). They then focus on, for example, pairs of long and short securities whose prices are out of historical alignment and are expected to experience mean reversion. To take advantage of idiosyncratic short-term mispricing between securities whose prices should otherwise be co-integrated, equity market-neutral hedge fund strategies take opposite (i.e., long and short) positions in similar or related equities that have divergent valuations, while also attempting to maintain a near net zero portfolio exposure to the market.

C is incorrect because opportunistic strategies do have risk exposure to market directionality, also called trendiness. Opportunistic strategies are based on macro themes and multi-asset relationships on a global basis; therefore, broad themes, global relationships, market trends, and cycles affect their returns. Generally, the key source of returns in global macro strategies revolves around correctly discerning and capitalizing on trends in global markets. For example, global macro managers typically hold views on trends in inflation (among other things). Global macro strategies are typically top down and use a range of macroeconomic and fundamental models to express a view regarding the direction or relative value of an asset or asset class. If the hedge fund manager is making a directional bet, then directional models will use fundamental data regarding a specific market or asset to determine whether it is undervalued or overvalued relative to history and the expected macro trend.

3. C is correct. For equity-related strategies, the IC considers low volatility to be more important than negative correlation. Dedicated short selling and short-biased strategies have return goals that are typically less than those for most other hedge fund strategies but with a negative correlation benefit. In addition, they are more volatile than a typical long/short equity hedge fund because of their short beta exposure. As a result, Mukilteo should avoid dedicated short selling and short-biased strategies.

   A is incorrect because long/short equity is a lower-volatility strategy. A long/short equity manager aims to achieve a standard deviation that is 50% lower than a long-only approach while achieving average annual returns roughly equivalent to a long-only approach. Since the IC considers low volatility important, this is not a strategy that Mukilteo should necessarily avoid.

   B is incorrect because equity market-neutral strategies generally have high levels of diversification and lower standard deviations of returns than many other strategies across normal market conditions. Because they typically deliver returns that are steadier and less volatile than those of many other hedge strategy areas, equity market-neutral managers generally are more useful for portfolio allocation during periods of non-trending or declining markets. Equity market-neutral managers neutralize market risk by constructing their portfolios such that the expected portfolio beta is approximately equal to zero. Over time, their conservative and constrained approach typically results in less volatile overall returns than those of managers who accept beta exposure. (The exception to this norm is when the use of significant leverage may cause forced portfolio downsizing.) Since the IC considers low volatility important, this is not a strategy that Mukilteo should necessarily avoid.

4. B is correct. The event-driven strategy that Mukilteo researches is a stock-for-stock merger arbitrage strategy. In this strategy, because the management of the acquiring company (AA) believes its shares to be overvalued, it

will offer AA shares in exchange for target company (TT) shares in a specified ratio. The merger arbitrage fund manager will then buy TT shares and sell AA shares in the same ratio as the offer, hoping to earn the spread on successful deal completion.

For most acquisitions, the initial announcement of a deal will cause the target's share price to rise toward the acquisition price and the acquirer's share price to fall (either because of the potential dilution of its outstanding shares or the use of cash for purposes other than a dividend payment). If the acquisition is unsuccessful, the manager faces losses if the target's share price has already risen and/or the acquirer's share price has already fallen in anticipation of the acquisition. When merger deals do fail, the initial price rise of the target's shares and the initial price fall of the acquirer's shares are typically reversed. Arbitrageurs who jumped into the merger situation after its initial announcement stand to incur substantial losses on their long positions in the target's shares and their short positions in the acquirer's shares.

To manage the risk of the acquisition failing, the manager can buy out-of-the-money calls on AA shares (to cover the short position) and buy out-of-the money puts on TT shares (to protect against loss in value). Such a position will provide protection that would likely satisfy the IC's concern about losses with this strategy.

A is incorrect because protecting against loss with this strategy requires buying out-of-the-money calls (not puts) on AA and buying out-of-the-money puts (not calls) on TT.

C is incorrect because it represents the payoff profile of this merger arbitrage strategy, not a way to protect the strategy against loss should the acquisition fail. The payoff profile of this merger arbitrage strategy resembles that of a riskless bond combined with a short put option on AA shares and a long call option on TT shares. The short put on the AA shares reflects the need to cover the short position in AA when the share price rises. The long call on TT shares becomes valuable if and when another interested acquirer (i.e., White Knight) makes a higher bid for TT before the initial merger proposal is completed.

5. A is correct. Carry trades involve going long a higher-yielding security and shorting a lower-yielding security with the expectation of receiving the positive carry and of profiting on long and short sides of the trade when the temporary relative mispricing reverts to normal. A classic example of a fixed-income arbitrage trade involves buying lower-liquidity, off-the-run government securities and selling higher-liquidity, duration-matched, on-the-run government securities. Interest rate and credit risks are hedged because long and short positions have the same duration and credit exposure. So, the key concern is liquidity risk. Under normal conditions, as time passes, the more (less) expensive on-the-run (off-the-run) securities will decrease (increase) in price as the current on-the-runs are replaced by a more liquid issue of new on-the-run bonds that then become off-the-run bonds.

   B is incorrect because Mukilteo considers a carry trade, not a yield curve trade. For yield curve trades, the prevalent calendar spread strategy involves taking long and short positions at different points on the yield curve where the relative mispricing of securities offers the best opportunities, such as in a curve flattening or steepening, to profit. Perceptions and forecasts of macroeconomic conditions are the backdrop for these types of trades. The positions can be in fixed-income securities of the same issuer; in that case, most credit and liquidity risks would likely be hedged, making interest rate risk the main concern. Alternatively, longs and shorts can be taken in the securities of different issuers—but typically ones operating in the same industry or sector. In this case, differences in credit quality, liquidity, volatility, and issue-specific characteristics would likely drive the relative mispricing. In either case, the hedge fund manager aims to profit as the mispricing reverses (mean reversion occurs) and the longs rise and shorts fall in value within the targeted time frame.

C is incorrect because Mukilteo considers a carry trade, not a long/short credit trade. In a long/short credit trade, valuation differences result from differences in credit quality—for example, investment-grade versus non-investment-grade securities. It involves the relative credit risks across different security issuers and tends to be naturally more volatile than the exploitation of small pricing differences within sovereign debt alone.

6. C is correct. The strategy under consideration is a managed futures strategy—specifically, a cross-sectional momentum approach. Such an approach is generally implemented with securities in the same asset class, which is corporate bonds in this case. The strategy is to take long positions in contracts for bonds that have risen the most in value relative to the others (the bonds with the narrowing spreads) and short positions in contracts for bonds that have fallen the most in value relative to the others (the bonds with the widening spreads). Cross-sectional momentum strategies generally result in holding a net zero or market-neutral position. In contrast, positions for assets in time-series momentum strategies are determined in isolation, independent of the performance of the other assets in the strategy and can be net long or net short depending on the current price trend of an asset.

   A is incorrect because the opportunistic strategy under consideration is more likely to be described as a managed futures strategy—specifically, a cross-sectional momentum approach—rather than a global macro strategy. Global macro strategies are typically top down and generally focus on correctly discerning and capitalizing on trends in global financial markets, which does not describe the strategy under consideration. In contrast, managed futures strategies that use a cross-sectional momentum approach are implemented with a cross-section of assets (generally within an asset class, which in this case is highly rated corporate bonds) by going long those that are rising in price the most and by shorting those that are falling the most.

   B is incorrect because the strategy under consideration is a managed futures strategy—specifically, a cross-sectional (not time-series) momentum approach. Time-series trading strategies are driven by the past performance of the individual assets. The manager will take long positions for assets that are rising in value and short positions for assets that are falling in value. Positions are taken on an absolute basis, and individual positions are determined independent of the performance of the other assets in the strategy. This approach is in contrast to cross-sectional strategies, where the position taken in an asset depends on that asset's performance relative to the other assets. With time-series momentum strategies, the manager can be net long or net short depending on the current price trend of an asset.

7. C is correct. Mukilteo needs to recommend a specialist hedge fund strategy that can help PWPF maintain a high Sharpe ratio even in a crisis when equity markets fall. Buying longer-dated out-of-the-money options on VIX index futures is a long equity volatility position that works as a protective hedge, particularly in an equity market crisis when volatility spikes and equity prices fall. A long volatility strategy is a useful potential diversifier for long equity investments (albeit at the cost of the option premium paid by the volatility buyer). Because equity volatility is approximately 80% negatively correlated with equity market returns, a long position in equity volatility can substantially reduce the portfolio's standard deviation, which would serve to increase its Sharpe ratio. Longer-dated options will have more absolute exposure to volatility levels (i.e., vega exposure) than shorter-dated options, and out-of-the-money options will typically trade at

higher implied volatility levels than at-the-money options.

A is incorrect because cross-asset volatility trading, a type of relative value volatility trading, may often involve idiosyncratic, macro-oriented risks that may have adverse effects during an equity market crisis.

B is incorrect because the volatility seller is the provider of insurance during crises, not the beneficiary of it. Selling volatility provides a volatility risk premium or compensation for taking on the risk of providing insurance against crises for holders of equities and other securities. On the short side, option premium sellers generally extract steadier returns in normal market environments.

8. A is correct. FoFs have double layers of fees without being able to net performance fees on individual managers. The FoF investor always faces netting risk and is responsible for paying performance fees that are due to winning underlying funds while suffering return drag from the performance of losing underlying funds. Even if the FoF's overall performance (aggregated across all funds) is flat or down, FoF investors must still pay incentive fees that are due to the managers of the winning underlying funds.

   The fee structure is more investor friendly at MSFs, where the general partner absorbs the netting risk arising from the divergent performance of the fund's different strategy teams. This is an attractive outcome for the MSF investor because (1) the GP is responsible for netting risk and (2) the only investor-level incentive fees paid are those due on the total fund performance after netting the positive and negative performances of the various strategy teams.

   However, if the MSF operates with a pass-through fee model, the investor will pay for a portion of the netting risk. Using this model, the MSF may charge no management fee but instead pass through the costs of paying individual teams (inclusive of salary and incentives fees earned by each team) before an added manager-level incentive fee is charged to the investor on total fund performance. In this instance, the investor does implicitly pay for a portion of netting risk.

   B is incorrect because MSFs have a tactical allocation advantage over FoFs. MSFs can reallocate capital into different strategy areas more quickly and efficiently than is possible in FoFs, allowing MSFs to react faster to real-time market impacts. This shorter tactical reaction time, combined with MSFs' better strategy transparency, makes MSFs more resilient than FoFs in preserving capital.

   C is incorrect because MSFs have higher manager-specific operational risks than FoFs. In MSFs, teams of managers dedicated to running different hedge fund strategies share operational and risk management systems under the same roof. This means that the MSF's operational risks are not well diversified because all operational processes are performed under the same fund structure. FoFs, in contrast, have less operational risk because each separate underlying hedge fund is responsible for its own risk management.

9. C is correct. The equity market-neutral strategy makes for a combined portfolio that has a standard deviation below the maximum specified and has the highest Sortino ratio.

   The primary consideration is that the variance of the combined portfolio must be less than 90% of that of the current portfolio. Since variance is the square of standard deviation, the maximum variance allowed is

$$\sigma_{\text{max}}^2 = \left(\sigma_{\text{current}}\right)^2 \times 90\%$$

$$\sigma_{\text{max}}^2 = (7.95)^2 \times 90\% = 63.20 \times 0.9 = 56.88$$

   And standard deviation is the square root of variance, so the maximum standard deviation allowed is

$$\sigma_{max} = \sqrt{\sigma_{max}^2}$$

$$\sigma_{max} = \sqrt{56.88} = 7.54$$

All three portfolios are below the maximum specified variance.

The next consideration is that the portfolio should maximize the risk-adjusted return with the expectation of large negative events. For hedge fund strategies with large negative events, the Sortino ratio is a more appropriate measure of risk-adjusted return than the Sharpe ratio. The Sharpe ratio measures risk-adjusted performance, where risk is defined as standard deviation, so it penalizes both upside and downside variability. The Sortino ratio measures risk-adjusted performance, where risk is defined as downside deviation, so it penalizes only downside variability below a minimum target return. Of the portfolios that meet the variance requirement, the one with the highest Sortino ratio is the portfolio with the equity market-neutral allocation, with a Sortino ratio of 1.80. Therefore, the portfolio with the equity market-neutral allocation is the most suitable portfolio for the considerations specified by the IC.

A is incorrect because the portfolio with an allocation to the merger arbitrage hedge fund strategy, while meeting the variance requirement, has a lower Sortino ratio (1.35) than the portfolio with an allocation to the equity market-neutral hedge fund strategy (1.80). Although the portfolio with the merger arbitrage allocation has the lowest value of maximum drawdown (5.60), the relevant measure of downside risk is the Sortino ratio. As a result, the portfolio with the equity market-neutral allocation is the most suitable portfolio given the considerations specified by the IC.

B is incorrect because the portfolio with an allocation to the systematic futures hedge fund strategy, while meeting the variance requirement, has a lower Sortino ratio (1.68) than the portfolio with an allocation to the equity market-neutral hedge fund strategy. As a result, the portfolio with the equity market-neutral allocation is the most suitable portfolio given the considerations specified by the IC.

10. C is correct. Global macro investing may introduce natural benefits of asset class and investment approach diversification, but they come with naturally higher volatility in the return profiles typically delivered. The exposures selected in any global macro strategy may not react to the global risks as expected because of either unforeseen contrary factors or global risks that simply do not materialize; thus, macro managers tend to produce somewhat lumpier and more uneven return streams than other hedge fund strategies.

    A is incorrect because relative value hedge fund strategies tend to use significant leverage that can be dangerous to limited partner investors, especially during periods of market stress. During normal market conditions, successful relative value strategies can earn credit, liquidity, or volatility premiums over time. However, in crisis periods when excessive leverage, deteriorating credit quality, illiquidity, and volatility spikes come to fruition, relative value strategies can result in losses.

    B is incorrect because long/short equity strategies tend to be exposed to some natural equity market beta risk but have less beta exposure than simple long-only beta allocations. Given that equity markets tend to rise over the long run, most long/short equity managers typically hold net long equity positions with some managers maintaining their short positions as a hedge against unexpected market downturns.

11. C is correct. Xu states that she prefers opportunistic hedge fund strategies that use high leverage, have high liquidity, and exhibit right-tail skewness. The two most common opportunistic hedge fund strategies are global macro and managed futures. Both global macro and managed futures are highly liquid. Further,

returns of managed futures strategies typically exhibit positive right-tail skewness in periods of market stress, whereas global macro strategies have delivered similar diversification in such stress periods but with more heterogeneous outcomes. Global macro and managed futures strategies can also use high leverage, either through the use of futures contracts, in which high leverage is embedded, or through the active use of options, which adds natural elements of leverage and positive convexity.

A and B are incorrect because both global macro and managed futures strategies can offer the three characteristics that Xu seeks in an opportunistic hedge fund strategy.

12. B is correct. Xu bought 22,500 shares of Taurus at €20 per share for a total cost of €450,000 and sold short 15,000 shares of Aqua at €45 per share for a total cost of €675,000. Given the offer ratio of two shares of Aqua for three shares of Taurus, the 22,500 shares of Taurus are economically equivalent to 15,000 shares of Aqua. Thus, assuming the deal closes, the payoff to Xu's trade is €675,000 – €450,000 = €225,000.

    A is incorrect because –€187,500 is the payoff if the merger fails and both companies' share prices revert back to their pre-merger prices. Xu bought 22,500 shares of Taurus at €20 per share for a total cost of €450,000 and sold short 15,000 shares of Aqua at €45 per share for a total cost of €675,000. If the merger fails and the share prices revert back to pre-announcement levels, Xu will have to sell 22,500 shares of Taurus at €15 per share for proceeds of €337,500, resulting in a loss on the Taurus stock of –€112,500 (€337,500 – €450,000). Xu will also have to close the short position by purchasing 15,000 shares of Aqua at €50 per share for a total cost of €750,000. This will result in a loss on Aqua of –€75,000 (€675,000 – €750,000). The total loss is –€112,500 + –€75,000 = –€187,500.

    C is incorrect because the initial pre-merger prices are used to compute the payoff: 22,500 shares of Taurus are bought for €15 per share for a total of €337,500, and 15,000 shares of Aqua are sold short at €50 per share for a total of €750,000. The payoff is €750,000 – €337,500 = €412,500.

13. C is correct. Xu's decision to short ZMD and take a long position in Tarreras with equal beta-weighted exposure is an example of a pairs trade or an equity-market-neutral strategy. Xu is neutralizing market risk by constructing a strategy where the expected portfolio beta is zero. Since her strategy does not take beta risk and attempts to neutralize many other factor risks, Xu must apply leverage to the long and short positions to achieve a meaningful expected return from the stock selection.

    A is incorrect because in a short-biased hedge fund strategy, the manager aims to sell expensively priced equities but may balance the short exposure with some modest long exposure. Xu, however, has entered into an equity-market-neutral pairs trade that takes opposite long and short positions in an attempt to eliminate market exposure. Her positions do not have a short bias.

    B is incorrect because long/short equity managers buy equities of companies they expect will rise and sell short equities of companies they believe will fall in value. When long and short positions are placed together into a portfolio, the market exposure is the net of the beta-adjusted long and short exposures; however, the target beta is typically not zero. Xu is neutralizing market risk by constructing a strategy where the expected portfolio beta is zero.

14. A is correct. The classic convertible bond arbitrage strategy is to buy the relatively undervalued convertible bond and take a short position in the relatively overvalued underlying stock. If the convertible bond's current price is near the conversion value, then the combination of a long convertible and short equity

delta exposure will create a situation where for small changes in the share price and ignoring dividends and borrowing costs, the profit/loss will be the same.

The current conversion price of the AVC convertible bond is €1,000 × (115/100)/50 = €23, and the current AVC share price is €28. Thus, by purchasing the convertible bond, selling short the shares, exercising the conversion option, and selling the shares at the current market price, a profit of €5 can be locked in regardless of changes in the share price. The following table demonstrates this result by showing the same trade profit of €5 for three different stock prices:

	Profit on:		**Total Profit**
AVC New Share Price	Long Stock via Convertible Bond at $23/Sh.	Short Stock at $28/Sh.	
€26	€3	€2	**€5**
€28	€5	€0	**€5**
€34	€11	–€6	**€5**

where

Long stock via convertible bond profit
= New share price – Current conversion price

Short stock profit = Current share price – New share price

Total profit = Long stock via convertible bond profit + Short stock profit

Thus, regardless of the share price, the total profit on the convertible arbitrage trade is €5.

B is incorrect because if the convertible bond's current price is near the conversion value, then the combination of a long convertible and short equity delta exposure will create a situation where the profit/loss will be the same (not higher if the share price decreases).

C is incorrect because if the convertible bond's current price is near the conversion value, then the combination of a long convertible and short equity delta exposure will create a situation where for small changes in equity price, the profit/loss will be the same (not higher if the share price increases).

15. B is correct. Hedge funds look for policies in which the ongoing premium payments to keep the policy active are relatively low, so Characteristic 2 is correct. Hedge funds also look for life settlements where the surrender value offered to the insured individual is also relatively low and the probability that the designated insured person is likely to die earlier than predicted by standard actuarial methods is relatively high.

    A is incorrect because hedge funds look for policies in which the surrender value offered to the insured individual is relatively low (not high) in order to enhance return by purchasing at a lower price.

    C is incorrect because hedge funds look for settlements in which the probability that the designated insured person is likely to die *earlier* than predicted by standard actuarial methods is relatively high. This means the hedge fund's cash outflows to pay the ongoing premium will be less than predicted, which will enhance return.

16. A linear factor model can provide insights into the intrinsic characteristics and risks in a hedge fund investment. Since hedge fund strategies are dynamic, a conditional model allows for the analysis in a specific market environment to determine whether hedge fund strategies are exposed to certain risks under

abnormal market conditions. A conditional model can show whether hedge fund risk exposures to equities that are insignificant during calm periods become significant during turbulent market periods. During normal periods when equities are rising, the desired exposure to equities (S&P 500 Index) should be long (positive) to benefit from higher expected returns. However, during crisis periods when equities are falling sharply, the desired exposure to equities should be short (negative).

17. Shaindy should employ an equity market-neutral (EMN) equity strategy. Overall, EMN managers are more useful for portfolio allocation during periods of non-trending or declining markets. EMN hedge fund strategies take opposite (long and short) positions in similar or related equities having divergent valuations while attempting to maintain a near net zero portfolio exposure to the market. EMN managers neutralize market risk by constructing their portfolios such that the expected portfolio beta is approximately equal to zero. Moreover, EMN managers often choose to set the betas for sectors or industries as well as for common risk factors (e.g., market size, price-to-earnings ratio, and book-to-market ratio) equal to zero. Since these portfolios do not take beta risk and attempt to neutralize many other factor risks, they typically must apply leverage to the long and short positions to achieve a meaningful return profile from their individual stock selections.

    EMN strategies typically deliver return profiles that are steadier and less volatile than those of many other hedge strategy areas. Over time, their conservative and constrained approach typically results in a less dynamic overall return profile than those of managers who accept beta exposure. Despite the use of substantial leverage and because of their more standard and overall steady risk/return profiles, equity market-neutral managers are often a preferred replacement for fixed-income managers during periods when fixed-income returns are unattractively low.

18.

    i. At the current share prices of $55 for Sellshom and $22 for Meura, Patel would receive $1,100,000 from short selling 20,000 shares of Sellshom and would pay $880,000 to buy 40,000 shares of Meura. This provides a net spread of $220,000 to Patel if the merger is successfully completed.

    ii. If the merger fails, then prices should revert back to their pre-merger announcement levels of $18 per share for Meura and $60 per share for Sellshom. The manager would need to buy back 20,000 shares of Sellshom at $60 per share, for a total of $1,200,000, to close the short position. Patel would then sell the long position of 40,000 shares of Meura at $18 per share for a total of $720,000. This net loss would be $260,000, calculated as: (Sellshom: $1,100,000 – $1,200,000 = –$100,000) + (Meura: –$880,000 + $720,000 = –$160,000).

19.

	Describe how each of the following circumstances can create concerns for Stein's proposed hedge fund strategy:
Short selling	Since Hedge Fund 1 employs a convertible arbitrage strategy, the fund buys the convertible bond and takes a short position in the underlying security. When short selling, shares must be located and borrowed; as a result, the stock owner may want his/her shares returned at a potentially inopportune time, such as during stock price run-ups or when supply for the stock is low or demand for the stock is high. This situation, particularly a short squeeze, can lead to substantial losses and a suddenly unbalanced exposure if borrowing the underlying equity shares becomes too difficult or too costly for the arbitrageur.
Credit issues	Credit issues may complicate valuation since bonds have exposure to credit risk. When credit spreads widen or narrow, there would be a mismatch in the values of the stock and convertible bond positions that the convertible manager may or may not have attempted to hedge away.
Time decay of call option	The convertible bond arbitrage strategy can lose money due to time decay of the convertible bond's embedded call option during periods of reduced realized equity volatility and/or due to a general compression of market implied volatility levels.
Extreme market volatility	Convertible arbitrage strategies have performed best when convertible issuance is high (implying a wider choice among convertible securities as well as downward price pressure and cheaper prices), general market volatility levels are moderate, and the liquidity to trade and adjust positions is sufficient. Extreme market volatility typically implies heightened credit risks. Convertibles are naturally less-liquid securities, so convertible managers generally do not fare well during such periods. Because hedge funds have become the natural market makers for convertibles and typically face significant redemption pressures from investors during crises, the strategy may have further unattractive left-tail risk attributes during periods of market stress.

20. Hedge Fund 2 would be most appropriate for Puten because it follows a global macro strategy, which is consistent with Puten's preferences. Global macro managers use both fundamental and technical analysis to value markets, and they use discretionary and systematic modes of implementation. The key source of returns in global macro strategies revolves around correctly discerning and capitalizing on trends in global markets.

    Global macro strategies are typically top-down and employ a range of macroeconomic and fundamental models to express a view regarding the direction or relative value of a particular asset or asset class. Positions may comprise a mix of individual securities, baskets of securities, index futures, foreign exchange futures/forwards, fixed-income products or futures, and derivatives or options on any of the above. If the hedge fund manager is making a directional bet, then directional models will use fundamental data regarding a specific market or asset to determine if it is undervalued or overvalued relative to history and the expected macro-trend.

    Hedge Fund 1 follows a relative value strategy with a focus on convertible arbitrage, which is not aligned with Puten's preferences. In a convertible bond arbitrage strategy, the manager strives to extract "cheap" implied volatility by buying the relatively undervalued convertible bond and taking a short position in the relatively overvalued common stock. Convertible arbitrage managers are typically neither using fundamental and technical analysis to value markets nor employing top-down strategies to express a view regarding the direction or relative value of an asset.

21. Hedge Fund A's volatility trading strategy can be implemented by following multiple paths. One path is through simple exchange-traded options. The maturity of such options typically extends to no more than two years. In terms of expiry, the longer-dated options will have more absolute exposure to volatility levels than shorter-dated options, but the shorter-dated options will exhibit more delta

sensitivity to price changes.

A second, similar path is to implement the volatility trading strategy using OTC options. In this case, the tenor and strike prices of the options can be customized. The tenor of expiry dates can then be extended beyond what is available with exchange-traded options.

A third path is to use VIX futures or options on VIX futures as a way to more explicitly express a pure volatility view without the need for constant delta hedging of an equity put or call for isolating the volatility exposure.

A fourth path for implementing a volatility trading strategy would be to purchase an OTC volatility swap or a variance swap from a creditworthy counterparty. A volatility swap is a forward contract on future realized price volatility. Similarly, a variance swap is a forward contract on future realized price variance, where variance is the square of volatility. Both volatility and variance swaps provide "pure" exposure to volatility alone, unlike standardized options in which the volatility exposure depends on the price of the underlying asset and must be isolated and extracted via delta hedging.

22.

a. Multi-strategy managers like Hedge Fund B can reallocate capital into different strategy areas more quickly and efficiently than would be possible by a fund-of-funds (FoF) manager like Hedge Fund C. The multi-strategy manager has full transparency and a better picture of the interactions of the different teams' portfolio risks than would ever be possible for FoF managers to achieve. Consequently, the multi-strategy manager can react faster to different real-time market impacts—for example, by rapidly increasing or decreasing leverage within different strategies depending upon the perceived riskiness of available opportunities.

b. The fees paid by investors in a multi-strategy fund can be structured in a number of ways, some of which can be very attractive when compared to the FoFs' added fee layering and netting risk attributes. Conceptually, FoF investors always face netting risk, whereby they are responsible for paying performance fees due to winning underlying funds while suffering return drag from the performance of losing underlying funds. Even if the FoF's overall performance is flat or down, FoF investors must still pay incentive fees due to the managers of winning funds.

23. Based on the investment committee's considerations, Singh should view a 10% allocation to the global macro hedge fund strategy as most suitable for the Foundation. Such an allocation would result in a decrease in standard deviation (volatility) and significant increases in the combined portfolio's Sharpe and Sortino ratios (these are the highest such ratios among the strategies presented). In addition, the lower maximum drawdown (15.0%) indicates less downside risk in the combined portfolio than with any of the other strategy choices.

Glossary

Abnormal earnings See *residual income.*

Abnormal return The amount by which a security's actual return differs from its expected return, given the security's risk and the market's return.

Absolute convergence The idea that developing countries, regardless of their particular characteristics, will eventually catch up with the developed countries and match them in per capita output.

Absolute valuation model A model that specifies an asset's intrinsic value.

Absolute version of PPP An extension of the law of one price whereby the prices of goods and services will not differ internationally once exchange rates are considered.

Accounting estimates Estimates used in calculating the value of assets or liabilities and in the amount of revenue and expense to allocate to a period. Examples of accounting estimates include, among others, the useful lives of depreciable assets, the salvage value of depreciable assets, product returns, warranty costs, and the amount of uncollectible receivables.

Accuracy The percentage of correctly predicted classes out of total predictions. It is an overall performance metric in classification problems.

Acquisition When one company, the acquirer, purchases from the seller most or all of another company's (the target) shares to gain control of either an entire company, a segment of another company, or a specific group of assets in exchange for cash, stock, or the assumption of liabilities, alone or in combination. Once an acquisition is complete, the acquirer and target merge into a single entity and consolidate management, operations, and resources.

Activation function A functional part of a neural network's node that transforms the total net input received into the final output of the node. The activation function operates like a light dimmer switch that decreases or increases the strength of the input.

Active factor risk The contribution to active risk squared resulting from the portfolio's different-than-benchmark exposures relative to factors specified in the risk model.

Active return The return on a portfolio minus the return on the portfolio's benchmark.

Active risk The standard deviation of active returns.

Active risk squared The variance of active returns; active risk raised to the second power.

Active share A measure of how similar a portfolio is to its benchmark. A manager who precisely replicates the benchmark will have an active share of zero; a manager with no holdings in common with the benchmark will have an active share of one.

Active specific risk The contribution to active risk squared resulting from the portfolio's active weights on individual assets as those weights interact with assets' residual risk.

Activist short selling A hedge fund strategy in which the manager takes a short position in a given security and then publicly presents his/her research backing the short thesis.

Adjustable rate Interest rate for a mortgage or other loan that combines a fixed-rate period with a variable-rate period, which fluctuates based on market reference rates.

Adjusted funds from operations Funds from operations adjusted to remove any non-cash rent reported under straight-line rent accounting and to subtract maintenance-type capital expenditures and leasing costs, including leasing agents' commissions and tenants' improvement allowances.

Adjusted present value As an approach to valuing a company, the sum of the value of the company, assuming no use of debt, and the net present value of any effects of debt on company value.

Adjusted R^2 Goodness-of-fit measure that adjusts the coefficient of determination, R^2, for the number of independent variables in the model.

Advanced set An arrangement in which the reference interest rate is set at the time the money is deposited.

Advanced settled An arrangement in which a forward rate agreement (FRA) expires and settles at the same time, at the FRA expiration date.

Agglomerative clustering A bottom-up hierarchical clustering method that begins with each observation being treated as its own cluster. The algorithm finds the two closest clusters, based on some measure of distance (similarity), and combines them into one new larger cluster. This process is repeated iteratively until all observations are clumped into a single large cluster.

Akaike's information criterion (AIC) A statistic used to compare sets of independent variables for explaining a dependent variable. It is preferred for finding the model that is best suited for prediction.

Allowance for loan losses A balance sheet account; it is a contra asset account to loans.

Alpha The return on an asset in excess of the asset's required rate of return. Sometimes referred to as an *abnormal return*.

American Depositary Receipt A negotiable certificate issued by a depositary bank that represents ownership in a non-US company's deposited equity (i.e., equity held in custody by the depositary bank in the company's home market).

Analysis of variance (ANOVA) A table that presents the sums of squares, degrees of freedom, mean squares, and F-statistic for a regression model.

Application programming interface (API) A set of well-defined methods of communication between various software components and typically used for accessing external data.

Appraisals Professional estimates of current market value for a real estate property.

Arbitrage (1) The simultaneous purchase of an undervalued asset or portfolio and sale of an overvalued but equivalent asset or portfolio in order to obtain a riskless profit on the price differential. Taking advantage of a market inefficiency in a risk-free manner. (2) The condition in a financial market in which equivalent assets or combinations of assets sell for two different prices, creating an opportunity to profit at no risk with no commitment of money. In a well-functioning financial market, few arbitrage opportunities are possible. (3) A risk-free operation that earns an expected positive net profit but requires no net investment of money.

Arbitrage opportunity An opportunity to conduct an arbitrage; an opportunity to earn an expected positive net profit without risk and with no net investment of money.

Arbitrage portfolio The portfolio that exploits an arbitrage opportunity.

Arbitrage-free models Term structure models that project future interest rate paths that emanate from the existing term structure. Resulting prices are based on a no-arbitrage condition.

Arbitrage-free valuation An approach to valuation that determines security values consistent with the absence of any opportunity to earn riskless profits without any net investment of money.

Arm's-length transaction Both buyer and seller act independently without any preexisting relationship that may sway their decision making.

Asset-based approach Approach that values a private company based on the values of the underlying assets of the entity less the value of any related liabilities.

Asset-based valuation An approach to valuing natural resource companies that estimates company value on the basis of the market value of the natural resources the company controls.

At market contract When a forward contract is established, the forward price is negotiated so that the market value of the forward contract on the initiation date is zero.

Authorized participants (APs) A special group of institutional investors who are authorized by the ETF issuer to participate in the creation/redemption process. APs are large broker/dealers, often market makers.

Autocorrelations The correlations of a time series with its own past values.

Autoregressive model (AR) A time series regressed on its own past values in which the independent variable is a lagged value of the dependent variable.

Back-testing The process that approximates the real-life investment process, using historical data, to assess whether an investment strategy would have produced desirable results.

Backward propagation The process of adjusting weights in a neural network, to reduce total error of the network, by moving backward through the network's layers.

Backwardation A downward-sloping, or inverted, forward curve in a futures market.

Bag-of-words (BOW) A collection of a distinct set of tokens from all the texts in a sample dataset. BOW does not capture the position or sequence of words present in the text.

Balance sheet restructuring Altering the composition of the balance sheet by either shifting the asset composition, changing the capital structure, or both.

Bankruptcy Legal proceedings, which vary by jurisdiction, allowing a firm whose liabilities exceed its assets to restructure existing debt obligations or liquidate assets in an orderly manner.

Barbell portfolio Fixed-income portfolio that combines short and long maturities.

Base error Model error due to randomness in the data.

Basic earnings per share (EPS) Net earnings available to common shareholders (i.e., net income minus preferred dividends) divided by the weighted average number of common shares outstanding during the period.

Basis The difference between the spot price and the futures price. As the maturity date of the futures contract nears, the basis converges toward zero.

Basis trade A trade based on the pricing of credit in the bond market versus the price of the same credit in the CDS market. To execute a basis trade, go long the "underpriced" credit and short the "overpriced" credit. A profit is realized as the implied credit prices converge.

Bearish flattening Term structure shift in which short-term bond yields rise more than long-term bond yields, resulting in a flatter yield curve.

Benchmark value of the multiple In using the method of comparables, the value of a price multiple for the comparison asset; when we have comparison assets (a group), the mean or median value of the multiple for the group of assets.

Bias error Describes the degree to which a model fits the training data. Algorithms with erroneous assumptions produce high bias error with poor approximation, causing underfitting and high in-sample error.

Bill-and-hold basis Sales on a bill-and-hold basis involve selling products but not delivering those products until a later date.

Blockage factor An illiquidity discount that occurs when an investor sells a large amount of stock relative to its trading volume (assuming it is not large enough to constitute a controlling ownership).

Bond indenture A legal document between a bond issuer and investors that governs each party's rights and responsibilities.

Bond risk premium The expected excess return of a default-free long-term bond less that of an equivalent short-term bond.

Bond yield plus risk premium (BYPRP) approach An estimate of the cost of common equity that is produced by summing the before-tax cost of debt and a risk premium that captures the additional yield on a company's stock relative to its bonds.

Bonus issue of shares A type of dividend in which a company distributes additional shares of its common stock to shareholders instead of cash.

Book value Shareholders' equity (total assets minus total liabilities) minus the value of preferred stock; common shareholders' equity.

Book value of equity Shareholders' equity (total assets minus total liabilities) minus the value of preferred stock; common shareholders' equity.

Book value per share The amount of book value (also called carrying value) of common equity per share of common stock, calculated by dividing the book value of shareholders' equity by the number of shares of common stock outstanding.

Bootstrap aggregating (or bagging) A technique whereby the original training dataset is used to generate n new training datasets or bags of data. Each new bag of data is generated by random sampling with replacement from the initial training set.

Bootstrapping The use of a forward substitution process to determine zero-coupon rates by using the par yields and solving for the zero-coupon rates one by one, from the shortest to longest maturities.

Breakup value The value derived using a sum-of-the-parts valuation.

Breusch–Godfrey (BG) test A test used to detect autocorrelated residuals up to a predesignated order of the lagged residuals.

Breusch–Pagan (BP) test A test for the presence of heteroskedasticity in a regression.

Bullet portfolio A fixed-income portfolio concentrated in a single maturity.

Bullish flattening Term structure change in which the yield curve flattens in response to a greater decline in long-term rates than short-term rates.

Bullish steepening Term structure change in which short-term rates fall by more than long-term yields, resulting in a steeper term structure.

Buy-side analysts Analysts who work for investment management firms, trusts, bank trust departments, and similar institutions.

Buyback A transaction in which a company buys back its own shares. Unlike stock dividends and stock splits, share repurchases use corporate cash.

Callable bond A bond containing an embedded call option that gives the issuer the right to buy the bond back from the investor at specified prices on predetermined dates.

Canceled shares Shares that were issued, subsequently repurchased by the company, and then retired (cannot be reissued).

Capital asset pricing model (CAPM) An equation describing the expected return on any asset (or portfolio) as a linear function of its beta relative to the market portfolio.

Capital charge The company's total cost of capital in money terms.

Capital deepening An increase in the capital-to-labor ratio.

Capitalization rate The rate used to discount expected NOI, which combines the required rate of return on similar properties with an implied constant growth rate.

Capitalized cash flow method In the context of private company valuation, a valuation model based on an assumption of a constant growth rate of free cash flow to the firm or a constant growth rate of free cash flow to equity. Also called *capitalized cash flow model.*

Capped floater Floating-rate bond with a cap provision that prevents the coupon rate from increasing above a specified maximum rate. It protects the issuer against rising interest rates.

Carry arbitrage model A no-arbitrage approach in which the underlying instrument is either bought or sold along with an opposite position in a forward contract.

Carry benefits Benefits that arise from owning certain underlyings; for example, dividends, foreign interest, and bond coupon payments.

Carry costs Costs that arise from owning certain underlyings. They are generally a function of the physical characteristics of the underlying asset and also the interest forgone on the funds tied up in the asset.

Cash available for distribution See *adjusted funds from operations.*

Cash settlement A procedure used in certain derivative transactions that specifies that the long and short parties settle the derivative's difference in value between them by making a cash payment.

Catalyst An event or piece of information that causes the marketplace to re-evaluate the prospects of a company.

CDS spread A periodic premium paid by the buyer to the seller that serves as a return over a market reference rate required to protect against credit risk.

Ceiling analysis A systematic process of evaluating different components in the pipeline of model building. It helps to understand what part of the pipeline can potentially improve in performance by further tuning.

Centroid The center of a cluster formed using the *k*-means clustering algorithm.

Chain rule of forecasting A forecasting process in which the next period's value as predicted by the forecasting equation is substituted into the right-hand side of the equation to give a predicted value two periods ahead.

Cheapest-to-deliver The debt instrument that can be purchased and delivered at the lowest cost yet has the same seniority as the reference obligation.

Classification and regression tree A supervised machine learning technique that can be applied to predict either a categorical target variable, producing a classification tree, or a continuous target variable, producing a regression tree. CART is commonly applied to binary classification or regression.

Clean surplus relation The relationship between earnings, dividends, and book value in which ending book value is equal to the beginning book value plus earnings less dividends, apart from ownership transactions.

Closed DB plan A DB plan that is not accepting new enrollees.

Club convergence The idea that only rich and middle-income countries sharing a set of favorable attributes (i.e., are members of the "club") will converge to the income level of the richest countries.

Cluster A subset of observations from a dataset such that all the observations within the same cluster are deemed "similar."

Clustering The sorting of observations into groups (clusters) such that observations in the same cluster are more similar to each other than they are to observations in other clusters.

Cobb–Douglas production function A function of the form $Y = K^{\alpha} L^{1-\alpha}$ relating output (Y) to labor (L) and capital (K) inputs.

Coefficient of determination A measure of how well data points fit a linear statistical model, indicated in percentage terms from 0 to 100%. Also known as *R-squared* (R^2).

Cointegrated Describes two time series that have a long-term financial or economic relationship such that they do not diverge from each other without bound in the long run.

Collateral return The component of the total return on a commodity futures position attributable to the yield for the bonds or cash used to maintain the futures position. Also called *collateral yield.*

Collection frequency (CF) The number of times a given word appears in the whole corpus (i.e., collection of sentences) divided by the total number of words in the corpus.

Commodity swap A type of swap involving the exchange of payments over multiple dates as determined by specified reference prices or indexes relating to commodities.

Company fundamental factors Factors related to the company's internal performance, such as factors relating to earnings growth, earnings variability, earnings momentum, and financial leverage.

Company share-related factors Valuation measures and other factors related to share price or the trading characteristics of the shares, such as earnings yield, dividend yield, and book-to-market value.

Comparables Assets used as benchmarks when applying the method of comparables to value an asset. Also called *comps*, *guideline assets*, or *guideline companies*.

Compiled financial statements Financial statements that are not accompanied by an auditor's opinion letter.

Complexity A term referring to the number of features, parameters, or branches in a model and to whether the model is linear or non-linear (non-linear is more complex).

Composite variable A variable that combines two or more variables that are statistically strongly related to each other.

Comprehensive income All changes in equity other than contributions by, and distributions to, owners; income under clean surplus accounting; includes all changes in equity during a period except those resulting from investments by owners and distributions to owners. Comprehensive income equals net income plus other comprehensive income.

Comps Assets used as benchmarks when applying the method of comparables to value an asset.

Concentrated ownership Ownership structure consisting of an individual shareholder or a group (controlling shareholders) with the ability to exercise control over the corporation.

Conditional convergence The idea that convergence of per capita income is conditional on the countries having the same savings rate, population growth rate, and production function.

Conditional heteroskedasticity A condition in which the variance of residuals of a regression are correlated with the value of the independent variables.

Conditional VaR (CVaR) The weighted average of all loss outcomes in the statistical (i.e., return) distribution that exceed the VaR loss. Thus, CVaR is a more comprehensive measure of tail loss than VaR is. Sometimes referred to as the *expected tail loss* or *expected shortfall*.

Confirmation bias A type of cognitive bias that makes individuals view information that confirms beliefs they already hold as more salient.

Confusion matrix A grid used for error analysis in classification problems, it presents values for four evaluation metrics including true positive (TP), false positive (FP), true negative (TN), and false negative (FN).

Conglomerate discount When an issuer is trading at a valuation lower than the sum of its parts, which is generally the result of diseconomies of scale or scope or the result of the capital markets having overlooked the business and its prospects.

Constant dividend payout ratio policy A policy in which a constant percentage of net income is paid out in dividends.

Constant returns to scale The condition that if all inputs into the production process are increased by a given percentage, then output rises by that same percentage.

Contango Refers to spot price below forward price in a futures market.

Contingent consideration Potential future payments to the seller that are contingent on the achievement of certain agreed-on occurrences.

Continuing earnings Earnings excluding nonrecurring components. Also referred to as *core earnings*, *persistent earnings*, or *underlying earnings*.

Continuing residual income Residual income after the forecast horizon.

Continuing value The analyst's estimate of a stock's value at a particular point in the future.

Contraction risk The risk of earlier repayment of a mortgage-backed security than expected.

Control premium An increment or premium to value associated with a controlling ownership interest in a company.

Convergence The property by which as expiration approaches, the price of a newly created forward or futures contract will approach the price of a spot transaction. At expiration, a forward or futures contract is equivalent to a spot transaction in the underlying.

Conversion period The period over which a convertible bond may be exchanged for equity at a predetermined price.

Conversion price Predetermined share price at which convertible debt may be fully exchanged for common shares during the conversion period.

Conversion rate (or ratio) For a convertible bond, the number of shares of common stock that a bondholder receives from converting the bond into shares.

Conversion value The current contingency feature value derived by comparing a convertible bond's price with its value if a bondholder were to exchange bonds for shares.

Convertible bond A bond that gives the bondholder the right to exchange the bond for a specified number of common shares in the issuing company.

Convexity The second order, usually a positive change in the price of a bond for a given change in yield, which can be negative for a callable bond such as a high-yield bond.

Core earnings Earnings excluding nonrecurring components. Also referred to as *continuing earnings*, *persistent earnings*, or *underlying earnings*.

Core real estate Real estate investments in well-developed, stable-income-producing commercial and residential properties.

Corpus A collection of text data in any form, including list, matrix, or data table forms.

Cost of carry model A model that relates the forward price of an asset to the spot price by considering the cost of carry (also referred to as future-spot parity model).

Cost of debt The required return on debt financing for a company, such as when it issues a bond, takes out a bank loan, or leases an asset through a finance lease.

Cost of equity The return required by equity investors to compensate for both the time value of money and the risk. Also referred to as the required rate of return on common stock or the required return on equity.

Cost restructuring Actions to reduce costs by improving operational efficiency and profitability, often to raise margins to a historical level or to those of comparable industry peers.

Country risk premium (CRP) The additional return required by investors to compensate for the risk associated with investing in a foreign country relative to the investor's domestic market.

Country risk rating (CRR) The rating of a country based on many risk factors, including economic prosperity, political risk, and ESG risk.

Covariance stationary Describes a time series when its expected value and variance are constant and finite in all periods and when its covariance with itself for a fixed number of periods in the past or future is constant and finite in all periods.

Covered bonds A senior debt obligation of a financial institution that gives recourse to the originator/issuer and a predetermined underlying collateral pool.

Covered interest rate parity The relationship among the spot exchange rate, the forward exchange rate, and the interest rates in two currencies that ensures that the return on a hedged (i.e., covered) foreign risk-free investment is the same as the return on a domestic risk-free investment. Also called *interest rate parity*.

Cox-Ingersoll-Ross model A general equilibrium term structure model that assumes interest rates are mean reverting and interest rate volatility is directly related to the level of interest rates.

Creation basket The list of securities (and share amounts) the authorized participant (AP) must deliver to the ETF manager in exchange for ETF shares. The creation basket is published each business day.

Creation units Large blocks of ETF shares transacted between the authorized participant (AP) and the ETF manager that are usually but not always equal to 50,000 shares of the ETF.

Creation/redemption The process in which ETF shares are created or redeemed by authorized participants transacting with the ETF issuer.

Credit correlation The correlation of credit (or default) risks of the underlying single-name CDS contained in an index CDS.

Credit curve The credit spreads for a range of maturities of a company's debt.

Credit default swap A derivative contract between two parties in which the buyer makes a series of cash payments to the seller and receives a promise of compensation for credit losses resulting from the default.

Credit derivative A derivative instrument in which the underlying is a measure of the credit quality of a borrower.

Credit event An occurrence that triggers the settlement of a CDS contract, including failure to make a debt payment, debt restructuring, or a bankruptcy filing.

Credit protection buyer One party to a credit default swap; the buyer makes a series of cash payments to the seller and receives a promise of compensation for credit losses resulting from the default.

Credit protection seller One party to a credit default swap; the seller makes a promise to pay compensation for credit losses resulting from the default.

Credit risk The expected economic loss under a potential borrower default over the life of the contract.

Credit spread The compensation for the risk of default in a debt security, typically measured by the yield-to-maturity difference between a bond and a comparable government benchmark security.

Credit valuation adjustment The value of the credit risk of a bond in present value terms.

Cross-sectional momentum A managed futures trend following strategy implemented with a cross-section of assets (within an asset class) by going long those that are rising in price the most and by shorting those that are falling the most. This approach generally results in holding a net zero (market-neutral) position and works well when a market's out- or underperformance is a reliable predictor of its future performance.

Cross-validation A technique for estimating out-of-sample error directly by determining the error in validation samples.

Cumulative preferred stock Preferred stock that requires that the dividends be paid in full to preferred stock owners for any missed dividends prior to any payment of dividends to common stock owners.

Current exchange rate For accounting purposes, the spot exchange rate on the balance sheet date.

Current rate method Approach to translating foreign currency financial statements for consolidation in which all assets and liabilities are translated at the current exchange rate. The current rate method is the prevalent method of translation.

Curvature One of the three factors (the other two are level and steepness) that empirically explain most of the changes in the shape of the yield curve. A shock to the curvature factor affects mid-maturity interest rates, resulting in the term structure becoming either more or less hump-shaped.

Curve trade Buying a CDS of one maturity and selling a CDS on the same reference entity with a different maturity.

Customer concentration risk The risk associated with sales dependent on a few customers.

Cyclical businesses Businesses with high sensitivity to business- or industry-cycle influences.

Data preparation (cleansing) The process of examining, identifying, and mitigating (i.e., cleansing) errors in raw data.

Data snooping The subconscious or conscious manipulation of data in a way that produces a statistically significant result (i.e., the p-value is sufficiently small or the t-statistic sufficiently large to indicate statistical significance), such as by running multiple simulations and naively accepting the best result. Also known as p-hacking.

Data wrangling (preprocessing) This task performs transformations and critical processing steps on cleansed data to make the data ready for ML model training (i.e., preprocessing), and includes dealing with outliers, extracting useful variables from existing data points, and scaling the data.

Debt service coverage ratio A key indicator of credit performance equal to the ratio of net operating income to debt service.

Dedicated short-selling A hedge fund strategy in which the manager takes short-only positions in equities deemed to be expensively priced versus their deteriorating fundamental situations. Short exposures may vary only in terms of portfolio sizing by, at times, holding higher levels of cash.

Deep learning An area of artificial intelligence in which a system uses neural networks to perform multistage, non-linear data processing to identify patterns. Also called *deep learning nets.*

Deep neural networks Neural networks with many hidden layers—at least 2 but potentially more than 20—that have proven successful across a wide range of artificial intelligence applications.

Default risk See *credit risk.*

Delta The sensitivity of the derivative price to a small change in the value of the underlying asset.

Dendrogram A type of tree diagram used for visualizing a hierarchical cluster analysis; it highlights the hierarchical relationships among the clusters.

Depository Trust and Clearinghouse Corporation A US-headquartered entity providing post-trade clearing, settlement, and information services.

Depreciable base Total construction or original acquisition cost plus any property improvements less the cost of land written down over the estimated useful life, as in the case of a company's fixed assets.

Diluted earnings per share (Diluted EPS) Net income, minus preferred dividends, divided by the weighted average number of common shares outstanding considering all dilutive securities (e.g., convertible debt and options); the EPS that would result if all dilutive securities were converted into common shares.

Dilution An increase in the number of shares outstanding from share issuance that decreases the percentage of shares owned by existing shareholders.

Dimension reduction A set of techniques for reducing the number of features in a dataset while retaining variation across observations to preserve the information contained in that variation.

Diminishing marginal productivity When each additional unit of an input, keeping the other inputs unchanged, increases output by a smaller increment.

Direct capitalization method Valuation approach that estimates the value of an income-producing property using a discounted cash flow approach based on a single year's net operating income.

Discount To reduce the value of a future payment in allowance for how far away it is in time; to calculate the present value of some future amount. Also, the amount by which an instrument is priced below its face value.

Discount factor The price equivalent of a zero rate. Also may be stated as the present value of a currency unit on a future date.

Discount for lack of control An amount or percentage deducted from the pro rata share of 100% of the value of an equity interest in a business to reflect the absence of some or all of the powers of control.

Discount for lack of marketability An amount of percentage deducted from the value of an ownership interest to reflect the relative absence of marketability.

Discount function Discount factors for the range of all possible maturities. The spot curve can be derived from the discount function and vice versa.

Discounted abnormal earnings model A model of stock valuation that views intrinsic value of stock as the sum of book value per share plus the present value of the stock's expected future residual income per share.

Discounted cash flow method A valuation method involving a series of income projections discounted to the present with a terminal value.

Discounted cash flow model A model of intrinsic value that views the value of an asset as the present value of the asset's expected future cash flows.

Dispersed ownership Ownership structure consisting of many shareholders, none of which has the ability to individually exercise control over the corporation.

Divestiture When a seller sells a company, segment of a company, or group of assets to an acquirer. Once complete, control of the target is transferred to the acquirer.

Dividend coverage ratio The ratio of net income to dividends.

Dividend discount model (DDM) The model of the value of stock that is the present value of all future dividends, discounted at the required return on equity.

Dividend displacement of earnings The concept that dividends paid now displace earnings in all future periods.

Dividend imputation tax system A taxation system that effectively assures corporate profits distributed as dividends are taxed just once and at the shareholder's tax rate.

Dividend index point A measure of the quantity of dividends attributable to a particular index.

Dividend payout ratio The ratio of cash dividends paid to earnings for a period.

Dividend policy The strategy a company follows with regard to the amount and timing of dividend payments.

Dividend rate The annualized amount of the most recent dividend.

Dividend recapitalization A change in the mix of debt and equity outstanding for an existing corporate issuer which increases leverage via debt-financed dividends or share repurchases to benefit existing shareholders.

Dividend yield Annual dividends per share divided by share price.

Dividends Distributions of profits and/or net assets from a corporation to its shareholders. While often in cash, dividends can be also be paid in stock or assets, such as property.

Divisive clustering A top-down hierarchical clustering method that starts with all observations belonging to a single large cluster. The observations are then divided into two clusters based on some measure of distance (similarity). The algorithm then progressively partitions the intermediate clusters into smaller ones until each cluster contains only one observation.

Document frequency (DF) The number of documents (texts) that contain a particular token divided by the total number of documents. It is the simplest feature selection method and often performs well when many thousands of tokens are present.

Document term matrix (DTM) A matrix where each row belongs to a document (or text file), and each column represents a token (or term). The number of rows is equal to the number of documents (or text files) in a sample text dataset. The number of columns is equal to the number of tokens from the BOW built using all the documents in the sample dataset. The cells typically contain the counts of the number of times a token is present in each document.

Dominance An arbitrage opportunity when a financial asset with a risk-free payoff in the future must have a positive price today.

Double taxation system Corporate earnings are taxed twice when paid out as dividends. First, corporate pretax earnings are taxed regardless of whether they will be distributed as dividends or retained at the corporate level. Second, dividends are taxed again at the individual shareholder level.

Downstream A transaction between two related companies, an investor company (or a parent company) and an associate company (or a subsidiary) such that the investor company records a profit on its income statement. An example is a sale of inventory by the investor company to the associate or by a parent to a subsidiary company.

Dual-class shares Shares that grant one share class superior or even sole voting rights, whereas the other share class has inferior or no voting rights.

Due diligence Investigation and analysis in support of an investment action, decision, or recommendation.

Dummy variable An independent variable that takes a value of either 1 or 0, depending on a specified condition. Also known as an *indicator variable*.

Duration The first-order, linear change in a bond's price for a given yield change in yield, which is a negative or inverse relationship.

Durbin–Watson (DW) test A test for the presence of first-order serial correlation.

Dutch disease A situation in which currency appreciation driven by strong export demand for resources makes other segments of the economy (particularly manufacturing) globally uncompetitive.

Earnings surprise The difference between reported EPS and expected EPS. Also referred to as *unexpected earnings*.

Earnings yield EPS divided by price; the reciprocal of the P/E.

Economic profit Equal to accounting profit less the implicit opportunity costs not included in total accounting costs; the difference between total revenue (TR) and total cost (TC). Also called *abnormal profit* or *supernormal profit*.

Economic sectors Large industry groupings.

Economic value added (EVA®) A commercial implementation of the residual income concept; the computation of EVA® is the net operating profit after taxes minus the cost of capital, where these inputs are adjusted for a number of items.

Edwards–Bell–Ohlson model A model of stock valuation that views intrinsic value of stock as the sum of book value per share plus the present value of the stock's expected future residual income per share.

Effective convexity An interest rate risk statistic that measures the non-linear/second-order effect of changes in the benchmark yield curve on a bond's price.

Effective duration The sensitivity of the bond's price to an instantaneous parallel shift in a benchmark yield curve—for example, the government par curve.

Effective gross income Gross rent plus other income minus deductions for vacancies or concessions.

Eigenvalue A measure that gives the proportion of total variance in the initial dataset that is explained by each eigenvector.

Eigenvector A vector that defines new mutually uncorrelated composite variables that are linear combinations of the original features.

Embedded options Contingency provisions found in a bond's indenture representing rights that enable their holders to take advantage of interest rate movements. They can be exercised by the issuer, by the bondholder, or automatically depending on the course of interest rates.

Ensemble learning A technique of combining the predictions from a collection of models to achieve a more accurate prediction.

Ensemble method The method of combining multiple learning algorithms, as in ensemble learning.

Enterprise value A measure of a company's total market value from which the value of cash and short-term investments have been subtracted.

Enterprise value multiple A valuation multiple that relates the total market value of all sources of a company's capital (net of cash) to a measure of fundamental value for the entire company (such as a pre-interest earnings measure).

Equity charge The estimated cost of equity capital in money terms.

Equity dividend rate Equityholder return that considers the first-year return on equity on an income-producing property involving the before-tax cash flow divided by the property purchase price less the mortgage loan outstanding.

Equity investment A company purchasing another company's equity but less than 50% of its shares. The two companies maintain their independence, but the investor company has investment exposure to the investee and, in some cases depending on the size of the investment, can have representation on the investee's board of directors to influence operations.

Equity REITs REITs that primarily own and operate properties and distribute dividends to shareholders.

Equity swap A swap transaction in which at least one cash flow is tied to the return to an equity portfolio position, often an equity index.

Error autocorrelations The autocorrelations of the error term.

ESG integration The inclusion of ESG considerations within financial analysis and investment decisions. This may be done in various ways, tailored to the investment style and approach of the fund manager.

***Ex ante* tracking error** A measure of the degree to which the performance of a given investment portfolio might be expected to deviate from its benchmark; also known as *relative VaR*.

***Ex ante* version of PPP** The hypothesis that expected changes in the spot exchange rate are equal to expected differences in national inflation rates. An extension of relative purchasing power parity to expected future changes in the exchange rate.

Ex-dividend Trading ex-dividend refers to shares that no longer carry the right to the next dividend payment.

Ex-dividend date The first date that a share trades without (i.e., "ex") the right to receive the declared dividend for the period.

Excess earnings method Income approach that estimates the value of all intangible assets of the business by capitalizing future earnings in excess of the estimated return requirements associated with working capital and fixed assets.

Excess tax benefit The amount by which the tax deduction associated with a share-based award exceeds the cumulative share-based compensation expense recognized in accordance with US GAAP or IFRS. Excess tax benefits occur when the value of a share-based award at settlement exceeds the value at the grant date.

Exercise value The value of an option if it were exercised. Also sometimes called *intrinsic value*.

Expanded CAPM An adaptation of the CAPM that adds to the CAPM a premium for small size and company-specific risk.

Expectations approach A procedure for obtaining the value of an option derived from discounting at the risk-free rate its expected future payoff based on risk neutral probabilities.

Expected exposure The projected amount of money an investor could lose if an event of default occurs, before factoring in possible recovery.

Expected shortfall The average loss conditional on exceeding the VaR cutoff; sometimes referred to as *conditional VaR* or *expected tail loss*.

Expected tail loss See *conditional VaR*.

Exploratory data analysis (EDA) The preliminary step in data exploration, where graphs, charts, and other visualizations (heat maps and word clouds) as well as quantitative methods (descriptive statistics and central tendency measures) are used to observe and summarize data.

Exposure to foreign exchange risk The risk of a change in value of an asset or liability denominated in a foreign currency due to a change in exchange rates.

Extendible bond Bond with an embedded option that gives the bondholder the right to keep the bond for a number of years after maturity, possibly with a different coupon.

Extension risk The risk of later repayment of a mortgage-backed security than expected.

Extra dividend A dividend paid by a company that does not pay dividends on a regular schedule, or a dividend that supplements regular cash dividends with an extra payment.

F1 score The harmonic mean of precision and recall. F1 score is a more appropriate overall performance metric (than accuracy) when there is unequal class distribution in the dataset and it is necessary to measure the equilibrium of precision and recall.

Factor A common or underlying element with which several variables are correlated.

Factor betas An asset's sensitivity to a particular factor; a measure of the response of return to each unit of increase in a factor, holding all other factors constant.

Factor portfolio See *pure factor portfolio*.

Factor price The expected return in excess of the risk-free rate for a portfolio with a sensitivity of 1 to one factor and a sensitivity of 0 to all other factors.

Factor risk premium The expected return in excess of the risk-free rate for a portfolio with a sensitivity of 1 to one factor and a sensitivity of 0 to all other factors. Also called *factor price*.

Factor risk premiums The expected return in excess of the risk-free rate for a portfolio with a sensitivity of 1 to one factor and a sensitivity of 0 to all other factors. Also called factor price.

Failure to pay When a borrower does not make a scheduled payment of principal or interest on any outstanding obligations after a grace period.

Fair market value The price, expressed in terms of cash equivalents, at which a property (asset) would change hands between a hypothetical willing and able buyer and a hypothetical willing and able seller, acting at "arm's length" in an open and unrestricted market, when neither is under compulsion to buy or sell and when both have reasonable knowledge of the relevant facts. Fair market value is most often used in a tax reporting context in the United States.

Fair value A market-based measure of an investment based on observable or derived assumptions to determine a price that market participants would use to exchange an asset or liability in an orderly transaction at a specific time.

Fama–French models Factor models that explain the drivers of returns related to three, four, or five factors.

Feature engineering A process of creating new features by changing or transforming existing features.

Feature selection A process whereby only pertinent features from the dataset are selected for model training. Selecting fewer features decreases model complexity and training time.

Features The independent variables (X's) in a labeled dataset.

Finance (or capital) lease A lease that is viewed as a financing arrangement.

Financial buyer An owner seeking to earn investment returns from an existing company without identifying or capitalizing on synergies from a controlling interest.

Financial leverage The use of debt in the capital structure. Measured using ratios such as operating income to operating income less interest expense, total assets to total equity, or debt to equity.

First-differencing A transformation that subtracts the value of the time series in period $t - 1$ from its value in period t.

First-order serial correlation The correlation of residuals with residuals adjacent in time.

Fitting curve A curve which shows in- and out-of-sample error rates (E_{in} and E_{out}) on the y-axis plotted against model complexity on the x-axis.

Fixed price tender offer Offer made by a company to repurchase a specific number of shares at a fixed price that is typically at a premium to the current market price.

Fixed-rate perpetual preferred stock Non-convertible, non-callable preferred stock with a specified dividend rate that has a claim on earnings senior to the claim of common stock, and no maturity date.

Flight to quality During times of market stress, investors sell higher-risk asset classes such as stocks and commodities in favor of default-risk-free government bonds.

Float Amounts collected as premium and not yet paid out as benefits.

Floored floater Floating-rate bond with a floor provision that prevents the coupon rate from decreasing below a specified minimum rate. It protects the investor against declining interest rates.

Flotation cost Fees charged to companies by investment bankers and other costs associated with raising new capital.

Forced conversion For a convertible bond, when the issuer calls the bond and forces bondholders to convert their bonds into shares, which typically happens when the underlying share price increases above the conversion price.

Foreign currency transactions Transactions that are denominated in a currency other than a company's functional currency.

Forward curve The term structure of forward rates for loans made on a specific initiation date.

Forward dividend yield A dividend yield based on the anticipated dividend during the next 12 months.

Forward P/E A P/E calculated on the basis of a forecast of EPS; a stock's current price divided by next year's expected earnings.

Forward price Represents the price agreed upon in a forward contract to be exchanged at the contract's maturity date, T. This price is shown in equations as $F_0(T)$.

Forward pricing model The model that describes the valuation of forward contracts.

Forward propagation The process of adjusting weights in a neural network, to reduce total error of the network, by moving forward through the network's layers.

Forward rate An interest rate determined today for a loan that will be initiated in a future period.

Forward rate agreement An over-the-counter forward contract in which the underlying is an interest rate on a deposit. A forward rate agreement (FRA) calls for one party to make a fixed interest payment and the other to make an interest payment at a rate to be determined at contract expiration.

Forward rate model The forward pricing model expressed in terms of spot and forward interest rates.

Forward rate parity The proposition that the forward exchange rate is an unbiased predictor of the future spot exchange rate.

Forward value The monetary value of an existing forward contract.

Forward-looking estimates Estimates based on current and expectations. Also referred to as ex ante estimates.

Franchising A situation where an owner of an asset and associated intellectual property divests the asset and licenses intellectual property to a third-party operator (franchisee) in exchange for royalties. Franchisees operate under the constraints of a franchise agreement.

Franking credit A tax credit received by shareholders for the taxes that a corporation paid on its distributed earnings.

Free cash flow to equity The cash flow available to a company's common shareholders after all operating expenses, interest, and principal payments have been made and necessary investments in working and fixed capital have been made.

Free cash flow to equity model A model of stock valuation that views a stock's intrinsic value as the present value of expected future free cash flows to equity.

Free cash flow to the firm The cash flow available to the company's suppliers of capital after all operating expenses (including taxes) have been paid and necessary investments in working and fixed capital have been made.

Free cash flow to the firm model A model of stock valuation that views the value of a firm as the present value of expected future free cash flows to the firm.

Frequency analysis The process of quantifying how important tokens are in a sentence and in the corpus as a whole. It helps in filtering unnecessary tokens (or features).

Frozen DB plan A DB plan that is no longer accruing benefits for employee service.

Fulcrum securities Partially-in-the-money claims (not expected to be repaid in full) whose holders end up owning the reorganized company in a corporate reorganization situation.

Functional currency The currency of the primary economic environment in which an entity operates.

Fund of funds Funds that hold a portfolio of hedge funds; also called *funds of hedge funds*.

Fundamental factor models A multifactor model in which the factors are attributes of stocks or companies that are important in explaining cross-sectional differences in stock prices.

Fundamentals Economic characteristics of a business, such as profitability, financial strength, and risk.

Funded status The present value of the DB obligation less the fair value of plan assets (if any).

Funds available for distribution See *adjusted funds from operations*.

Funds from operations Net income (computed in accordance with generally accepted accounting principles) *plus* (1) gains and losses from sales of properties and (2) depreciation and amortization.

Futures price The pre-agreed price at which a futures contract buyer (seller) agrees to pay (receive) for the underlying at the maturity date of the futures contract.

Futures value The monetary value of an existing futures contract.

FX carry trade An investment strategy that involves taking long positions in high-yield currencies and short positions in low-yield currencies.

Gamma A numerical measure of how sensitive an option's delta (the sensitivity of the derivative's price) is to a change in the value of the underlying.

General linear *F*-test A test statistic used to assess the goodness of fit for an entire regression model, so it tests all independent variables in the model.

Generalize When a model retains its explanatory power when predicting out-of-sample (i.e., using new data).

Global CAPM (GCAPM) A single-factor model with a global index representing the single factor.

Going-concern assumption The assumption that the business will maintain its business activities into the foreseeable future.

Going-concern value A business's value under a going-concern assumption.

Going-in cap rate The capitalization rate based on the first year of ownership used to discount the initial annual cash flow from a real estate property.

Goodwill An intangible asset that represents the excess of the purchase price of an acquired company over the value of the net identifiable assets acquired.

Gordon growth model A DDM that assumes dividends grow at a constant rate into the future.

Green bond Bonds in which the proceeds are designated by issuers to fund a specific project or portfolio of projects that have environmental or climate benefits.

Greenmail The purchase of the accumulated shares of a hostile investor by a company that is targeted for takeover by that investor, usually at a substantial premium over market price.

Greenwashing The risk that a green bond's proceeds are not actually used for a beneficial environmental or climate-related project.

Grid search A method of systematically training a model by using various combinations of hyperparameter values, cross validating each model, and determining which combination of hyperparameter values ensures the best model performance.

Gross domestic product The market value of all final goods and services produced within the economy during a given period (output definition) or, equivalently, the aggregate income earned by all households, all companies, and the government within the economy during a given period (income definition).

Gross potential rental income Equal to the current market rent of a property at full occupancy.

Gross rent The average lease or rental price realized per square foot multiplied by the total rentable space.

Ground truth The known outcome (i.e., target variable) of each observation in a labelled dataset.

Growth accounting equation The production function written in the form of growth rates. For the basic Cobb–Douglas production function, it states that the growth rate of output equals the rate of technological change plus α multiplied by the growth rate of capital plus $(1 - \alpha)$ multiplied by the growth rate of labor.

Guideline assets Assets used as benchmarks when applying the method of comparables to value an asset.

Guideline companies Assets used as benchmarks when applying the method of comparables to value an asset.

Guideline public companies Public-company comparables for the company being valued.

Guideline public company method A variation of the market approach; establishes a value estimate based on the observed multiples from trading activity in the shares of public companies viewed as reasonably comparable to the subject private company.

Guideline transactions method A variation of the market approach; establishes a value estimate based on pricing multiples derived from the acquisition of control of entire public or private companies that were acquired.

Hard-catalyst event-driven approach An event-driven approach in which investments are made in reaction to an already announced corporate event (mergers and acquisitions, bankruptcies, share issuances, buybacks, capital restructurings, re-organizations, accounting changes) in which security prices related to the event have yet to fully converge.

Harmonic mean A type of weighted mean computed as the reciprocal of the arithmetic average of the reciprocals.

Hazard rate The probability that an event will occur, given that it has not already occurred.

Hedonic index A real estate index that is not based on repeat sales of the same property but, rather, that controls for differences in property characteristics, such as size, age, quality of construction, and location, for the properties sold in each period.

Heteroskedastic When the variance of the residuals differs across observations in a regression.

Heteroskedasticity Non-constant variance across all observations.

Hierarchical clustering An iterative unsupervised learning procedure used for building a hierarchy of clusters.

High-leverage point An observation of an independent variable that has an extreme value and is potentially influential.

Historical exchange rates For accounting purposes, the exchange rates that existed when the assets and liabilities were initially recorded.

Historical scenario analysis A technique for exploring the performance and risk of investment strategies in different structural regimes.

Historical simulation A simulation method that uses past return data and a random number generator that picks observations from the historical series to simulate an asset's future returns.

Historical simulation method The application of historical price changes to the current portfolio.

Historical stress testing The process that tests how investment strategies would perform under some of the most negative (i.e., adverse) combinations of events and scenarios.

Holding period return The single-period internal rate of return for a real estate property that includes property income and the change in property value over the period.

Holdout samples Data samples that are not used to train a model.

Homoskedasticity Constant variance across all observations.

Horizontal ownership Companies with mutual business interests (e.g., key customers or suppliers) that have cross-holding share arrangements with each other.

Household formation An economic statistic which tracks the establishment of new residences as a group of people (or household) decide to live together, which increases housing demand.

Ho–Lee model The first arbitrage-free term structure model. The model is calibrated to market data and uses a binomial lattice approach to generate a distribution of possible future interest rates.

Human capital The present value of an individual's future expected labor income.

Hyperparameter A parameter whose value must be set by the researcher before learning begins.

I-spreads Shortened form of "interpolated spreads" and a reference to a linearly interpolated yield.

Illiquidity discount A reduction or discount to value that reflects the lack of depth of trading or liquidity in that asset's market.

Impairment Diminishment in value as a result of carrying (book) value exceeding fair value and/or recoverable value.

Impairment of capital rule A legal restriction that dividends cannot exceed retained earnings.

Implied volatility The standard deviation that causes an option pricing model to give the current option price.

In-sample forecast errors The residuals from a fitted time-series model within the sample period used to fit the model.

iNAVs "Indicated" net asset values are intraday "fair value" estimates of an ETF share based on its creation basket.

Income approach A valuation approach that values an asset as the present discounted value of the income expected from it. In the context of real estate, this approach estimates the value of a property based on an expected rate of return. The estimated value is the present value of the expected future income from the property, including proceeds from resale at the end of a typical investment holding period.

Incremental borrowing rate (IBR) The rate of interest that the lessee would have to pay to borrow using a collateralized loan over the same term as a lease.

Incremental VaR (IVaR) A measure of the incremental effect of an asset on the VaR of a portfolio by measuring the difference between the portfolio's VaR while including a specified asset and the portfolio's VaR with that asset eliminated.

Indenture A written contract between a lender and borrower that specifies the terms of the loan, such as interest rate, interest payment schedule, or maturity.

Independent board directors Directors with no material relationship with the company with regard to employment, ownership, or remuneration.

Index CDS A type of credit default swap that involves a combination of borrowers.

Indexed rents Contractually agreed periodic rent changes based on an observed market variable, such as the consumer price index.

Industry risk premium (IP) The additional return that is required to bear industry -specific risk.

Industry shocks Unexpected changes to an industry from regulations or the legal environment, technology, or changes in the growth rate of the industry.

Industry structure An industry's underlying economic and technical characteristics.

Influential observation An observation in a statistical analysis whose inclusion may significantly alter regression results.

Information gain A metric which quantifies the amount of information that the feature holds about the response. Information gain can be regarded as a form of non-linear correlation between Y and X.

Information ratio The ratio of mean active return to standard deviation (active return).

Insiders Corporate managers and board directors who are also shareholders of a company.

Intangible assets Assets without a physical form, such as patents and trademarks.

Inter-temporal rate of substitution The ratio of the marginal utility of consumption *s* periods in the future (the numerator) to the marginal utility of consumption today (the denominator).

Interaction term A term that combines two or more independent variables and represents their joint influence on the dependent variable.

Intercept dummy An indicator variable that allows a single regression model to estimate two lines of best fit, each with differing intercepts, depending on whether the dummy takes a value of 1 or 0.

Interest rate risk The risk that interest rates will rise and therefore the market value of current portfolio holdings will fall so that their current yields to maturity then match comparable instruments in the marketplace.

Interlocking directorates Corporate structure in which individuals serve on the board of directors of multiple corporations.

International CAPM (ICAPM) A two-factor model with a global index and a wealth-weighted currency index.

International Fisher effect The proposition that nominal interest rate differentials across currencies are determined by expected inflation differentials.

Intrinsic value The amount gained (per unit) by an option buyer if an option is exercised at any given point in time. May be referred to as the exercise value of the option.

Inverse price ratio The reciprocal of a price multiple—for example, in the case of a P/E, the "earnings yield" E/P (where P is share price and E is earnings per share).

Investment value The value to a specific buyer, taking account of potential synergies based on the investor's requirements and expectations.

ISDA Master Agreement A standard or "master" agreement published by the International Swaps and Derivatives Association. The master agreement establishes the terms for each party involved in the transaction.

Joint test of hypotheses The test of hypotheses that specify values for two or more independent variables in the hypotheses.

Joint venture Two or more companies form and control a new, separate company to achieve a business objective. Each participant contributes assets, employees, know-how, or other resources to the joint venture company. The participants maintain their independence otherwise and continue to do business apart from the joint venture, but they share in the joint venture's profits or losses.

Justified (fundamental) P/E The price-to-earnings ratio that is fair, warranted, or justified on the basis of forecasted fundamentals.

Justified price multiple The estimated fair value of the price multiple, usually based on forecasted fundamentals or comparables.

***K*-fold cross-validation** A technique in which data (excluding test sample and fresh data) are shuffled randomly and then are divided into k equal sub-samples, with $k - 1$ samples used as training samples and one sample, the kth, used as a validation sample.

***K*-means** A clustering algorithm that repeatedly partitions observations into a fixed number, k, of non-overlapping clusters.

***K*-nearest neighbor** A supervised learning technique that classifies a new observation by finding similarities ("nearness") between this new observation and the existing data.

Kalotay–Williams–Fabozzi (KWF) model An arbitrage-free term structure model that describes the dynamics of the log of the short rate and assumes constant drift, no mean reversion, and constant volatility.

Key rate durations Sensitivity of a bond's price to changes in specific maturities on the benchmark yield curve. Also called *partial durations*.

***k*th-order autocorrelation** The correlation between observations in a time series separated by k periods.

Labeled dataset A dataset that contains matched sets of observed inputs or features (X's) and the associated output or target (Y).

Labor force Everyone of working age (ages 16 to 64) who either is employed or is available for work but not working.

Labor force participation rate The percentage of the working age population that is in the labor force.

Labor productivity The quantity of real GDP produced by an hour of labor. More generally, output per unit of labor input.

Labor productivity growth accounting equation States that potential GDP growth equals the growth rate of the labor input plus the growth rate of labor productivity.

Lack of marketability discount An extra return to investors to compensate for lack of a public market or lack of marketability.

LASSO Least absolute shrinkage and selection operator is a type of penalized regression which involves minimizing the sum of the absolute values of the regression coefficients. LASSO can also be used for regularization in neural networks.

Law of one price A principle that states that if two investments have the same or equivalent future cash flows regardless of what will happen in the future, then these two investments should have the same current price.

Leading dividend yield Forecasted dividends per share over the next year divided by current stock price.

Leading P/E A P/E calculated on the basis of a forecast of EPS; a stock's current price divided by next year's expected earnings.

Learning curve A curve that plots the accuracy rate (= 1 – error rate) in the validation or test samples (i.e., out-of-sample) against the amount of data in the training sample, which is thus useful for describing under- and overfitting as a function of bias and variance errors.

Learning rate A parameter that affects the magnitude of adjustments in the weights in a neural network.

Lessee Tenant or property user that enters a lease with a property owner or lessor.

Lessor Property owner or manager that leases a property to a tenant or property user.

Level One of the three factors (the other two are steepness and curvature) that empirically explain most yield curve shape changes. A shock to the level factor changes the yield for all maturities by an almost identical amount.

Leverage A measure for identifying a potentially influential high-leverage point.

Leveraged buyout (LBO) A transaction in which a private acquiror uses equity and a high proportion of debt to acquire a public or private company in order to make changes to increase value over an investment period.

Libor–OIS spread The difference between Libor and the overnight indexed swap rate.

Life settlement The sale of a life insurance contract to a third party. The valuation of a life settlement typically requires detailed biometric analysis of the individual policyholder and an understanding of actuarial analysis.

Likelihood ratio (LR) test A method to assess the fit of logistic regression models that is based on the log-likelihood metric that describes the model's fit to the data.

Linear classifier A binary classifier that makes its classification decision based on a linear combination of the features of each data point.

Linear trend A trend in which the dependent variable changes at a constant rate with time.

Liquidating dividend A dividend that is a return of capital rather than a distribution from earnings or retained earnings.

Liquidation value The value of a company if the company were dissolved and its assets sold individually.

Liquidity preference theory A term structure theory that asserts liquidity premiums exist to compensate investors for the added interest rate risk they face when lending long term.

Liquidity premium The compensation for liquidity risk that increases in proportion to the investment's illiquidity.

Loan-to-value ratio A primary measure of leverage involving the ratio of mortgage principal outstanding to the property's current value.

Local currency The currency of the country where a company is located.

Local expectations theory A term structure theory that contends the return for all bonds over short periods is the risk-free rate.

Log odds The natural log of the odds of an event or characteristic happening. Also known as the *logit function*.

Log-linear model With reference to time-series models, a model in which the growth rate of the time series as a function of time is constant.

Logistic regression (logit) A regression in which the dependent variable uses a logistic transformation of the event probability.

Logistic transformation The log of the probability of an occurrence of an event or characteristic divided by the probability of the event or characteristic not occurring.

Long/short credit trade A credit protection seller with respect to one entity combined with a credit protection buyer with respect to another entity.

Look-ahead bias The bias created by using information that was unknown or unavailable in the time periods over which backtesting is conducted. Survivorship bias is a type of look-ahead bias.

Lookback period The time period used to gather a historical data set.

Loss given default The amount that will be lost if a default occurs.

Loss to lease The difference between rental rates on existing leases and current market rents.

Macroeconomic factor model A multifactor model in which the factors are surprises in macroeconomic variables that significantly explain equity returns.

Macroeconomic factors Factors related to the economy, such as the inflation rate, industrial production, or economic sector membership.

Majority shareholders Shareholders that own more than 50% of a corporation's shares.

Majority-vote classifier A classifier that assigns to a new data point the predicted label with the most votes (i.e., occurrences).

Marginal VaR (MVaR) A measure of the effect of a small change in a position size on portfolio VaR.

Market approach Valuation approach that values an asset based on pricing multiples from sales of assets viewed as similar to the subject asset.

Market condition A performance condition that is related to the market price (or value) of the entity's equity instruments such as attaining a specified share price or a specified target based on the market price (or value) of the entity's equity instruments relative to an index of market prices of other companies.

Market conditions Interest rates, inflation rates, and other economic characteristics that comprise the macroeconomic environment.

Market conversion premium per share For a convertible bond, the difference between the market conversion price and the underlying share price, which allows investors to identify the premium or discount payable when buying a convertible bond rather than the underlying common stock.

Market conversion premium ratio For a convertible bond, the market conversion premium per share expressed as a percentage of the current market price of the shares.

Market efficiency A finance perspective on capital markets that deals with the relationship of price to intrinsic value. The traditional efficient markets formulation asserts that an asset's price is the best available estimate of its intrinsic value. The rational efficient markets formulation asserts that investors should expect to be rewarded for the costs of information gathering and analysis by higher gross returns.

Market model A regression model with the return on a stock as the dependent variable and the returns on a market index as the independent variable.

Market value of invested capital The market value of debt and equity.

Mature growth rate The earnings growth rate in a company's mature phase; an earnings growth rate that can be sustained long term.

Maximum drawdown The worst cumulative loss ever sustained by an asset or portfolio. More specifically, maximum drawdown is the difference between an asset's or a portfolio's maximum cumulative return and its subsequent lowest cumulative return.

Maximum likelihood estimation (MLE) A method that estimates values for the intercept and slope coefficients in a logistic regression that make the data in the regression sample most likely.

Mean reversion The tendency of a time series to fall when its level is above its mean and rise when its level is below its mean; a mean-reverting time series tends to return to its long-term mean.

Metadata Data that describes and gives information about other data.

Method based on forecasted fundamentals An approach to using price multiples that relates a price multiple to forecasts of fundamentals through a discounted cash flow model.

Method of comparables An approach to valuation that involves using a price multiple to evaluate whether an asset is relatively fairly valued, relatively undervalued, or relatively overvalued when compared to a benchmark value of the multiple.

Minority interest The proportion of the ownership of a subsidiary not held by the parent (controlling) company.

Minority shareholders Particular shareholders or a block of shareholders holding a small proportion of a company's outstanding shares, resulting in a limited ability to exercise control in voting activities.

Mispricing Any departure of the market price of an asset from the asset's estimated intrinsic value.

Mixed-use development Commercial real estate properties that combine more than one tenant type and economic use.

Model specification The set of independent variables included in a model and the model's functional form.

Molodovsky effect The observation that P/Es tend to be high on depressed EPS at the bottom of a business cycle and tend to be low on unusually high EPS at the top of a business cycle.

Momentum indicators Valuation indicators that relate either price or a fundamental (such as earnings) to the time series of their own past values (or in some cases to their expected value).

Monetary assets and liabilities Assets and liabilities with value equal to the amount of currency contracted for, a fixed amount of currency. Examples are cash, accounts receivable, accounts payable, bonds payable, and mortgages payable. Inventory is not a monetary asset. Most liabilities are monetary.

Monetary/non-monetary method Approach to translating foreign currency financial statements for consolidation in which monetary assets and liabilities are translated at the current exchange rate. Non-monetary assets and liabilities are translated at historical exchange rates (the exchange rates that existed when the assets and liabilities were acquired).

Monetizing Unwinding a position to either capture a gain or realize a loss.

Monte Carlo simulation A technique that uses the inverse transformation method for converting a randomly generated uniformly distributed number into a simulated value of a random variable of a desired distribution. Each key decision variable in a Monte Carlo simulation requires an assumed statistical distribution; this assumption facilitates incorporating non-normality, fat tails, and tail dependence as well as solving high-dimensionality problems.

Multi-class trading An equity market-neutral strategy that capitalizes on misalignment in prices and involves buying and selling different classes of shares of the same company, such as voting and non-voting shares.

Multi-manager fund Can be of two types—one is a multi-strategy fund in which teams of portfolio managers trade and invest in multiple different strategies within the same fund; the second type is a fund of hedge funds (or fund-of-funds) in which the manager allocates capital to separate, underlying hedge funds that themselves run a range of different strategies.

Multi-strategy fund A fund in which teams of portfolio managers trade and invest in multiple different strategies within the same fund.

Multicollinearity When two or more independent variables are highly correlated with one another or are approximately linearly related.

Multiple linear regression Modeling and estimation method that uses two or more independent variables to describe the variation of the dependent variable. Also referred to as *multiple regression*.

Mutual information Measures how much information is contributed by a token to a class of texts. MI will be 0 if the token's distribution in all text classes is the same. MI approaches 1 as the token in any one class tends to occur more often in only that particular class of text.

N-grams A representation of word sequences. The length of a sequence varies from 1 to n. When one word is used, it is a unigram; a two-word sequence is a bigram; and a 3-word sequence is a trigram; and so on.

***n*-Period moving average** The average of the current and immediately prior $n - 1$ values of a time series.

Naked credit default swap A position where the owner of the CDS does not have a position in the underlying credit.

Name entity recognition An algorithm that analyzes individual tokens and their surrounding semantics while referring to its dictionary to tag an object class to the token.

Negative serial correlation A situation in which residuals are negatively related to other residuals.

Nested models Models in which one regression model has a subset of the independent variables of another regression model.

Net asset balance sheet exposure When assets translated at the current exchange rate are greater in amount than liabilities translated at the current exchange rate. Assets exposed to translation gains or losses exceed the exposed liabilities.

Net asset value per share Net asset value divided by the number of shares outstanding.

Net liability balance sheet exposure When liabilities translated at the current exchange rate are greater assets translated at the current exchange rate. Liabilities exposed to translation gains or losses exceed the exposed assets.

Net operating income A commonly used measure of income-producing property returns prior to the inclusion of financing costs or income taxes.

Network externalities The impact that users of a good, a service, or a technology have on other users of that product; it can be positive (e.g., a critical mass of users makes a product more useful) or negative (e.g., congestion makes the product less useful).

Neural networks A type of computer program design based on how the human brain learns and processes information.

No-arbitrage approach A procedure for obtaining the value of an option based on the creation of a portfolio that replicates the payoffs of the option and deriving the option value from the value of the replicating portfolio.

No-growth company A company without positive expected net present value projects.

No-growth value per share The value per share of a no-growth company, equal to the expected level amount of earnings divided by the stock's required rate of return.

Non-cash rent An amount equal to the difference between the average contractual rent over a lease term (the straight-line rent) and the cash rent actually paid during a period. This figure is one of the deductions made from FFO to calculate AFFO.

Non-convergence trap A situation in which a country remains relatively poor, or even falls further behind, because it fails to implement necessary institutional reforms and/or adopt leading technologies.

Non-monetary assets and liabilities Assets and liabilities that are not monetary assets and liabilities. Non-monetary assets include inventory, fixed assets, and intangibles, and non-monetary liabilities include deferred revenue.

Non-renewable resources Finite resources that are depleted once they are consumed; oil and coal are examples.

Nonearning assets Cash and investments (specifically cash, cash equivalents, and short-term investments).

Normal EPS The EPS that a business could achieve currently under mid-cyclical conditions. Also called *normalized EPS*.

Normal Q-Q plot A visual used to compare the distribution of the residuals from a regression to a theoretical normal distribution.

Normalized earnings The expected level of mid-cycle earnings for a company in the absence of any unusual or temporary factors that affect profitability (either positively or negatively).

Normalized EPS The EPS that a business could achieve currently under mid-cyclical conditions. Also called *normal EPS*.

Normalized P/E P/E based on normalized EPS data.

Notional amount The amount of protection being purchased in a CDS.

NTM P/E Next 12-month P/E: current market price divided by an estimated next 12-month EPS.

Off-the-run Seasoned government bonds that are often less liquid.

Offshoring Refers to relocating operations from one country to another, mainly to reduce costs through lower labor costs or to achieve economies of scale through centralization, but still maintaining operations within the corporation.

Omitted variable bias Bias resulting from the omission of an important independent variable from a regression model.

On-the-run Most recently issued, and liquid, government bonds.

One hot encoding The process by which categorical variables are converted into binary form (0 or 1) for machine reading. It is one of the most common methods for handling categorical features in text data.

One-sided durations Effective durations when interest rates go up or down, which are better at capturing the interest rate sensitivity of bonds with embedded options that do not react symmetrically to positive and negative changes in interest rates of the same magnitude.

One-tier board Board structure consisting of a single board of directors, composed of executive (internal) and non-executive (external) directors.

Opportunistic real estate Real estate investments primarily in commercial and/or residential properties involving major redevelopment, repurposing of assets, taking on large vacancies, or speculating on significant improvement in market conditions.

Opportunity cost Reflects the foregone opportunity of investing in a different asset. It is typically denoted by the risk-free rate of interest, *r*.

Option-adjusted spread or OAS for a bond is its Z-spread adjusted for the value of an embedded option.

Orderly liquidation value The estimated gross amount of money that could be realized from the liquidation sale of an asset or assets, given a reasonable amount of time to find a purchaser or purchasers.

Other comprehensive income Changes to equity that bypass (are not reported in) the income statement; the difference between comprehensive income and net income.

Other post-employment benefits (OPEB) DB post-employment benefit plans other than plans that pay cash retirement benefits (e.g., retiree medical care benefit plans).

Out-of-sample forecast errors The differences between actual and predicted values of time series outside the sample period used to fit the model.

Outlier An observation that has an extreme value of the dependent variable and is potentially influential.

Outsourcing Shifting internal business services to a subcontractor that can offer services at lower costs by scaling to serve many clients.

Overage rent Contractual sale-based rental adjustments that result in higher rent if a tenant's sales exceed a pre-agreed minimum target.

Overfitting When a machine learning model learns the input and target dataset too precisely, making the system more likely to discover false relationships or unsubstantiated patterns that will lead to prediction errors.

Overfunded plan A DB plan with a positive funded status; the present value of the DB obligation is less than the fair value of plan assets.

Overnight indexed swap (OIS) rate An interest rate swap in which the periodic floating rate of the swap equals the geometric average of a daily unsecured overnight rate (or overnight index rate).

Pairs trading An equity market-neutral strategy that capitalizes on the misalignment in prices of pairs of similar under- and overvalued equities. The expectation is the differential valuations or trading relationships will revert to their long-term mean values or their fundamentally-correct trading relationships, with the long position rising and the short position declining in value.

Par curve A hypothetical yield curve for coupon-paying Treasury securities that assumes all securities are priced at par.

Par swap A swap in which the fixed rate is set so that no money is exchanged at contract initiation.

Parametric method A method of estimating VaR that uses the historical mean, standard deviation, and correlation of security price movements to estimate the portfolio VaR. Generally assumes a normal distribution but can be adapted to non-normal distributions with the addition of skewness and kurtosis. Sometimes called the *variance–covariance method* or the *analytical method*.

Partial regression coefficient Coefficient that describes the effect of a one-unit change in the independent variable on the dependent variable, holding all other independent variables constant. Also known as *partial slope coefficient*.

Parts of speech An algorithm that uses language structure and dictionaries to tag every token in the text with a corresponding part of speech (i.e., noun, verb, adjective, proper noun, etc.).

Payout amount The loss given default times the notional.

Payout policy The principles by which a company distributes cash to common shareholders by means of cash dividends and/or share repurchases.

Payouts Cash dividends and the value of shares repurchased in any given year.

PEG ratio The P/E-to-growth ratio, calculated as the stock's P/E divided by the expected earnings growth rate.

Penalized regression A regression that includes a constraint such that the regression coefficients are chosen to minimize the sum of squared residuals *plus* a penalty term that increases in size with the number of included features.

Pension obligation The present value, without deducting any plan assets, of expected future payments required to settle the obligation resulting from employee service in the current and prior periods.

Perfect capital markets Markets in which, by assumption, there are no taxes, no transaction costs, and no bankruptcy costs and in which all investors have equal ("symmetric") information.

Performance condition A vesting condition comprising a service condition and the meeting of a specified performance target during the service period. A performance target is typically defined as an accounting measure or a market condition.

Performance shares Needs Definition

Perpetuity A perpetual annuity, or a set of never-ending level sequential cash flows, with the first cash flow occurring one period from now.

Persistent earnings Earnings excluding nonrecurring components. Also referred to as *core earnings, continuing earnings*, or *underlying earnings*.

Physical settlement Involves actual delivery of the debt instrument in exchange for a payment by the credit protection seller of the notional amount of the contract.

Point-in-time data Data consisting of the exact information available to market participants as of a given point in time. Point-in-time data is used to address look-ahead bias.

Portfolio balance approach A theory of exchange rate determination that emphasizes the portfolio investment decisions of global investors and the requirement that global investors willingly hold all outstanding securities denominated in each currency at prevailing prices and exchange rates.

Positive serial correlation A situation in which residuals are positively related to other residuals.

Potential GDP The maximum amount of output an economy can sustainably produce without inducing an increase in the inflation rate. The output level that corresponds to full employment with consistent wage and price expectations.

Precision In error analysis for classification problems it is ratio of correctly predicted positive classes to all predicted positive classes. Precision is useful in situations where the cost of false positives (FP), or Type I error, is high.

Preferred habitat theory A term structure theory that contends that investors have maturity preferences and require yield incentives before they will buy bonds outside of their preferred maturities.

Premium leg The series of payments the credit protection buyer promises to make to the credit protection seller.

Premiums Amounts paid by the purchaser of insurance products.

Prepayment risk The risk that the some or all of a mortgage-backed security's principal is repaid at a different speed than expected, either in the form of contraction risk (or earlier repayment than expected) or extension risk (later repayment).

Present value model A model of intrinsic value that views the value of an asset as the present value of the asset's expected future cash flows.

Present value of growth opportunities The difference between the actual value per share and the no-growth value per share. Also called *value of growth*.

Presentation currency The currency in which financial statement amounts are presented.

Price momentum A valuation indicator based on past price movement.

Price multiples The ratio of a stock's market price to some measure of value per share.

Price-to-earnings ratio (P/E) The ratio of share price to earnings per share.

Priced risk Risk for which investors demand compensation for bearing (e.g., equity risk, company-specific factors, macroeconomic factors).

Principal components analysis (PCA) An unsupervised ML technique used to transform highly correlated features of data into a few main, uncorrelated composite variables.

Principle of no arbitrage In well-functioning markets, prices will adjust until there are no arbitrage opportunities.

Prior transaction method A variation of the market approach; considers actual transactions in the stock of the subject private company.

Private market value The value derived using a sum-of-the-parts valuation.

Pro forma financial statements Financial statements that include the effect of a corporate restructuring.

Probability of default The likelihood that a borrower defaults or fails to meet its obligation to make full and timely payments of principal and interest.

Probability of survival The probability that a bond issuer will meet its contractual obligations on schedule.

Projection error The vertical (perpendicular) distance between a data point and a given principal component.

Property classes A relative ranking of properties based on a combination of features such as location, property age, local income levels, recent property appreciation, and relative condition.

Property maintenance allowance Expenses incurred to maintain a property's current level of income generation.

Prospective P/E A P/E calculated on the basis of a forecast of EPS; a stock's current price divided by next year's expected earnings.

Protection leg The contingent payment that the credit protection seller may have to make to the credit protection buyer.

Protection period Period during which a bond's issuer cannot call the bond.

Provision for loan losses An income statement expense account that increases the amount of the allowance for loan losses.

Pruning A regularization technique used in CART to reduce the size of the classification or regression tree—by pruning, or removing, sections of the tree that provide little classifying power.

Purchasing power gain A gain in value caused by changes in price levels. Monetary liabilities experience purchasing power gains during periods of inflation.

Purchasing power loss A loss in value caused by changes in price levels. Monetary assets experience purchasing power loss during periods of inflation.

Purchasing power parity (PPP) The idea that exchange rates move to equalize the purchasing power of different currencies.

Pure expectations theory A term structure theory that contends the forward rate is an unbiased predictor of the future spot rate. Also called the *unbiased expectations theory*.

Pure factor portfolio A portfolio with sensitivity of 1 to the factor in question and a sensitivity of 0 to all other factors.

Putable bond Bond that includes an embedded put option, which gives the bondholder the right to put back the bonds to the issuer prior to maturity, typically when interest rates have risen and higher-yielding bonds are available.

Qualitative dependent variable A dependent variable that is discrete (binary). Also known as a *categorical dependent variable*.

Quality of earnings analysis The investigation of issues relating to the accuracy of reported accounting results as reflections of economic performance. Quality of earnings analysis is broadly understood to include not only earnings management but also balance sheet management.

Quantitative market-neutral An approach to building market-neutral portfolios in which large numbers of securities are traded and positions are adjusted on a daily or even an hourly basis using algorithm-based models.

Random forest classifier A collection of a large number of decision trees trained via a bagging method.

Random walk A time series in which the value of the series in one period is the value of the series in the previous period plus an unpredictable random error.

Rate implicit in the lease (RIIL) The discount rate that equates the present value of the lease payment with the fair value of the leased asset, considering also the lessor's direct costs and the present value of the leased asset's residual value.

Rational efficient markets formulation See *market efficiency*.

Readme files Text files provided with raw data that contain information related to a data file. They are useful for understanding the data and how they can be interpreted correctly.

Real estate cycle Phases of recovery, expansion, oversupply, and recession that combine short-term adjustments in lease rates and occupancy in response to changing market conditions.

Real estate investment trusts Investment vehicles that directly own and operate real estate properties or debt investments and distribute dividends and other income to shareholders.

Real estate operating companies Corporate issuers whose primary activity is in the construction, development, operation, and servicing of real estate.

Real interest rate parity The proposition that real interest rates will converge to the same level across different markets.

Real options Refers to the right but not the obligation to take future action. The existence of such options may affect the value of a real estate investment.

Rebalance return A return from rebalancing the component weights of an index.

Recall Also known as *sensitivity*, in error analysis for classification problems it is the ratio of correctly predicted positive classes to all actual positive classes. Recall is useful in situations where the cost of false negatives (FN), or Type II error, is high.

Recency bias The behavioral tendency to place more relevance on recent events.

Reconstitution When dealers recombine appropriate individual zero-coupon securities and reproduce an underlying coupon Treasury.

Recovery rate The percentage of the loss recovered.

Redemption basket The list of securities (and share amounts) the authorized participant (AP) receives when it redeems ETF shares back to the ETF manager. The redemption basket is published each business day.

Reference entity The borrower (debt issuer) covered by a single-name CDS.

Reference obligation A particular debt instrument issued by the borrower that is the designated instrument being covered.

Regime The governing set of relationships (between variables) that stem from technological, political, legal, and regulatory environments. Changes in such environments or policy stances can be described as changes in regime.

Regular expression (regex) A series of texts that contains characters in a particular order. Regex is used to search for patterns of interest in a given text.

Regularization A term that describes methods for reducing statistical variability in high-dimensional data estimation problems.

Reinforcement learning Machine learning in which a computer learns from interacting with itself or data generated by the same algorithm.

Reinvestment rate A company's rate of investment in working capital and long-term assets necessary to maintain operations and support assumed growth.

Related-party transactions A business transaction between parties which share economic or other interests and may not take place at fair market value.

Relative valuation models A model that specifies an asset's value relative to the value of another asset.

Relative value volatility arbitrage A volatility trading strategy that aims to source and buy cheap volatility and sell more expensive volatility while netting out the time decay aspects normally associated with options portfolios.

Relative VaR The minimum portfolio loss expected to occur over a given time period at a specific confidence level based on a portfolio containing active positions minus benchmark holdings.

Relative version of PPP The hypothesis that changes in (nominal) exchange rates over time are equal to national inflation rate differentials.

Relative-strength indicators Valuation indicators that compare a stock's performance during a period either to its own past performance or to the performance of some group of stocks.

Renewable resources Resources that can be replenished, such as a forest.

Rental price of capital The cost per unit of time to rent a unit of capital.

Reorganization A court-supervised restructuring process available in some jurisdictions for companies facing insolvency from burdensome debt levels. A bankruptcy court assumes control of the company and oversees an orderly negotiation process between the company and its creditors for asset sales, conversion of debt to equity, refinancing, and so on.

Repeat sales index A real estate price index that relies on multiple sales of the same property.

Replacement cost Estimate of expenses associated with purchasing land and building a new property on a site with the same features and economic use as a property being appraised.

Required rate of return on equity The minimum rate of return required by an investor to invest in an asset, given the asset's riskiness. Also known as the required return on equity.

Residual autocorrelations The sample autocorrelations of the residuals.

Residual income Earnings for a given period, minus a deduction for common shareholders' opportunity cost in generating the earnings. Also called *economic profit* or *abnormal earnings*.

Residual income model (RIM) A model of stock valuation that views intrinsic value of stock as the sum of book value per share plus the present value of the stock's expected future residual income per share. Also called *discounted abnormal earnings model* or *Edwards–Bell–Ohlson model*.

Restricted model A regression model with a subset of the complete set of independent variables.

Restricted stock Needs Definition

Restricted stock units (RSUs) An instrument used in share-based compensation plans that represents the right to receive a common share upon vesting. RSUs are not tradeable, nor do they have voting rights or participate in dividends.

Restructuring Reorganizing the capital structure of a firm.

Return on invested capital A measure of the profitability of a company relative to the amount of capital invested by the equity- and debtholders.

Reverse carry arbitrage A strategy involving the short sale of the underlying and an offsetting opposite position in the derivative.

Reverse stock split A reduction in the number of shares outstanding with a corresponding increase in share price but no change to the company's underlying fundamentals.

Reverse stress testing A risk management approach in which the user identifies key risk exposures in the portfolio and subjects those exposures to extreme market movements.

Reviewed financial statements A type of non-audited financial statements; typically provide an opinion letter with representations and assurances by the reviewing accountant that are less than those in audited financial statements.

Rho The change in a given derivative instrument for a given small change in the risk-free interest rate, holding everything else constant. Rho measures the sensitivity of the option to the risk-free interest rate.

Risk budgeting The establishment of objectives for individuals, groups, or divisions of an organization that takes into account the allocation of an acceptable level of risk.

Risk decomposition The process of converting a set of holdings in a portfolio into a set of exposures to risk factors.

Risk factors Variables or characteristics with which individual asset returns are correlated. Sometimes referred to simply as *factors.*

Risk parity A portfolio allocation scheme that weights stocks or factors based on an equal risk contribution.

Risk-based models Models of the return on equity that identify risk factors or drivers and sensitivities of the return to these factors.

Risk-free rate The minimum rate of return expected on a security that has no default risk.

Robust standard errors Method for correcting residuals for conditional heteroskedasticity. Also known as *heteroskedasticity-consistent standard errors* or *White-corrected standard errors.*

Roll When an investor moves its investment position from an older series to the most current series.

Roll return The component of the return on a commodity futures contract attributable to rolling long futures positions forward through time. Also called *roll yield.*

Rolling down the yield curve A maturity trading strategy that involves buying bonds with a maturity longer than the intended investment horizon. Also called *riding the yield curve.*

Rolling windows A backtesting method that uses a rolling-window (or walk-forward) framework, rebalances the portfolio after each period, and then tracks performance over time. As new information arrives each period, the investment manager optimizes (revises and tunes) the model and readjusts stock positions.

Rollover risk The likelihood that a property owner will lose an existing tenant and forgo income until a new one is found.

Root mean squared error (RMSE) The square root of the average squared forecast error; used to compare the out-of-sample forecasting performance of forecasting models.

Sale-leaseback A situation in which a company sells the building it owns and occupies to a real estate investor and the company then signs a long-term lease with the buyer to continue to occupy the building. At the end of the lease, use of the property reverts to the landlord.

Sales comparison approach Real estate valuation approach that considers the price at which similar or comparable properties (comparables) are purchased and sold in the current market; also referred to as the *market approach.*

Sales risk The uncertainty regarding the price and number of units sold of a company's products.

Scaled earnings surprise Unexpected earnings divided by the standard deviation of analysts' earnings forecasts.

Scaling The process of adjusting the range of a feature by shifting and changing the scale of the data. Two of the most common ways of scaling are normalization and standardization.

Scatterplot matrix A visualization technique that shows the scatterplots between different sets of variables, often with the histogram for each variable on the diagonal. Also referred to as a *pairs plot.*

Schwarz's Bayesian information criterion (BIC or SBC) A statistic used to compare sets of independent variables for explaining a dependent variable. It is preferred for finding the model with the best goodness of fit.

Scree plots A plot that shows the proportion of total variance in the data explained by each principal component.

Screening The application of a set of criteria to reduce a set of potential investments to a smaller set having certain desired characteristics.

Seasonality A characteristic of a time series in which the data experience regular and predictable periodic changes; for example, fan sales are highest during the summer months.

Secured overnight financing rate (SOFR) A daily volume-weighted index of rates on qualified cash borrowings collateralized by US Treasuries that is expected to replace Libor as a floating reference rate for swaps.

Security selection risk See *active specific risk.*

Segmented markets theory A term structure theory that contends yields are solely a function of the supply and demand for funds of a particular maturity.

Sell-side analysts Analysts who work at brokerages.

Sensitivity analysis A form of analysis used to determine the impact of a change in one or more key variables affecting investment returns or valuation.

Sentence length The number of characters, including spaces, in a sentence.

Serial correlation A condition found most often in time series in which residuals are correlated across observations. Also known as *autocorrelation.*

Serial-correlation consistent standard errors Method for correcting serial correlation. Also known as *serial correlation and heteroskedasticity adjusted standard errors, Newey–West standard errors*, and *robust standard errors.*

Service condition A vesting condition that requires the employee to complete a period of service provision to the employer. A service condition does not require a performance target to be met.

Settled in arrears An arrangement in which the interest payment is made (i.e., settlement occurs) at the maturity of the underlying instrument.

Settlement The closing date at which the counterparties of a derivative contract exchange payment for the underlying as required by the contract.

Shadow banking Lending by financial institutions that are not regulated as banks.

Shaping risk The sensitivity of a bond's price to the changing shape of the yield curve.

Share repurchase A transaction in which a company buys back its own shares. Unlike stock dividends and stock splits, share repurchases use corporate cash.

Shareholder activism A range of actions by a corporation's shareholders that are intended to result in some change in the corporation, typically a change in the board of directors, management, or business strategy.

Shareholders' equity Assets less liabilities; the residual interest in the assets after subtracting the liabilities.

Short biased These strategies use quantitative, technical, and fundamental analysis to short overvalued equity securities with limited or no long-side exposures.

Simulation A technique for exploring how a target variable (e.g. portfolio returns) would perform in a hypothetical environment specified by the user, rather than a historical setting.

Single-manager fund A fund in which one portfolio manager or team of portfolio managers invests in one strategy or style.

Single-name CDS Credit default swap on one specific borrower.

Sinking fund bond A bond that requires the issuer to set aside funds over time to retire the bond issue, thus reducing credit risk.

Size premium (SP) Additional return compensation for bearing the additional risk associated with smaller companies.

Slope dummy An indicator variable that allows a single regression model to estimate two lines of best fit, each with differing slopes, depending on whether the dummy takes a value of 1 or 0.

Soft margin classification An adaptation in the support vector machine algorithm which adds a penalty to the objective function for observations in the training set that are misclassified.

Soft-catalyst event-driven approach An event-driven approach in which investments are made proactively in anticipation of a corporate event (mergers and acquisitions, bankruptcies, share issuances, buybacks, capital restructurings, re-organizations, accounting changes) that has yet to occur.

Sovereign yield spread The spread between the yield on a foreign country's sovereign bond and a similar-maturity domestic sovereign bond.

Special dividend A dividend paid by a company that does not pay dividends on a regular schedule, or a dividend that supplements regular cash dividends with an extra payment.

Specific-company risk premium (SCRP) Additional return required by investors for bearing non-diversifiable company-specific risk.

Spin off When a company separates a distinct part of its business into a new, independent company. The term is used to describe both the transaction and the separated component, while the company that conducts the transaction and formerly owned the spin off is known as the parent.

Split-rate tax system In reference to corporate taxes, a split-rate system taxes earnings to be distributed as dividends at a different rate than earnings to be retained. Corporate profits distributed as dividends are taxed at a lower rate than those retained in the business.

Spot curve Yields-to-maturity on a series of default-risk-free zero-coupon bonds.

Spot price The current price of an asset or security. For commodities, the current price to deliver a physical commodity to a specific location or purchase and transport it away from a designated location.

Spot rate The interest rate that is determined today for a risk-free, single-unit payment at a specified future date.

Spot yield curve The term structure of spot rates for loans made today.

Stabilized NOI Normalized or expected long-term level of net operating income level used to value real estate properties.

Stable dividend policy A policy in which regular dividends are paid that reflect long-run expected earnings. In contrast to a constant dividend payout ratio policy, a stable dividend policy does not reflect short-term volatility in earnings.

Standardized beta With reference to fundamental factor models, the value of the attribute for an asset minus the average value of the attribute across all stocks, divided by the standard deviation of the attribute across all stocks.

Standardized unexpected earnings Unexpected earnings per share divided by the standard deviation of unexpected earnings per share over a specified prior time period.

Statistical factor model A multifactor model in which statistical methods are applied to a set of historical returns to determine portfolios that best explain either historical return covariances or variances.

Steady-state rate of growth The constant growth rate of output (or output per capita) that can or will be sustained indefinitely once it is reached. Key ratios, such as the capital–output ratio, are constant on the steady-state growth path.

Steepness The difference between long-term and short-term yields that constitutes one of the three factors (the other two are level and curvature) that empirically explain most of the changes in the shape of the yield curve.

Step-up clauses Pre-specified contractual future rent increases.

Stock dividend A type of dividend in which a company distributes additional shares of its common stock to shareholders instead of cash.

Stop-loss limit Constraint used in risk management that requires a reduction in the size of a portfolio, or its complete liquidation, when a loss of a particular size occurs in a specified period.

Straight bond An underlying option-free bond with a specified issuer, issue date, maturity date, principal amount and repayment structure, coupon rate and payment structure, and currency denomination.

Straight debt Debt with no embedded options.

Straight voting A shareholder voting process in which shareholders receive one vote for each share owned.

Straight-line rent The average annual rent under a multi-year lease agreement that contains contractual increases in rent during the life of the lease.

Straight-line rent adjustment See *non-cash rent*.

Stranded assets A resource that is no longer economically valuable owing to changes in demand, regulations, or availability of substitutes—for example, a newly discovered oil well that will not be brought into production.

Strategic buyer An investor seeking to capitalize on synergies by extending the value creation process initiated by a GP, combining a business with another portfolio company, or taking other actions to increase firm value.

Stress tests A risk management technique that assesses the portfolio's response to extreme market movements.

Stripping A dealer's ability to separate a bond's individual cash flows and trade them as zero-coupon securities.

Stub trading An equity market-neutral strategy that capitalizes on misalignment in prices and entails buying and selling stock of a parent company and its subsidiaries, typically weighted by the percentage ownership of the parent company in the subsidiaries.

Studentized deleted residual A deleted residual divided by its estimated standard deviation.

Studentized residuals t-distributed statistics that are used to detect outliers.

Subject property A real estate property that is being appraised.

Succession event A change of corporate structure of the reference entity, such as through a merger, a divestiture, a spinoff, or any similar action, in which ultimate responsibility for the debt in question is unclear.

Sum-of-the-parts valuation A valuation approach that considers the value of a firm's business segments if they are sold separately.

Summation operator A functional part of a neural network's node that multiplies each input value received by a weight and sums the weighted values to form the total net input, which is then passed to the activation function.

Supernormal growth Above-average or abnormally high growth rate in earnings per share.

Supervised learning A type of machine learning in which the system attempts to learn to model relationships based on labeled training data.

Support vector machine A linear classifier that determines the hyperplane that optimally separates the observations into two sets of data points.

Survivorship bias Relates to the inclusion of only current investment funds in a database. As such, the returns of funds that are no longer available in the marketplace (have been liquidated) are excluded from the database. Also see *backfill bias*.

Sustainable growth rate The rate of dividend (and earnings) growth that can be sustained over time for a given level of return on equity, keeping the capital structure constant and without issuing additional common stock.

Swap curve The term structure of swap rates.

Swap rate The fixed rate to be paid by the fixed-rate payer specified in a swap contract.

Swap rate curve The term structure of swap rates.

Swap spread The difference between the fixed rate on an interest rate swap and the rate on a Treasury note with equivalent maturity; it reflects the general level of credit risk in the market.

Synergies The combination of two companies being more valuable than the sum of the parts. Generally, synergies take the form of lower costs ("cost synergies") or increased revenues ("revenue synergies") through combinations that generate lower costs or higher revenues, respectively.

Systematic risk Risk that affects the entire market or economy; it cannot be avoided and is inherent in the overall market. Systematic risk is also known as *non-diversifiable* or *market risk*.

Tail risk The possibility of extreme losses.

Takeover premium The amount by which the per-share takeover price exceeds the unaffected price expressed as a percentage of the unaffected price. It reflects the amount shareholders require to relinquish their control of the company to the acquirer.

Tangible assets Identifiable, physical assets such as property, plant, and equipment.

Tangible book value per share Common shareholders' equity minus intangible assets reported on the balance sheet, divided by the number of shares outstanding.

Target In machine learning, the dependent variable (Y) in a labeled dataset; the company in a merger or acquisition that is being acquired.

Target capital structure Management's desired proportions of debt and equity financing, usually stated on a book value basis or indirectly using a financial leverage metric, such as net or gross debt to EBITDA or credit rating.

Target payout ratio A strategic corporate goal representing the long-term proportion of earnings that the company intends to distribute to shareholders as dividends.

Taxable REIT subsidiaries Subsidiaries that pay income taxes on earnings from non-REIT-qualifying activities, such as merchant development or third-party property management.

Technical indicators Momentum indicators based on price.

TED spread A measure of perceived credit risk determined as the difference between Libor and the T-bill yield of matching maturity.

Temporal method A variation of the monetary/non-monetary translation method that requires not only monetary assets and liabilities, but also non-monetary assets and liabilities that are measured at their current value on the balance sheet date to be translated at the current exchange rate. Assets and liabilities are translated at rates consistent with the timing of their measurement value. This method is typically used when the functional currency is other than the local currency.

Term frequency (TF) Ratio of the number of times a given token occurs in all the texts in the dataset to the total number of tokens in the dataset.

Term premium The additional return required by lenders to invest in a bond to maturity net of the expected return from continually reinvesting at the short-term rate over that same time horizon.

Terminal cap rate Capitalization rate for a real estate property used to discount a final projected NOI that typically incorporates a constant future growth rate.

Terminal price multiples The price multiple for a stock assumed to hold at a stated future time.

Terminal share price The share price at a particular point in the future.

Terminal value of the stock The analyst's estimate of a stock's value at a particular point in the future. Also called *continuing value of the stock*.

Test sample A data sample that is used to test a model's ability to predict well on new data.

Theta The change in a derivative instrument for a given small change in calendar time, holding everything else constant. Specifically, the theta calculation assumes nothing changes except calendar time. Theta also reflects the rate at which an option's time value decays.

Time series A set of observations on a variable's outcomes in different time periods.

Time-series momentum A managed futures trend following strategy in which managers go long assets that are rising in price and go short assets that are falling in price. The manager trades on an absolute basis, so be net long or net short depending on the current price trend of an asset. This approach works best when an asset's own past returns are a good predictor of its future returns.

Tobin's *q* The ratio of the market value of debt and equity to the replacement cost of total assets.

Token The equivalent of a word (or sometimes a character).

Tokenization The process of representing ownership rights to physical assets on a blockchain or distributed ledger.

Total factor productivity (TFP) A multiplicative scale factor that reflects the general level of productivity or technology in the economy. Changes in total factor productivity generate proportional changes in output for any input combination.

Total invested capital The sum of market value of common equity, book value of preferred equity, and face value of debt.

Tracking error The standard deviation of the differences between a portfolio's returns and its benchmark's returns; a synonym of active risk.

Tracking risk The standard deviation of the differences between a portfolio's returns and its benchmarks returns. Also called *tracking error.*

Trailing dividend yield The reciprocal of current market price divided by the most recent annualized dividend.

Trailing P/E A stock's current market price divided by the most recent four quarters of EPS (or the most recent two semi-annual periods for companies that report interim data semi-annually). Also called *current P/E.*

Training sample A data sample that is used to train a model.

Tranche CDS A type of credit default swap that covers a combination of borrowers but only up to pre-specified levels of losses.

Transaction exposure The risk of a change in value between the transaction date and the settlement date of an asset of liability denominated in a foreign currency.

Treasury shares/stock Shares that were issued and subsequently repurchased by the company.

Trend A long-term pattern of movement in a particular direction.

Triangular arbitrage An arbitrage transaction involving three currencies that attempts to exploit inconsistencies among pairwise exchange rates.

Trimming Also called truncation, it is the process of removing extreme values and outliers from a dataset.

Two-tier board Board structure consisting of a supervisory board that oversees a management board.

Unbiased expectations theory A term structure theory that contends the forward rate is an unbiased predictor of the future spot rate. Also called the *pure expectations theory.*

Unconditional heteroskedasticity When heteroskedasticity of the error variance is not correlated with the regression's independent variables.

Uncovered interest rate parity The proposition that the expected return on an uncovered (i.e., unhedged) foreign currency (risk-free) investment should equal the return on a comparable domestic currency investment.

Underlying earnings Earnings excluding nonrecurring components. Also referred to as *continuing earnings, core earnings,* or *persistent earnings.*

Unexpected earnings The difference between reported EPS and expected EPS. Also referred to as an *earnings surprise.*

Unfunded Post-employment plans for which the sponsor has not set aside assets to pay benefits. Benefits for unfunded plans are paid from company cash

Unit root A time series that is not covariance stationary is said to have a unit root.

Units of comparison Measure used to compare the current market value of real estate properties, such as purchase price per square meter or square foot of leasable area or total area.

Unrestricted model A regression model with the complete set of independent variables.

Unsupervised learning A type of machine learning in which the system tries to learn the structure of unlabeled data.

Upfront payment The difference between the credit spread and the standard rate paid by the protection buyer if the standard rate is insufficient to compensate the protection seller. Also called *upfront premium.*

Upfront premium See *upfront payment.*

Upstream A transaction between two related companies, an investor company (or a parent company) and an associate company (or a subsidiary company) such that the associate company records a profit on its income statement. An example is a sale of inventory by the associate to the investor company or by a subsidiary to a parent company.

Validation sample A data sample that is used to validate and tune a model.

Valuation The process of determining the value of an asset or service either on the basis of variables perceived to be related to future investment returns or on the basis of comparisons with closely similar assets.

Value additivity An arbitrage opportunity when the value of the whole equals the sum of the values of the parts.

Value at risk (VaR) The minimum loss that would be expected a certain percentage of the time over a certain period of time given the assumed market conditions.

Value of growth The difference between the actual value per share and the no-growth value per share.

Variance error Describes how much a model's results change in response to new data from validation and test samples. Unstable models pick up noise and produce high variance error, causing overfitting and high out-of-sample error.

Variance inflation factor (VIF) A statistic that quantifies the degree of multicollinearity in a model.

Vasicek model A partial equilibrium term structure model that assumes interest rates are mean reverting and interest rate volatility is constant.

Vega A measure of the sensitivity of an option's price to changes in the underlying's volatility.

Vertical ownership Ownership structure in which a company or group that has a controlling interest in two or more holding companies, which in turn have controlling interests in various operating companies.

Vesting The process of an employee becoming unconditionally entitled to, and an employer becoming obligated to pay, compensation.

Visibility The extent to which a company's operations are predictable with substantial confidence.

Voting caps Legal restrictions on the voting rights of large share positions.

Web spidering (scraping or crawling) programs Programs that extract raw content from a source, typically web pages.

Weighted harmonic mean See *harmonic mean.*

Weighted-average cost of capital (WACC) A weighted average of the after-tax required rates of return on a company's equity, debt, preferred stock, and other long-term financing sources, where the weights are the fraction of each source of financing in the company's current market value or management's target capital structure.

Winsorization The process of replacing extreme values and outliers in a dataset with the maximum (for large value outliers) and minimum (for small value outliers) values of data points that are not outliers.

Write-down A reduction in the value of an asset as stated in the balance sheet.

Yield curve factor model A model or a description of yield curve movements that can be considered realistic when compared with historical data.

Zero A bond that does not pay a coupon but is priced at a discount and pays its full face value at maturity.

Zero-coupon bonds Bonds that do not pay interest during their life. They are issued at a discount to par value and redeemed at par. Also called pure discount bond.